Pro J2ME Polish

Open Source Wireless Java Tools Suite

ROBERT VIRKUS

Apress®

Pro J2ME Polish: Open Source Wireless Java Tools Suite

Softcover re-print of the Hardcover 1st edition 2005
Lead Editor: Steve Anglin
Technical Reviewer: Thomas Kraft

Associate Publisher: Grace Wong
Project Manager: Beth Christmas
Copy Edit Manager: Nicole LeClerc
Copy Editors: Marilyn Smith, Kim Wimpsett, Nicole LeClerc
Assistant Production Director: Kari Brooks-Copony
Production Editor: Ellie Fountain
Compositor: Dina Quan
Proofreader: Linda Seifert
Indexer: John Collin
Artist: Kinetic Publishing Services, LLC
Cover Designer: Kurt Krames
Manufacturing Manager: Tom Debolski

Virkus, Robert, 1949-
Pro J2ME Polish : open source wireless Java tools suite / Robert Virkus.
p. cm.
Includes index.

ISBN 1-4302-1197-0 (hardcover : alk. paper)
1. Java (Computer program language) 2. Wireless communication systems--Programming. I. Title.

QA76.73.J38V57 2005
005.13'3--dc22

2005016571

Distributed to the book trade in the United States by Springer-Verlag New York, Inc., 233 Spring Street, 6th Floor, New York, NY 10013, and outside the United States by Springer-Verlag GmbH & Co. KG, Tiergartenstr. 17, 69112 Heidelberg, Germany.

In the United States: phone 1-800-SPRINGER, fax 201-348-4505, e-mail orders@springer-ny.com, or visit http://www.springer-ny.com. Outside the United States: fax +49 6221 345229, e-mail orders@springer.de, or visit http://www.springer.de.

For information on translations, please contact Apress directly at 2560 Ninth Street, Suite 219, Berkeley, CA 94710. Phone 510-549-5930, fax 510-549-5939, e-mail info@apress.com, or visit http://www.apress.com.

The source code for this book is available to readers at http://www.apress.com in the Downloads section.

This book is dedicated to the people who fight against software patents and for a better world.

Contents at a Glance

Foreword . . . xvi
About the Author . . . xviii
About the Technical Reviewer . . . xix
Acknowledgments . . . xx
Introduction . . . xxi

PART 1 ■ ■ ■ Getting Ready

CHAPTER 1 Quick Setup Guide . . . 3
CHAPTER 2 Installing the Prerequisites . . . 7
CHAPTER 3 Installing J2ME Polish . . . 11
CHAPTER 4 Integrating J2ME Polish into IDEs . . . 19

PART 2 ■ ■ ■ Using J2ME Polish

CHAPTER 5 Getting to Know J2ME Polish . . . 29
CHAPTER 6 The Device Database . . . 39
CHAPTER 7 Building Applications . . . 55
CHAPTER 8 Preprocessing . . . 101
CHAPTER 9 The Logging Framework . . . 123
CHAPTER 10 Using the Utilities . . . 133
CHAPTER 11 Game Programming with J2ME Polish . . . 145
CHAPTER 12 Working with the GUI . . . 159
CHAPTER 13 Extending J2ME Polish . . . 231

PART 3 ■ ■ ■ Programming in the Real World

CHAPTER 14 Overview of the Wireless Market 273

CHAPTER 15 Dancing Around Device Limitations 283

CHAPTER 16 Optimizing Applications 325

PART 4 ■ ■ ■ Appendix

APPENDIX 351

INDEX 419

Contents

Foreword . . . xvi
About the Author . . . xviii
About the Technical Reviewer . . . xix
Acknowledgments . . . xx
Introduction . . . xxi

PART 1 ■ ■ ■ Getting Ready

CHAPTER 1 Quick Setup Guide . . . 3

Installing J2ME Polish . . . 4
Launching the Sample Applications . . . 4
Exploring the Sample Applications . . . 5
Summary . . . 6

CHAPTER 2 Installing the Prerequisites . . . 7

The Java 2 SDK . . . 7
The Wireless Toolkit . . . 8
 WTK Versions . . . 8
 WTK for Mac OS X . . . 8
IDE . . . 8
Ant . . . 9
Vendor-Specific Emulators . . . 9
Summary . . . 10

CHAPTER 3 Installing J2ME Polish . . . 11

J2ME Polish Installation Guide . . . 11
 License Selection . . . 11
 WTK Directory Selection . . . 12
 Component Selection . . . 13
 The Installation . . . 14

External Tools 15
J2ME Polish Sample Applications 15
  Testing the Sample Applications 16
  Troubleshooting Sample Application Errors 17
Summary 17

CHAPTER 4 **Integrating J2ME Polish into IDEs** 19

Recognizing Common Integration Issues 19
Using Eclipse 20
  Integrating Eclipse with Ant 20
  Troubleshooting Integration Issues 22
  Installing the J2ME Polish Plug-Ins 22
Using NetBeans 23
Using JBuilder 24
Using IntelliJ 24
Summary 26

PART 2 ■■■ **Using J2ME Polish**

CHAPTER 5 **Getting to Know J2ME Polish** 29

J2ME Polish from 500 Miles Above 29
Managing the Application Life Cycle with J2ME Polish 30
  Designing the Architecture 31
  Implementing the Application 32
  Building Your Application 32
  Testing the Application 32
  Optimizing Your Application 33
  Deploying Your Application 33
  Updating Your Application 36
Summary 38

CHAPTER 6 **The Device Database** 39

Understanding the XML Format 39
  Defining Devices 40
  Defining Vendors 44
  Defining Groups 44
  Defining Libraries 45

Describing Known Issues 47
Defining Complementing Capabilities and Features 48
Using the Device Database 49
Selecting Your Target Devices 50
Selecting Resources for Your Target Devices 50
Optimizing for Your Target Devices 51
Changing and Extending the Device Database 52
Summary 53

CHAPTER 7 **Building Applications** 55

Taking an Ant Crash Course 55
Creating a "Hello, J2ME Polish World" Application 58
Introducing the Build Phases 64
Selecting the Target Devices 65
Preprocessing 66
Compilation 66
Obfuscation 67
Preverification 68
Packaging 68
Invoking Emulators 68
Packaging Your Application 68
Resource Assembling 68
Managing JAD and Manifest Attributes 74
Signing MIDlets 77
Using Third-Party Packagers 78
Building for Multiple Devices 80
Selecting Devices 80
Minimizing the Number of Target Devices 83
Building Localized Applications 84
The <localization> Element and Localized Resource Assembling 84
Managing Translations 85
Coping with Dates and Currencies 88
Avoiding Common Mistakes 89
Localizing the J2ME Polish GUI 90
Integrating Third-Party APIs 92
Integrating Source Code Third-Party APIs 92
Integrating Binary Third-Party APIs 93
Integrating Device APIs 94

Obfuscating Applications . . . 94
Using the Default Package . . . 95
Combining Several Obfuscators . . . 95
Debugging Applications . . . 96
Using Conditions . . . 96
Using J2ME Polish As a Compiler . . . 98
Summary . . . 100

CHAPTER 8 Preprocessing . . . 101

Why Preprocessing? . . . 101
Preprocessing Directives . . . 104
Branching Your Code . . . 105
Defining Temporary Symbols and Variables . . . 109
Including Values of Variables in Your Code . . . 110
Using Several Variable Values Individually . . . 111
Including External Code . . . 112
Analyzing the Preprocessing Phase . . . 112
Hiding Statements . . . 112
Logging . . . 113
Setting CSS Styles . . . 113
Nesting Directives . . . 114
Managing Variables and Symbols . . . 114
Using Standard Preprocessing Symbols and Variables . . . 114
Setting Symbols and Variables . . . 115
Transforming Variables with Property Functions . . . 117
Preprocessing to the Rescue! . . . 118
Using Optional and Device-Specific Libraries . . . 118
Changing the Class Inheritance . . . 119
Configuring Applications . . . 119
Using Hard-Coded Values . . . 120
Circumventing Known Issues . . . 121
Summary . . . 121

CHAPTER 9 The Logging Framework . . . 123

Logging Messages . . . 123
Adding Debug Code for Specific Log Levels . . . 125
Controlling the Logging . . . 125
Viewing the Log on Real Devices . . . 128
Forwarding Log Messages . . . 130
Summary . . . 131

CHAPTER 10 **Using the Utilities** 133

Utility Classes 133
The ArrayList Class 134
The TextUtil Class 135
The BitMapFont Class 136
Other Utility Classes 138
Stand-Alone Utilities 138
The Binary Editor 139
The Font Editor 142
The SysInfo MIDlet 143
Summary 143

CHAPTER 11 **Game Programming with J2ME Polish** 145

Using the Game Engine 145
Optimizing the Game Engine 146
Running Your Game in Full-Screen Mode 147
Using a Back Buffer in the TiledLayer 148
Splitting an Image into Single Tiles 149
Defining the Grid Type of a TiledLayer 149
Using the Game Engine for MIDP 2.0 Devices 150
Working Around the Limitations of the Game Engine 150
Porting an MIDP 2.0 Game to the MIDP 1.0 Platform 152
Porting Low-Level Graphics Operations 152
Porting Sound Playback 155
Controlling Vibration and the Display Light 156
Summary 157

CHAPTER 12 **Working with the GUI** 159

Introducing Interface Concepts 160
Controlling the GUI 161
Activating the GUI 161
Configuring the J2ME Polish GUI 162
Programming the GUI 170
Using Correct import Statements 170
Setting Styles 171
Using Dynamic and Predefined Styles 173
Porting MIDP 2.0 Applications to MIDP 1.0 Platforms 173
Programming Specific Items and Screens 174

Designing the GUI ... 181
- Designing for Specific Devices and Device Groups ... 182
- Using Dynamic, Static, and Predefined Styles ... 183
- Extending Styles ... 187
- Reviewing CSS Syntax ... 187
- Common Design Attributes ... 189
- Designing Screens ... 199
- Designing Items ... 215
- Using Animations ... 228

Summary ... 229

CHAPTER 13 Extending J2ME Polish ... 231

Extending the Build Tools ... 231
- Understanding the Extension Mechanism ... 231
- Creating Your Own Preprocessor ... 239
- Setting the Compiler ... 243
- Using a Postcompiler ... 244
- Integrating Your Own Obfuscator ... 244
- Integrating a Preverifier ... 245
- Copying and Transforming Resources ... 245
- Using Different Packagers ... 246
- Integrating Finalizers ... 247
- Integrating Emulators ... 247
- Adding Property Functions ... 248

Extending the J2ME Polish GUI ... 248
- Writing Your Own Custom Items ... 248
- Loading Images Dynamically ... 261
- Creating Your Own Background ... 265
- Adding a Custom Border ... 269

Extending the Logging Framework ... 269

Summary ... 270

PART 3 ■■■ Programming in the Real World

CHAPTER 14 Overview of the Wireless Market ... 273

Introducing Device Differences ... 273
- Hardware ... 273
- Profiles and Configurations ... 274

Optional Packages . . . 276
The JTWI Specification and Mobile Service Architecture . . . 278
Supported Formats . . . 279
Device Modifications . . . 279
Device Issues . . . 280
The Emulator Trap . . . 280
Examining the Current Market . . . 280
Telecom Market . . . 280
J2ME Market . . . 282
Summary . . . 282

CHAPTER 15 Dancing Around Device Limitations . . . 283

Identifying Vendor Characteristics . . . 283
Nokia . . . 283
Motorola . . . 287
Samsung . . . 288
Siemens . . . 289
LG Electronics . . . 290
Sony Ericsson . . . 290
RIM BlackBerry . . . 291
Other Vendors . . . 292
Identifying Carriers . . . 292
Identifying Platforms . . . 292
MIDP Platforms . . . 293
DoJa Platforms . . . 294
WIPI Platforms . . . 294
Writing Portable Code . . . 294
Using the Lowest Common Denominator . . . 295
Using Dynamic Code . . . 295
Using Preprocessing . . . 298
Using Different Source Files . . . 300
Solving Common Problems . . . 303
Using the Appropriate Resources . . . 303
Circumventing Known Issues . . . 304
Implementing the User Interface . . . 308
Networking . . . 310
Playing Sounds . . . 313
Using Floating-Point Arithmetic . . . 314
Using Trusted MIDlets . . . 317
Identifying Devices . . . 318

Getting Help 321
Honoring Netiquette 321
Exploring J2ME Polish Forums 322
Exploring Vendor Forums 322
Exploring General J2ME Forums and Mailing Lists 322
Summary 323

CHAPTER 16 **Optimizing Applications** 325

Optimization Overview 325
Improving Performance 326
Measuring Performance 326
Performance Tuning 329
Improving Perceived Performance 338
Reducing Memory Consumption 341
Measuring Memory Consumption 341
Improving the Memory Footprint 342
Decreasing the Size of JAR Files 344
Improving the Class Model 344
Handling Resources 349
Obfuscating and Packaging Your Application 350
Summary 350

PART 4 **Appendix**

APPENDIX 353
JAD and Manifest Attributes 353
MIDP 1.0 Attributes 353
MIDP 2.0 Attributes 354
Vendor-Specific Attributes 355
Runtime Properties 356
System Properties 356
Bluetooth Properties 358
3D Properties 359
Permissions for Signed MIDlets 360

The J2ME Polish Ant Settings 363
<info> Section 363
Device Requirements Section 365
Build Section 366
Emulator Section 388
Standard Preprocessing Variables and Symbols 389
Device-Specific Symbols 389
Device-Specific Variables 390
Configuration Variables 392
Symbols and Variables for Reading the Settings 397
Preprocessing Directives 398
Property Functions 399
The J2ME Polish GUI 400
Backgrounds 400
Borders 412
J2ME Polish License 417
Abbreviations Glossary 417

INDEX 419

Foreword

So, you are a developer, you write applications for mobile devices, and you've been asked by a network operator to get your application working on their list of preferred devices, otherwise they won't deal with you. That all sounds familiar and, initially, it all sounds pretty easy—we are developing applications in Java, and as we all know, Java is platform independent and we just "write once, run anywhere."

OK, now that you've picked yourself up off the floor and stopped laughing after that statement, you've probably realized the big deal about writing mobile applications is that there are so many little differences between devices and the Java implementations on those devices that it's a mammoth task to support many devices.

How do we get around these "inconsistencies"?

How do we avoid having device-specific source code for everything we write?

These are among the *really* important questions for mobile application developers. When I started writing applications for mobile devices, we were still learning about these inconsistencies and still finding things that made us want to tear our hair out.

I would like to suggest that your first port of call should always be the API specifications. You see, that's why they are there: to show you exactly what *should* happen and how you *should* handle things—but as you know, if you sit a thousand monkeys in front of typewriters, you certainly don't end up with the works of Shakespeare. Well, the same applies here. If you give all the device manufacturers the specifications for the application management software, you certainly can't expect them to work in exactly the same way. (Now, I'm not saying it's all their fault—I mean, it's not always exactly the same hardware, and miracles don't happen.)

So, how *do* we get around these inconsistencies? Well, that's where this book and J2ME Polish come in. I recommend going straight to the "Programming in the Real World" section and having a quick read through it. Then you should have a better appreciation for the problems at hand, and you'll realize that you need some help to control the mass of workarounds that you're likely to need. Of course, that help comes in the form of J2ME Polish, and this book explains how to use it.

As I mentioned earlier, when I started writing mobile device applications, we were still figuring out the problems, and to a certain extent we still are. I used to have my own custom Ant scripts for individual builds of an application for individual devices. I just looked at one of the device benchmark sites and it already has results for over 400 devices! I certainly don't want to have 400 versions of source code for one application. I first came across J2ME Polish when I was looking for a better way to implement my build system, and since then I've found it to be an extremely useful addition to my entire development process. Tools like this are what will keep us developing applications in a reasonable amount of time for multiple devices, which keeps the network operators and publishers happy—and you want to keep them happy, because this mobile applications industry is one of the fastest-growing industries in the world.

So if you want to be successful, keep your knowledge up to date, keep your eye on the ball, and keep enjoying the ride. J2ME Polish keeps developers happy and able to make everything work.

Welcome to your world—make it a good one!

Kirk Bateman
Managing Director/Lead Developer
Synaptic Technologies Limited (UK)

About the Author

ROBERT VIRKUS is the architect and lead programmer for the open source project J2ME Polish. He is an internationally recognized J2ME expert and is a member of Mobile Solutions Group, Bremen, Germany.

After studying law and computer science in Bremen, Germany, and Sheffield, England, Robert began working in the mobile industry in 1999. He followed WAP and J2ME from their very beginnings and developed large-scale mobile betting applications.

In 2003, he founded Enough Software, the company behind J2ME Polish.

In his spare time, Robert enjoys the company of his girlfriend, Jinny, and his dog, Benny. Other spare-time favorites are going to concerts of soul, ska, and punk-rock bands, and playing around with old computers like Atari 400, Commodore 8296, and MCS Alpha 1.

About the Technical Reviewer

THOMAS KRAFT is a managing director of Synyx, a company located in Karlsruhe, Germany. Synyx specializes in developing business solutions based on open source frameworks. Thomas has many years of experience developing Java applications, with a focus on business solutions and J2ME applications. He is also an expert in the open source content management system OpenCms. Thomas has written several articles about J2ME developing, mostly GUI related. Thomas resides in the beautiful city of Karlsruhe and can be reached via e-mail at *kraft@synyx.de*.

Acknowledgments

Writing this book was hard work, but also a lot of fun. Thanks to everyone who made it possible, especially Jinny Verdonck, Thomas Kraft, Ricky Nkrumah, Kirk Bateman, and the whole Apress crew. A big thanks goes also to the community that continuously extends and improves J2ME Polish!

Introduction

This book introduces J2ME Polish, a collection of open source tools for creating "polished" wireless Java applications. J2ME Polish is best known for its build tools and its user interface—but more about that later. In this book, you will learn how to use J2ME Polish to your advantage. You will also learn about the challenges you will encounter in the real world of wireless Java programming and how J2ME Polish can help you to master these problems, by circumventing device bugs, integrating the best matching resources, and more.

The first part of this book helps you to install and integrate J2ME Polish in your development system. The second part of the book deals with the various tools included in J2ME Polish, including the following:

- Device database (Chapter 6)
- Build tools (Chapter 7)
- Preprocessor (Chapter 8)
- Logging framework (Chapter 9)
- Utilities (Chapter 10)
- Game engine (Chapter 11)
- User interface (Chapter 12)

You can also extend J2ME Polish in almost every aspect, which I discuss in Chapter 13. In the third and last part of the book, you will learn about differences between J2ME devices, known issues, and typical challenges of J2ME programming in the real world.

In this book, I assume that you are already familiar with J2ME development, so you should know what a MIDlet is, what the Mobile Media API is used for, and so forth. This book will not teach J2ME programming; instead, it focuses on how you can get the most out of your programming.

Please feel free to get in touch with me at *robert@enough.de*.

PART 1

Getting Ready

Creating mobile Java applications is great fun. Use this part for learning how to install J2ME Polish and other necessary or useful tools for J2ME programming. If you already have J2ME Polish up and running, I suggest that you skim through this part, so you don't miss out on the additional tips and tricks.

CHAPTER 1

Quick Setup Guide

In this chapter:

- Download J2ME Polish (*http://www.j2mepolish.org*).
- Install J2ME Polish (double-click the downloaded file or call `java -jar j2mepolish-[version].jar`).
- Check out the sample applications (call `ant` or `ant test j2mepolish` in the *samples/menu* or *samples/roadrunner* directory), if you have Ant and the Wireless Toolkit (WTK) installed.

About two years ago, I was working on yet another mobile application and experienced the agony of J2ME development: the application worked fine on the emulators, but not in the crude real world. Then it worked on one device, but not another. After a while, my coworkers and I managed to get it running on all our target devices (five different handsets), but we had to split up the application into a different branch for each device we targeted. Then we needed to incorporate any changes into each branch. What a headache! We used way too much time coding device adjustments—more time than we devoted to the actual application itself. Being good programmers, we managed it in the end, of course. Then we presented our finished project. Although the application itself was regarded as good, the design was utterly rejected. So, we had to redo the code, once again in every branch.

This scenario probably sounds familiar to you. And, as a programmer, you probably wondered, as I did, if it really had to be that way. Why should you create yet another application branch just for incorporating device-specific adjustments? Why should you do these adjustments in the first place? And last, but not least, why should you, as a programmer, be forced to design the user interface of the application yourself? These are the types of problems that J2ME Polish was designed to address.

In this chapter, you'll get a quick start with J2ME Polish. Here, I assume that you have set up Ant and the Wireless Toolkit already. Please refer to the following chapters for a detailed step-by-step guide.

Installing J2ME Polish

The installation of J2ME Polish is done in three distinct phases:

1. Install the Java Software Development Kit (SDK) 1.4 or higher, the Wireless Toolkit (WTK), and a Java integrated development environment (IDE) or Ant.
2. Install J2ME Polish.
3. Integrate J2ME Polish into your favorite IDE.

You can download J2ME Polish from *http://www.j2mepolish.org* and start the installation by either double-clicking the downloaded *.jar* file or by calling

```
java -jar j2mepolish-[version].jar
```

from the command line. (Sanity note: Please substitute the `[version]` with the actual version number of J2ME Polish.) You should now be presented with the screen similar to Figure 1-1.

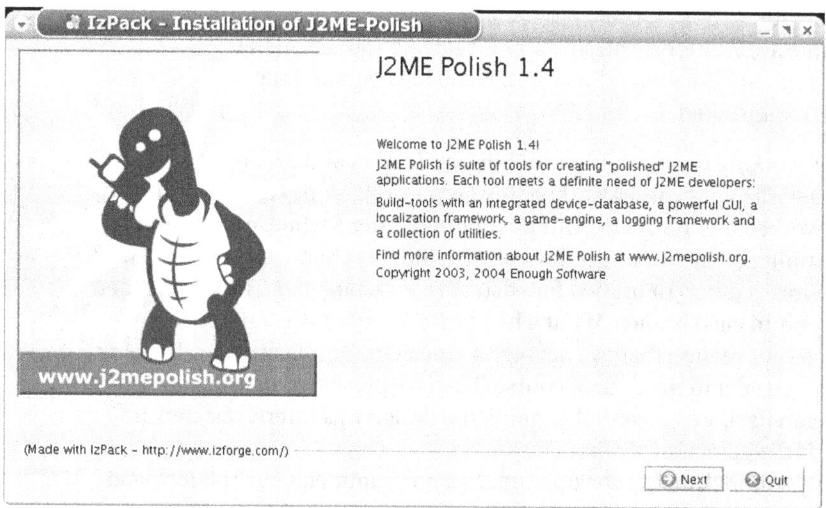

Figure 1-1. *Installing J2ME Polish*

Launching the Sample Applications

After you have installed J2ME Polish to any directory, which I refer to as *${polish.home}*, you can check out the sample applications, which can be found in the *samples* directory. Change (`cd`) to one of the directories, such as *samples/menu*, and call Ant from the command line:

```
ant test j2mepolish
```

The default WTK emulator should pop up when J2ME Polish has finished processing the application, as shown in Figure 1-2.

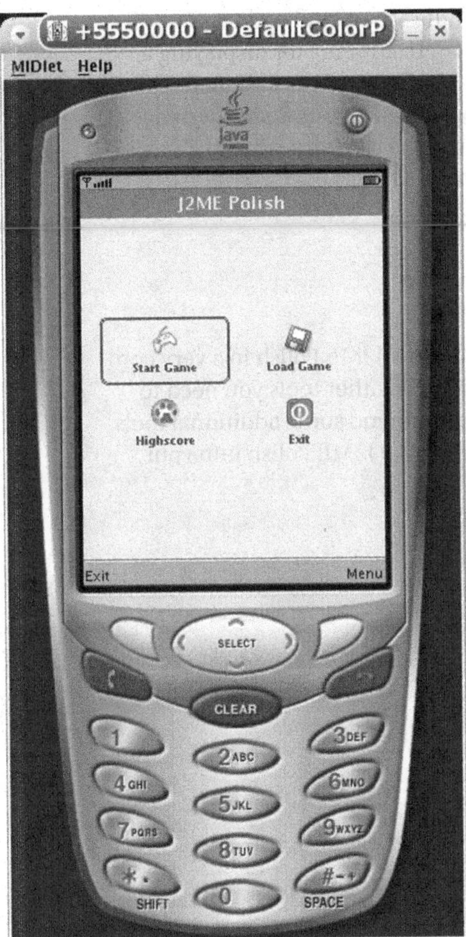

Figure 1-2. *The sample menu application in the WTK emulator*

If you see any error messages, most likely your Ant setup or your path to the WTK is not correct. See the "Troubleshooting Sample Application Errors" section in Chapter 3 for help.

You can also start J2ME Polish from within any Java IDE. You need to mount the sample project, right-click the *build.xml* file within it, and select Run Ant, Execute, or a similar menu command to launch J2ME Polish. If you want to start the emulator, make sure that you have selected the `test` target first, followed by the `j2mepolish` target.

Exploring the Sample Applications

If you wonder how the sample applications are made, you can take a peek at the *build.xml* file in either the *samples/menu* or *samples/roadrunner* directory. This standard Ant file controls the build process and uses the `<j2mepolish>` task for creating the application.

If you take a look at the code itself in the *src* directory of the Menu application, you will find a very simple application that uses a `javax.microedition.lcdui.List` for displaying a menu. Open the *resources/polish.css* file to find out how this application was designed. This file contains the design information in a human-readable format. To gain your first experience with J2ME Polish, change the `fontColor` in the `colors` section on the top from `rgb( 30, 85, 86 )` to `red`, and then restart J2ME Polish by calling `ant test j2mepolish`!

Congratulations, you are now ready to rumble!

Summary

This chapter explained the necessary steps for installing and using J2ME Polish in a very condensed manner. The following chapters describe how to install the other tools you need to run J2ME Polish, detail the J2ME Polish installation steps, recommend some additional tools that you might find helpful, and show how you can tightly integrate J2ME Polish into your favorite IDE.

CHAPTER 2

Installing the Prerequisites

In this chapter:

- Install the Java SDK (*http://java.sun.com/j2se*).
- Install the WTK (*http://java.sun.com/products/j2mewtoolkit*, or the Mac OS X version from *http://mpowers.net/midp-osx*).
- Obtain an IDE (such as Eclipse, *http://www.eclipse.org*), if you don't already have one.
- Install Ant (*http://ant.apache.org*).
- Obtain device emulators (from vendors, such as *http://forum.nokia.com*, *http://motocoder.com*, and *http://developer.samsungmobile.com*).

J2ME Polish relies on several open-source and free tools. You need to have the Java 2 Software Development Kit (SDK), the Wireless Toolkit (WTK), and Ant—either stand-alone or as part of your integrated development environment (IDE). You should also install device emulators from several vendors for testing your applications. Even though these are not strictly needed for developing great applications, they make your programming life a good deal easier. This chapter covers the installation of these tools.

The Java 2 SDK

J2ME Polish is a solution for creating wireless Java applications. So, it's only natural that you need Java itself as well. Java comes in three editions for catering to different needs:

- The Java 2 Standard Edition (J2SE) runs on your desktop computer and is needed by J2ME Polish for generating the actual mobile applications.
- The Java 2 Micro Edition (J2ME) runs on mobile phones, but also on television set-top boxes, personal digital assistants (PDAs), and embedded devices.
- The Java 2 Enterprise Edition (J2EE) runs on servers and is used for powering web applications or delivering mobile applications over the air.

If you do not have J2SE installed, please download the latest 1.4.*x* version now from *http://java.sun.com/j2se* and install it. You can also use Java 5.0 (1.5.*x*), but many mobile emulators require J2SE 1.4, so I recommend that you to stick to the 1.4 branch for now.

■ **Tip** See *Beginning J2ME: From Novice to Professional, Third Edition*, by Jonathan Knudsen (Apress, 2005) for a great introduction to J2ME development.

The Wireless Toolkit

The Wireless Toolkit (WTK) provides not only a generic emulator of a Java-enabled mobile phone, but also a preverification tool, which you need to make a J2ME application ready for deployment.

The installation is straightforward once you have downloaded it from *http://java.sun.com/products/j2mewtoolkit*. Just install it into the default directory, and you're ready to go.

WTK Versions

Several versions of the WTK are available, notably the old 1.0.4 version for Mobile Information Device Profile (MIDP) 1.0 phones and the latest version from the 2.*x* branch. Usually, you should go with the latest version, but you can also use the 1.0.4 version if you prefer it. The main difference is that you need to compile the code to Java 1.1 when you use the older WTK, whereas Java 1.2 is used by default when WTK 2.*x* is available. In theory, this shouldn't make a difference, but sometimes you might encounter really mind-boggling bugs that seem to be linked to overloading problems. In such cases, the `javac` target can make a difference, so just keep in mind that you can change it when you use WTK 2.*x*, but not when you use WTK 1.0.4.

WTK for Mac OS X

The standard WTK is not available for Mac OS X, but you can use a port that is provided by mpowers LLC at *http://mpowers.net/midp-osx*. To do so, you need to have X11 installed as well, which you can obtain at *http://www.apple.com/macosx/x11*.

The WTK itself is delivered as a disc image, which is mounted automatically when you double-click it. Just install it by dragging the mounted disc image onto the desktop first, and then into the *Applications* folder. If you don't have administrator's rights, you can move the disc image into the *Applications* folder within your home folder (create that folder if necessary).

IDE

In case you don't use an IDE yet, I recommend the Eclipse IDE, which is available for free from *http://www.eclipse.org*. Eclipse provides a modular and powerful environment based on plug-ins. J2ME Polish also brings along some Eclipse plug-ins that help you to write preprocessing code, manage emulators, and so on. Chapter 3 discusses the possible integration in more detail. Refer to *http://eclipse-tutorial.dev.java.net/* to learn more about developing Java programs with Eclipse.

Other popular IDEs include NetBeans (*http://www.netbeans.org/*) and JBuilder (*http://www.borland.com/jbuilder/*).

Ant

Ant forms the well-established standard for building any Java applications. You can use Ant from the command line or from within any serious IDE, such as Eclipse, NetBeans, JBuilder, or IDEA.

If you want to use Ant from the command line, you should download the binary distribution from *http://ant.apache.org* and extract it. You then need to adjust your PATH environment variable, so that the ant command from the *bin* directory can be found.

If you have installed Ant into *C:\tools\ant*, enter the following command on your Windows command line (or your shell script):

```
SET PATH=%PATH%;C:\tools\ant\bin
```

You can change the PATH variable permanently in the System Settings of Windows (Start ➤ Settings ➤ Control Center ➤ System ➤ Advanced ➤ Environment Variables).

Also set the JAVA_HOME environment variable, which needs to point to the installation directory of the Java 2 SDK:

```
SET JAVA_HOME=C:\j2sdk1.4.2_06
```

Under Unix/Linux/Mac OS X, use the export command instead of the SET command:

```
export PATH=$PATH:/home/user/tools/ant/bin
export JAVA_HOME=/opt/java
```

You can set any environment variable automatically by editing the *.bashrc* script, found in your home folder.

Now you should be able to test your Ant setup by querying the installed version:

```
> ant -version
Apache Ant version 1.6.2 compiled on September 11 2004
```

■ **Note** Please refer to the "Ant Crash Course" section in Chapter 7 for a guide to getting started with Ant. It's not that difficult!

Vendor-Specific Emulators

Emulators let you check out the look and feel of an application, and sometimes even help you find bugs. Some emulators are little more than the standard WTK with another skin, but some do reproduce the actual behavior of the device quite well.

■ **Caution** Beware of the "But it works in the emulator" trap! Never rely on an emulator. Test as early and as often as possible on the real device.

You can usually download emulators directly from the vendors' web sites, such as listed in Table 2-1. Some vendors provide additional services, such as discussion forums and the like. Most sites require you to register before you can download any resources. Sometimes, carriers and operating system developers provide emulators too. Most emulators are available for Windows only; some are available for Linux as well. For Mac OS X, you can use the mpowerplayer SDK (*http://mpowerplayer.com*).

Table 2-1. *Emulator Vendors*

Vendor	URL	Remarks
Nokia	*http://forum.nokia.com*	Look for Java tools and SDKs for getting several emulators. Most common are the Series 60 and the Series 40 developer kits.
Motorola	*http://motocoder.com*	The Motorola SDK contains several emulators for most J2ME-enabled devices. Go to Tools ➤ SDK to download the SDK.
Samsung	*http://developer.samsungmobile.com*	The Samsung site supports only Microsoft Internet Explorer 6.0 and above. KDE's Konqueror also works, but Mozilla-based browsers cannot be used. Check out the Resources section for downloading the SDKs.
Sony Ericsson	*http://developer.sonyericsson.com*	You can download the SDK from Docs & Tools ➤ Java.
Siemens	*http://communication-market.siemens.de/portal/main.aspx?pid=1*	Download the toolkit by choosing Resources ➤ Tools.
Symbian	*http://www.symbian.com/developer*	Download the emulators from the SDKs section.

Summary

In this chapter, we looked at the various basic tools that you need in order to use J2ME Polish. In the next chapter, you will learn how to install and set up J2ME Polish itself, so that you can start developing professional mobile applications!

CHAPTER 3

Installing J2ME Polish

In this chapter:

- Get the J2ME Polish installer (*http://www.j2mepolish.org*).
- Invoke the installer (by calling `java -jar j2mepolish-[version].jar`).
- Use the provided sample applications.

Thanks to the graphical installer, the setup of J2ME Polish is relatively painless. This chapter describes the installation of J2ME Polish, as well as some third-party tools that you can use with J2ME Polish.

J2ME Polish Installation Guide

You can download the J2ME Polish installer from *http://www.j2mepolish.org*. Just select Download from the main page.

Tip While you're at *http://www.j2mepolish.org*, you can also subscribe to the mailing lists by selecting Discussion, then Mailing Lists. The polish-users list provides help and general discussions about J2ME Polish. The polish-announce list keeps you updated about new releases.

You can invoke the installer either by double-clicking the downloaded file or by calling `java -jar j2mepolish-[version].jar` from the command line. You need to substitute the `[version]` part with the real version number, such as `j2mepolish-1.4.1.jar`. Now the installer should start.

The installer is a simple wizard that needs your input for some steps. It presents three critical screens: license selection, WTK directory selection, and component selection.

License Selection

The license selection screen, shown in Figure 3-1, asks you to decide which license you want to use. The license will be included in the *build.xml* files, which control the actual build process. So, you can change the license at any time by modifying these files.

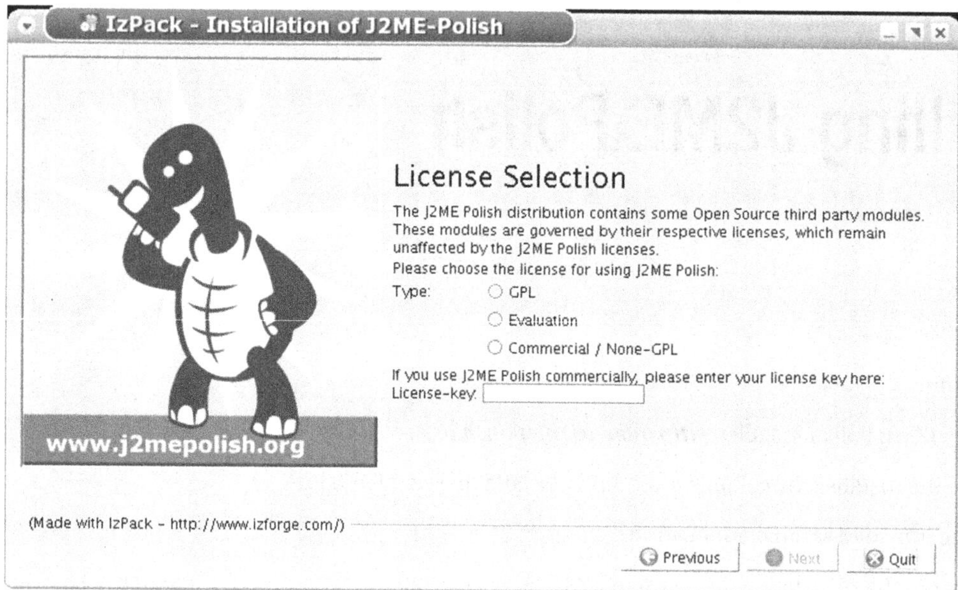

Figure 3-1. *Selecting a license in the installer*

The license screen offers the following choices:

GPL: If you want to publish your J2ME applications under the open source GNU General Public License (GPL), you should select the GPL option. You can also choose the GPL option when you use J2ME Polish commercially in closed-source products, but in that case, you are not allowed to use many modules like the GUI, the debugging framework, or any of the provided client APIs. You can, however, use the general building facilities of J2ME Polish, including the resource assembling, multiple device builds, and powerful preprocessing tools.

Evaluation: If you just want to check out J2ME Polish, choose the Evaluation option.

Commercial/None-GPL: If you already have a commercial license key, select the Commercial/None-GPL option. In that case, you need to enter your license key into the provided text box.

WTK Directory Selection

Another important installer screen requests that you select the directory in which the WTK is installed, as shown in Figure 3-2.

On Windows, a typical installation directory is *C:\WTK22*. On Mac OS X, you need to select the directory (usually called *MIDPv1.0.3 for OS X*), and then click Choose in the file selection dialog box.

Like the license information, the WTK location information is included into the provided *build.xml* files, so you can change it later by modifying the `${wtk.home}` property in those files.

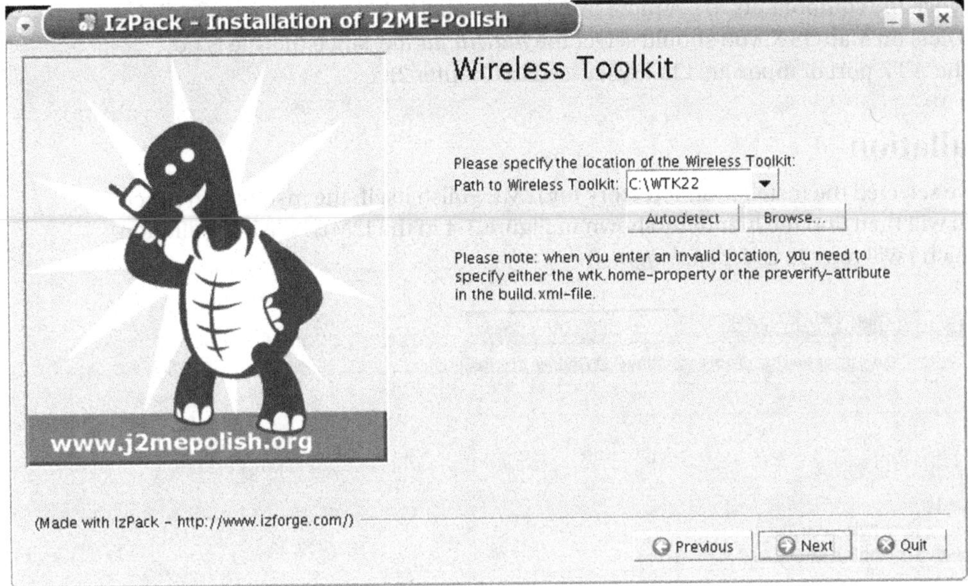

Figure 3-2. *Specifying the WTK directory location*

Component Selection

The last important screen of the installer is the one where you select the components to be installed, as shown in Figure 3-3.

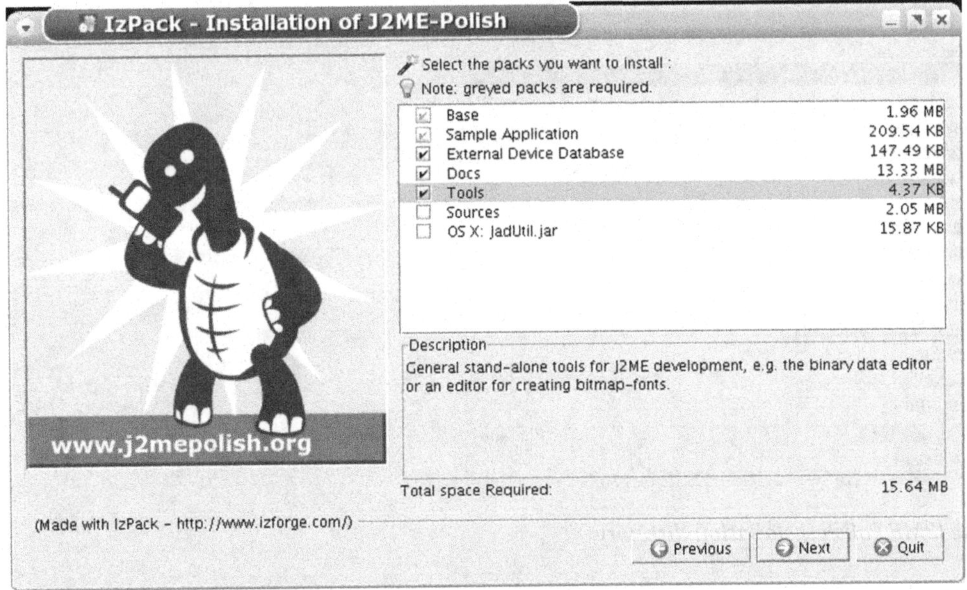

Figure 3-3. *Selecting the components you want to install*

You can click the components to get more information about them. If you want to digitally sign MIDlets on Mac OS X, you should select the *JadUtil.jar* file, since this file is not available in the WTK port of mpowers LLC (discussed in Chapter 2).

The Installation

After you have selected the installation directory for J2ME Polish itself, the installation process is started. You will then find the hierarchy shown in Figure 3-4 in the J2ME Polish installation directory (which I will refer to as *${polish.home}*).

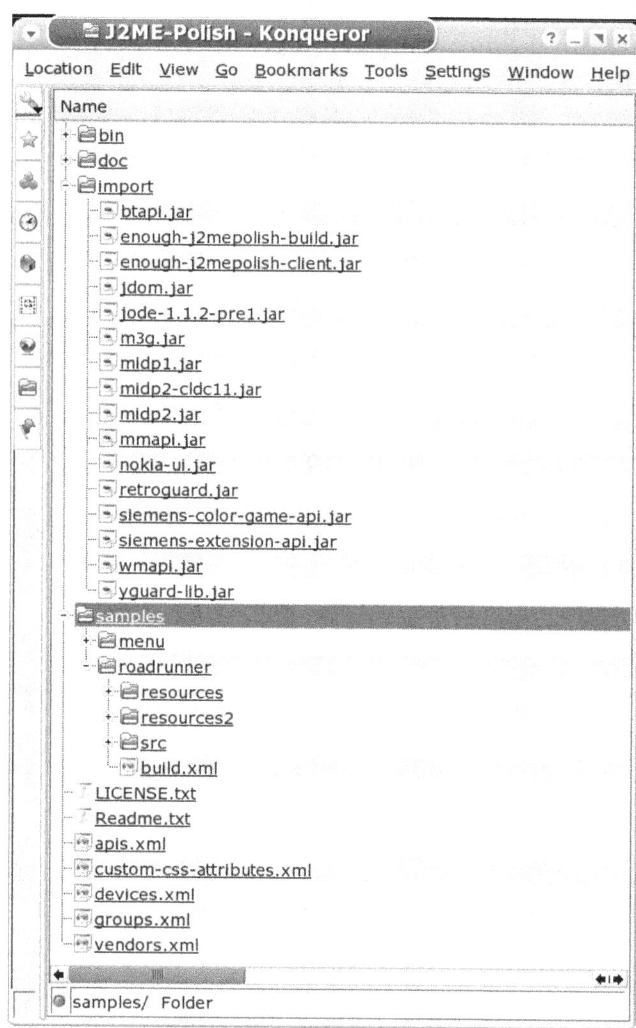

Figure 3-4. *The J2ME Polish installation directory*

The J2ME Polish installation directory contains the following folders:

- The *bin* folder contains some stand-alone tools, such as the editor for binary data files and the tool for creating bitmap fonts from True Type fonts.
- The *doc* folder contains the HTML and the PDF documentation.
- The *import* folder contains the core libraries of J2ME Polish, along with many standard J2ME libraries and vendor-specific API extensions. These APIs are used during the build process and can also be used for the classpath of your J2ME project in your favorite IDE.
- The *samples* directory contains the sample applications.
- The root directory (*${polish.home}*) contains the device database, which consists of the files *devices.xml, vendors.xml, groups.xml, bugs.xml,* and *apis.xml.* The file *custom-css-attributes.xml* can be used to describe your own extensions to the GUI of J2ME Polish.

External Tools

While you're in the install mode, you should also consider installing the following third-party tools:

Jad: Jad (*http://www.kpdus.com/jad.html*) is a free Java decompiler. It is useful for resolving stack traces shown within emulators. Such stack traces show only the bytecode instruction offset within a method. J2ME Polish can show the actual positions in the source code when Jad is either in the PATH or in the *${polish.home}/bin* folder.

ProGuard: ProGuard (*http://proguard.sourceforge.net*) is the best open-source obfuscator, which protects and shrinks your code at the same time. Copy the *proguard.jar* file to *${polish.home}/import.*

7-Zip: J2ME Polish can use 7-Zip (*http://7-zip.org,* or *http://p7zip.sourceforge.net* for Linux and Mac OS X systems) for packaging the application, which might result in smaller file sizes. Install 7-Zip to *${polish.home}/bin* so that J2ME Polish can find it automatically. You can download 7-Zip for Linux and Mac OS X at *http://p7zip.sourceforge.net.*

KZIP: J2ME Polish can also use the KZIP packager (*http://advsys.net/ken/utils.htm#kzip*). When you install KZIP to *${polish.home}/bin,* J2ME Polish can find it automatically.

Pngcrush, PNGOUT, and PNGGauntlet: Pngcrush (*http://pmt.sourceforge.net/pngcrush*) and PNGOUT (*http://advsys.net/ken/utils.htm#pngout*) optimize PNG images. You must use these tools manually. PNGGauntlet (*http://numbera.com/software/pnggauntlet.aspx*) provides a GUI for PNGOUT. Install these tools anywhere on your system.

J2ME Polish Sample Applications

You will find sample applications in the *samples* folder of the J2ME Polish installation directory *${polish.home}* (see Figure 3-4). You can use these sample applications as a blueprint for your own projects. Each sample application contains the following:

- The *resources* folder stores all images, design settings, and so forth.
- The *resources2* folder stores an alternative design for the application.
- The *src* folder contains the actual source code of the sample application.
- The *build.xml* file controls how J2ME Polish should build the sample applications.

Note In this section, I assume that you are using Ant from the command line. Of course, you can build the sample application from within your IDE as well. Often, it is enough to create a new project with the sample application as its root, right-click *build.xml* within it, and select Run ➤ Ant or a similar menu command in the IDE. See the next chapter for details on integrating J2ME Polish into common IDEs.

Testing the Sample Applications

The Menu application just displays a typical menu of any J2ME game. Test this application in the emulator from the command line with the following commands:

```
> cd C:\Programs\J2ME-Polish\samples\menu
> ant test j2mepolish
```

Adjust the path to your installation directory of J2ME Polish accordingly.

So what happens here? When Ant is called, it looks for the file *build.xml* in the current directory (so it uses *samples/menu/build.xml* in this example). The parameters `test` and `j2mepolish` denote targets within *build.xml*, which are executed by Ant. The `test` target sets an Ant property to `true`, which is evaluated by the `j2mepolish` target. When `test` is `true`, J2ME Polish will build the application for only one device and will also launch the appropriate emulator after the successful build. When everything works out, you should see the sample application (see Figure 1-2 in Chapter 1).

The RoadRunner sample application features a full-blown game, in which a frog needs to be guided through crowded streets (sound familiar?). By default, the RoadRunner game is built for the Nokia/Series60 in the test mode. Before building it, make sure that you have installed that emulator, which you can get from *http://forum.nokia.com.* Depending on your setup, you might need to define the Ant property `${nokia.home}` in the *build.xml* file, for example:

```
<property name="nokia.home" value="C:\Nokia" />
```

A commented-out version of this property can be found at the beginning of the *build.xml* file.

Treat yourself to a successful installation and play a round of RoadRunner now:

```
> cd C:\Programs\J2ME-Polish\samples\roadrunner
> ant test j2mepolish
```

Use the correct path for the `cd` command.

Figure 3-5 shows the main RoadRunner menu.

Figure 3-5. *The main menu of the RoadRunner game*

Troubleshooting Sample Application Errors

If you get an error message when you build a sample application, check your Ant setup. The following are common errors:

Command not found: To resolve this, set your `PATH` environment variable so that it includes the *bin* directory of your Ant setup; for example, `SET PATH=%PATH%;C:\ant\bin`, or on Unix systems, `export PATH=$PATH:/home/ant/bin`.

Java Compiler cannot be found: To resolve this, make sure that you have set the `JAVA_HOME` environment variable correctly (using the preceding `SET` or `export` command).

`${wtk.home}` can be set incorrectly: If you did not specify the installation directory of the WTK correctly during the installation, J2ME Polish will complain about the wrong `${wtk.home}` property. In that case, you need to open the *build.xml* file and adjust this Ant property; for example, `<property name="wtk.home" value="C:\WTK22" />`.

When you call `ant` without any parameters from the command line, only the `j2mepolish` target will be executed. Since the `test` property has not been set to `true`, J2ME Polish will create the sample application for several target devices and will not launch the emulator. In that case, you will find the created applications within the newly created *dist* folder.

Summary

With the help of this chapter, you have now installed J2ME Polish and maybe even some other useful tools as well. In the next chapter, you will learn how to integrate your J2ME Polish installation into your favorite IDE.

CHAPTER 4

Integrating J2ME Polish into IDEs

In this chapter:

- Understand common integration issues when using J2ME Polish.
- Learn how to integrate J2ME Polish into Eclipse, NetBeans, JBuilder, and IntelliJ.

You can integrate J2ME Polish into any integrated development environment (IDE) that supports Ant, which nowadays means you can integrate J2ME Polish into all professional IDEs. In this chapter, I will first discuss common options you can set in every IDE, and then I will discuss how to integrate into Eclipse, NetBeans, and JBuilder in detail.

Recognizing Common Integration Issues

You must pay attention to certain issues regardless of which IDE you use. Rather than repeating these issues in the discussions of each IDE, I will summarize them in this section.

The easiest way to integrate J2ME Polish is to use one of the sample applications to get started (for example, *${polish.home}/samples/menu*). Depending on your IDE, you can just mount that application folder or copy it onto your IDE's workspace. You can then invoke the provided *build.xml* file within the Menu application for building it with J2ME Polish. In case you want to start the emulator, select the `emulator` target in *build.xml*.

If you want to use J2ME Polish for an existing project, just copy the *${polish.home}/samples/menu/build.xml* script to your project's folder and adjust at least the `<midlet>` definition in it. You may also want to change the `<deviceRequirements>` and `<resources>` settings in the *build.xml* file.

When you're working in a team and using a version control system such as CVS (*http://www.cvshome.org*), Subversion (*http://subversion.tigris.org*), and the like, make sure you do not share the temporary *build* and *dist* folders. These are created and used by J2ME Polish during the build phase and thus change with every run. Usually, you can disable the sharing of these folders by right-clicking (Command+click on Mac OS X) the *build* and *dist* folders and then choosing Add to .cvsignore (or similar).

■ **Note** In the following discussions, I will use the term *right-click*. This is equivalent to Command+click on Mac OS X.

Using Eclipse

Eclipse (*http://www.eclipse.org*) is a popular IDE among code-centric Java developers. It has great refactoring support and is highly extensible thanks to its plug-in concept. If you are not sure what IDE to use, test Eclipse first.

Integrating Eclipse with Ant

For creating your first J2ME Polish project, copy the complete *${polish.home}/samples/menu* folder into your Eclipse workspace directory. Then create a new project called Menu in Eclipse, and confirm each step. In case you have built the Menu application already on the command line, make sure you select only the *source/src* folder as your source directory (see Figure 4-1). Eclipse then automatically integrates all source files and sets the classpath accordingly. You will find the sample application now in the package `de.enough.polish.example`.

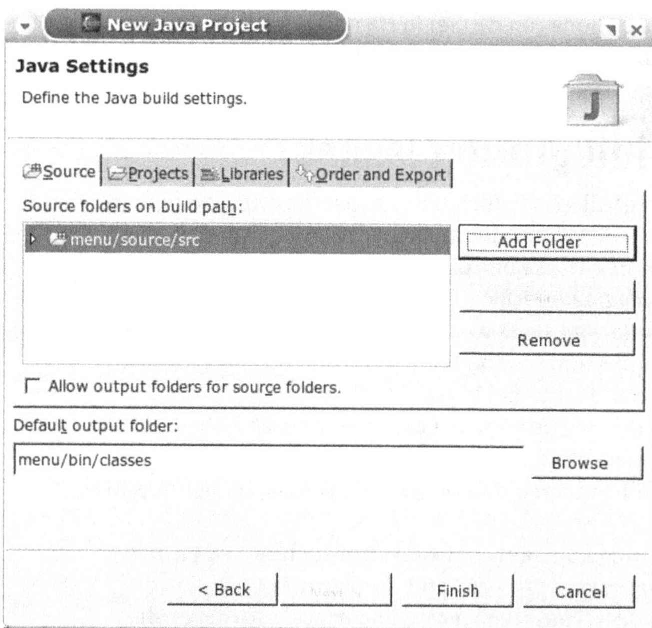

Figure 4-1. *Confirming the correct source folder in Eclipse*

You can now start J2ME Polish and create the JAR and JAD files by right-clicking the *build.xml* file and selecting Run Ant. After J2ME Polish has finished the build, you can find the JAR and JAD files in the *dist* folder of your project. If you want to access them from within Eclipse, you may need to refresh your project: right-click the project, and select Refresh.

For starting the emulator, just choose the `emulator` target in the Run Ant dialog box. After you have started it once, you can use the External Tools button shown in Figure 4-2 for quickly running the last Ant target again.

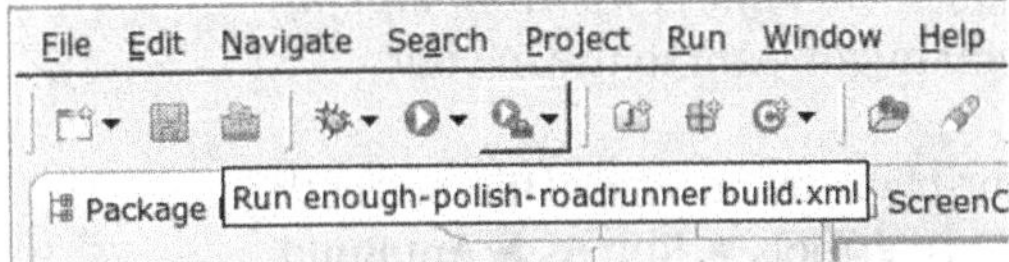

Figure 4-2. *Running the last Ant target again in Eclipse*

ENFORCING NAMING SCHEMES WITH ECLIPSE

Eclipse is not only one of the most flexible IDEs but also contains many useful features that can help you produce better code.

Take, for example, the many different naming schemes that are used to distinguish instance variables from local variables. Some people start local variables with a specific character, others start instance variables with a fixed character, and a third group starts local variables with one and instance variables with another character. While such naming schemes might help you or a small group of developers, they are problematic in two ways:

- Enforcing naming schemes is not a trivial task; you might need to check all source code regularly.
- New programmers need to learn your specific naming scheme first.

The Java standard provides a wonderful alternative to such naming schemes: use `this` to qualify instance variables. In contrast to your own naming scheme, every Java programmer knows that `this.variableName` refers to an instance variable. Furthermore, Eclipse enforces this scheme automatically for you when you activate the corresponding compiler warning (or error depending on your needs) under Window ➤ Preferences ➤ Java ➤ Compiler ➤ Unqualified Access to Instance Field. Check the other settings in the Compiler dialog box; Eclipse can enforce many other code conventions ranging from criticizing invalid JavaDoc comments to warning about variables that are never used.

If that is not enough for you, check out the available Eclipse plug-ins at *http://eclipse-plugins.info*. You will find almost anything for your development needs.

Troubleshooting Integration Issues

Sometimes you might encounter difficulties while integrating J2ME Polish in Eclipse.

In case the sources have not been integrated automatically, set the source directory of your project manually: select Project ➤ Properties ➤ Java Build Path ➤ Source, and add the source folder *source/src* there.

If Eclipse complains about unknown classes, the classpath of your project is not set correctly. Please include the following JAR files from the *${polish.home}/import* folder in your classpath: *import/midp2.jar*, *import/enough-j2mepolish-client.jar*, *import/mmapi.jar*, *import/nokia-ui.jar*, *import/wmapi.jar*, and any others you might want to use in your application such as *m3g.jar* or *pdaapi.jar*.

If the Run Ant command is not shown when you right-click the *build.xml* file, select the *build.xml* script, open the Run menu, and then select External Tools ➤ Run As ➤ Ant Build.

When the build process is aborted with a message that no suitable Java compiler was found, you need to make sure a valid Java SDK (not a JRE) is used for the build. Switch to the JRE tab in the Run Ant dialog box, and check the Runtime JRE setting. In most cases, you can run Ant in the same JRE as the workspace. When this does not work, check if the JRE is pointing to a Java SDK by clicking the Installed JREs button in the JRE tab.

Installing the J2ME Polish Plug-Ins

J2ME Polish has some optional Eclipse plug-ins for handling source code with preprocessing directives and *polish.css* files. From August 2005 onward, a debugger and several other tools are planned.

You can install the J2ME Polish plug-ins by selecting Help ➤ Software Updates ➤ Search for New Features to Install. In the dialog box that appears, create a new remote site with the URL *http://www.j2mepolish.org/eclipse*, select that site, and install the features.

After restarting the workspace, you can now open Java source files in the J2ME Polish editor by right-clicking them and selecting Open With ➤ J2ME Polish Editor. Figure 4-3 shows the syntax highlighting and marking of preprocessing blocks in action. When you stay within an `#if` directive for a couple of seconds, all corresponding `#else` and `#endif` directives are marked, for example. Other features include autocompletion and indenting of directives.

■ **Note** The EclipseME project (*http://eclipseme.org*) provides a popular plug-in for creating J2ME applications with Eclipse. With a bit of tweaking, you can use J2ME Polish along with the EclipseME plug-in; check out the compiler mode settings of the `<build>` element in the appendix for more information. As soon as J2ME Polish also provides a debugger plug-in, you should stick to J2ME Polish only for best compatibility.

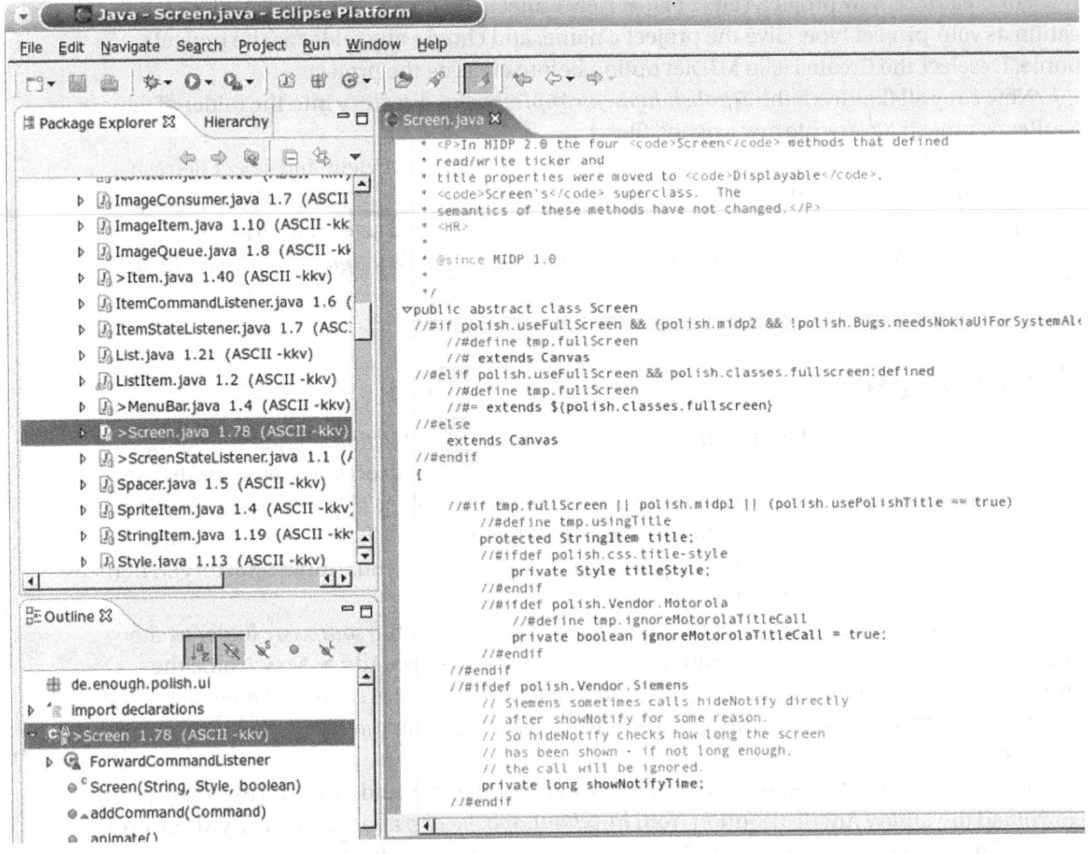

Figure 4-3. *The J2ME Polish editor can mark directive groups.*

Using NetBeans

NetBeans (*http://www.netbeans.org*) is another impressive free and open-source IDE for Java development. It is quite popular with J2ME developers because it integrates nicely with the Wireless Toolkit thanks to its Mobility Pack.

For integrating J2ME Polish with NetBeans 4, create a new project and copy the contents of *${polish.home}/samples/menu* into your new project with a file manager. Right-click *build.xml*, and choose Run Target ➤ j2mepolish for building the application or Run Target ➤ emulator for invoking the emulator.

For creating a new project, select File ➤ New Project and choose Mobile ➤ Mobile Application as your project type. Give the project a name, and choose any folder as the project's home. Deselect the Create Hello MIDlet option before creating the project.

Now copy all files from the *${polish.home}/samples/menu* directory into the folder of your NetBeans project. Overwrite any existing files.

Return to NetBeans, right-click your new project in the project view, and select Refresh Folders. You can now view the sample application in the `de.enough.polish.example` package.

Right-click your project again, choose Properties ➤ Build, and select Libraries and Resources. Click Add Jar/Zip, and add the *${polish.home}/import/enough-j2mepolish-client.jar* file to your project.

Using JBuilder

Borland's commercial JBuilder IDE (*http://www.borland.com/mobile/jbuilder*) is still going strong and provides a specialized IDE for J2ME development. This section shows how to use the freely available, general-purpose Foundation version of JBuilder.

To integrate J2ME Polish into JBuilder, copy the *${polish.home}/samples/menu* sample application into your workspace (usually to the *jbproject* folder in your home directory). Then start JBuilder, and create a new Menu project.

In the project dialog box, select the appropriate path and set the *source/src* folder as the main source folder. Switch to the Required Libraries tab, and select Add ➤ New. Name the library "MIDP-Development" or something similar, and add the files *enough-j2mepolish-client.jar*, *midp2.jar*, *mmapi.jar*, *wmapi.jar*, and *nokia-ui.jar* from the *${polish.home}/import* folder to the library path.

In the free Foundation edition of JBuilder, you need to install and integrate Ant first. Download the binary Ant distribution from *http://ant.apache.org*, and extract it anywhere on your system (now referred to as *${ant.home}*). Now adjust the JBuilder Ant setup in Project ➤ Project Properties ➤ Ant ➤ Build. Set the Ant home directory to *${ant.home}*.

Now create the new project, and integrate the *build.xml* file: select Project ➤ Add ➤ Add Files/Packages/Classes. In the dialog box that appears, choose the file *build.xml* from the project's root. Now *build.xml* appears in the project view. You need to deactivate the Borland compiler for building the actual applications: right-click the *build.xml* script, select Properties, and deselect the Use Borland Java Compiler check box.

You can now build the sample application by right-clicking the *build.xml* file and selecting Make. You will find the created J2ME application files in the *dist* folder of your project, after you have switched to the File Browser view.

To invoke the emulator, open the *build.xml* file by clicking the handle, right-click the `emulator` target, and select Make.

Using IntelliJ

IntelliJ of JetBrains (*http://www.jetbrains.com*) is famous for being the workhorse of code-centric developers.

To integrate J2ME Polish, just copy the complete directory of the Menu sample application from *${polish.home}/samples/menu* to your IntelliJ project folder, usually *IdeaProjects* in your home folder. Now create a new Menu project (File ➤ New Project). Use any JDK to choose a single module project to complete the project setup. IntelliJ is intelligent enough to automatically detect that the *source/src* folder contains the source files, so just confirm this setup.

You now adjust the classpath of your project by opening the project view, right-clicking the project, and selecting Module Settings. Switch to the Libraries (Classpath) tab, and create a new global library by selecting Edit in the Used Global Libraries section. Give it the name J2ME, and select all needed libraries from *${polish.home}/import* (for example, *midp2.jar*, *enough-j2mepolish-client.jar*, *wmapi.jar*, *m3g.jar*, *pdaapi.jar*, and *nokia-ui.jar*).

For building the project, right-click the *build.xml* file in the root of the project view and choose to add this file as an Ant build file. The Ant view will now open, and you can right-click the "j2mepolish" target and choose Run Target to build the application.

During the development you often have to launch the emulator. In IntelliJ it is easy to assign a shortcut to this task. Right-click the "emulator" target in the Ant view, and select Assign Shortcut. Now copy the Default keymap first, and activate it by selecting Set Active. Now you can assign any shortcut to it; Figure 4-4 shows how to assign Ctrl+E. From now on, just press the keys Ctrl and E simultaneously to invoke the emulator.

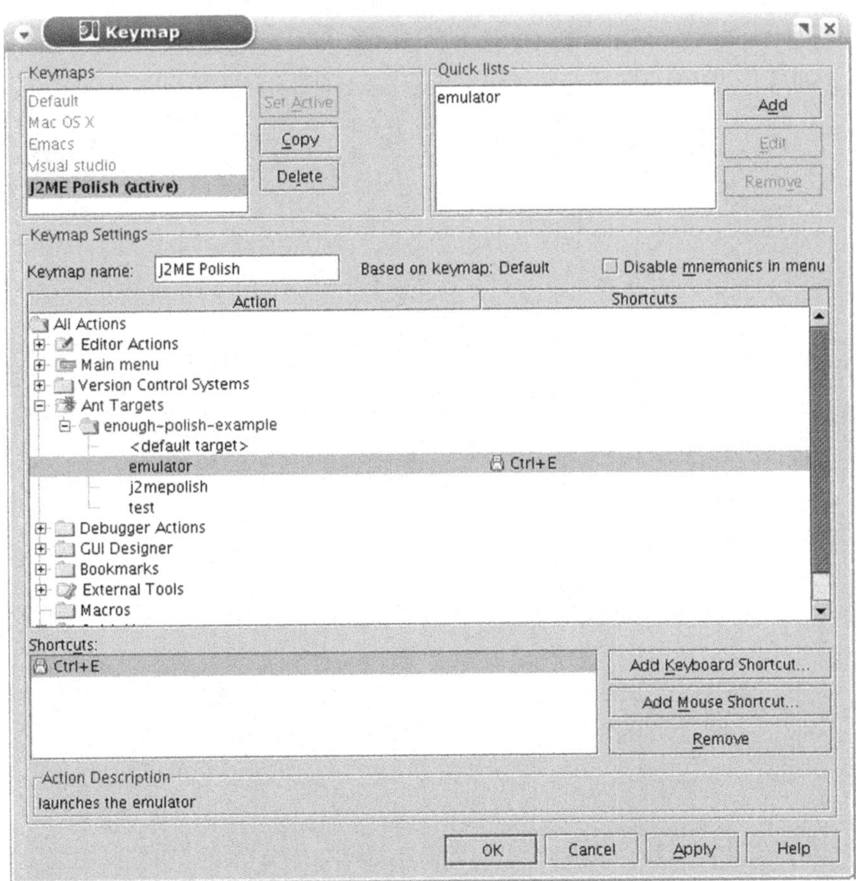

Figure 4-4. *Assigning a shortcut to the emulator Ant target in IntelliJ*

Summary

Thanks to the Ant support of all good Java IDEs, integrating J2ME Polish is quite easy. Apart from the discussed IDEs, you can use many others, as long as they can call Ant scripts. So, if you are a Unix guru, you can even use Emacs without any problems.

Now you are ready to start using J2ME Polish fully. In the next chapter, you will learn how you can use the device database of J2ME Polish not only for learning about your target devices but also for adjusting your application, circumventing device issues, and more.

PART 2

Using J2ME Polish

J2ME Polish is a collection of tools for the development of wireless Java applications. In this part, you will learn how to use and tweak the different tools, such as the build framework, the GUI, and the stand-alone tools.

CHAPTER 5

Getting to Know J2ME Polish

In this chapter:

- Get to know the architecture of J2ME Polish—the build framework, client API, IDE plug-ins, and stand-alone tools layers.
- Learn how J2ME Polish can help you with the development of wireless Java applications, as you design, implement, build, test, optimize, and deploy each J2ME application.

This chapter provides you with an overview of the architecture of J2ME Polish. It also shows you how J2ME Polish helps you in the different phases of the development of your J2ME applications.

J2ME Polish from 500 Miles Above

J2ME Polish is collection of components for the development of wireless Java applications. The various components can be separated into four different layers, as shown in Figure 5-1.

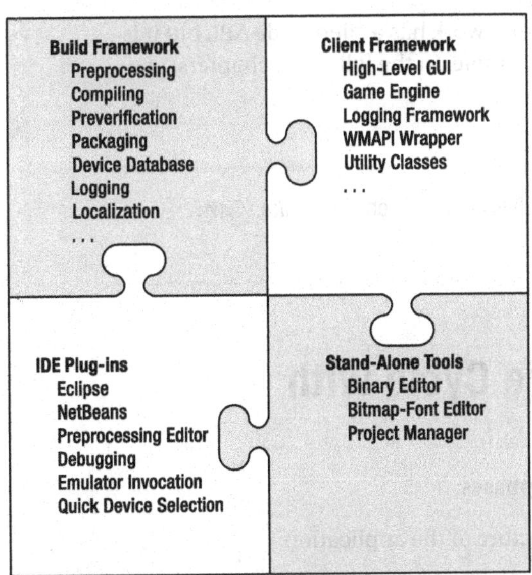

Figure 5-1. *The four layers of J2ME Polish*

Each layer features several components:

Build framework: You use the build framework to build your J2ME applications. This Ant-based framework allows you to preprocess your source code before it is compiled, and it compiles, preverifies, and packages your application for multiple devices and locales. A logging mode can be used for tracing errors in your application. Take advantage of the device database and the preprocessing to adjust your application to various handsets, without losing the portability of your application.

Client framework: The client framework provides APIs for enhancing your wireless Java application. It includes an alternative to the high-level Mobile Information Device Profile (MIDP) user interface. The J2ME Polish GUI is designed outside the application code using simple Cascading Style Sheets (CSS) text files. The game engine allows the usage of the MIDP 2.0 game API on MIDP 1.0 devices, so you can easily port games to MIDP 1.0 platforms. The WMAPI wrapper enables you to use the Wireless Messaging API, even on devices that support only vendor proprietary methods for sending and receiving messages. Last, but not least, the utility classes provide common functionalities, such as the `TextUtil` or the `BitMapFont` classes. Thanks to the build framework, the client framework is automatically adjusted to the target devices, so that you can use a full-screen mode on almost all phones, for example.

IDE plug-ins: The IDE plug-ins ease the development of J2ME applications in the popular Eclipse IDE. The preprocessing-aware Java editor plug-in provides syntax highlighting for preprocessing statements, for example. Since the build framework is based on Ant, you can still use J2ME Polish from within any IDE or even from the command line.

Stand-alone tools: J2ME Polish also includes several stand-alone tools. The binary data editor is specialized for creating and modifying structured binary files, like level data, while the font editor creates bitmap fonts out of any True Type.

These layers are tightly integrated. The logging framework has a client-side API, but it is controlled with the help of the build framework, for example. In the following chapters, you will get to know each layer intimately.

■ **Note** J2ME Polish is growing constantly, so make sure to check out the web site at *http://www.j2mepolish.org* to learn about the latest additions.

Managing the Application Life Cycle with J2ME Polish

Creating a J2ME application involves several distinct phases:

Design: In the design phase, you plan the architecture of the application.

Implementation: In the implementation phase, you realize the design and write the source code.

Build: In the build phase, you compile your source code and create the application bundles (JAR and JAD files).

Testing: In the testing phase, you check the implementation.

Optimization: In the optimization phase, you improve the application, focusing on performance, memory consumption, application size, and device adjustments.

Deployment: Finally, you install your application on the device in the deployment phase.

Here, we will take a closer look at each phase of the application life cycle. You'll see how you can use J2ME Polish for fast turnaround times in these phases, as well as learn some tips for each phase of the application life cycle.

Designing the Architecture

When you design the architecture of your application, you should strive to make it as simple as possible. You might already know that the pure object-oriented approach is not always the best one when designing a J2ME application. Each class adds overhead, and every abstraction slows down your application. But even so, you should try to create a clean and logical structure for your application, so that later changes do not result in unintentional side effects.

Bear the following recommendations in mind when you design your application (but do not follow them slavishly):

- Try to avoid abstract classes and interfaces. Often, you'll find preprocessing more effective for keeping your application flexible without using abstraction.
- Remember that each class increases your application size, so try to group functionalities to minimize the number of classes.
- Implement interfaces only when it is necessary. Instead of implementing the `CommandListener` interface in every screen, consider using a single dispatcher or controller class that is responsible for the application flow, for example. And don't create your own abstract event-handling system.
- Design for reusability by defining independent classes or modules, which can be used in other contexts and applications. Check if you can parameterize them, and don't be afraid of using different packages. The obfuscation step and J2ME Polish will take care of putting all classes into the default package, so that the size of the application is minimized.
- Do not overoptimize the design, such as by putting the complete application into one class. Leave drastic optimizations to the optimization phase, and remember that some devices accept classes only up to 16KB.
- Do not duplicate functionality. If you're using the J2ME Polish GUI for example, try to use these classes instead of implementing your own additional GUI classes.
- Try to use proven and stable third-party APIs instead of creating your own implementations, unless the needed functionality belongs to the core of your business. Thanks to the different behavior of the devices, creating stable APIs for J2ME is quite a challenging and complex task.

So to summarize these tips, your goal is to design a solid and clean architecture, but not overengineer it by using a heavy object-oriented approach.

Implementing the Application

You realize your application in the implementation phase. Along with the source code itself, you often need to create resources such as images and server-side application code.

For programming the actual source code, you can use an IDE or even a simple text editor, depending on your preferences. If you are new to Java programming, make sure to check out the free Eclipse and NetBeans IDEs. Both offer quite powerful environments and are excellent for J2ME programming. If you're using Eclipse, have a look at the compiler options under Window ➤ Preferences ➤ Java ➤ Compiler. You can activate many different warnings, which will help you to create clean code.

J2ME Polish helps you to implement your application by providing a powerful API that covers the user interface, network, and utilities tasks. The IDE plug-ins ease the programming of preprocessing code and allow fast turnaround times in the implementation phase.

Building Your Application

Building J2ME applications is necessary for running them, either on the emulator or on the actual device. At the very least, you need to compile your source, preverify the classes, package the classes and resources into a JAR file, and create the Java Application Descriptor (JAD) file. Often, you also need to choose the appropriate resources, translate your application, preprocess the source code, and obfuscate your application.

Does this sound like hard work? It is, but fortunately, it is completely automated by J2ME Polish. Chapter 7 discusses the details of building your applications.

Testing the Application

After implementing and building your application, you are ready to test it by running it on emulators and real devices. J2ME Polish can invoke emulators automatically for you, so that you can test your application with a single mouse click. When your application encounters an exception, stack traces given out in the emulators often show only the binary offset of the code, such as at `com.company.MyClass.myMethod(+20)`. J2ME Polish resolves such stack traces automatically when the Jad decompiler (discussed in Chapter 3) is installed.

■ **Caution** Testing your application on real devices is crucial to its success. Never rely on an emulator. Test as early and as often as possible on the real device.

J2ME Polish also provides a logging framework, which offers different logging levels and the ability to view logging messages on real devices. You can specify logging levels for packages and classes, and deactivate the logging completely, so that no precious space is wasted in the final application.

You'll learn more about invoking emulators in Chapter 7, and you'll get to know the details of the logging framework in Chapter 9.

Optimizing Your Application

When you implement and test your first prototype, you usually discover shortcomings that need to be fixed in the optimization phase. Typical shortcomings include the following:

Device-specific bugs: You encounter bugs on some devices, but not on others. You can solve these problems by using preprocessing for circumventing device-specific bugs. Chapter 8 describes how to preprocess your application with J2ME Polish. In Chapter 15 you will learn what problems you might encounter in the real world and how you can solve them.

Application size: Your application is too large. Usually, you can use automatic resource assembling to optimize resources usage and adjust your application's architecture. The automatic assembling of resources is discussed in Chapter 7.

Application performance: The performance is not as good as expected. You can use a variety of techniques for improving your application's performance. Chapter 16 is devoted to optimization strategies.

Deploying Your Application

Deploying your application on real handsets is a crucial step in the lifetime of your application. You can use different methods for installing your application, ranging from data cables to over-the-air downloads.

Bluetooth, Infrared, and Data Cables

The easiest way to install your application is to use a Bluetooth connection, which most devices provide nowadays. Usually, it is sufficient to send the generated JAR file (which contains the classes and the resources of your application) to the phone. How this is done depends on your operating system and your setup. Often, you simply right-click the file and select Send to Bluetooth Device or a similar option. Modern devices start the installation automatically directly after they have received the JAR file, but sometimes you need to look in the phone's incoming messages folder and select the sent file to start the installation.

Very similar to using Bluetooth is using an infrared connection or data or USB cable. Please refer to the documentation of your device for instructions on setting up such connections.

Over-the-Air Provisioning

The only standardized way to deploy your J2ME application is the over-the-air (OTA) download. In this scenario, you need a web server that delivers the JAD and JAR files of your application.

In a simple case, you can use a simple Wireless Markup Language (WML) page like the one in Listing 5-1. That page can be accessed with the Wireless Application Protocol (WAP) browser of the device and just provides a link to the JAD file. When the device reads the JAD file, it will forward the control to the Application Manager System (AMS). The AMS then shows some details (title, vendor, and size of the application) and prompts the user to download the actual application file (the JAR).

Listing 5-1. *Sample WML Page That Links to a JAD File*

```
<?xml version="1.0" encoding="ISO-8859-1"?>
<!DOCTYPE wml PUBLIC "-//WAPFORUM//DTD WML 1.1//EN"
 "http://www.wapforum.org/DTD/wml_1.1.xml">
<wml>
  <card title="Download" id="main">
      <p>
        <a href="myapplication.jad">Download Application</a>
      </p>
  </card>
</wml>
```

Most web servers are already configured to handle JAR and JAD files correctly. If your device does not recognize those files, you just need to add the *text/vnd.sun.j2me.app-descriptor* MIME type for *.jad* files and the *application/java* type for *.jar* files to the configuration of your web server.

If you have problems accessing the WML page, check your connection settings on your device. Some WAP gateways do not allow ports other than 80, so test this port as well if you encounter difficulties.

In a more complex scenario, you can generate the WML pages on the fly for the current device by evaluating the `USER_AGENT` HTTP header and using a server-side scripting technology such as JavaServer Pages (JSP) or PHP. You could also send links to the JAD files via binary short messages (as a WAP link) or with simple text messages.

Also, third-party OTA servers are available. These usually offer different provisioning technologies, device recognition, and payment solutions.

■ **Note** Using OTA in the development phase is a pain, since you need to copy the application first to the web server, and then download it from the server again. This takes quite a lot of time and can be costly as well. So check if there are other installation options available for your device.

Multimedia Message Provisioning

Some devices can also receive J2ME applications by using the Multimedia Messaging Service (MMS). Users find this much more convenient than bothering with normal OTA downloads, since no additional interaction is required (apart from selecting the application and the device on a web page). You will need a Short Message Service (SMS) center to send those messages for you.

Tracking Your Installations

If you publish your application on the Internet, it isn't easy to find out how many times it has been installed. Fortunately, the J2ME standard allows notifications at each installation as well as removal of your application. The optional JAD attribute `MIDlet-Install-Notify` contains the HTTP address, which should be invoked after the application has been installed. The device will try to call the given address and report the status in its content, such as `900 Success`. If the web server sets a cookie during the installation, this cookie might also be returned in the installation notification, as demonstrated in Listing 5-2.

Listing 5-2. *A Notification of a Successful Installation*

```
POST http://foo.bar.com/status HTTP/1.1
Host: foo.bar.com
Cookie: Name="abc"; Domain=".foo.bar"; Path="/app-dir"; \
        JSESSIONID="123"; VERSION="1"
Content-Length: 13

900 Success
```

Table 5-1 lists the possible status codes.

Table 5-1. *Status Codes of the Installation Notification*

Status Code	Status Message
900	Success
901	Insufficient Memory
902	User Cancelled
903	Loss of Service
904	JAR Size Mismatch
905	Attribute Mismatch
906	Invalid Descriptor
907	Invalid JAR
908	Incompatible Configuration or Profile
909	Application Authentication Failure
910	Application Authorization Failure
911	Push Registration Failure
912	Deletion Notification

You can also track the deletion of your application by setting the JAD attribute `MIDlet-Delete-Notify`. The device will then try to send a `POST` request stating `912 Deletion Notification` upon removal.

You can specify `MIDlet-Install-Notify` and `MIDlet-Delete-Notify` by defining the `<info>` attributes `installNotify` and `deleteNotify` in J2ME Polish. You'll learn more about setting attributes in Chapter 7.

Caution Do not rely on receiving each installation or deletion notification. Network failures and user interactions can suppress this mechanism.

Updating Your Application

Updates are quite important for business applications, but they can be equally desirable for long-running networked games. Update options depend on the platform.

MIDP 1.0 Platforms

Unfortunately, on MIDP 1.0 platforms, there is no way to trigger an update from within your application. Here are a few update strategies to consider:

- Query the current version whenever you make your first handshake with the server-side application. Depending on the business requirements, you could then notify the user that an update is available, or the server can deliver content specific to the version of your client J2ME application. When an active user chooses to update the application, you could send an SMS text message containing the link to the latest JAD file on the server. Most devices can now identify HTTP-based links in SMS messages and start the WAP browser directly.
- Send a binary message that contains a WAP-link to the user. The user can then save and invoke that link.
- Send the complete application via an MMS message to the user's handset. This is the most user-friendly way, but not all devices support deployment via MMS.

MIDP 2.0 Platforms

On MIDP 2.0 platforms, you can start the update process directly from within your application by issuing a platform request. Since platform requests are handled differently by real-world devices, you should prepare to exit your application after requesting an update. In any case, your application will be shut down before the update is actually put into place. Listing 5-3 shows an example of a MIDlet that persists its current version in a `RecordStore` so that it can detect updates.

Listing 5-3. *Issuing an Update Request from Your Application (MIDP 2.0)*

```
package com.apress.update;

import javax.microedition.io.ConnectionNotFoundException;
import javax.microedition.midlet.MIDlet;
import javax.microedition.midlet.MIDletStateChangeException;
import javax.microedition.rms.RecordStore;
import javax.microedition.rms.RecordStoreException;


public class UpdateMidlet extends MIDlet {

   private static final int VERSION = 125; // 1.2.5
```

```
public UpdateMidlet() {
   super();
}

protected void startApp() throws MIDletStateChangeException {
   try {
      RecordStore versionStore = RecordStore.openRecordStore( "version", false );
      versionStore.closeRecordStore();
      byte[] versionData = versionStore.getRecord(
                                    versionStore.getNextRecordID() - 1 );
      String versionStr = new String( versionData );
      int version = Integer.parseInt( versionStr );
      if ( version != VERSION ) {
         // app has been updated:
         showUpdateMessage();
         // remove version record store:
         RecordStore.deleteRecordStore("version");
         return;
      }
   } catch (RecordStoreException e) {
      // no update has been requested
   }
   showMainMenu();
}

protected void requestUpdate() {
   //#ifdef polish.midp2
      try {
         // request update:
         //#if updateUrl:defined
            //#= platformRequest( "${updateUrl}" );
         //#else
            platformRequest( "http://www.company.com/app/update.jad" );
         //#endif
         // persist current version:
         RecordStore versionStore = RecordStore.openRecordStore(
                                                   "version", true );
         byte[] versionData = Integer.toString( VERSION ).getBytes();
         versionStore.addRecord( versionData, 0, versionData.length );
         versionStore.closeRecordStore();
      } catch (ConnectionNotFoundException e) {
         //#debug error
         System.out.println("Unable to issue update request" + e );
      } catch (RecordStoreException e) {
         //#debug error
         System.out.println("Unable to persist current version" + e );
```

```
        }
      //#endif
   }

   protected void showMainMenu() {
      // TODO implement showMainMenu
   }

   protected void showUpdateMessage() {
      // TODO implement showUpdateMessage
   }

   protected void pauseApp() {
      // ignore
   }

   protected void destroyApp(boolean unconditional) throws
         MIDletStateChangeException {
      // exit gracefully
   }

}
```

Devices should ask users whether they want to keep the data when an update is installed. In most cases, it is at least possible to keep the data that has been stored in the record store. Depending on your application's needs, you should also consider storing the user data on the server before an update is requested. You can then add the user's ID to the JAD file that is used for the update. When your application is started and there is no user data, you can check that ID and download the data from the server.

Obviously, there are some security risks here, because JAD files can be changed very easily. So you need to ensure both that the user is really the intended user (authentication) and that any valid user who ended up with an invalid ID for some reason can change that ID.

Summary

The chapter introduced you to the general architecture of J2ME Polish. You gained an insight in the four main layers: the build framework, client framework, IDE plug-ins, and stand-alone tools. You also learned about the life cycle of wireless Java applications and how J2ME Polish can help you in each phase.

In the next chapter, we will take a look at the device database that provides the foundation for almost every module of J2ME Polish.

CHAPTER 6

The Device Database

In this chapter:

- Learn more about your target devices with the J2ME Polish device database.
- Get to know the XML format of the files in the device database: *devices.xml, vendors.xml, groups.xml, apis.xml,* and *bugs.xml.*
- Discover how to use the device database to select your target devices, assemble device-specific resources, and optimize your applications.

In this chapter, you will learn about the J2ME Polish device database. This database forms the basis of J2ME Polish and is essential for building and preprocessing applications. You can use the defined features and capabilities of the devices for selecting target devices in the build process and for adjusting your application to different handsets with preprocessing. Knowing the structure and uses of the device database is crucial for getting the most out of J2ME Polish.

Understanding the XML Format

The J2ME device database consists of different XML files that reside in the installation folder of J2ME Polish by default. The following files are included in the device database:

- *devices.xml*: Describes the capabilities and known issues of many J2ME capable devices.
- *vendors.xml*: Lists all vendors and manufacturers of J2ME devices.
- *groups.xml*: Describes the device groups. Each device can belong to an arbitrary number of groups.
- *apis.xml*: Lists optional and vendor-specific libraries, such as the Mobile Media API (MMAPI).
- *bugs.xml*: Describes known issues associated with devices.

Note From J2ME Polish 1.3 onwards, the *configurations.xml*, *platforms.xml*, and *capabilities.xml* files are also included in the device database. In the *configurations.xml* file, you can define configurations like CLDC 1.0 and CLDC 1.1. Use the *platforms.xml* file for defining profiles like MIDP 1.0, DoJa 4.0, and WIPI 2.0.

All of the files in the device database use a similar XML format and include common elements like <features> and <capability>. Features and capabilities can be inherited; some are overwritten, and others are supplemented. Here, we'll look at how to define devices, vendors, groups, libraries, and known issues.

Defining Devices

The *${polish.home}/devices.xml* file specifies the capabilities of most known J2ME devices, as well as some virtual devices. The database contains a couple of virtual phones that can be used to prepare your application for yet unknown devices. Listing 6-1 shows the definition of the Nokia 6600 and the virtual Java Technology for the Wireless Industry (JTWI) phones. The database contains a couple of virtual phones that can be used to prepare your application for yet unknown devices.

Listing 6-1. *Defining a Generic Phone and the Nokia 6600 Phone in devices.xml*

```
<devices>
   <device supportsPolishGui="true">
      <identifier>Generic/jtwi</identifier>
      <features>isVirtual</features>
      <capability name="JavaPlatform" value="MIDP/2.0" />
      <capability name="JavaConfiguration" value="CLDC/1.0" />
      <capability name="JavaPackage" value="mmapi,wmapi,jtwi" />
      <capability name="SoundFormat" value="midi, amr" />
   </device>
   <device>
      <identifier>Nokia/6600</identifier>
      <groups>Series60</groups>
      <features>hasCamera</features>
      <capability name="JavaPlatform" value="MIDP/2.0" />
      <capability name="JavaPackage" value="mmapi, wmapi, btapi, jtwi" />
      <capability name="OS" value="Symbian OS 7.0s"/>
      <capability name="ScreenSize" value="176x208"/>
      <capability name="BitsPerPixel" value="16"/>
      <capability name="VideoFormat" value="3gpp, mpeg-4, realvideo" />
      <capability name="SoundFormat"
                  value="midi, midi24, true tones, amr, wb-amr" />
      <capability name="HeapSize" value="3mb" />
      <capability name="MaxJarSize" value="dynamic" />
      <capability name="CameraResolution" value="vga" />
      <capability name="CameraZoom" value="2" />
   </device>
</devices>
```

The root element <devices> contains all <device> elements that describe the actual devices.

The `<identifier>` element identifies the device uniquely by stating the names of the vendor and of the device, separated by a single slash. You can also define several devices at once by separating the identifiers with commas:

```
<identifier>Sony-Ericsson/K700, Sony-Ericsson/K700i</identifier>
```

Use the `<features>` element to describe simple Boolean capabilities of the device:

```
<features>hasCamera, hasPointerEvents</features>
```

Examples include the existence of a camera (`hasCamera`), the support of pen-based input methods (`hasPointerEvents`), and being a virtual device (`isVirtual`). To define several features, separate them with commas. Features behave like Boolean variables: either they are defined (`true`) or they are not defined (`false`).

For defining more complex device capabilities, you use the `<capability>` element, which always has a name and a value:

```
<capability name="ScreenSize" value="176x208"/>
```

Like the preceding elements, a `<capability>` can contain several values that are separated by commas:

```
<capability name="JavaPackage" value="mmapi, wmapi, btapi"/>
```

Capabilities behave like variables with values. You can define any kind of capability, but J2ME provides standardized capabilities, as listed in Table 6-1.

■ **Note** You can define a capability in different ways. The most common method is to use the short notation using the `name` and `value` attributes. An equally valid notation is to use the nested elements `<capability-name>` and `<capability-value>`. Even though that format is much more verbose and cannot be read as easily, it ensures compatibility with the J2EE Client Provisioning specification. You can find this specification at *http://jcp.org/en/jsr/detail?id=124*.

You can explicitly add the device to any groups by specifying the `<groups>` element:

```
<groups>Series60</groups>
```

Again, you can define several groups by separating them with commas. These groups can, in turn, define features and capabilities, so that you don't need to specify these capabilities in the corresponding devices. Groups are also integral to the automatic resource assembling of J2ME Polish. Along with these explicitly defined groups, J2ME Polish also uses *implicit groups*. Implicit groups are formed from specific capabilities, such as `JavaPlatform`, `JavaPackage`, or `BitsPerColor`. Implicit groups help you in the resource assembling step when you build your J2ME application. Table 6-1 also shows capabilities that create implicit groups.

Note Whether or not a capability results in an implicit group will be defined in the *capabilities.xml* file from J2ME Polish 1.3 onwards.

Sometimes, it is useful to extend other devices. Consider, for example, the device modifications of some carriers like Vodafone. Such carriers often add some libraries like the Vodafone Service Class Library (VSCL) and market the device under a different name. One example in the device database is the Sony-Ericsson K500i, which is marketed by Vodafone as the F500i. For such cases, you can use the `<parent>` element, in which you specify the original device:

```
<parent>Sony-Ericsson/K500i</parent>
```

All features and capabilities of the parent device are inherited automatically. When you extend another device, you need to make sure that the parent device is defined above the child device; otherwise, J2ME Polish won't be able to resolve the inheritance correctly and will abort the processing.

You can specify the `supportsPolishGui` attribute of the `<device>` element to explicitly allow the use of the J2ME Polish GUI for the corresponding device. Normally, J2ME Polish checks automatically if a device has the recommended capabilities, such as supporting more than 256 colors and having a heap size greater than 500KB. By default, the J2ME Polish GUI is used only for devices that do have the recommended capabilities. The `supportsPolishGui` attribute allows you to override the automatic checking for GUI support.

Tip You can override the GUI indicators by setting the `usePolishGui` attribute in your *build.xml* file to `always` instead of `yes`. Then the J2ME Polish GUI will be used for all target devices, regardless of the settings in the device database.

Table 6-1. *Common Capabilities of the Device Database*

Capability	Explanation	Preprocessing Access	Groups
`BitsPerPixel`	Color depth: 1 = monochrome 4 = 16 colors 8 = 256 colors 12 = 4096 colors 16 = 65,536 colors 18 = 262,144 colors 24 = 16,777,216 colors	Variable: `polish.BitsPerPixel` Symbols: `polish.BitsPerPixel.1`, `polish.BitsPerPixel.4`, `polish.BitsPerPixel.16`, etc.	At 8 bits per pixel, e.g., `BitsPerPixel.4+` and `BitsPerPixel.8`

`ScreenSize`	Width times height of the screen resolution in pixels, e.g., 176×208	Variables: `polish.ScreenSize`,
		`polish.ScreenWidth`,
		`polish.ScreenHeight`
		Symbols (example):
		`polish.ScreenSize.176x208`,
		`polish.ScreenWidth.176`,
		`polish.ScreenHeight.208`	

Capability	Explanation	Preprocessing Access	Groups
`CanvasSize`	Width times height of an MIDP canvas	Like `ScreenSize`	
`FullCanvasSize`	Width times height of an MIDP canvas in full-screen mode	Like `ScreenSize`	
`JavaPlatform`	Supported Java platform, e.g., MIDP 1.0 or MIDP 2.0	Variable: `polish.JavaPlatform` Symbols: `polish.midp1`, `polish.midp2`	`midp1` or `midp2`
`JavaConfiguration`	Supported Java configuration, e.g., CLDC 1.0 or CLDC 1.1	Variable: `polish.JavaConfiguration` Symbols: `polish.cldc1.0`, `polish.cldc1.1`	`cldc1.0` or `cldc1.1`
`JavaPackage`	Supported APIs, e.g., Nokia UI and MMAPI	Variables: `polish.api`, `polish.JavaPackage` Symbols: `polish.api.nokia-ui`, `polish.api.mmapi`, etc.	Respectively, the name of the supported API, e.g., `nokia-ui` or `mmapi` (one group for each supported API)
`JavaProtocol`	Supported data exchange protocols*	Variable: `polish.JavaProtocol` Symbols: `polish.JavaProtocol.serial`, `polish.JavaProtocol.https`, etc.	
`HeapSize`	Maximum heap size, e.g., 500KB or 1.2MB	Variable: `polish.HeapSize`	
`MaxJarSize`	Maximum size of the MIDlet JAR bundle, e.g., 100KB or 2MB	Variable: `polish.MaxJarSize`	
`StorageSize`	Maximum size for all applications and data, e.g., 4MB	Variable: `polish.StorageSize`	
`OS`	Operating system of the device, e.g., Symbian OS 6.1	Variable: `polish.OS`	
`VideoFormat`	Supported video formats of the device, e.g., 3 GPP or MPEG-4	Variable: `polish.VideoFormat` Symbols: `polish.video.3gpp`, `polish.video.mpeg-4`, `polish.VideoFormat.3gpp`, `polish.VideoFormat.mpeg-4`, etc.	One group for each supported video format, e.g., `3gpp` and `mpeg-4`
`SoundFormat`	Supported sound formats of the device, e.g., MIDI and WAV	Variable: `polish.SoundFormat` Symbols: `polish.audio.midi`, `polish.audio.wav`, `polish.SoundFormat.midi`, `polish.SoundFormat.wav`, etc.	One group for each supported audio format, e.g., `midi` and `wav`
`Bugs`	Short names of known bugs	Variable: `polish.Bugs` Symbols: `polish.Bugs.drawRgbOrigin`, `polish.Bugs.ImageIOStream➥AutoClose`, etc.	

**All MIDP 1.0 devices support HTTP. All MIDP 2.0 devices additionally support HTTPS.*

Defining Vendors

The *${polish.home}/vendors.xml* file defines the manufacturers of devices. You need to ensure that every device vendor that is present in the *devices.xml* file is also listed in the *vendors.xml* file.

The `<vendors>` element contains all `<vendor>` definitions. Its nested `<name>` element specifies the name of the manufacturer. You can also define common capabilities and features that are valid for all devices of that vendor. Listing 6-2 demonstrates the definition of the Nokia and Siemens vendors.

Listing 6-2. *Defining the Nokia and Siemens Manufacturers in vendors.xml*

```
<vendors>
   <vendor>
      <name>Nokia</name>
      <features></features>
      <capability name="key.ClearKey" value="-8" />
      <capability name="key.ChangeInputModeKey" value="35" />
   </vendor>
   <vendor>
      <name>Siemens</name>
      <features></features>
      <capability name="Emulator.Class" value="SiemensEmulator" />
   </vendor>
<vendors>
```

Defining Groups

Device groups provide you with a handy way to define features and capabilities for many devices at once. For example, consider the popular Series 40 phones from Nokia, which share many common capabilities. Using the `<groups>` element in the *devices.xml* file and the corresponding definitions in the *groups.xml* file, it is quite easy to group devices. You can also use groups for selecting the appropriate resources, such as images or sound files for your application.

The `<groups>` root element contains all `<group>` elements that define the actual groups. Use the `<name>` element to define the name of the group. You can add features and capabilities, just as for devices and vendors. Devices belonging to this group inherit these features automatically. You can also extend another group with the `<parent>` element that contains the name of the extended group. Again, the child group will inherit all features and capabilities of the extended group. Listing 6-3 shows the definitions of the `Nokia-UI` group and the `Series40` group, in which the `Series40` group extends the `Nokia-UI` group.

■ **Note** In *groups.xml*, you find only the explicit groups; that is, groups that devices refer to with the `<groups>` element. There are also implicit groups formed from the device capabilities `JavaPlatform`, `JavaConfiguration`, `JavaPackage`, `SoundFormat`, `VideoFormat`, and `BitsPerPixel`, as listed in Table 6-1.

Listing 6-3. *Defining Device Groups in groups.xml*

```
<groups>
   <group>
      <name>Nokia-UI</name>
      <features>supportSpriteTransformation, hasCommandKeyEvents</features>
      <capability name="classes.fullscreen" value="com.nokia.mid.ui.FullCanvas" />
      <capability name="JavaPackage" value="nokia-ui" />
      <capability name="key.LeftSoftKey" value="-6" />
      <capability name="key.RightSoftKey" value="-7" />
   </group>
   <group>
      <name>Series40</name>
      <parent>Nokia-UI</parent>
      <capability name="JavaPlatform" value="MIDP/1.0" />
      <capability name="ScreenSize" value="128x128" />
      <capability name="FullCanvasSize" value="128x128" />
      <capability name="JavaConfiguration" value="CLDC/1.0" />
      <capability name="Emulator.Class" value="NokiaEmulator" />
      <capability name="Emulator.Skin" value="Nokia_S40_DP20_SDK_1_0" />
   </group>
</groups>
```

Defining Libraries

In *${polish.home}/apis.xml*, you can specify where to find device libraries. J2ME Polish includes these libraries automatically in the compilation and obfuscation steps when you build your application.

You define the supported libraries of a device by setting the `JavaPackage` capability in *devices.xml, groups.xml,* or *vendors.xml*:

```
<capability name="JavaPackage" value="mmapi, wmapi" />
```

When a supported library is not defined in the *apis.xml* file, J2ME Polish searches for the library in the project's *import* folder, and then in *${polish.home}/import* using the library name and the extension *.jar* and *.zip*. For example, for the Wireless Messaging API (WMAPI), it would first search for the *wmapi.jar* file, and then for the *wmapi.zip* file.

The case is different, however, when you define the library in *apis.xml*. For starters, you can define several possible file names and where these files are located. You can also specify which preprocessing symbol is set for that API. The `<apis>` element contains all actual `<api>` definitions. The nested `<name>` element specifies the name of the library, such as `Mobile Media API`. You should also describe the library using the `<description>` element. The `<names>` element lists all of the names under which the library is known, such as `mmapi` and `JSR-135`. This ensures that you always refer to the same library, no matter which of the possible names is used in the `JavaPackage` capability.

The `<symbol>` element specifies the preprocessing symbol that is defined for devices that support this library. (Preprocessing is covered in Chapter 8.) If you set the symbol to `mmapi` for example, you can check for that library using the `//#if polish.api.mmapi` construct. More generally speaking, for each library with the name `[api-name]` the preprocessing symbol polish.api.[*api-name*] is defined so that you can use it in the preprocessing step. The symbol is also the name of the implicit group to which devices belong when they support that library. Implicit groups can be used to select the appropriate resources for your application.

You can also extend other libraries by using the <parent> element. In this element, you specify one of the names of the parent library. When a library extends another library, it inherits all of the symbols of the extended libraries. Listing 6-4 shows how WMAPI 2.0 extends the original WMAPI. Devices that support WMAPI 2.0 now automatically belong to both the wmapi and wmapi2.0 groups, and have the preprocessing symbols polish.api.wmapi and polish.api.wmapi2.0 defined. When you extend another library, you need to ensure that the parent library is defined above the child library; otherwise, J2ME Polish will not be able to find it and will abort the build.

You specify the file names of the library with the <files> element. You can specify the default path of the library as well by using the <path> element.

J2ME Polish includes many empty libraries for your convenience. These include the Bluetooth API, the MIDP 1.0 API, the Mobile 3D Graphics API, and others.

Listing 6-4. *Specifying Libraries in apis.xml*

```
<apis>
   <api>
      <name>Mobile Media API</name>
      <description>The Mobile Media API provides
      functionalities for playing and capturing sounds and videos.
      </description>
      <names>mmapi,mm-api, JSR-135, JSR135</names>
      <symbol>mmapi</symbol>
      <files>j2me-mmapi.jar, mma.zip</files>
      <path>import/j2me-mmapi.jar</path>
   </api>
   <api>
      <name>Wireless Messaging API</name>
      <description>The Wireless Messaging API provides
      functionalities for sending and receiving messages (SMS).
      </description>
      <names>wmapi, wm-api, JSR-120, JSR120, wma</names>
      <symbol>wmapi</symbol>
      <files>j2me-wmapi.jar, wma.zip</files>
      <path>import/j2me-wmapi.jar</path>
   </api>
   <api>
      <name>Wireless Messaging API 2.0</name>
      <description>The Wireless Messaging API 2.0 provides
      functionalities for sending and receiving text and
      multimedia messages (SMS and MMS).
      </description>
      <names>wmapi2.0, wmapi2, JSR-205, JSR205</names>
      <symbol>wmapi2.0</symbol>
      <parent>wmapi</parent>
```

```
      <files>j2me-wmapi-2.0.jar, wma_2_0.zip</files>
      <path>import/j2me-wmapi-2.0.jar</path>
   </api>
</apis>
```

Describing Known Issues

You can find typical device issues in the device database as well. Such issues are defined using the `Bugs` capability in the *devices.xml* file. You can refer to *${polish.home}/bugs.xml* to get more information about each issue.

Each issue is described using a `<bug>` element. The nested element `<name>` equals the value given in the `Bugs` capability in *devices.xml*. You must not use any spaces within the name, and you should use meaningful names in camel notation; for example, `drawRgbOrigin`. The `<description>` element explains the issue in clear English, and the `<area>` element defines which area the bug belongs to; for example, `ui`, `multimedia`, or `rms`. The optional `<solution>` element describes how to circumvent the issue, if possible. Listing 6-5 shows an example of the issue database.

Listing 6-5. *Clarifying Device Bugs in bugs.xml*

```
<bugs>
   <bug>
      <name>drawRgbOrigin</name>
      <description>The Graphics.drawRGB(..) method does not use a
      translated origin, but starts always at the top-left 0,0 origin.
      </description>
      <area>ui</area>
      <solution>
      Use the top-left 0,0 origin for devices with this bug:
      //#ifdef polish.Bugs.drawRgbOrigin
         x += g.getTranslateX();
         y += g.getTranslateY();
      //#endif
      g.drawRGB( rgbData, offset, scanlength, x, y, width, height, processAlpha);
      </solution>
   </bug>
   <bug>
      <name>ImageIOStreamAutoClose</name>
      <description>The Image.createImage( InputStream in ) should not close
      the given input stream according to the specification. Devices with this
      bug close the input stream.
      </description>
      <area>io</area>
      <solution>Move any image which should be loaded from an input stream to
      the last position in the corresponding stream.
      </solution>
   <bug>
</bugs>
```

■ **Note** Even though an issue might be described in the *bugs.xml* file, that doesn't mean that it is really an error. Sometimes, behavior that is not expected but valid according to the specification is also noted. So the name *bugs.xml* can be a bit misleading. See Chapter 15 for some real-world examples of known issues.

Defining Complementing Capabilities and Features

You can define capabilities and features in the *vendors.xml*, *groups.xml*, and *devices.xml* files. A device automatically inherits all features and capabilities of its vendor and of all groups to which the device belongs. Such a hierarchy can become quite complex, as shown in Figure 6-1.

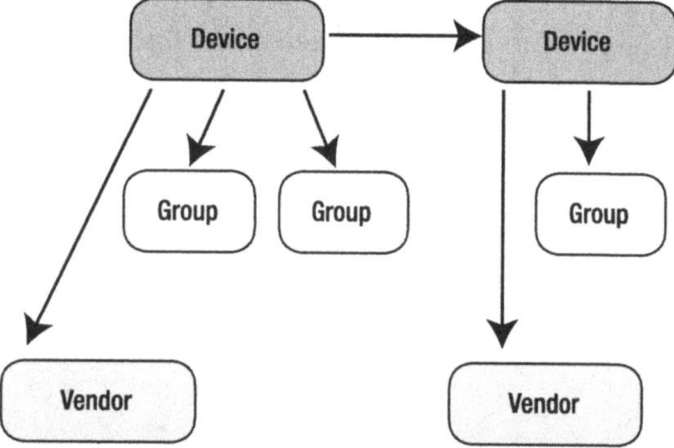

Figure 6-1. *A device can have a complex hierarchy.*

Any defined features are additive. This means that if a device's vendor defines *x*, a device's group defines *y*, and the device itself defines *z*, your device will end up with all the features: *x*, *y*, and *z*.

Capabilities are usually overwritten when they are defined in several places. Capabilities in *groups.xml* overwrite the same capabilities in *vendors.xml*, and capabilities in *devices.xml* overwrite those that are defined elsewhere. Phones from Nokia's popular Series 40 usually have a screen size of 128×128 pixels, so you find the corresponding definition in the `Series40` group in *groups.xml*:

```
<capability name="ScreenSize" value="128x128" />
```

Some devices from the Series 40 do have a different screen size, however. In that case, you can just define the `ScreenSize` capability in *devices.xml* with a different value for the corresponding devices.

Some capabilities, however, are cumulative, just like features. If you define the `JavaPackage`, `JavaProtocol`, `SoundFormat`, `VideoFormat`, and `Bugs` capabilities in several places along the hierarchy of a device, they will all add up. For example, the `JavaPackage` capability defines the supported libraries of a device. All Series 60 phones support the Nokia UI API, so the `Series60` group defines this:

```
<capability name="JavaPackage" value="nokia-ui" />
```

The `Series60` group actually inherits this setting from the `Nokia-UI` group. Take a look at any device definition that belongs to the `Series60` group in the *devices.xml* file, and you will see that the `nokia-ui` value is not repeated in the `JavaPackage` capability, because that value is inherited automatically.

Note From J2ME Polish 1.3 onwards, you can define whether a capability adds or replaces previously set values in the *capabilities.xml* file.

Using the Device Database

So now you know how the J2ME Polish device database works, but what can it be used for? Here are some of the things you can do with the device database:

- Select your target devices with the `<deviceRequirements>` element.
- Use automatic resource assembling by putting your images and other resource files into the *resources* directory and its subfolders.
- Optimize your application by evaluating and using device features and capabilities taken from the database.
- Adjust the database to your own needs without affecting other projects.

KNOW YOUR TARGET DEVICES

When you develop your application for a specific device, you may encounter problems or even device bugs. To get information about your target devices, take a look at the device database at *http://www.j2mepolish.org/devices-overview.html*. This is basically a fancy view of the *devices.xml* file and related files, which allows you to navigate easily between different devices, groups, vendors and so on. If you don't have online access, you can also view the devices at *${polish.home}/doc/html/devices-overview.html*.

Make sure to check out the known issues of your target device. Often, this helps you to solve any problems more quickly. You can also browse all devices that support a needed API of your application, which is important when you plan the architecture of your application.

Selecting Your Target Devices

With J2ME Polish, you can build and optimize your application for many target devices at once. You can do this by specifying requirements for your target devices in your *build.xml* file. The `<deviceRequirements>` element is responsible for selecting your target devices. (You will learn all the details about building applications for multiple devices in Chapter 7.)

You can use any `<capability>` or `<feature>` that has been defined in the device database for selecting your target devices. To demonstrate, Listing 6-6 shows how to select all devices that support a stylus *and* the MIDP 2.0 platform.

Listing 6-6. *Selecting All Devices Supporting a Stylus and the MIDP 2.0 Platform*

```
<deviceRequirements>
   <requirement name="JavaPlatform" value="MIDP/2.0+" />
   <requirement name="Feature" value="hasPointerEvents" />
</deviceRequirements>
```

Selecting Resources for Your Target Devices

J2ME Polish can automatically choose the correct resources, such as images and sound files, for your application. All you need to do is put the resources in the appropriate subfolder of the *resources* directory in your project. You can put common resources directly into the *resources* folder and specialized resources into the *resources/[vendor]*, *resources/[group]*, or *resources/[vendor]/[device]* folder. J2ME Polish will then pick the correct version of the resource and include it in the final application bundle. The details of this process are described in Chapter 7.

The key to resource assembling is the device database. Every device belongs to one vendor and can belong to several implicit and explicit groups. J2ME Polish always chooses the most specialized version of a resource, in this order:

1. J2ME Polish adds all resources from the common *resources* folder.
2. It adds all resources from the *resources/[vendor-name]* folder, such as *resources/Nokia*.
3. It adds all resources from the *resources/[group]* folder for each explicit and implicit group that the device belongs to. Examples are *resources/Series60* for devices belonging to Series 60, *resources/BitsPerPixel.16+* for devices having a color depth of at least 16 bits per pixel, and *resources/midi* for devices supporting the MIDI sound format.
4. It adds all resources from the *resources/[vendor]/[device]* folder, such as *resources/Nokia/6600* or *resources/Sony-Ericsson/K700*.

In each step, the more specialized resources override the more common resources. For example, suppose that you have a background picture called *bg.png* in the *resources* folder, as well as in the *resources/Nokia* and *resources/Nokia/3230* directories. If you build your application for non-Nokia devices, the image from the *resources* folder is added to the JAR file. Nokia devices get the image from *resources/Nokia*, but the application for the Nokia 3230 phone gets the image from the *resources/Nokia/3230* folder.

Note Explicit groups are the ones that devices refer to with the `<groups>` element in the `devices.xml` file. Implicit groups result from the device capabilities `JavaPlatform`, `JavaConfiguration`, `SoundFormat`, `VideoFormat`, and `BitsPerPixel`. You can view all implicit and explicit groups of a device in the online device database at *http://www.j2mepolish.org/devices-overview.html*. The groups are ordered hierarchically, so, for example, the `BitsPerColor.16` group is more specific than the `BitsPerColor.16+` group when a device supports exactly 16 bits per color. This order is also shown in the online database; the priority is increasing for each listed group, so the most specific group is the last one.

Optimizing for Your Target Devices

One of the best features of the device database is that you can detect and evaluate all features and capabilities in the source code of your application. This is done in the preprocessing step, which transforms the Java code before it is compiled. You control the preprocessing step with different directives, like `//#if`, `//#foreach`, or `//#=`. This section discusses only the general usage of the device database in the preprocessing phase. See Chapter 8 to learn more about the specifics of preprocessing.

All features of a device are translated into preprocessing symbols starting with `polish.` and ending with the name of the feature. When a device has pointer events, the preprocessing symbol `polish.hasPointerEvents` is defined, for example. Preprocessing symbols can be checked in your code with the `//#if` or the `//#ifdef` directive. As an example, Listing 6-7 shows how to check if a device is stylus-based.

Listing 6-7. *Checking for Pointer Events in Your Application*

```
//#ifdef polish.hasPointerEvents
   callPointerMethod();
//#else
   callPlainMethod();
//#endif
```

The capabilities of the current target device can also be evaluated and used in your source code. Each capability is available under `polish.[`*`capability-name`*`]`. You can compare capabilities with the `//#if` directive; for example, `//#if polish.BitsPerPixel >= 16` or `//#if polish.identifier == Nokia/6600`. When a capability is defined, you can check a corresponding preprocessing symbol `polish.[`*`capability-name`*`]:defined`. This is especially useful when you use the capability with the `//#=` directive, as in Listings 6-8 and 6-9.

Listing 6-8. *Changing Class Inheritance in Your Application*

```
public class SplashScreen
//#ifdef polish.classes.fullscreen:defined
   //#= extends ${ polish.classes.fullscreen }
//#else
   extends Canvas
//#endif
```

Listing 6-9. *Determining the Canvas Height with the Device Capabilities*

```
//#ifdef polish.FullCanvasHeight:defined
   //#= int height = ${ polish.FullCanvasHeight };
//#else
   int height = getHeight();
//#endif
```

J2ME Polish also defines the symbol `polish.[capability-name].[value]` for each value of a capability. When you have the `JavaProtocol` capability with the values `https, socket`, for example, both the symbols `polish.JavaProtocol.https` and `polish.JavaProtocol.socket` are defined and can be checked with `//#if` and `//#ifdef` directives.

The capabilities `JavaPlatform`, `JavaConfiguration`, `JavaPackage`, `SoundFormat`, and `VideoFormat` also trigger additional preprocessing symbols. Devices that support the MIDP 1.0 platform have the `polish.midp1` symbol, and the `polish.midp2` symbol is defined for all MIDP 2.0 devices. Similarly, the `polish.cldc1.0` symbol is defined for all CLDC 1.0 devices, and the `polish.cldc1.1` symbol is defined for all CLDC 1.1 devices. For each supported `JavaPackage`, the `polish.api.[api-name]` symbol is defined; for example, `polish.api.mmapi`. Also for each supported `SoundFormat`, the symbol `polish.audio.[format]` is defined. When your device supports MIDI sound, the `polish.audio.midi` symbol is defined. The same is true for all video formats, so you can check whether the current target device supports MPEG-4 videos by checking for `polish.video.mpeg-4`.

Changing and Extending the Device Database

Thanks to the XML format of the device database, you can read and write these files with any text editor. You can make changes globally by editing the device database XML file in the installation folder, such as *${polish.home}/custom-devices.xml*, but you can also do them locally only for the current project by copying the relevant file into the base directory of your project before editing it.

■ **Note** Consider contributing any of your device database changes to the J2ME Polish community, so that everyone can profit from them. If you do not contribute these changes, you might need to merge your own version with the official database, because the database is updated in every release of J2ME Polish.

After you have made changes to the database, you might need to make a clean build when you are using the changed definitions during the preprocessing step. Just call the `clean` target of the *build.xml* file with Ant or remove the temporary *build* folder before starting another build.

■ **Note** On Windows, you need a decent text editor for reading and writing the XML files. The line endings are written in Unix style, so in Notepad, you'll see only one seemingly endless text line. Consider using the Crimson editor (*http://www.crimsoneditor.com*) or any editor in a Java IDE like Eclipse (*http://www.eclipse.org*).

Summary

This chapter discussed J2ME Polish's XML-based device database and its formats. We took a quick look at using the database for information, building for multiple devices, selecting the appropriate resources, and optimizing applications. In the following chapter, you'll learn all about building applications with J2ME Polish.

CHAPTER 7

Building Applications

In this chapter:

- Get an overview of the basic concepts of Ant, on which J2ME Polish is based.
- Learn about the various build phases, ranging from preprocessing to packaging the application.
- Learn how to build for multiple devices, create localized applications, integrate third-party libraries, and obfuscate and debug your applications.

J2ME Polish makes it easy to use one application source code as the base for targeting various devices at the same time. This is often necessary because the devices may support the MIDP 1.0 or MIDP 2.0 standard, support proprietary APIs such as the Nokia UI API, support different sound formats, and so on.

Building J2ME applications is quite a complex task nowadays. Of course, the application needs to be compiled for the correct Java version, preverified, and packaged, but usually some other steps are involved as well, such as preprocessing or obfuscating the application.

J2ME Polish's main focus is to build J2ME applications, so it provides a flexible and powerful framework for doing so. In the following section, I will freshen up your Ant knowledge first; because J2ME Polish is based on Ant, understanding the basic Ant concepts is crucial. I will discuss the different build phases subsequently; then you will learn the various handles and switches of J2ME Polish. In addition, in this chapter, I will discuss typical user scenarios such as building your application for multiple devices and for several localizations.

Taking an Ant Crash Course

Apache Ant describes itself quite modestly as " . . . a Java-based build tool. In theory, it is kind of like Make, but without Make's wrinkles."[1] If you consider the sheer number of available Ant tasks, this is a noble understatement. Ant is *the* standard for building Java applications. With it, you can build applications, deploy them via FTP or any other network protocol to remote servers, enforce code style guides, and much more.

Ant interprets and executes the file *build.xml* in the current directory by default. The basic element of an Ant build file is a *project*, which basically contains *targets* and *tasks*. A *target* can be called from outside, for example, from the command line. Each target usually

1. *http://ant.apache.org*

contains one or more task, which is responsible for carrying out the real actions. Listing 7-1 shows a complete example.

Listing 7-1. *A Complete build.xml Example*

```
<project name="example" default="hello">
   <target name="hello">
      <echo message="hello world!" />
   </target>
</project>
```

Congratulations—you have created your first Ant script! Now let's take a closer look at it.

The `<project>` tag is the top element of the *build.xml* script. The attribute `default` describes which target should be called when no target has been specified on the command line. In this example, it points to the `hello` target. This target uses the `<echo>` task for printing information on the standard output. Figuring out what the `<echo>` task prints on the screen is left as an exercise to the reader.

When you now call Ant from the command line, you should see similar output to that in Listing 7-2.

Listing 7-2. *The Output of Your First Ant Script*

```
> ant
Buildfile: build.xml

hello:
     [echo] hello world!

BUILD SUCCESSFUL
Total time: 3 seconds
```

Well done—you have executed your first Ant script! If you are curious about what Ant tasks are already available, please refer to the Ant documentation at *http://ant.apache.org/manual/*. You will also find a list of external tasks such as J2ME Polish at *http://ant.apache.org/external.html*.

So, what else can you find in *build.xml*? The most important concepts you will encounter are *properties*. You can define properties outside a target at the beginning of the script or within a target. A property is a constant that can be set only once, as demonstrated in Listing 7-3.

Listing 7-3. *Using Ant Properties*

```
<project name="example" default="greetuser">
   <target name="robert">
      <property name="user" value="Robert" />
   </target>
   <target name="jinny">
      <property name="user" value="Jinny" />
   </target>
```

```
  <target name="greetuser">
    <echo message="hello ${user}" />
  </target>
</project>
```

Listing 7-3 provides three targets: robert, jinny, and greetuser. In the greetuser target, it uses the property ${user} within the message attribute.

■ **Note** With J2ME Polish you can use all Ant properties in your source code by setting the includeAntProperties and replacePropertiesWithoutDirective attributes of the <variables> element to true.

You can invoke any target just by giving the name of the target as a parameter, for example, ant robert greetuser. In this example, the robert target will be invoked first. It sets the ${user} property to Robert. Then the greetuser target is executed, which will print "hello Robert" in this case. It is easy to imagine what happens when you call ant jinny greetuser. But what happens when you call ant jinny robert hello? Thanks to the "write-once" nature of Ant properties, the printed message will be "hello Jinny" in this case.

You can define properties on the command line as well using the -D option, which is useful for providing a script with passwords. For example:

```
ant -Duser=Benny
```

This "write-once" capability of Ant properties might be confusing at first, but it is really useful for developing in teams where some people might want to use different settings. You can load user-specific properties with the file attribute of the <property> element, as demonstrated in Listing 7-4.

Listing 7-4. *Loading Ant Properties*

```
<project name="example" default="showpaths">
  <property file="${user.name}-build.properties" />
  <property name="wtk.home" location="C:\WTK22" />
  <property name="polish.home" location="C:\programs\J2ME-Polish" />
  <target name="showpaths">
    <echo message="wtk.home=${wtk.home}" />
    <echo message="polish.home=${polish.home}" />
  </target>
</project>
```

Listing 7-4 uses the predefined Ant property ${user.name} to determine the name of the properties file. So, if your username is "kirk" on your system, you can provide the properties file *kirk-build.properties* for defining your own settings. The properties file needs to have the common Java properties format, so you separate property names and values with the equals character:

```
wtk.home=/home/kirk/WTK21
```

Another important feature of Ant is the dependencies between several targets. Before you can deploy an application, you need to make sure it has been built first, for example. Listing 7-5 ensures this dependency.

Listing 7-5. *Dependencies Between Ant Targets*

```
<project name="example" default="build">
   <target name="build">
      <echo message="building application..." />
   </target>
   <target name="deploy" depends="build">
      <echo message="deploying application..." />
   </target>
</project>
```

When you call the deploy target with ant deploy, the build target executes first, even though you did not specify it on the command line.

■ Tip The *build.xml* script is—as you probably noticed—an XML file, so you can use XML comments like `<!-- invoking J2ME Polish -->`. You also need to encode special characters. If you need to specify a quotation mark within an attribute or property, just write `"` instead. If you need the ampersand character, &, use `&`, and so on.

Creating a "Hello, J2ME Polish World" Application

Since you know now how to handle Ant, let's say "hello" in the J2ME sort of way. Listing 7-6 shows a simple MIDlet with a menu, of which only the Exit button works.

Listing 7-6. *A Simple MIDlet Showing a Menu*

```
package com.apress.roadrunner;

import javax.microedition.lcdui.*;
import javax.microedition.midlet.MIDlet;
import javax.microedition.midlet.MIDletStateChangeException;

public class Roadrunner extends MIDlet implements CommandListener {
   List menuScreen;
   Command startGameCmd = new Command( "Start game", Command.ITEM, 8 );
   Command quitCmd = new Command( "Quit", Command.EXIT, 10 );
   Display display;

   public Roadrunner() {
      super();
      this.menuScreen = new List( "Hello World", List.IMPLICIT );
```

```
      this.menuScreen.append( "Start game", null );
      this.menuScreen.append( "Settings", null );
      this.menuScreen.append( "Highscore", null );
      this.menuScreen.append( "Quit", null );
      this.menuScreen.addCommand( this.startGameCmd );
      this.menuScreen.addCommand( this.quitCmd );
      this.menuScreen.setCommandListener( this );
   }
   protected void startApp() throws MIDletStateChangeException {
      this.display = Display.getDisplay( this );
      this.display.setCurrent( this.menuScreen );
   }
   protected void pauseApp() {
      // ignore
   }
   protected void destroyApp(boolean unconditional)
   throws MIDletStateChangeException {
      // just quit
   }
   public void commandAction(Command cmd, Displayable screen) {
      if ( screen == this.menuScreen ) {
         if ( cmd == List.SELECT_COMMAND ) {
         int selectedItem =
                         this.menuScreen.getSelectedIndex();
         if ( selectedItem == 3 ) {
            notifyDestroyed();
         }
      } else if ( cmd == this.quitCmd ) {
         notifyDestroyed();
      }
   }
   }
}
```

In the constructor, the MIDlet is initialized and the `List menuScreen` is populated. Also, the MIDlet registers itself as the `CommandListener` for the `menuScreen`. The `commandAction` method determines which action has been triggered and calls the appropriate code. In this book, I assume you know the basics of J2ME programming already. Do not despair in case you do not—many great books on this subject are available; for example, try *Beginning J2ME: From Novice to Professional, Third Edition*, by Jonathan Knudsen and Sing Li (Apress, 2005).

You should use the IDE of your choice from now on, because you start with the coding. Please create a shiny new project, and adjust the classpath of the project so it includes the MIDP 2.0 API. You will find this API, for example, at *${polish.home}/import/midp2.jar*. In Eclipse you can do this by right-clicking the project and then selecting Properties ➤ Java Build Path ➤ Libraries. Now select Add JARs, and include the *midp2.jar* file.

Please create the class `com.apress.roadrunner.Roadrunner`, which extends `javax.microedition.midlet.MIDlet`, and implement the code shown in Listing 7-6 now.

Tip I recommend using the folder *source/src* for the source files and the folder *bin/classes* for the compiled classfiles. Later you can use the *source/test* folder for implementing JUnit tests and the *bin/test* folder for the compiled test classes. In Eclipse you can change this setting by right-clicking the project and selecting Java Build Path ➤ Source. Apply these settings permanently in Window ➤ Preferences ➤ Java ➤ Build Path. In any case, you should never store the source code and the classes in the same folder.

Now let's build this MIDlet with J2ME Polish. Create a new file in the project root, and call it *build.xml*. Implement the script shown in Listing 7-7. Alternatively, you could just copy and adjust a *build.xml* file from one of the sample applications, but then you might miss all the gory details.

Listing 7-7. *The Build Script for the Simple Menu MIDlet*

```
<project name="roadrunner" default="j2mepolish">
   <!-- define the installation folder of J2ME Polish -->
   <property name="polish.home" location="C:\programs\J2ME-Polish" />
   <!-- define the installation folder of the WTK -->
   <property name="wtk.home" location="C:\WTK22" />
   <!-- define the J2ME Polish task, classpath on one line please -->
   <taskdef name="j2mepolish"
      classname="de.enough.polish.ant.PolishTask"
      classpath="${polish.home}/import/enough-j2mepolish-build.jar:
      ${polish.home}/import/jdom.jar"/>
   <!-- start the build with J2ME Polish -->
   <target name="j2mepolish">
      <j2mepolish>
         <info
            license="GPL"
            name="Roadrunner"
            vendorName="A reader."
            version="0.0.1"
            jarName="${polish.vendor}-${polish.name}-roadrunner.jar"
         />
         <deviceRequirements>
            <requirement name="Identifier" value="Generic/midp1" />
         </deviceRequirements>
         <build
            usePolishGui="false"
         >
            <midlet class="com.apress.roadrunner.Roadrunner" />
         </build>
         <emulator />
      </j2mepolish>
   </target>
   <target name="clean">
```

```
      <delete dir="build" />
      <delete dir="dist" />
   </target>
</project>
```

Let's now look at the *build.xml* script in detail.

The properties `${wtk.home}` and `${polish.home}` define the locations of the Wireless Toolkit and of J2ME Polish (you *have* adjusted those values to your system, right?).

■ **Note** Even though the `${wtk.home}` property is not used directly in the script, it is needed by J2ME Polish for finding the preverify tool.

The `<taskdef>` element tells Ant about the J2ME Polish task and how to find it. Please make sure you have put the `classpath` attribute on a single line without any spaces in it.

The real J2ME Polish task is invoked in the `j2mepolish` target. The task contains the four sections `<info>`, `<deviceRequirements>`, `<build>`, and `<emulator>`.

The `<info>` section describes general information about the MIDlet, which is written into the generated JAD and Manifest files. The most important attribute is `jarName`, which specifies the name of the JAR file that is generated. Listing 7-7 uses the properties `${polish.vendor}` (the vendor of a device) and `${polish.name}` (the name of a device) without having these properties defined anywhere. They are defined automatically by J2ME Polish and change with each processed device.

In the `<deviceRequirements>` section, the target devices are selected for which the application is built. For each target device, an application bundle consisting of a JAD and JAR file is created in the *dist* folder of your project. You can select devices by names or by defining needed capabilities such as "all devices that support the Bluetooth API and the Mobile Media API." In this example, you will build the application for the "Generic/midp1" device, which represents a typical device supporting the MIDP 1.0 profile.

The following `<build>` section controls the actual build process. In this example, you merely inform J2ME Polish about the `MIDlet` class using the nested `<midlet>` element. You also specify that the J2ME Polish GUI should not be used by setting the `usePolishGui` attribute to `false`.

The last section of the `<j2mepolish>` task is the `<emulator>` one. This section is responsible for invoking the emulator for the target device.

The `clean` target is used in case you want to do a clean rebuild. It just removes the *build* and *dist* folders in your project. J2ME Polish uses the *build* folder as a temporary work folder. Preprocessed source codes and compiled classes are stored here, for example. The *dist* directory contains the final JAR and JAD files of your application. Doing a clean build is necessary in certain cases, for example, when you have changed device definitions. In principle you could always do a clean build, but in that case J2ME Polish would need a bit more time, because all source files would need to be compiled again.

Now that you know the basics of J2ME Polish, you can execute the Ant script either from within your IDE or from the command line: in Eclipse, right-click the *build.xml* file, and select Run ➤ Ant Build. If the Ant Build command is not shown, click the *build.xml* file, open the

Eclipse Run menu, and select External Tools ➤ Run As ➤ Ant Build. In other IDEs you can usually right-click the *build.xml* file and select Execute or something similar (refer to Chapter 4 for details). From the command line, you just need to call `ant`.

Now J2ME Polish starts and builds the application. When J2ME Polish has finished the build, it will invoke the WTK emulator, as shown in Figure 7-1.

Figure 7-1. *The MIDlet in action*

The application works smoothly, meaning the Exit button works as expected. But the appearance is not very convincing, so let's improve it a bit.

Normally you cannot alter the design or layout of applications that use the MIDP high-level GUI, because the design is left to the Virtual Machine on the device. On MIDP 2.0 phones you can alter the design a bit, but most implementations are not very convincing and differ from device to device. When the J2ME Polish GUI is activated, however, it will "weave" its own wrapper API between the application and the JVM to create a far superior design.

Please create a new file called *polish.css* within the *resources* folder. This directory is created automatically by J2ME Polish in case it does not exist. You might need to refresh your project to find it. The *polish.css* file is used for designing an application with J2ME Polish. Listing 7-8 shows an example design.

Listing 7-8. *Designing the Simple Menu MIDlet*

```
colors {
   bgColor: #eef1e5;
   highlightedBgColor: #848f60;
   fontColor: rgb( 30, 85, 86 );
   highlightedFontColor: white;
}
title {
   padding-top: 15;
   font-color: fontColor;
   font-style: bold;
   font-size: large;
```

```
    font-face: proportional;
    layout: expand | center;
}
.mainMenu {
    padding: 10;
    background-color: bgColor;
    layout: horizontal-center | vertical-center;
}
.mainMenuItem {
    font-color: fontColor;
    font-style: bold;
    font-size: medium;
    layout: expand | center;
}
focused {
    background-color: highlightedBgColor;
    font-style: bold;
    font-size: medium;
    border-color: highlightedBgColor;
    border-width: 2;
    font-color: highlightedFontColor;
    layout: expand | center;
}
```

You specify all design settings in the *polish.css* file. The first section defines the colors you use in the styles. This makes it easy to change all colors in one place. It is always a good idea to give the colors names that relate to what they are used for and not to the color they represent. This way you can change the colors later without losing their meaning. A good color name is, for example, `highlightedTextColor`, whereas the name `darkPinkText` is not very flexible.

The `title` style is responsible for designing—who would have guessed it?—the title. I will use the `.mainMenu` and `.mainMenuItem` styles for this list and the list items, respectively. The dot at the beginning of their names qualify them as so-called custom, or static, styles, by the way. In contrast, dynamic and predefined styles also exist. Last but not least, the `focused` style designs the currently focused item. Do not worry too much about the applied settings here; I will explain all the gory details in Chapter 12.

You also need to adjust the constructor of your MIDlet so that J2ME Polish knows which styles to apply to which items. For this purpose, use the `#style` preprocessing directive, as shown in Listing 7-9.

Listing 7-9. *Applying CSS Styles in the MIDlet Constructor*

```
public Roadrunner() {
    super();
    //#style mainMenu
    this.menuScreen = new List( "Hello World", List.IMPLICIT );
    //#style mainMenuItem
    this.menuScreen.append( "Start game", null );
    //#style mainMenuItem
```

```
    this.menuScreen.append( "Settings", null );
    //#style mainMenuItem
    this.menuScreen.append( "Highscore", null );
    //#style mainMenuItem
    this.menuScreen.append( "Quit", null );
    this.menuScreen.addCommand( this.startGameCmd );
    this.menuScreen.addCommand( this.quitCmd );
    this.menuScreen.setCommandListener( this );
}
```

■ **Note** You could also use dynamic styles such as `list` and `listitem` instead of the static styles `.mainMenu` and `.mainMenuItem`. In that case, you would not need to change the source code at all. Dynamic styles are applied during runtime, whereas static ones are applied during the compilation phase. The drawback of dynamic styles is that you can use only one style for a specific `Item` or `Screen` type. They are also more resource hungry. This is why I use only static and predefined styles in this book.

You also need to change the `usePolishGui` attribute of the `<build>` element in the *build.xml* script so the styles defined in the *polish.css* file are applied to your application.

When you now restart J2ME Polish, you will get the much nicer GUI shown in Figure 7-2.

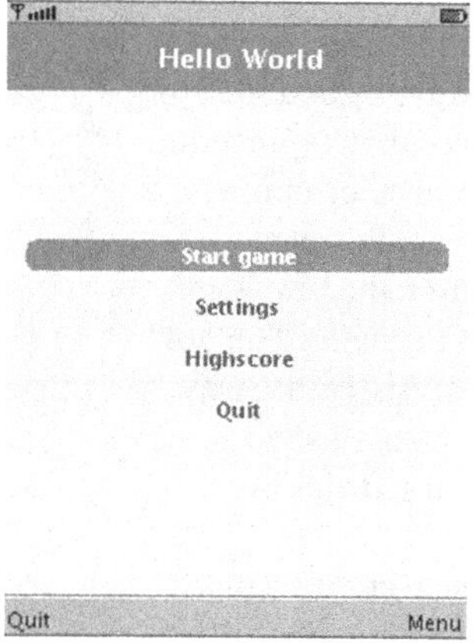

Figure 7-2. *The improved MIDlet*

Introducing the Build Phases

In each build, you will pass through the phases shown in Figure 7-3. You can control each phase by modifying the *build.xml* file. The following sections describe each phase and the available options in J2ME Polish.

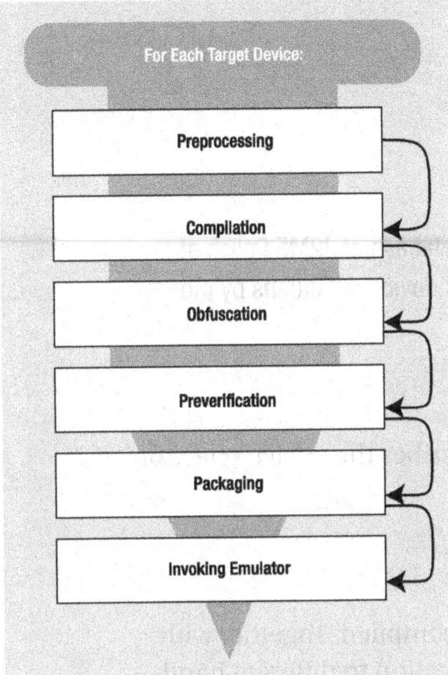

Figure 7-3. *Building your application with J2ME Polish*

Selecting the Target Devices

Each build starts with selecting the target devices for which the application is built. All subsequent phases are passed through for each device for which the application is built. The `<deviceRequirements>` section is responsible for selecting the target devices. You can select devices by listing their names or by specifying their needed capabilities, such as support for APIs, color depths, and so on.

Listing 7-10 shows a simple device selection; the application is being built for two target devices.

Listing 7-10. *Selecting Single Devices in the <deviceRequirements> Section*

```
<j2mepolish>
   <info
      license="GPL"
      name="Roadrunner"
      vendorName="A reader."
      version="0.0.1"
      jarName="${polish.vendor}-${polish.name}-roadrunner.jar"
   />
   <deviceRequirements>
      <requirement name="Identifier" value="Generic/midp1, Nokia/Series60" />
   </deviceRequirements>
   <build
      usePolishGui="false"
   >
```

```
        <midlet class="com.apress.roadrunner.Roadrunner" />
    </build>
    <emulator />
</j2mepolish>
```

■ **Tip** If you want to know what devices you can target, refer to the device database of J2ME Polish at *http://www.j2mepolish.org/devices-overview.html*. You can also use your own device definitions by modifying the file *${polish.home}/custom-devices.xml*, as discussed in Chapter 6.

The "Building for Multiple Devices" section of this chapter describes the device selection in full detail.

Preprocessing

In the preprocessing phase, the source code is changed before it is compiled. Together with the device database of J2ME Polish, you can easily adapt your application to different handsets without creating incompatibilities. You can utilize a whole armada of preprocessing directives for customizing your application to different environments. Each device defines capabilities and symbols that you can exploit in the preprocessing step. Refer to *http://www.j2mepolish.org/devices-overview.html* to learn the available preprocessing symbols and variables for each device.

Listing 7-11 demonstrates how you can use preprocessing to distinguish between devices that might support audio playback. Note that each preprocessing directive starts with the characters `//#`. This ensures that your IDE is not confused about those directives. Chapter 8 discusses all the options of preprocessing.

Listing 7-11. *Using Preprocessing to Distinguish Devices That Might Support Audio Playback*

```
//#if polish.api.mmapi || polish.midp2
   // okay, the MMAPI can be used for audio playback.
   //#if polish.audio.midi
      // play back the MIDI file...
   //#elif polish.audio.wav
      // play back the WAV  file...
   //#endif
//#endif
```

Compilation

During the compilation phase, the source code is translated into binary bytecode. J2ME Polish automatically includes all optional APIs that are supported by your target devices, such as MMAPI, for example. It also sets the `javactarget` to either 1.1 or 1.2 depending on the used WTK; from WTK 2.0 onward, the 1.2 `javac-target` is preferred. The `javac-target` ensures the compatibility of the compiled classfiles with your device. You can also set the target directly by specifying the `javacTarget` attribute of the `<build>` element. Debug information is not added unless the debugging mode is enabled with the `<debug>` element.

You can also use J2ME Polish as a compiler, in which case only the preprocessing, the compilation, and optionally the preverification (see the "Preverification" section) steps are executed. This can be useful for interacting with available J2ME plug-ins such as EclipseME or J2ME-enabled IDEs such as NetBeans. Activate the compiler mode by using the `compilerMode`, `compilerDestDir`, and `compilerModePreverify` attributes, as shown in Listing 7-12.

Listing 7-12. *Using J2ME Polish As a Compiler*

```
<j2mepolish>
  <info
    license="GPL"
    name="Roadrunner"
    vendorName="A reader."
    version="0.0.1"
    jarName="${polish.vendor}-${polish.name}-roadrunner.jar"
  />
  <deviceRequirements>
  <requirement name="Identifier" value="Generic/midp1" />
  </deviceRequirements>
  <build
    compilerMode="true"
    compilerModePreverify="true"
    compilerDestDir="preverified"
  >
    <midlet class="com.apress.roadrunner.Roadrunner" />
  </build>
  <emulator />
</j2mepolish>
```

If you need full control of the compiler settings, you can also use the `<compiler>` element, which is a nested element of the `<build>` section. This allows you to enable the insertion of debug information directly, for example. The `<compiler>` element accepts all attributes and nested elements of the original `<javac>` task; please consult *http://ant.apache.org/manual* for more information.

Obfuscation

Obfuscating your J2ME application is good for two reasons: it makes your application more difficult to decompile, and it reduces the size of your application by removing all unused classes, methods, and fields and renaming the remaining ones.

J2ME Polish supports many different obfuscators, and you can even use several obfuscators at once. The "Obfuscating Applications" section in this chapter describes all the available options and their implications.

Preverification

To ensure the integrity and security of the application, Java classes are verified by the Java Virtual Machine while loading the class. Since this step is computing intensive, the J2ME standard mandates that all classes need to be verified *before* they are installed on the J2ME device. This preverification step alters the bytecode and inserts additional information that ensures the validity and integrity of the bytecode. J2ME Polish uses the preverifier supplied with the WTK by default.

Packaging

In the packaging step, the final application bundles are created for each target device. They consist of one JAR file with the application code and one JAD file with the metadata needed for installation on the handheld. J2ME Polish assembles the resources specifically for each target device and for each locale and creates the needed JAD and Manifest files automatically. You can use third-party packagers such as 7-Zip or KZIP for decreasing the JAR file size a bit more. The "Packaging Your Application" section of this chapter discusses all these possibilities in full detail.

Invoking Emulators

J2ME Polish can invoke most emulators for testing the application. Just include an `<emulator>` element as the last element of the `<j2mepolish>` task. Please refer to the "Debugging Applications" section of this chapter for more information about invoking emulators.

Packaging Your Application

In the packaging phase for each target device, a JAD and a JAR file are generated. This step accomplishes several tasks, such as selecting the appropriate resources, managing JAD or Manifest attributes, and signing the application.

Resource Assembling

J2ME Polish provides sophisticated ways for including only the needed and appropriate resources for each target device. The base for resource assembling is the *resources* folder, in which all resources reside by default. Figure 7-4 shows an example.

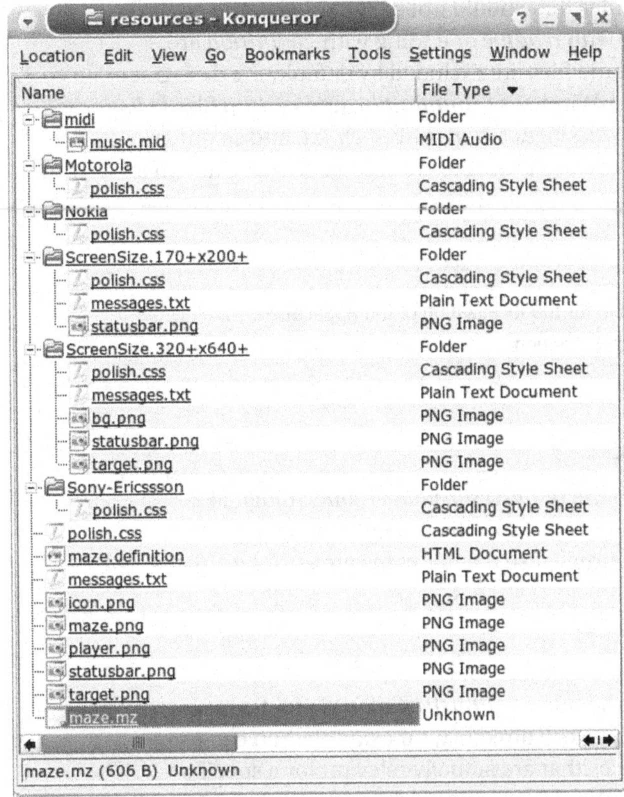

Figure 7-4. *Managing your images, sounds, and other data files in the resources folder*

Concepts

In the *resources* folder all common resources are placed. These are included unless more specific resources replace them. You can specify which folder is used for the resources with the `dir` attribute of the `<resources>` element, as demonstrated in Listing 7-13. By using a different resources folder, you can change the appearance of an application easily and drastically.

Listing 7-13. *Using a Different Resources Folder*

```
<build>
   <resources
      dir="resources/modern"
      excludes="readme*, *.definition"
   />
   <midlet class="com.apress.roadrunner.Roadrunner" />
</build>
```

Use the `excludes` attribute to specify any files that should not be included in the application bundle. In Listing 7-13, all files starting with *readme* or ending with *.definition* are excluded from the final application JAR file. Some files are excluded by default: the design settings (*polish.css*), the temporary files created by Windows (*Thumbs.db*), any backup files (**.bak* and **~*), and the files used for the localization (*messages.txt*, *messages_en.txt*, and so on) are excluded by default. The names given in the `excludes` attribute are case-sensitive, even on a Windows machine.

■ **Note** The `<resources>` element is also responsible for the localization of the application, which is discussed in the following "Building Localized Applications" section.

Using Vendor- and Device-Specific Resources

You can put resources for specific vendors into the *resources/[vendor-name]* folder, like *resources/Nokia* for Nokia devices. Place resources for a specific device into the *resources/[vendor-name]/[device-name]* directory; for example, use the folder *resources/Nokia/6600* for Nokia 6600 devices.

Including Group-Specific Resources

Use groups for a higher abstraction layer. Use the *resources/BitsPerColor.16+* folder for high-color images, or put MIDI files into the *resources/midi* directory, for example. You can use groups efficiently to include only those resources that are actually relevant for a specific device. A device can belong to an arbitrary number of groups, which are defined either implicitly by the capabilities of that device or explicitly by setting the `<groups>` element in the *${polish.home}/devices.xml* file. Chapter 6 discussed groups in full detail. Table 7-1 lists the most useful groups for resource assembling.

Table 7-1. *Useful Groups for Assembling Resources*

Group	Type	Default Folder	Explanation
`midp1`	Platform	*resources/midp1*	If a device supports the MIDP 1.0 profile, resources for this device can be placed in the *resources/midp1* folder.
`midp2`	Platform	*resources/midp2*	For devices supporting the MIDP 2.0 profile.
`cldc1.0`	Configuration	*resources/cldc1.0*	For devices supporting the CLDC 1.0 configuration.

Group	Type	Default Folder	Explanation
`cldc1.1`	Configuration	*resources/cldc1.1*	For devices supporting the CLDC 1.1 configuration.
`mmapi`	API	*resources/mmapi*	When a device supports the Mobile Media API, resources that need this API can be placed in the *resources/mmapi* folder.
`nokia-ui`	API	*resources/nokia-ui*	For devices that support the Nokia User Interface API.
`midi`	Audio	*resources/midi*	For devices that support the MIDI sound format.
`wav`	Audio	*resources/wav*	For devices that support WAV sound.
`mp3`	Audio	*resources/mp3*	For devices that support MPR3 sound.
`amr`	Audio	*resources/amr*	For devices that support AMR sound.
`mpeg-4`	Video	*resources/mpeg-4*	For devices that support the MPEG-4 video format.
`h.263`	Video	*resources/h.263*	For devices that support H.263 video.
`3gpp`	Video	*resources/3gpp*	For devices that support 3GPP video.
`ScreenSize`	Screen	*resources/ScreenSize.150+x200+*	For devices with a screen size of at least 150×200 pixels.
`ScreenSize`	Screen	*resources/ScreenSize.176x208*	For devices with a screen size of exactly 176×208 pixels.
`BitsPerColor.12+`	Colors	*resources/BitsPerColor.12+*	For devices with a color depth of at least 12 bits per color.
`BitsPerColor.16`	Colors	*resources/BitsPerColor.16*	For devices with a color depth of exactly 16 bits per color.

■ **Note** Explicit groups are the ones that devices refer to with the `<groups>` element in the *${polish.home}/devices.xml* file. Implicit groups result from the device capabilities `JavaPlatform`, `JavaConfiguration`, `JavaPackage`, `SoundFormat`, `VideoFormat`, and `BitsPerPixel`. You can view all implicit and explicit groups of a device in the online device database at *http://www.j2mepolish.org/devices-overview.html*. The groups are ordered hierarchically, so the `BitsPerColor.16` group is more specific than the `BitsPerColor.16+` group when a device supports exactly 16 bits per color. This order is also shown in the online database.

Using Locale-Specific Resources

Another possible hook for using different resources in your application is the localization. You can differentiate between English and Spanish resources by putting the Spanish resources into the *resources/es* folder, for example. The section "Building Localized Applications" of this chapter elaborates this point further.

Selecting and Loading Resources

All resources will be copied to the root of the application, and more specific resources will overwrite the common resources: if you have a picture named *background.png* in the *resources* folder as well as in the *resources/Nokia* and *resources/Nokia/6600* folders, the version in the *resources* folder will be used for all non-Nokia devices, and the version contained in the *resources/Nokia* folder will be used for all Nokia devices. However, the image *resources/Nokia/6600/background.png* will be used for the application that is built for the Nokia 6600 phone. In the application code, you can load the `Image.createImage( "/background.png" )` image from the root, no matter where the resource was copied from.

Because of this assembling mechanism, no subfolders can be used within an application. This means the application cannot load resources from a subfolder but only from the root, /, of the application. This is not a bug but a feature, since subfolders only add overhead to an application.

So, instead of calling this:

```
InputStream is = getClass().getResourceAsStream( "/levels/level.map" );
```

you need to use the following code:

```
InputStream is = getClass().getResourceAsStream( "/level.map" );
```

Subdirectories in the *resources* folder are merely used to distinguish different devices, device groups, and locales.

Fine-Tuning the Resource Assembling

Sometimes it is necessary to adjust the automatic resource assembling. You can do so by using nested `<fileset>` elements in your *build.xml* script.

Imagine that your application uses AMR sound files when the device supports AMR and uses MIDI sound files when the device supports MIDI. In the source code, you can use the preprocessing symbols `polish.audio.amr` and `polish.audio.midi` to distinguish between these cases, as demonstrated in Listing 7-14.

Listing 7-14. *Distinguishing Between Several Audio Formats*

```
//#ifdef polish.audio.amr
   // play the amr sound
//#elifdef polish.audio.midi
   // play midi sound instead
//#endif
```

The situation is different in the resource assembling step, though. Obviously, you can put all AMR files in the *resources/amr* folder and all MIDI files into the *resources/midi* folder so these resources are available when they are needed. But for devices that support both AMR and MIDI sounds, the application will contain the MIDI files as well, even though only the AMR files are actually needed. This is a waste of space and can be prevented by fine-tuning the resource assembling with nested `<fileset>` elements, as outlined in Listing 7-15.

Listing 7-15. *Fine-Tuning the Resource Assembling with <fileset>*

```
<resources
   dir="resources"
   excludes="readme*, *.definition"
>
   <fileset
      dir="resources/multimedia"
      includes="*.amr"
      if="polish.audio.amr"
   />
   <fileset
      dir="resources/multimedia"
      includes="*.mid"
      if="polish.audio.midi and not polish.audio.amr"
   />
</resources>
```

In the previous example, MIDI files are included only when two conditions are met:

- The device supports MIDI sound (so the `polish.audio.midi` symbol will be defined).
- The device does not support AMR sound (so the `polish.audio.amr` symbol will not be defined).

In this way, an application contains either AMR files or MIDI files or no sound files at all so your application does not contain any redundant resources anymore.

Note You might have noticed the usage of `and` as well as `not` in the `if` attribute. This is done because you would need to XML encode the normally used && operator otherwise. You can use this notation in every place where complex terms are allowed, for example, in `#if` preprocessing terms.

Managing JAD and Manifest Attributes

JAD and Manifest attributes are needed during the installation and can contain user-defined properties for configuring your application. Some attributes are mandatory, such as the name of the application, and some are optional, such as the description. Sometimes you might need to define vendor- or carrier-specific attributes as well.

■ **Tip** Consider using preprocessing for configuring your application instead of using user-defined attributes and calling `MIDlet.getAppProperty(String)` during runtime. You can include any variables with the #= preprocessing directive, for example, `//#= private final static String START_URL = "${start-url}";`. You can define your configuration variables using the `<variables>` element in the `<build>` section.

You can specify attributes in three ways:

- By specifying attributes in the `<info>` section of the `<j2mepolish>` task
- By using the `<jad>` element of the `<build>` section
- By defining preprocessing variables in the `<variables>` element of the `<build>` section or in the *messages.txt* files that are used in the localization step

Standard attributes are defined in the `<info>` section, whereas the `<jad>` element is used for defining nonstandard attributes. Your defined preprocessing variables can override the values of any attributes that you have defined in the `<info>` section. This is useful for setting locale-specific attributes such as the name of your application. Chapter 8 discusses how you can define your own variables.

In every attribute value, you can use any variables from the device database or from your own preprocessing variables.

Listing 7-16 shows how attributes are defined using the `<info>` and `<jad>` elements.

Listing 7-16. *Defining JAD and Manifest Attributes in Your build.xml Script*

```
<j2mepolish>
   <info
      license="GPL"
      name="Roadrunner"
      vendorName="HighTech Ltd."
      version="0.0.1"
      jarName="${polish.vendor}-${polish.name}-roadrunner.jar"
   />
   <deviceRequirements>
      <requirement name="Identifier" value="Generic/midp1" />
   </deviceRequirements>
   <build>
      <midlet class="com.apress.roadrunner.Roadrunner" />
```

```
      <jad>
         <attribute
            name="Nokia-MIDlet-Category"
            value="Game"
            if="polish.group.Series40"
         />
         <attribute
            file="config/${polish.vendor}.attributes"
         />
      </jad>
   </build>
   <emulator />
</j2mepolish>
```

Each <attribute> element supports the XML attributes name, value, file, target, if, and unless.

Except when you use the optional file XML attribute, you do not have to set the name and the value of the attribute. With the file option, you specify the file that contains one or more attributes, in which colons separate name and values of the attribute: Nokia-MIDlet-Category: Game. Listing 7-16 included all attributes defined in the *config/${polish.vendor}.attributes* file. The ${polish.vendor} property contains the name of the vendor of the current target device, so when you build your application for the Siemens SK65 phone, you would include the *config/Siemens.attributes* file.

With the XML attribute target, you can control whether the attribute should be added to the JAD (target="jad"), the Manifest (target="manifest"), or both (target="jad,manifest"). When you omit the target setting, the attribute is added to both the JAD file and the Manifest. This is the default behavior of J2ME Polish even though the MIDP standard suggests putting user-defined attributes only into the JAD file. Some devices do, however, use the JAD file only during the installation and remove it afterwards.

With the optional if and unless terms, you can control whether the attribute should be added for the current target device. Listing 7-16 added the Nokia-MIDlet-Category attribute only when the target device belongs to the "Series40" group, because it would be ignored on all other devices anyway.

Sorting and Filtering Attributes

Some resellers (also called *aggregators*) and carriers mandate which attributes you can use in what order. You can comply to these conditions by sorting and filtering JAD attributes with the <jadFilter> element, as demonstrated in Listing 7-17. This listing also demonstrates how to use the <manifestFilter> element, which sorts and filters the attributes of the Manifest.

Listing 7-17. *Filtering JAD and Manifest Attributes*

```
<j2mepolish>
   <info
      license="GPL"
      name="Roadrunner"
      vendorName="A reader."
      version="0.0.1"
```

```
      jarName="${polish.vendor}-${polish.name}-roadrunner.jar"
   />
   <deviceRequirements>
      <requirement name="Identifier" value="Generic/midp1" />
   </deviceRequirements>
   <build>
      <midlet class="com.apress.roadrunner.Roadrunner" />
      <jad>
         <attribute
            name="Nokia-MIDlet-Category"
            value="Game"
            if="polish.group.Series40"
         />
         <jadFilter>
         MIDlet-Name, MIDlet-Version,
         MIDlet-Vendor, MIDlet-Jar-URL, MIDlet-Jar-Size,
         MIDlet-Description?, MIDlet-Icon?, MIDlet-Info-URL?,
         MIDlet-Data-Size?, MIDlet-*, *
         </jadFilter>
      </jad>
      <manifestFilter>
      Manifest-Version, MIDlet-Name, MIDlet-Version, MIDlet-Vendor,
      MIDlet-1, MIDlet-2?, MIDlet-3?, MIDlet-4?, MIDlet-5?,
      MicroEdition-Profile, MicroEdition-Configuration,
      MIDlet-Description?, MIDlet-Icon?, MIDlet-Info-URL?,
      MIDlet-Data-Size?
      </manifestFilter>
   </build>
   <emulator />
</j2mepolish>
```

Both the `<jadFilter>` and `<manifestFilter>` elements accept a list of comma-separated names defining the allowed attributes in the desired order. When an attribute name ends with a question mark like `MIDlet-Description?`, it is considered optional. In that case, it is included only if it has been defined. You can select several attributes at the same time by ending an attribute name with an asterisk, as in `MIDlet-*`. In that case, all remaining attributes that start with `MIDlet-` are included at that position. Last but not least, you can select all remaining attributes by just using an asterisk, as in `*`. This obviously has to be the last item in the list.

You can apply a filter for specific devices only by using the `if` or `unless` attributes, for example, `<jadFilter if="polish.Vendor == Samsung" />`.

Caution When you use `<manifestFilter>`, always ensure that you list the `Manifest-Version` as the first element. Otherwise, you end up with an invalid Manifest.

By default, J2ME Polish includes all defined JAD attributes by using the following filter:

```
MIDlet-Name, MIDlet-Version, MIDlet-Vendor, MIDlet-Jar-URL, MIDlet-Jar-Size,
MIDlet-Description?, MIDlet-Icon?, MIDlet-Info-URL?, MIDlet-Data-Size?, MIDlet-*, *
```

The default Manifest filter is the same one but starts with the necessary `Manifest-Version` and skips the `MIDlet-Jar-URL` and `MIDlet-Jar-Size` attributes:

```
Manifest-Version, MIDlet-Name, MIDlet-Version, MIDlet-Vendor, MIDlet-Description?,
MIDlet-Icon?, MIDlet-Info-URL?, MIDlet-Data-Size?, MIDlet-*, *
```

Signing MIDlets

The MIDP 2.0 standard distinguishes between trusted and untrusted applications. An application is considered untrusted by default, unless it contains a valid digital signature. Whenever an untrusted application accesses security-sensitive resources such as sending text messages, the user will be asked for permission. Certain actions such as low-level network access might be entirely forbidden for untrusted applications. In contrast, the user is asked only once during the installation to allow certain actions for trusted applications. With J2ME Polish you can automate the signing of your application when you have a valid digital certificate.

■ **Note** Chapter 15 covers how to sign MIDlets in the real world in detail. In most cases you will need to certify your application by the Java Verified initiative (*http://www.javaverified.com*). This will involve further costs. You can define any required permissions with the `permissions` attribute and optional operations with the `optionalPermissions` attribute of the `<info>` element, as shown in Listing 7-18. Please refer to the appendix for getting a list of available permissions.

When the application is signed, the SHA1 hash value of the JAR file is calculated and added to the JAD file. The certificate that is used for the calculation is added to the JAD file, too. The JAR file itself is not changed and must not be modified afterward.

For testing purposes, you do not need to purchase a certificate. Such MIDlets cannot be installed on real devices, however, unless you manage to import the certificate on your device. This seems to be difficult, to say the least. Generate a temporary key with Java's `keytool` on the command line:

```
> keytool -genkey -alias SignMIDlet -keystore midlets.ks -keyalg RSA
```

You can now sign your MIDlet using the `<sign>` element, which is nested in the `<build>` section, as shown in Listing 7-18. This example assumes you have purchased and imported an appropriate certificate into the keystore named *midlets.ks* with the key named `SignMIDlet`.

Listing 7-18. *Signing MIDlets*

```
<j2mepolish>
   <info
      license="GPL"
      name="Roadrunner"
```

```
        vendorName="A reader."
        version="0.0.1"
        jarName="${polish.vendor}-${polish.name}-roadrunner.jar"
        permissions="javax.microedition.io.Connector.http"
        optionalPermissions="javax.microedition.io.Connector.bluetooth.client"
    />
    <deviceRequirements>
        <requirement name="Identifier" value="Generic/midp2" />
    </deviceRequirements>
    <build>
        <midlet class="com.apress.roadrunner.Roadrunner" />
        <sign
            keystore="midlets.ks"
            key="SignMIDlet"
            password="${password}"
        />
    </build>
    <emulator />
</j2mepolish>
```

The application is signed only when the current device supports the MIDP 2.0 standard. It is assumed that the *midlets.ks* keystore is situated in the same directory as the *build.xml* file.

Please note that the password is specified using an Ant property in Listing 7-18. You can define this property on the command line using the `-Dpassword=[value]` option:

```
> ant -Dpassword=secret
```

Using Third-Party Packagers

Usually, the standard, compliant, internal J2ME Polish packager is used for creating the final application bundles. External packagers can reduce the size of JAR files by using optimized zip algorithms. Use the `<packager>` element for working with a different packaging program, and integrate any packager by specifying the attributes `executable` and `arguments`. Use the `executable` attribute for defining the actual packager program. In the `arguments` attribute, you can separate several arguments by using two semicolons, as demonstrated in Listing 7-19.

Listing 7-19. *Using the JAR Packager*

```
<j2mepolish>
    <info
        license="GPL"
        name="Roadrunner"
        vendorName="A reader."
        version="0.0.1"
        jarName="${polish.vendor}-${polish.name}-roadrunner.jar"
    />
    <deviceRequirements>
        <requirement name="Identifier" value="Generic/midp1" />
```

```
  </deviceRequirements>
  <build>
    <midlet class="com.apress.roadrunner.Roadrunner" />
    <packager
      executable="jar"
      arguments="cvfM;;${polish.jarPath};;-C;;${polish.packageDir};;."
    />
  </build>
  <emulator />
</j2mepolish>
```

As demonstrated in Listing 7-19, the *${polish.packageDir}* directory (the directory in which all classes and resources reside) and the *${polish.jarPath}* file (the file that should be created) are useful for specifying the arguments for the packager.

Of course, you can also use any other Ant or J2ME Polish properties as well.

You can use the popular 7-Zip and KZIP packagers just by defining the appropriate name attribute (either 7zip or kzip). Please note that these packagers use optimized zip algorithms that are not accepted by every J2ME device. Listing 7-20 uses the 7-Zip packager for generating the JAR file. The packager supports the optional parameters compression (either maximum, normal, or none), passes (the number of compression runs, a number between 1 and 4), and fastbytes (the size of internal compression chunks, a number between 3 and 255). Set the ${7zip.home} Ant property when the 7-Zip packager is neither on the path of your system nor in the *${polish.home}/bin* folder.

Listing 7-20. *Using the 7-Zip Packager*

```
<j2mepolish>
  <info
    license="GPL"
    name="Roadrunner"
    vendorName="A reader."
    version="0.0.1"
    jarName="${polish.vendor}-${polish.name}-roadrunner.jar"
  />
  <deviceRequirements>
    <requirement name="Identifier" value="Generic/midp1" />
  </deviceRequirements>
  <build>
    <midlet class="com.apress.roadrunner.Roadrunner" />
    <packager name="7zip" >
      <parameter name="compression" value="maximum" />
      <parameter name="passes" value="4" />
      <parameter name="fastbytes" value="212" />
    </packager>
  </build>
  <emulator />
</j2mepolish>
```

Similarly, you can invoke the KZIP packager, which supports the optional parameter `blocksplit` with a value between 0 and 2048. You might want to experiment with values such as 128, 256, 512, 1024, and 2048 for better compression. When J2ME Polish cannot find the KZIP executable, make sure to define the `${kzip.home}` property on your system or install KZIP to *${polish.home}/bin*. For using KZIP, just set the `name` attribute to `kzip`, like so:

```
<packager name="kzip" />
```

Building for Multiple Devices

In today's diverse J2ME world, it is necessary to provide specialized application bundles for different devices. Consider, for example, the usage of device-specific APIs or the usage of resources such as images and sound files: it is not necessary to include sound files for devices that do not support that format. On some devices, you cannot use classes that are not available on that device, even when you reference them only dynamically using the `Class.forName(String)` pattern. Last but not least, you should always use optimized applications when you use J2ME Polish, since that API is highly optimized for each target device. Pointer events are, for instance, evaluated only when the target device is a pen-based device. Also, workarounds for device-specific issues can be incorporated only when you build your application for the affected device.

Selecting Devices

The `<deviceRequirements>` section is responsible for selecting the devices for which the application is built. You can select target devices just by listing their names, or you can use more complex selections by stating required capabilities. You can use any device capabilities or features that are defined in the device database. Listing 7-21 demonstrates how to select all devices that support the MIDP 2.0 platform or the Nokia UI API.

■ **Note** The `<deviceRequirements>` section is optional. When it is omitted, the application is built for all known devices. This might take some time.

Listing 7-21. *Using <deviceRequirements> for Selecting Several Target Devices*

```
<j2mepolish>
   <info
      license="GPL"
      name="Roadrunner"
      vendorName="A reader."
      version="0.0.1"
      jarName="${polish.vendor}-${polish.name}-roadrunner.jar"
   />
   <deviceRequirements>
      <or>
```

```
            <requirement name="JavaPlatform" value="MIDP/2.0+" />
            <requirement name="JavaPackage" value="nokia-ui" />
        </or>
    </deviceRequirements>
    <build>
        <midlet class="com.apress.roadrunner.Roadrunner" />
    </build>
    <emulator />
</j2mepolish>
```

The actual selection of devices is done with <requirement> elements. When you just list the requirements, all of them need to be fulfilled by the target devices. You can use nested <or>, <and>, <not>, and <xor> elements to make the requirements very flexible. You can even use a hierarchy of nested elements, as shown in Listing 7-22.

Listing 7-22. *Using Nested <requirement> Elements*

```
<deviceRequirements>
    <or>
        <and>
            <requirement name="JavaPlatform" value="MIDP/2.0+" />
            <requirement name="SoundFormat" value="midi" />
        </and>
        <and>
            <requirement name="JavaPackage" value="nokia-ui" />
            <requirement name="BitPerPixel" value="16+" />
        </and>
    </or>
</deviceRequirements>
```

In Listing 7-22, the application is built for devices that support the MIDP 2.0 standard and the MIDI sound format or that alternatively support the Nokia UI API and have a color depth of at least 16 bits per pixel (that's 65,000 colors).

In the previous examples, the application is built for more than 50 devices, which can be annoying when you just want to test the application during development. You can, therefore, use different sets of device requirements by using the `if` or `unlesss` attribute. Listing 7-23 demonstrates this.

Listing 7-23. *Using Different Sets of <deviceRequirements>*

```
<deviceRequirements unless="test">
    <or>
        <requirement name="JavaPlatform" value="MIDP/2.0+" />
        <requirement name="JavaPackage" value="nokia-ui" />
    </or>
</deviceRequirements>
<deviceRequirements if="test">
    <requirement name="Identifier" value="Nokia/Series60" />
</deviceRequirements>
```

When the Ant property `test` is set to `true` in Listing 7-23, the application will be built only for the "Nokia/Series60" device. You now need to inform the build script about which set should be used. You can do this either by including and executing a new Ant target in which the `test` property is defined or by specifying the following property on the command line:

```
> ant -Dtest=true
```

Note The "Nokia/Series60" device exists only in the device database. It models a typical MIDP 1.0–based device from Nokia's Series 60. This is useful for not generating too many applications for basically the same devices. Similar virtual devices are "Nokia/Series60E2FP1," "Nokia/Series40," and "Nokia/Series40DP2." Chapter 15 discusses these device groups and their capabilities in detail.

You can use any capabilities and features defined in the device database for selecting your target devices. When you have numerical values, you can append a plus sign (+) for also allowing higher values, for example, `<requirement name="BitsPerPixel" value="4+" />`. Many requirements also allow different options that can be separated by commas, for example, `<requirement name="JavaPackage" value="nokia-ui, mmapi" />`. Table 7-2 lists some often-needed options for selecting devices.

Table 7-2. *Common Requirements for Selecting Target Devices*

<requirement>	Example	Description
`BitsPerPixel`	`<requirement name="BitsPerPixel" value="4+" />`	Needed color depth of the device: 1 is monochrome, 4 is 16 colors, 8 is 256 colors, 16 is 65,536 colors, and 24 is 16,777,216 colors.
`ScreenSize`	`<requirement name="ScreenSize" value="120+ x 100+" />`	Required width and height of the display.
`ScreenWidth`	`<requirement name="ScreenWidth" value="120+" />`	The needed horizontal resolution of the display.
`ScreenHeight`	`<requirement name="ScreenHeight" value="100+" />`	The needed vertical resolution of the display.
`CanvasSize`	`<requirement name="CanvasSize" value="120+ x 100+" />`	Required width and height of the MIDP `Canvas`.
`FullCanvasSize`	`<requirement name="FullCanvasSize" value="120+ x 100+" />`	Required width and height of the MIDP `Canvas` in full-screen mode.
`JavaPlatform`	`<requirement name="JavaPlatform" value="MIDP/2.0+" />`	The needed platform.
`JavaConfiguration`	`<requirement name="JavaConfiguration" value="CLDC/1.1+" />`	The needed configuration.
`JavaPackage`	`<requirement name="JavaPackage" value="nokia-ui, mmapi" />`	Needed APIs.
`JavaProtocol`	`<requirement name="JavaProtocol" value="serial,socket" />`	Needed data exchange protocols.

<requirement>	Example	Description
`HeapSize`	`<requirement name="HeapSize" value="200+kb" />`	The needed heap size of the device.
`Vendor`	`<requirement name="Vendor" value="Nokia, SonyEricsson" />`	The vendor of the device.
`Identifier`	`<requirement name="Identifier" value="Nokia/6600, SonyEricsson/P900" />`	The identifier of the device.
`Feature`	`<requirement name="Feature" value="hasPointerEvents" />`	A feature that needs to be supported by the device.
`SoundFormat`	`<requirement name="SoundFormat" value="midi" />`	The sound format that target devices need to support.
`VideoFormat`	`<requirement name="VideoFormat" value="3gpp" />`	The video format that target devices need to support.
`Term`	`<requirement name="Term" value="polish.mmapi and not polish.isVirtual" />`	You can use the `Term` requirement for selecting based on several conditions at once. This provides an easy way to check whether a device does *not* support a specific feature.

When you want to check other capabilities, you can specify the `type` attribute of the `<requirement>` element. The `type` needs to be either the name of the class that extends the `de.enough.polish.ant.requirements.Requirement` class or one of the base types, `Size`, `Int`, `String`, `Version`, or `Memory`:

```
<requirement name="MaxJarSize" value="100+ kb" type="Memory" />
```

■ Note Selecting the target devices is the first step for creating optimized applications. You can use resource assembling and preprocessing for optimizing your application for each target device. Please refer to the previous "Resource Assembling" section in this chapter, and see Chapter 8 for more information about creating device-optimized applications.

Minimizing the Number of Target Devices

Creating device-optimized applications is great, but it has two ramifications. First, it is more complex to distribute. Second, if you need to run through a verification process, you need to submit all versions of your application.

Whether you have only one or you have thirty versions of your application complicates the distribution. This may or may not be a problem, depending on your distribution plan. When you distribute your applications through carriers, aggregators, or device vendors, you just need to transmit the different application versions to your distribution partner. This is not a problem in today's fragmented device world, because professional distributors deploy capable platforms. When, however, you want to distribute your application on your own, you have to manage these different versions somehow and provide the best-suited versions to your clients. Take a look at the J2EE Provisioning Specification (see JSR 124 at *http://jcp.org/en/jsr/detail?id=124*) for getting ideas how to do this.

Another reason why you might want to minimize the number of different versions is the Java Verified process (*http://www.javaverified.com*). This Java Verified initiative tests and—more important—signs your application. Signing is required if you want to use certain security-sensitive options such as networking without asking the user for permission. Some areas such as low-level networking layers cannot even be used without having a valid signature. Unfortunately, the Java Verified initiative is one of the few available ways to sign your application. And it costs money for each tested version.

So, some situations require you to limit the number of different versions. J2ME Polish provides many virtual devices for this task. These allow you to build for certain classes of devices. These can be very unspecific like the "Generic/midp1" device, specific like the "Nokia/Series60" one, or very specific like "Nokia/Series60E2FP3" for a Series 60 device of the second edition that includes the Feature Pack 3. Refer to the device database at *http://www.j2mepolish.org/devices-overview.html* for getting to know the available virtual devices.

Building Localized Applications

Often applications should be marketed in not only one country or region but in several ones. The process of adjusting an application to a specific region is called *localization*.

With J2ME Polish you can manage the obvious needed translations and also adjust any kind of resources such as images or sounds to specific regions. Traditionally, localization involved loading the localized messages from a file during runtime and retrieving these messages with `Hashtable` keys. This slows down a localized application and also enlarges the application size. J2ME Polish embeds the translations directly into the source code by default, so in most cases a localized application has absolutely no overhead at all compared to a nonlocalized application—both in size as well as in performance.

The localization framework extends the concepts of resource assembling, so you can, for example, provide one Nokia-specific resource for each supported locale. The localization is controlled by the `<localization>` element, which is a subelement of the `<resources>` element (see the "Resource Assembling" section in this chapter).

The <localization> Element and Localized Resource Assembling

You can control the localization process with the `<localization>` element in your *build.xml* script. Listing 7-24 demonstrates how to use this element.

Listing 7-24. *Using <localization> for Supporting Several Locales*

```
<j2mepolish>
   <info
      license="GPL"
      name="Roadrunner"
      vendorName="A reader."
      version="0.0.1"
      jarName="${polish.vendor}-${polish.name}-${polish.locale}-roadrunner.jar"
   />
```

```
  <deviceRequirements>
    <requirement name="Identifier" value="Nokia/Series60" />
  </deviceRequirements>
  <build>
    <midlet class="com.apress.roadrunner.Roadrunner" />
    <resources>
      <localization
        locales="de_DE, en_US,"
        unless="test" />
      <localization locales="en_US" if="test" />
    </resources>
  </build>
  <emulator />
</j2mepolish>
```

Caution The `jarName` attribute of the `<info>` section uses the `${polish.locale}` property. This is necessary because otherwise different localizations would all end up in the same application bundle; and in that case, only the last locale could be used.

The `<localization>` element is responsible for defining which locales should be supported. The previous example uses the locales `de_DE` (German in Germany) and `en_US` (English in the United States), unless the test mode is active, in which case the application is built only for the US-English locale.

Locales are defined using the ISO standard of two lowercase letters for the language[2] (`en` for English, `de` for German, `fr` for French, and so on) and two optional uppercase letters for the country[3] (`US` for the United States, `DE` for Germany, `FR` for France, and so on). Possible combinations separate the language and the region with an underscore. You can localize your application for French-speaking Canadians by supporting the locale `fr_CA`, for example.

In each used *resources* folder, you can create a subfolder for a specific locale, for instance, *resources/en* for general English resources and *resources/en_US* for resources for the American English version of your application. The usual specification rules also apply here, so a more specific resource in *resources/Nokia/en* will override a resource with the same name in *resources/Nokia* when the English locale is used.

Managing Translations

It is easy to use translations in your application once you have the hang of it. In the following sections, you will learn how to do just that.

---

2. ISO-639; refer to *http://www.ics.uci.edu/pub/ietf/http/related/iso639.txt*
3. ISO-3166; refer to *http://www.chemie.fu-berlin.de/diverse/doc/ISO_3166.html*

Inserting Translations in Your Application

Use the `de.enough.polish.util.Locale` class for retrieving translations. It offers three methods for this purpose:

- `static String get( String name )`
- `static String get( String name, String parameter )`
- `static String get( String name, String[] parameters )`

Listing 7-25 illustrates how to use these methods.

Listing 7-25. *Using Locale for Localizing Your Application*

```
import de.enough.polish.util.Locale;

[...]

// getting a simple translation:
this.menuScreen.append( Locale.get( "menu.StartGame" ), null );
// getting a translation with one parameter:
this.menuScreen.setTitle( Locale.get( "title.Main", userName ) );
// getting a translation with several parameters:
String[] parameters = new String[2];
parameters[0] = userName;
parameters[1] = enemyName;
this.textField.setString( Locale.get( "messages.Introduction", parameters ) );
```

Note You need to add *${polish.home}/import/enough-polish-client.jar* on the classpath of your project to use the `Locale` class in your IDE.

All translations need to be defined in the *resources/messages.txt* file. You can use comments in this file by starting a line with the hash mark (#). You can use parameters in the translations by using curly parentheses; the first parameter is `{0}`, the second is `{1}`, and so on. You can also use any Java-specific characters, such as `\t` for a tab or `\"` for a quotation mark. Listing 7-26 shows an example translation file.

Listing 7-26. *Defining Translations in resources/messages.txt*

```
menu.StartGame=Start Tickle Fight
# the title of the main-screen with the user-name as the only parameter:
title.Main=Welcome {0}!
# the intro for a new game - with following parameters:
# {0}: the name of the player
# {1}: the name of the remote or computer player
messages.Introduction={1} threatens to tickle you!\n{0} against {1} is loading...
```

The translations are embedded in the actual code during the preprocessing phase; if you look at the preprocessed code, you will find code like in Listing 7-27.

Listing 7-27. *The Embedded Translations After the Preprocessing*

```
import de.enough.polish.util.Locale;

[...]

// getting a simple translation:
this.menuScreen.append( "Start Tickle Fight", null );
// getting a translation with one parameter:
this.menuScreen.setTitle( "Welcome " + userName + "!" );
// getting a translation with several parameters:
String[] parameters = new String[2];
parameters[0] = userName;
parameters[1] = enemyName;
this.textField.setString( Locale.get( 1, parameters ) );
```

Translations that contain no or one parameter are directly embedded into the source code, so there is no performance or size impact compared to a nonlocalized application at all for these kinds of translations. Only when a translation has more than one parameter is a call to the `Locale` class actually made. To improve the performance, the former `String` key, `messages.Introduction`, is transformed to a simple integer by J2ME Polish, thus saving valuable bytes as well as ensuring a fast retrieval of the resource in question.

Defining Translations

Use the *resources/messages.txt* file to define your default translations, *resources/de/messages.txt* to define your German translations, and *resources/fr_CA/messages.txt* to define your French Canadian translations. Instead of using subfolders, you can also use the files *resources/messages.txt*, *resources/messages_de.txt*, and *resources/messages_fr_CA.txt* if you prefer to have all translations in one folder. Translations follow the usual hierarchy of resource assembling, so if you have Nokia-specific translations, you can define these in *resources/Nokia/messages.txt*, and so on. For each translation key, the best matching translation is used. When an application is localized for the Nokia 6600 phone and the German `de` language, J2ME Polish tries to find a translation in the following places:

- *resources/Nokia/6600/de/messages.txt*
- *resources/Nokia/6600/messages_de.txt*
- *resources/[group-name]/de/messages.txt* (for example, *resources/Series60/de/messages.txt*)
- *resources/[group-name]/messages_de.txt* (for example, *resources/Series60/messages_de.txt*)
- *resources/Nokia/de/messages.txt*
- *resources/Nokia/messages_de.txt*

- *resources/de/messages.txt*
- *resources/messages_de.txt*

When the translation is still not found, the same hierarchy is searched again, but this time the default *messages.txt* file is used instead of the more specific *messages_de.txt* file.

Setting and Using Localized Variables

You can set localized variables just by defining them in the appropriate *messages* file. Variable definitions need to start with either `var:` or `variable:`, as follows:

```
var:VirtualCurrency=Nuggets
```

You can also use such variables within the translations (of course, you can also use normal variables), as shown in Listing 7-28.

Listing 7-28. *Using Variables Within the messages.txt File*

```
# The player has won some nuggets, {0} specifies the number of won nuggets,
# e.g. Congrats, you have won 3 Nokia-nuggets!
messages.YouHaveWon=Congrats! You have won {0} ${polish.Vendor}-${VirtualCurrency}!
```

Naturally, you can use the variables you have defined in the *messages.txt* file during the usual preprocessing in the Java source code as well:

```
//#= String virtualCurrency = "${VirtualCurrency}";
```

Using Localized Attributes

Some JAD or Manifest attributes need to be localized as well, for example, the description of the application. You can do this by defining these attributes in the appropriate *messages* file, as demonstrated in Listing 7-29.

Listing 7-29. *Defining JAD and Manifest Attributes in the messages.txt File*

```
MIDlet-Description=A game where you need to tickle your enemies!
MIDlet-Name=Tickle-Fight
```

Please refer to the "Managing JAD and Manifest Attributes" section in this chapter for more information about defining attributes.

Coping with Dates and Currencies

The `Locale` class can also help you deal with localized content; for most functions, you need to define a country as well in your `<localization>` element.

- `static String formatDate( Calendar calendar )` formats a date specific to the current locale; this method is also available for `Date` and `long`.
- `static String LANGUAGE` contains the ISO language code for the locale.

- static String COUNTRY holds the ISO country code. This is null when no country is used in the current locale.
- static String DISPLAY_LANGUAGE contains the localized language name; for example, use Deutsch for German.
- static String DISPLAY_COUNTRY contains the localized name of the country; for example, use Deutschland for Germany. This is null when no country is used in the current locale.
- static String CURRENCY_SYMBOL contains the symbol of the translation's currency; for example, use $ or €. This is null when no country is used in the current locale.
- static String CURRENCY_CODE holds the three-letter code of the used currency; for example, use USD or EUR. This is null when no country is used in the current locale.

Avoiding Common Mistakes

You have to pay attention to some issues when you want to localize your application.

Adjusting the JAR Name

You need to remember to adjust the JAR name of the application in the <info> section of *build.xml* so that the locale is included; otherwise, only the last localized application is actually written into the *dist* folder. You can use the variables ${polish.locale}, ${polish.language}, or ${polish.country} in the jarName attribute:

```
<info jarName="${polish.vendor}-${polish.name}-${polish.locale}-roadrunner.jar"
```

Using Quotation Marks and Other Special Characters in Translations

Some characters need to be Java encoded in your translation files. You can use quotation marks as well as any special character if you escape them correctly, usually with a backslash character (\) at the start; for example, you can use \" for quotation marks, \t for tabs, and \\ for backslashes.

Invalid Locale Calls

The Locale.get() method is a bit sensitive about its contents. Please ensure that the key of the translation is always given directly instead of using a variable; otherwise, J2ME Polish will not be able to embed the translation correctly, and you will end up with compile errors. Listing 7-30 shows how *not* to do it.

Listing 7-30. *Invalid Locale Call, Because the Key Is Not Given Directly*

```
// never do this:
String key = "menu.StartGame";
this.menuScreen.append( Locale.get( key ), null );
```

Instead, use the key directly in the call as in this example:

```
this.menuScreen.append( Locale.get( "menu.StartGame" ), null );
```

When you have several parameters, you need to give the parameters in a variable; otherwise, J2ME Polish is again unable to process the call correctly. Listing 7-31 shows the wrong way.

Listing 7-31. *Another Invalid Locale Call, Because Parameters Are Given Directly*

```
// never do this:
this.menuScreen.append( Locale.get( "game.StartMessage" ),
        new String[]{ userName, enemyname } );
```

Instead, define the parameters before the actual call, as shown in Listing 7-32.

Listing 7-32. *Corrected Locale Call*

```
// this is fine:
String[] parameters = new String[]{ userName, enemyname };
this.menuScreen.append( Locale.get( "game.StartMessage" ), parameters );
```

■ **Note** In a future version, J2ME Polish will use bytecode processing instead of embedding the translations during the preprocessing phase, so then you can use any call method that is allowed by Java.

Localizing the J2ME Polish GUI

The J2ME Polish GUI uses several texts, which can be localized using variables. Table 7-3 lists the variables that can be set either in *build.xml* or within any *messages.txt* file.

Table 7-3. *Localizing the J2ME Polish GUI*

Variable	Default	Explanation
`polish.command.ok`	OK	The label for the OK menu item.
`polish.command.cancel`	Cancel	The label for the Cancel menu item.
`polish.command.select`	Select	The label for the Select menu item, which is used by an implicit or exclusive `List` or `ChoiceGroup`.
`polish.command.mark`	Mark	The label for the Mark menu item of a multiple `List` or `ChoiceGroup`.
`polish.command.unmark`	Unmark	The label for the Unmark menu item of a multiple `List` or `ChoiceGroup`.
`polish.command.options`	Options	The label for the menu when several menu items are available.
`polish.command.delete`	Delete	The label for the Delete menu item, which is used by `TextFields`.

Variable	Default	Explanation
polish.command.clear	Clear	The label for the Clear menu item, which is used by TextFields.
polish.title.input	Input	The title of the native TextBox that is used for the actual input of text. This title is used only when the corresponding TextField item has no label. When the TextField has a label, that label is used as a title instead.

Listing 7-33 shows the definition of some of these variables within a *messages.txt* file.

Listing 7-33. *Localizing the GUI in a messages.txt File*

```
var:polish.command.cancel=Abbruch
var:polish.command.delete=Löschen
var:polish.title.input=Eingabe
```

You can also define translations for the J2ME Polish GUI in the *build.xml* file. This approach is useful only when no complete localization/internationalization should take place. Listing 7-34 demonstrates how to define some German translations.

Listing 7-34. *Localizing the GUI with the <variables> Element*

```
<j2mepolish>
   <info
      license="GPL"
      name="Roadrunner"
      vendorName="A reader."
      version="0.0.1"
      jarName="${polish.vendor}-${polish.name}-roadrunner.jar"
   />
   <deviceRequirements>
      <requirement name="Identifier" value="Nokia/Series60" />
   </deviceRequirements>
   <build>
      <midlet class="com.apress.roadrunner.Roadrunner" />
      <variables>
         <variable name="polish.command.cancel" value="Abbruch" />
         <variable name="polish.command.delete" value="L&ouml;schen" />
         <variable name="polish.title.input" value="Eingabe" />
      </variables>
   </build>
   <emulator />
</j2mepolish>
```

Integrating Third-Party APIs

Sometimes you need a third-party API in a project. You have to distinguish between APIs that are available as source code and APIs that are available in binary-only form. Another case is the so-called optional APIs that are already preinstalled on your target devices, such as the Wireless Messaging API or the Location API. Depending on the type of API, different actions are required for integrating the API.

■ **Note** Do not forget to add the library to the classpath of your project within your IDE.

Integrating Source Code Third-Party APIs

When a third-party API is available in source code, you can integrate it by modifying the `sourceDir` attribute of the `<build>` element in the *build.xml* file. Consider the case where your normal application code is in the *source/src* directory and the source code of the third-party API is in the *source/thirdparty* folder. You can now add the third-party API with the `<sources>` element, as shown in Listing 7-35. As most other elements, you can use `if` and `unless` conditions for your sources.

Listing 7-35. *Integrating a Source Code Third-Party API*

```
<j2mepolish>
   <info
      license="GPL"
      name="Roadrunner"
      vendorName="A reader."
      version="0.0.1"
      jarName="${polish.vendor}-${polish.name}-roadrunner.jar"
   />
   <deviceRequirements>
      <requirement name="Identifier" value="Nokia/Series60" />
      </deviceRequirements>
   <build
>
      <sources>
         <source dir="source/src" />
         <source dir="source/thirdparty" />
         <source dir="source/s60" if="polish.group.Series60" />
      </sources>
      <midlet class="com.apress.roadrunner.Roadrunner" />
   </build>
   <emulator />
</j2mepolish>
```

Tip Usually you do not need to specify where to find the sources, since J2ME Polish finds the source code automatically when it is situated in either the *source/src* or *src* folder.

Integrating Binary Third-Party APIs

When a third-party API is available only in binary form, you can integrate it with the `<libraries>` element of the `<build>` section in your *build.xml* script. This element can point to JAR or ZIP files or to a directory containing third-party libraries (either JAR files, ZIP files, or classfiles). When the libraries are situated in the *${polish.home}/import* folder, only the names of the libraries need to be given (instead of specifying the full path).

In Listing 7-36, the binary library TinyLine is integrated (*http://www.tinyline.com*). TinyLine provides specialized libraries for MIDP 2.0, Nokia Series 60, and Personal Profile J2ME devices, so you need make sure to include the correct library by using `if` or `unless` attributes.

Listing 7-36. *Integrating the TinyLine Binary Third-Party Package*

```
<j2mepolish>
   <info
      license="GPL"
      name="Roadrunner"
      vendorName="A reader."
      version="0.0.1"
      jarName="${polish.vendor}-${polish.name}-roadrunner.jar"
   />
   <deviceRequirements>
      <requirement name="Identifier" value="Nokia/Series60" />
   </deviceRequirements>
   <build
   >
      <midlet class="com.apress.roadrunner.Roadrunner" />
      <libraries>
         <library file="thirdparty/tinylines60.zip"
                  if="polish.group.Series60 and not polish.midp2" />
         <library file="thirdparty/tinylinemidp2.zip"
                  if="polish.midp2" />
         <library file="thirdparty/tinyline.zip"
                  if="polish.midp1 and not polish.group.Series60" />
      </libraries>
   </build>
   <emulator />
</j2mepolish>
```

Integrating Device APIs

Many devices provide additional optional APIs. A popular example is the Nokia UI API, which provides additional graphic and sound functions. When a device supports a specific API, this is noted with the `JavaPackage` capability of that device in the *${polish.home}/devices.xml* file.

Assuming that you want to use the Motorola Phonebook API, you just need to copy the corresponding library file *phonebook.jar* or *phonebook.zip* into the *${polish.home}/import* folder. It will then be used automatically for the devices that support the Phonebook API.

J2ME Polish already provides a large number of APIs ranging from MIDP 1.0 to vendor-specific APIs such as the Nokia UI API or the Siemens Extension API.

You can modify the *${polish.home}/apis.xml* file for specifying different library names, paths, or aliases. Chapter 6 describes this in more detail.

■ **Caution** You cannot use optional and vendor-specific APIs for devices that do not support them. So, if a device does not support the Wireless Messaging API, you cannot use that API for your application build for that device. Use preprocessing and the `polish.api.[api-name]` preprocessing symbol for making the necessary adjustments in your application.

Obfuscating Applications

Obfuscating is vitally important for J2ME applications not only because it makes reverse engineering more difficult but also because the application size is decreased—in some cases quite drastically. Obfuscators usually strip away any classes, methods, and fields that are not used by the application. In a further step, they rename all remaining classes. Because of this functionality, you need to define "entry points" that are not scrambled. J2ME Polish automatically adds all MIDlets that are defined with the `<midlet>` element to the list of entry points. With the nested `<keep>` element, you can define additional classes that must be kept, even though they are not used directly. This is the case for all classes you load with the `Class.forName( String )` mechanism, for example. Most obfuscators also accept additional parameters with nested `<parameter>` elements. Listing 7-37 demonstrates how to use the ProGuard obfuscator, in which the bytecode optimization of ProGuard is deactivated.

Listing 7-37. *Using the ProGuard Obfuscator*

```
<j2mepolish>
   <info
      license="GPL"
      name="Roadrunner"
      vendorName="A reader."
      version="0.0.1"
      jarName="${polish.vendor}-${polish.name}-roadrunner.jar"
   />
   <deviceRequirements>
      <requirement name="Identifier" value="Nokia/Series60" />
```

```
    </deviceRequirements>
    <build>
        <midlet class="com.apress.roadrunner.Roadrunner" />
        <obfuscator name="ProGuard" >
            <keep class="com.apress.roadrunner.DynamicClass" />
            <parameter name="optimize"  value="false" />
        </obfuscator>
    </build>
    <emulator />
</j2mepolish>
```

Using the Default Package

When you place your MIDlet and its related helper classes into different packages, you are maintaining a good architecture, but you might need to sacrifice some JAR size for that. J2ME Polish can move all your classes into the empty default package, which reduces the size of your JAR file. You can enable this option with any obfuscator by setting the `useDefaultPackage` option of the obfuscator to `true`: `<obfuscator name="ProGuard" useDefaultPackage="true" />`.

■ **Caution** Use `import` statements instead of fully qualified class names in your code; otherwise, J2ME Polish will not be able to resolve the imports correctly. So, *do not* extend a class without importing it. This code will not work: `class MyClass extends com.company.package.OtherClass`. But this code is fine: `import com.company.package.OtherClass; class MyClass extends OtherClass`.

Combining Several Obfuscators

You can combine several obfuscators at once just by specifying several `<obfuscator>` elements. When you use the `<keep>` subelement, you need to specify in only one of the `<obfuscator>` elements. J2ME Polish will then use the obfuscated output of one obfuscator as input for the following obfuscator. Listing 7-38 uses the ProGuard obfuscator together with the DashO obfuscator. Whether combining several obfuscators minimizes the JAR size depends on both the obfuscator and your application. In some cases, you might even end up with bigger JAR files than with using one obfuscator only. Your mileage may vary. You can obtain the DashO obfuscator from *http://www.preemptive.com.*

Listing 7-38. *Combining Several Obfuscators*

```
<j2mepolish>
    <info
        license="GPL"
        name="Roadrunner"
        vendorName="A reader."
        version="0.0.1"
        jarName="${polish.vendor}-${polish.name}-roadrunner.jar"
```

```
    />
    <deviceRequirements>
        <requirement name="Identifier" value="Nokia/Series60" />
    </deviceRequirements>
    <build>
        <midlet class="com.apress.roadrunner.Roadrunner" />
        <obfuscator name="ProGuard" />
        <obfuscator name="Dasho" />
    </build>
    <emulator />
</j2mepolish>
```

■ **Note** The appendix lists all supported obfuscators. You can integrate unsupported obfuscators by using the `antcall` mechanism, by which you can call another target within your *build.xml* script: `<obfuscator name="antcall" target="obfuscate" />`. Chapter 13 provides more details about this extension mechanism.

Debugging Applications

J2ME Polish's support for multiple devices, locales, and obfuscators is great for creating applications, but it is a bit heavyweight for the development phase. Fortunately, you can choose a lightweight approach by tweaking *build.xml* a bit.

One strategy for allowing fast builds is to use conditional `<deviceRequirements>`, `<localization>`, and `<obfuscation>` elements, which can be enabled and disabled by setting Ant properties.

Another strategy is to use J2ME Polish in the compiler mode. In that case, J2ME Polish only preprocesses, compiles, and possibly preverifies the application. This approach is useful for integrating J2ME Polish with the IDE or with an IDE plug-in such as EclipseME.

If you want to debug an application that is compiled by J2ME Polish, you need to enable the `<debug>` element so that debug information such as variable names and line numbers in the source code is included in the classfiles. Alternatively, you can provide your own `<compiler>` element.

In the following sections, I elaborate on these strategies.

Using Conditions

With conditions you can disable and enable elements in *build.xml*. You can use the Ant property `test` to differentiate between the test mode and the "real" build mode, in which everything is activated. Listing 7-39 provides a blueprint for your *build.xml* file.

Listing 7-39. *Using Conditions in J2ME Polish*

```
<project name="roadrunner" default="j2mepolish">
   <!-- define the installation folder of J2ME Polish -->
   <property name="polish.home" location="C:\programs\J2ME-Polish" />
   <!-- define the installation folder of the WTK -->
   <property name="wtk.home" location="C:\WTK22" />
   <!-- define the J2ME Polish task, classpath on one line please -->
   <taskdef name="j2mepolish"
      classname="de.enough.polish.ant.PolishTask"
      classpath="${polish.home}/import/enough-j2mepolish-build.jar:
      ${polish.home}/import/jdom.jar:
      ${polish.home}/import/proguard.jar"/>
   <!-- activate the test mode -->
   <target name="test">
      <property name="test" value="true" />
      <property name="work.dir" value="build/test" />
   </target>
   <!-- normal settings -->
   <target name="init">
      <property name="test" value="false" />
      <property name="work.dir" value="build/real" />
   </target>
   <!-- start the build with J2ME Polish -->
   <target name="j2mepolish" depends="init">
      <j2mepolish>
         <info
            license="GPL"
            name="Roadrunner"
            vendorName="A reader."
            version="0.0.1"
            jarName="${polish.vendor}-${polish.name}-${polish.locale}-app.jar"
         />
      <deviceRequirements if="test">
         <requirement name="Identifier" value="Nokia/Series60" />
      </deviceRequirements>
      <deviceRequirements unless="test">
         <requirement name="JavaPlatform" value="MIDP/2+.0+" />
      </deviceRequirements>
       <build workDir="${work.dir}" >
         <midlet class="com.apress.roadrunner.Roadrunner" />

         <resources
            dir="resources"
            excludes="*.definition"
         >
         <localization locales="de, en, fr_CA" unless="test" />
         <localization locales="en" if="test" />
```

```
            </resources>
        <debug level="error" if="test" />
        <obfuscator name="ProGuard" unless="test" />
        </build>
        <emulator if="test" />
    </j2mepolish>
    </target>
    <target name="clean">
        <delete dir="build" />
        <delete dir="dist" />
    </target>
</project>
```

In this example, you have the test target that sets the Ant property test to true and sets the working directory to *build/test*. This is recommended because you are also enabling the <debug> mode. The <j2mepolish> target depends on the <init> target, which sets the test property to false and defines another working directory. When the <test> target is executed first, these properties cannot be changed by the <init> target anymore:

```
> ant test j2mepolish
```

The elements <deviceRequirements>, <localization>, <debug>, <obfuscator>, and <emulator> all depend on the test property. When it is set to true, J2ME Polish will compile the application only for the "Nokia/Series60" device, use only the English en locale, enable the debug mode, skip the obfuscation, and start the emulator after the build. When the test property is false, J2ME Polish compiles the application for all MIDP 2.0 devices; uses the en, de, and fr_CA locales; disables the debug mode; and obfuscates the application.

Using J2ME Polish As a Compiler

You can use J2ME Polish as a compiler, in which case only the preprocessing, the compilation, and possibly the preverification steps are executed. This can be useful for interacting with available J2ME plug-ins such as EclipseME or J2ME-enabled IDEs such as NetBeans. The compiler mode is activated using the compilerMode-, compilerDestDir-, and compilerModePreverify attributes, as shown in Listing 7-40.

Listing 7-40. *Using J2ME Polish As a Compiler*

```
<j2mepolish>
    <info
        license="GPL"
        name="Roadrunner"
        vendorName="A reader."
        version="0.0.1"
        jarName="${polish.vendor}-${polish.name}-roadrunner.jar"
    />
```

```
  <deviceRequirements>
    <requirement name="Identifier" value="Generic/midp1" />
  </deviceRequirements>
  <build
    compilerMode="true"
    compilerModePreverify="true"
    compilerDestDir="preverified"
  >
      <midlet class="com.apress.roadrunner.Roadrunner" />
  </build>
  <emulator />
</j2mepolish>
```

J2ME Polish sets the javac-target to either 1.1 or 1.2 depending on the used WTK. You can also set the target directly by specifying the javacTarget attribute of the <build> element. Debug information is not added unless the debugging mode is enabled with the <debug> element.

If you need full control of the compiler settings, you can also use the <compiler> element, which is a nested element of the <build> section. Listing 7-41 demonstrates how to use the <compiler> element.

Listing 7-41. *Using the <compiler> Element*

```
<build
  compilerMode="true"
  compilerModePreverify="true"
  compilerDestDir="preverified"
>
  <midlet class="com.apress.roadrunner.Roadrunner" />
  <compiler
    compiler="jikes"
    debug="true"
    debuglevel="lines,vars,source"
    optimize="true"
  />
</build>
```

Note You can use the <compiler> element independently of the compiler mode; it supports all attributes and elements of the original Ant <javac> task.

Summary

In this chapter, you learned how to build applications with Ant and J2ME Polish. You can equip your applications with specific resources without touching the source code, use obfuscators to minimize the application size, localize your application, and integrate a third-party API.

In the next chapter, you will explore the possibilities of preprocessing. In contrast to the packaging solutions, preprocessing is used on the source code level of your application.

CHAPTER 8

Preprocessing

In this chapter:

- Learn why J2ME Polish uses preprocessing for its J2ME APIs.
- Control preprocessing with directives.
- Use the standard preprocessing variables supported by J2ME Polish.
- Define your own variables and symbols in J2ME Polish.
- Transform variable values using property functions.
- Explore some practical applications of preprocessing.

One of the greatest challenges of developing J2ME applications is to adjust them to work on many different devices. Along with the detailed device database you learned about in Chapter 6, J2ME Polish provides a powerful preprocessor to help you meet this challenge. Preprocessing is the key to optimizing your application without losing portability. This chapter equips you with the necessary knowledge to adjust your application to different environments, circumvent known issues, and exploit device-specific options.

Why Preprocessing?

Often, you need to use device-specific code to create optimal applications. For example, on Nokia's MIDP 1.0 devices, you can play back sounds and use a full-screen mode, but only when you use Nokia's UI API. But when you use this API, you cannot run your application on other handsets. So what can you do?

Java allows you to load classes dynamically. So, in theory, you could create several versions of your classes and load the correct one dynamically during the runtime of your application. Unfortunately, this quite drastically reduces the performance of your application and increases its size at the same time. Both results are not acceptable in the resource-constrained J2ME world. Also, some devices do not accept any applications that refer to unknown classes, even when those classes are loaded only via Java's reflection mechanism.

Another approach is to create a separate project for each target device, or at least for each device type. This solves the performance and size problems, but leaves you with a huge maintenance chore. Just imagine the work to implement a new feature in all those separate projects!

A third approach is to use static final variables and the compiler to adjust your code. You can use normal `if` branches like `if (Configuration.IS_NOKIA_SERIES60)` to distinguish between different configurations. When `Configuration.IS_NOKIA_SERIES60` is a `final static boolean` field and `false`, the compiler can eliminate the following dead code during the compile phase. The main problem here is that you need to create and include one `Configuration` class for each target device, and you need to integrate it somehow. Another problem is that you can use `if` branches only in the normal code, so you cannot take this approach for importing different APIs or using different fields, for example. Also, you need to make sure to recompile all classes whenever you change the `Configuration` class.

A more powerful solution is to use *aspects* for adjusting your application. In aspect-oriented programming, you code a plain-vanilla application and use aspects to inject additional code at specific positions in your source code, called *pointcuts*. Aspect-oriented development is quite powerful and allows you to do some amazing things, like changing the hierarchy of classes. However, this new paradigm is also enormously complex and difficult to learn. On the positive side, you end up with a very clean and easy-to-understand application. On the other hand, you need to provide a different set of aspects for each target device, meaning that you need to split up your application project again.

■ **Tip** In aspect-oriented development, you distinguish between the main cause of your application (for example, a banking application) and its secondary purposes (for example, to authenticate its users securely). Refer to *http://en.wikipedia.org/wiki/Aspect-oriented_programming* to learn more about aspect-oriented development. The AspectJ project (*http://eclipse.org/aspectj*) is a popular solution for the Java world.

A simple, yet effective, solution is to *preprocess* your application. Preprocessing changes your application code before it is compiled. You control this process with preprocessing directives, symbols, and variables. J2ME Polish not only includes a powerful preprocessor, but it also provides a standardized way to query and use the capabilities of the current target device. Thanks to the integrated device database, you can access the detailed configurations of more than 300 different handsets out of the box, so you don't need to create and maintain your own configurations. Preprocessing allows you to adjust your application to different devices and configurations without degrading runtime performance, creating incompatibilities, or splitting up your project.

Preprocessing sounds more complicated than it actually is. Listing 8-1 shows a code snippet that uses preprocessing for determining how a sound can be played.

Listing 8-1. *Playing Sound Only When the MMAPI or Nokia's UI API Is Available*

```
public void playAudio() {
   //#if polish.api.mmapi || polish.midp2
      try {
         Player player = Manager.createPlayer(
            getClass().getResourceAsStream("/music.mid"), "audio/midi");
         player.realize();
         player.prefetch();
```

```
            player.start();
         } catch (Exception e) {
            //#debug error
            System.out.println("Unable to start audio playback" + e);
         }
   //#elif polish.api.nokia-ui
         try {
            byte[] soundData = loadSoundData();
            Sound sound = new Sound( soundData, Sound.FORMAT_TONE );
            sound.play( 1 );
         } catch (IllegalArgumentException e) {
            //#debug error
            System.out.println("Unable to play Nokia sound" + e );
         }
   //#else
         System.out.println("No sound playback supported.");
   //#endif
}
```

When the device supports the MMAPI or the MIDP 2.0 profile, you can use the `javax.microedition.media.Player` for the audio playback. The statement `//#if polish.api.mmapi || polish.midp2` tests these requirements. Alternatively, you can use Nokia's UI API for playing sounds, so the code tests this option in the `//#elif polish.api.nokia-ui` statement.

Listing 8-2 demonstrates how you can use the J2ME Polish device database for checking the capabilities of the current target device. For each API that the device supports, the preprocessing symbol `polish.api.[`*`api-name`*`]` is defined. If the device supports the MIDP 1.0 platform, the `polish.midp1` symbol is defined. Similarly, the `polish.midp2` preprocessing symbol is defined when the MIDP 2.0 platform is supported by the target device.

Listing 8-2. *Preprocessed Code for Devices That Support Nokia's UI API*

```
public void playAudio() {
   //#if polish.api.mmapi || polish.midp2
      //# try {
      //#    Player player = Manager.createPlayer(
      //#       getClass().getResourceAsStream("/music.mid"), "audio/midi");
      //#    player.realize();
      //#    player.prefetch();
      //#    player.start();
      //# } catch (Exception e) {
      //#    //#debug error
      //#    System.out.println("Unable to start audio playback" + e);
      //# }
   //#elif polish.api.nokia-ui
      try {
         byte[] soundData = loadSoundData();
         Sound sound = new Sound( soundData, Sound.FORMAT_TONE );
```

```
            sound.play( 1 );
        } catch (IllegalArgumentException e) {
            //#debug error
            System.out.println("Unable to play Nokia sound" + e );
        }
    //#else
        //# System.out.println("No sound playback supported.");
    //#endif
}
```

So what happens when the device supports only Nokia's UI API, and not the MMAPI nor the MIDP 2.0 standard? In that case, J2ME Polish comments out all the code for the unavailable capabilities. Only the code between the `//#elif polish.api.nokia-ui` and the `//#else` directive is left active, as in Listing 8-2.

J2ME Polish calls the preprocessor automatically for you, by the way. So you need to include only the necessary preprocessing statements in your code. The rest is taken care of by J2ME Polish.

Preprocessing Directives

J2ME Polish equips you with powerful preprocessing directives for controlling the preprocessing phase. All directives start with the standard Java line comment characters (double slash) followed by a hash mark, so that they don't confuse your IDE and Java compiler. Table 8-1 lists all of the supported preprocessing directives. These are described in detail in the following sections.

Note You can also implement your own preprocessing directives, as described in Chapter 13.

Table 8-1. *J2ME Preprocessing Directives*

Directive	Description	Example
`//#ifdef`	Checks if a single preprocessing symbol is defined	`//#ifdef polish.api.mmapi`
`//#ifndef`	Checks if a single preprocessing symbol is not defined	`//#ifndef polish.api.mmapi`
`//#else`	Branches in an `//#ifdef` or `//#if` directive	`//#else`
`//#elifdef`	Branches and checks for another single preprocessing symbol	`//#elifdef polish.midp2`
`//#elifndef`	Branches and checks whether another single preprocessing symbol is not defined	`//#elifndef polish.midp2`
`//#endif`	Ends an `//#ifdef` or `//#if block`	`//#endif`

Directive	Description	Example
`//#if`	Checks several preprocessing symbols or compares preprocessing variables	`//#if polish.api.mmapi || polish.midp2`
`//#elif`	Branches and checks for other preprocessing symbols or preprocessing variables	`//#elif polish.BitsPerPixel > 10`
`//#condition`	Includes or excludes a complete file	`//#condition polish.usePolishGui || polish.midp2`
`//#define`	Defines temporary preprocessing symbols or variables	`//#define tmp.useSound`
`//#undefine`	Removes defined preprocessing symbols or variables	`//#undefine tmp.useSound`
`//#`	Comments out a statement within an `//#if` or `//#ifdef` block	`//# return true;`
`//#=`	Inserts preprocessing variables	`//#= int screenWidth = ${polish.ScreenWidth};`
`//#debug`	Uses the logging framework of J2ME Polish	`//#debug error`
`//#foreach`	Uses several values of a preprocessing variable	`//#foreach format in polish.SoundFormat`
`//#next`	Ends a `#foreach` block	`//#next format`
`//#style`	Assigns a J2ME Polish CSS style to the following item or screen	`//#style importantText`
`//#include`	Includes code fragments	`//#include ${polish.source}/includes/audioplayback.txt`
`//#message`	During the build phase, prints out messages	`//#message preprocessing for ${polish.Identifier}`
`//#todo`	During the build phase, prints out messages that automatically include the name and line of the source file	`//#todo implement playSound()`

The most important directives are the `#if` and the `#=` directives, so let's look at those first.

Branching Your Code

`If-then-else` branches are well-known programming constructs. The `#if` directive and its various relatives and relations allow you to adjust your source code to different handsets and configurations very effectively. The possibilities of these adjustments are endless. You can easily create tailor-made applications that use device-specific APIs, circumvent known issues of your target devices, or change the application flow depending on the configuration.

Checking for Single Preprocessing Symbols

Use the `#ifdef`, `#ifndef`, `#elifdef`, `#elifndef`, `#else`, and `#endif` directives to check for single preprocessing symbols. A preprocessing symbol is like a Boolean variable: either it is defined (`true`) or it is not defined (`false`). Preprocessing symbols are defined in the device database with the `<features>` of a device, such as `polish.hasPointerEvents`, and indirectly by device `<capability>` elements, such as `polish.CanvasSize:defined` and `polish.api.mmapi`. You can define your own project-specific symbols by using the `symbols` attribute of the `<build>` section in the *build.xml* file. Table 8-2 explains the meaning of the directives.

Table 8-2. *Directives for Checking Single Preprocessing Symbols*

Directive	Meaning	Explanation
`//#ifdef [symbol]`	`if [symbol]` is defined	The symbol `[symbol]` needs to be defined, when the next section should be compiled.
`//#ifndef [symbol]`	`if [symbol]` is not defined	The symbol `[symbol]` must not be defined, when the next section should be compiled.
`//#else`	`else`	When the corresponding `#if` clause failed, the following section will be compiled (and the other way around).
`//#elifdef [symbol]`	`else if [symbol]` is defined	The symbol `[symbol]` needs to be defined and the previous section needs to be false, when the next section should be compiled.
`//#elifndef [symbol]`	`else if [symbol]` is not defined	The symbol `[symbol]` must not be defined and the previous section needs to be false, when the next section should be compiled.
`//#endif`	End of the `if` block	End of every `#ifdef` and `#ifndef` block.

Every `//#ifdef` or `//#ifndef` directive needs to be closed by an `//#endif` statement. Use the `//#else`, `//#elifdef`, and `//#elifndef` directives to branch within an `//#ifdef` or `//#ifndef` block. Listing 8-3 shows an example of how to use the `#ifdef` directive to include a menu item on devices that have a camera.

Listing 8-3. *Including an Additional Menu Item Only for Devices with a Camera*

```
this.menuScreen = new List( "Menu", List.IMPLICIT );
this.menuScreen.append("Load Photos", null );
this.menuScreen.append("View Photos", null );
//#ifdef polish.hasCamera
   this.menuScreen.append("Create Photo", null );
//#endif
```

Checking for Multiple Symbols and Comparing Variables

Often, you need to check for several symbols at once or compare variables in your preprocessing code. You can do all that with the `#if`, `#elif`, `#else`, and `#endif` directives. Table 8-3 explains the meaning of these directives.

Table 8-3. *Directives for Checking Several Preprocessing Symbols and Comparing Variables*

Directive	Meaning	Explanation
`//#if [term]`	`if [term]` is true	The specified term must be true, if the next section should be compiled.
`//#else`	`else`	When the previous if clause failed, the following section will be compiled (and the other way around).
`//#elif [term]`	`else if [term]` is true	The specified term needs to be true and the previous section needs to be false, when the next section should be compiled.
`//#endif`	End of the `if` block	End of every `#if` block.

You have already seen the `#if` directive in action in Listings 8-1 and 8-2. You can use `#if` and `#elif` for checking single preprocessing symbols, too. The only difference is that `#ifdef` directives are processed slightly faster during the build phase, but on today's high-speed computers, you probably won't notice the difference.

You can use the normal Boolean operators (&&, ||, !, and ^) and parentheses for evaluating complex terms like this:

```
//#if (polish.api.mmapi || polish.api.nokia-ui) && !polish.hasPointerEvents
```

The arguments for Boolean operators are symbols that are `true` when they are defined and `false` otherwise. Table 8-4 explains these operators. If you prefer, you can also use the written operators `and`, `or`, `not`, and `xor` instead of the symbols. This is especially handy if you use or define such terms in your *build.xml* file, because some characters, like &, need to be XML-encoded (for example, to `&`).

Table 8-4. *Boolean Operators for Evaluating Terms*

Boolean Operator	Meaning	Explanation
`&&` or `and`	And	Both arguments/symbols need to be defined: `true && true = true`, `true && false = false`, `false && true = false`, `false && false = false`
`||` or `or`	Or	At least one argument/symbol must be defined: `true || true = true`, `true || false = true`, `false || true = true`, `false || false = false`
`^` or `xor`	Exclusive or (xor)	Only and at least one argument/symbol must be defined: `true ^ false = true`, `false ^ true = true`, `true ^ true = false`, `false ^ false = false`
`!` or `not`	Not	The argument/symbol must not be defined: `! false = true`, `! true = false`

You can also compare variables and constants in the `#if` directive, as demonstrated by Listing 8-4.

Listing 8-4. *Showing an Animation Only When the Device Has at Least 65,000 Colors*

```
public void startApp() {
   //#if polish.api.mmapi && (polish.BitsPerColor >= 16)
      showSplashVideo();
   //#else
      showSplashImage();
   //#endif
}
```

Compare variables with the ==, !=, >, <, <=, and >= comparators. Arguments for the comparators are variables or constants. A term can include both comparators and Boolean operators, if the sections are separated by parentheses. Table 8-5 explains the available comparators.

Table 8-5. *Comparators for Evaluating Terms*

Comparator	Meaning	Explanation	Example
`==`	Equal to	The left and the right argument must be equal. Integers and strings can be compared	`8 == 8 = true, Nokia == Nokia = true, //#if polish.BitsPerPixel == 8, //#if polish.vendor == Nokia`
`!=`	Not equal to	The left and the right argument must not be equal, integers and strings can be compared	`8 != 8 = false, Nokia != Sony-Ericsson = true, //#if polish.BitsPerPixel != 8, //#if polish.vendor != Nokia`
`>`	Greater than	The left argument must be greater than the right one. Only integers can be compared	`8 > 8 = false, 16 > 8 = true, //#if polish.BitsPerPixel > 8`
`<`	Less than	The left argument must be smaller than the right one. Only integers can be compared	`8 < 8 = false, 8 < 16 = true, //#if polish.BitsPerPixel < 8`
`>=`	Greater than or equal to	The left argument must be greater than or equal to the right one. Only integers can be compared	`8 >= 8 = true, 16 >= 8 = true, //#if polish.BitsPerPixel >= 8`
`<=`	Less than or equal to	The left argument must be smaller than or equal to the right one. Only integers can be compared	`8 <= 8 = true, 8 <= 16 = false, //#if polish.BitsPerPixel <= 8`

Some variables can use different units. The `polish.HeapSize` variable is sometimes defined in kilobytes and sometimes in megabytes, for example. You cannot compare such variables using the less-than or greater-than comparators, since these comparators accept only numerical values. In such situations, you can use property functions. When you use a function like this, you precede the function call with a dollar sign ($) and enclose it within curly parentheses. The following example compares the heap size of the current device using the bytes function:

```
//#if ${ bytes( polish.HeapSize ) } > 102400
```

The bytes function will return –1 when the given memory value is dynamic, so it might be necessary to test both cases:

```
//#if ( ${ bytes( polish.HeapSize ) } > 102400 ) or (polish.HeapSize == dynamic)
```

You can also use functions for constants like 100 kb, which often improves the readability of your code:

```
//#if ${ bytes( polish.HeapSize ) } > ${ bytes( 100 kb ) }
```

You will find more information about using property functions in the "Managing Variables and Symbols" section later in this chapter.

Excluding or Including Complete Classes

You can include or exclude complete classes or interfaces with the #condition directive. J2ME Polish uses this functionality to include its GUI wrapper classes only when the J2ME Polish GUI is actually used, for example. Another possible scenario is to include an audio player only when the target device supports the necessary requirements, as shown in Listing 8-5. The #condition directive accepts all arguments of the #if directive, so you can use logical operators and comparators in it. You can place the #condition directive anywhere in the file, but the recommended position is on the very first line.

Listing 8-5. *Including the Audio Player Class Only When the Device Can Play Sounds*

```
//#condition polish.api.mmapi || polish.api.nokia-ui

package com.company.j2me.audio;

public class AudioPlayer {
...
}
```

Note When you use #if directives to check if the device supports audio before you use the AudioPlayer class, you don't actually need the #condition directive, since the obfuscator takes care of removing any unused classes. But the #condition directive forces you to use these checks consistently; otherwise, you will get compiler errors.

Defining Temporary Symbols and Variables

You can define and remove preprocessing symbols and variables in your source code by using the #define and #undefine directives.

When you have a complex preprocessing term, you can test this term once, and then set a preprocessing symbol that indicates the result of the term. Later on, you need to check only that symbol. Such symbols are valid only in the file where they have been defined. To indicate that these symbols are temporary, you should start their names with `tmp.`. Listing 8-6 demonstrates how to define a temporary symbol and variable.

Listing 8-6. *Defining a Symbol and a Variable in Your Source Code*

```
//#if config.useFullScreen && (polish.midp2 || polish.classes.fullscreen:defined)
   //#define tmp.useFullScreen
   //#define tmp.message = Hello fullscreen World!
//#else
   //#define tmp.message = Hello World!
//#endif
```

With the `#undefine` directive, you can remove any symbols and variables. Usually, this is not necessary, since J2ME Polish removes all temporary symbols and variables automatically when it has finished preprocessing the corresponding source file.

■ **Tip** You can define conditional variables globally by defining them in the `<variables>` section of the *build.xml* file. Use the `if` or `unless` attribute for setting them: `<variable name="config.Message" value="Hello Moto" if="polish.Vendor == Motorola" />`.

Including Values of Variables in Your Code

You include the values of preprocessing variables in your code by using the #= directive. You can include your own variables, as well as any device capabilities of the device database.

Listing 8-7 shows how to use device-specific hard-coded values in your application. You can check whether a variable is available by testing the preprocessing symbol `[`*`variable-name`*`]:defined`, as in `//#if polish.ScreenWidth:defined`. When you include the variable, you need to surround the variable name with a dollar sign and curly parentheses, just like the Ant properties in the *build.xml* file.

Listing 8-7. *Using Device-Specific Hard-Coded Values*

```
//#ifdef polish.FullCanvasSize:defined
   //#= final int width = ${polish.FullCanvasWidth};
   //#= final int height = ${polish.FullCanvasHeight};
//#else
   final int width = myCanvas.getWidth();
   final int height = myCanvas.getHeight();
//#endif
```

Using Several Variable Values Individually

In the device database, many device capabilities contain several values. For example, the `polish.SoundFormat`, `polish.ImageFormat`, and `polish.VideoFormat` capabilities include several values, separated by commas. You can access each value individually with the `#foreach` directive. The logging framework of J2ME Polish uses this mechanism to include all registered log handlers, for example.

In the `#foreach` directive, you define a temporary loop variable that holds each value of the variable:

```
//#foreach format in polish.SoundFormat
```

You need to finish each `#foreach` block with the `#next [loop-var-name]` directive:

```
//#next format
```

You can loop through any variable that separates its values by commas.

Listing 8-8 demonstrates how you can loop through all supported sound formats of a device.

Listing 8-8. *Looping Through All Sound Formats of the Target Device*

```
String format;
//#foreach format in polish.SoundFormat
   format = "${ lowercase( format ) }";
   System.out.println( "The audio-format " + format + " is supported." );
//#next format
```

Caution The code fragment within the `#foreach` loop will be copied into the preprocessed source code as many times as there are values. This copying process has two implications: any variables should be defined outside the loop (but they can be set and used within the loop, of course), and when the application is debugged or compiled, breakpoints or errors can point to the wrong source code lines. If the variable is not defined, the complete block is commented out and not compiled at all.

You can use the `number` property function for retrieving the number of separate values within a variable. This is useful when you want to fill an array in the `#foreach` loop, for example. Listing 8-9 demonstrates a real-world example taken from the logging framework of J2ME Polish.

Listing 8-9. *Using the number Property Function to Determine the Number of Separate Entries*

```
//#if polish.log.handlers:defined
   private static LogHandler[] handlers;
   static {
      //#= handlers = new LogHandler[ ${ number( polish.log.handlers )} ];
      int i = 0;
      //#foreach handler in polish.log.handlers
```

```
            //#= handlers[i] = new ${ classname( handler )}();
            i++;
        //#next handler
    }
//#endif
```

Including External Code

You can include external code fragments with the #include directive. With this mechanism, you can create often-used code fragments only once, instead of using copy and paste to duplicate functionality.

The included fragment is loaded relative to the location of the *build.xml* file. You can use the polish.source variable for including files relative to the source directory:

```
//#include ${polish.source}/includes/standard.java
```

Analyzing the Preprocessing Phase

Preprocessing can be a complex business. The #message and #todo directives help you to follow the preprocessing logic by printing out messages during the build process.

You can include any variables in your message. These are replaced by their values when they are defined. The #todo directive also adds the name of the source code and the line number to the output. Listing 8-10 demonstrates the usage and output of both directives.

Listing 8-10. *Showing Messages During the Build Phase*

```
//#if polish.api.mmapi
   //#message The device ${polish.Identifier} supports the MMAPI.
//#else
   //#todo Implement audio playback for device ${polish.Identifier}.
//#endif

// output when you build it for the SE/K700:
MESSAGE: The device Sony-Ericsson/K700 supports the MMAPI.

// output when you build it for Nokia/7650:
TODO: com.company.package.ClassName line 55: Implement audio playback
for device Nokia/7650.
```

Hiding Statements

Hiding statements is a somewhat weird application of preprocessing, but nevertheless necessary at times so that the IDE is not confused.

Sometimes you have several return statements in one method. In such cases, you can comment out all but the last return statement by starting the line with //#, followed by a space and the actual statement. J2ME Polish will then activate the correct return statement when it preprocesses your source code. Listing 8-11 shows a method that caches images for quicker retrieval when the device has a heap size greater than 500 kilobytes.

Listing 8-11. *Hiding return Statements*

```
public Image loadImage( String url )
throws IOException
{
   //#if ${ bytes( polish.HeapSize ) } <= ${ bytes( 500 kb ) }
      //# return Image.createImage( url );
   //#else
      Image image = (Image) this.cachedImages.get( url );
      if (image == null) {
         image = Image.createImage( url );
         this.cachedImages.put( url, image );
      }
      return image;
   //#endif
}
```

Logging

J2ME Polish contains a logging framework that allows you to view logged messages on the device and to enable different logging levels (or none at all). You can log a message with the `#debug` directive. The following `System.out.println()` message is then forwarded to the logging system. Listing 8-12 demonstrates the usage of the logging system. Chapter 9 covers the details of the logging framework.

Listing 8-12. *Logging an Error Message*

```
try {
   this.optionalImage = Image.createImage( "/optional.png" );
} catch (IOException e) {
   //#debug
   System.out.println("Unable to load optional.png" + e );
}
```

Setting CSS Styles

You can apply CSS styles for UI items with the `#style` directive. When you use the advanced GUI of J2ME Polish, you can define such styles in the *resources/polish.css* file. This whole process is discussed in detail in Chapter 12. Listing 8-13 shows how to apply a style for a `StringItem`.

Listing 8-13. *Setting a Style for a UI Item*

```
//#style text
StringItem item = new StringItem( null, "Hello World!" );
```

Nesting Directives

You can nest and mix directives up to any level, so you can check for special cases within #if branches. Listing 8-14 shows an example.

Listing 8-14. *Nesting Directives*

```
//#ifdef polish.group.Series40
   doSomething( 40 );
   //#if polish.Identifier != Nokia/6230
      doAnotherThing();
   //#endif
//#elifdef polish.group.Series60
   doSomething( 60 );
//#endif
```

Managing Variables and Symbols

Most preprocessing directives need preprocessing symbols or variables on which to operate. Many symbols and variables are defined in the device database, but you are free to define your own variables and symbols as well.

For each preprocessing variable, several symbols are defined automatically: the symbol [*variable-name*]:defined is set for each defined variable, and one [*variable-name*].[*value*] symbol is defined for each value that the variable holds. For example, for the fictitious variable config.Locations with the equally fictitious values London, New-York, Moscow, the following symbols would be defined automatically:

- config.Locations:defined
- config.Locations.London
- config.Locations.New-York
- config.Locations.Moscow

The same mechanism is used when there is only one value in the variable. If, for example, only London were set for the config.Locations variable, the preprocessing symbols config.Locations:defined and config.Locations.London would be defined.

As well as defining your own symbols and variables, you may need to transform variables before you use or compare them. J2ME Polish provides property functions for this task. In this section, you will learn how to define and transform symbols and variables. But first, let's take a look at the symbols that are already defined in the J2ME Polish device database.

Using Standard Preprocessing Symbols and Variables

Thanks to the device database of J2ME Polish, many often-needed symbols and variables are already defined out of the box. Each device feature results in the corresponding preprocessing symbol, and each capability is represented by its respective preprocessing variable. Table 8-6 lists the most commonly needed variables and symbols. (See Chapter 6 for details on the XML-based device database.)

Table 8-6. *Standard Preprocessing Variables and Symbols*

Variable	Symbol	Explanation
polish.BitsPerPixel	polish.BitsPerPixel.4, polish.BitsPerPixel.16, etc.	Color depth: 1=monochrome, 4=16 colors, 8 = 256 colors, 12 = 4,096 colors, 16 = 65,536 colors, 18 = 262,144 colors, 24 = 16,777,216 colors
polish.ScreenSize	polish.ScreenSize.176x208, polish.ScreenWidth.176, polish.ScreenHeight.208	Width times height of the screen resolution in pixels, e.g., 176X208
polish.CanvasSize	Like ScreenSize	Width times height of an MIDP canvas
polish.FullCanvasSize	Like ScreenSize	Width times height of an MIDP canvas in full-screen mode
polish.JavaPlatform	polish.midp1 or polish.midp2	Supported Java platform, e.g., MIDP 1.0 or MIDP 2.0
polish.JavaConfiguration	polish.cldc1.0 or polish.cldc1.1	Supported Java configuration, e.g., CLDC 1.0 or CLDC 1.1.
polish.JavaPackage	polish.api.nokia-ui, polish.api.mmapi, etc.	Supported APIs, e.g., Nokia UI or MMAPI
polish.JavaProtocol	polish.JavaProtocol.serial, polish.JavaProtocol.https	Supported data exchange protocols*
polish.HeapSize		Maximum heap size, e.g., 500KB or 1.2MB
polish.MaxJarSize		Maximum size of the MIDlet JAR bundle, e.g., 100KB or 2MB**
polish.StorageSize		Maximum size for all applications and data, e.g., 4MB
polish.OS	polish.OS.Motorola, polish.OS.Symbian, etc.	Operating system of the device, e.g., Symbian
polish.VideoFormat	polish.video.3gpp, polish.video.mpeg-4	Supported video formats of the device, e.g., 3gpp and MPEG-4
polish.SoundFormat	polish.audio.midi, polish.audio.wav	Sound formats that are supported by the device, e.g., MIDI and WAV
polish.Bugs	polish.Bugs.drawRgbOrigin, polish.Bugs.ImageIOStreamAutoClose, etc.	The short names of known issues

**All MIDP 1.0 devices support HTTP. All MIDP 2.0 devices also support HTTPS.*
***Note that these are sometimes just a recommendation (Motorola, Siemens).*

Setting Symbols and Variables

You can define your own variables and symbols at various places. You can also set variables conditionally for greater flexibility.

In the *build.xml* file, you can define variables with the `<variables>` element and symbols with the `symbols` attribute of the `<build>` element, as shown in Listing 8-15.

Listing 8-15. *Defining Variables and Symbols in build.xml*

```
<j2mepolish>
   <info
      license="GPL"
      name="Roadrunner"
      vendorName="A reader."
      version="0.0.1"
      jarName="${polish.vendor}-${polish.name}-roadrunner.jar"
   />
   <deviceRequirements>
      <requirement name="Identifier" value="Generic/midp1" />
   </deviceRequirements>
   <build
      usePolishGui="true"
      symbols="mySymbol1, mySymbol2"
   >
      <midlet class="com.apress.roadrunner.Roadrunner" />
      <variables includeAntProperties="true">
         <variable
            name="config.BaseUrl"
            value="http://www.server.com"
         />
         <variable
            name="config.WelcomeMessage"
            value="Welcome!"
         />
      </variables>
   </build>
   <emulator />
</j2mepolish>
```

The `<variable>` element also supports the `file` attribute for specifying the file that holds the variable definitions. Collecting variable definitions in a single file is sometimes easier than managing them in the quite complex *build.xml* script. In the external file, you can list any number of variables, separating the name and value by an equal sign. You can use comments by starting a line with a hash mark. Listing 8-16 shows an example of a file that can be used by including `<variable file="filename.settings" />` in the *build.xml* file.

Listing 8-16. *Defining Variables in an External File*

```
# The base URL of the application:
config.BaseUrl=http://www.server.com
# The message that is displayed on the splash screen:
config.WelcomeMessage=Welcome!
```

You can set variables conditionally by specifying the `if` or `unless` attribute of the `<variable>` element. You can use any preprocessing term in the condition. Remember that you can use `and`, `or`, `xor`, and `not` as logical operators, because the equivalent `&&`, `||`, `^`, and `!` operators need to be XML-encoded in the *build.xml* file. For example, use the *nokia.midp2.settings* file only for Nokia devices that support the MIDP 2.0 profile:

```
<variable file="nokia.midp2.settings" if="(polish.Vendor == Nokia) and ➥
polish.midp2" />.
```

Tip You can use preprocessing variables and property functions in the `file` attribute of the `<variable>` element. This allows you to set variables for specific devices very easily. For example, include the file *cfg/nokia.properties* for Nokia devices and *cfg/sony-ericsson.properties* for Sony Ericsson devices with this definition: `<variable file="cfg/${ lowercase(polish.vendor) }.properties" />`.

When you localize your application with J2ME Polish (as discussed in Chapter 7), you can define variables in the *resources/messages.txt* file and its localized versions as well. Any variables that are defined here will override previous definitions. The variables are defined in the *messages.txt* file by starting them with `var:`, as shown in Listing 8-17.

Listing 8-17. *Defining Variables in the resources/messages.txt File*

```
# The base URL of the application:
var:config.BaseUrl = http://www.server.com
# The message that is displayed on the splash screen:
var:config.WelcomeMessage = Willkommen!
# Some places:
var:config.Places = "Home", "Work", "School"
```

In your code, you can then include the values with the #= directive:

```
//#= String[] placesOfInterest = new String[]{ ${config.Places} };
```

Transforming Variables with Property Functions

J2ME Polish provides a set of property functions for transforming variable values, which can be useful for comparisons, for example.

Each function goes within the curly parentheses, with the variable enclosed by normal parentheses:

```
//#= private String url = "${ lowercase( config.BaseUrl ) }";.
```

When using a property function, you do not necessarily need a variable. You can also use a constant as an argument. Doing so can improve the readability of your source code:

```
//#if ${ bytes( polish.HeapSize ) } > ${ bytes(100 kb) }.
```

Table 8-7 lists the available property functions.

Table 8-7. *Functions for Transforming Variable Values*

Function	Purpose
`uppercase`	Translates the given value into uppercase. `aBc` becomes `ABC`, for example.
`lowercase`	Translates the given value into lowercase. `AbC` becomes `abc`, for example.
`classname`	Retrieves the fully qualified name for the given class. When you activate the `useDefaultPackage` option of the `<obfuscator>` element, all source files will be moved into the empty default package. In that case, `${ classname( com.apress.ImageLoader ) }` returns `ImageLoader`. When the `useDefaultPackage` option is not active or the obfuscator is not enabled, the function returns `com.apress.ImageLoader`.
`bytes`	Calculates the number of bytes of the given memory value. For example, `1 kb` becomes `1024`. The memory value `dynamic` returns `-1`.
`kilobytes`	Calculates the (double) number of kilobytes of the given memory value. The value can contain a point and decimal places. For example, `512 bytes` becomes `0.5`, `1024 bytes` becomes, `1` and so on.
`megabytes`	Calculates the (double) number of megabytes of the given memory value.
`gigabytes`	Calculates the (double) number of gigabytes of the given memory value.
`number`	Retrieves the number of separate values within the variable.

Tip You can define your own property functions by extending the `de.enough.polish.propertyfunctions.PropertyFunction` class and registering this class in *${polish.home}/custom-extensions.xml*. Check out Chapter 13 for details.

Preprocessing to the Rescue!

In this section, you will learn solutions for some frequently encountered tasks:

- Use device-specific libraries.
- Change the class inheritance.
- Configure your application.
- Use hard-coded values.
- Circumvent known issues with preprocessing.

Using Optional and Device-Specific Libraries

A typical challenge for J2ME applications is to exploit optional libraries that are not available on every device. Even though your application might be usable on devices without the library in question, you should take advantage of the available libraries if they improve the functionality or usability of your product.

Fortunately, preprocessing, combined with the device database, makes this task quite trivial. As you learned in Chapter 6, you can use the *${polish.home}/apis.xml* file for defining any optional libraries. For each supported library, the preprocessing symbol `polish.api.[library-name]` is defined and can be checked with the `#if` or `#ifdef` directive:

```
//#if polish.api.mmapi
```

Listing 8-18 demonstrates how to use the MMAPI for playing a sound without restricting the portability of your application.

Listing 8-18. *Playing a Sound with the MMAPI*

```
//#if polish.api.mmapi || polish.midp2
     try {
        Player player = Manager.createPlayer(
           getClass().getResourceAsStream("/music.mid"), "audio/midi");
        player.realize();
        player.prefetch();
        player.start();
     } catch (Exception e) {
        //#debug error
        System.out.println("Unable to start audio playback" + e);
     }
//#endif
```

Changing the Class Inheritance

You can use preprocessing for changing the inheritance of your class. One example is using Nokia's `FullCanvas` class for splash screens. Listing 8-19 demonstrates this application, and also shows how to hide the first `extends` statement, so that your IDE will not complain about an invalid class definition.

Listing 8-19. *Extending Nokia's FullCanvas When It Is Available*

```
public class SplashScreen
   //#if polish.api.nokia-ui
      //# extends com.nokia.mid.ui.FullCanvas
   //#else
      extends Canvas
   //#endif
```

Configuring Applications

Most developers use the JAD file for storing configuration settings and `MIDlet.getAppProperty( String key )` to retrieve those settings. As you learned in Chapter 7, J2ME Polish supports the setting of JAD attributes with the `<jad>` element. The advantage of this approach is that you can easily change the settings later on, but it also has several critical drawbacks:

- You need extra processing time and additional code for determining the configuration during the runtime.
- A few devices remove the JAD file and all its settings after the installation.
- Malicious users can easily intercept and change the JAD file.

As an alternative, you can use preprocessing for configuring your application. Specify your configuration settings with the `<variable>` element in the *build.xml* file:

```
<variable name="config.BaseUrl" value="http://www.specific.com" />
```

Now you can use your variables with the #= directive. Best practice is to use default values in case no settings have been specified. As shown in Listing 8-20, you can check whether a variable has been defined by testing the `[variable-name]:defined` preprocessing symbol that is automatically defined for all variables.

Listing 8-20. *Using Preprocessing for Configuring an Application*

```
//#ifdef config.BaseUrl:defined
   //#= private static final String BASE_URL = "${config.BaseUrl}";
//#else
   private static final String BASE_URL = "http://www.default.com";
//#endif
```

While using preprocessing for configuring your application is often the smarter solution than using JAD attributes, it has also a drawback: it is harder to use dynamic settings. It's easier to generate a JAD file on the fly than to build the complete application on request. An example of dynamic settings is the inclusion of the customer's phone number for later identification. You can use both approaches with J2ME Polish: use preprocessing for the normal configuration values and dynamic JAD generation for settings that change frequently.

Using Hard-Coded Values

Using device-specific hard-coded values is another challenge that you can cope with preprocessing variables. Why would you want to do that? One reason is that you can circumvent some device issues with this approach. Some Nokia devices, for example, do not report the correct canvas height when they are in the full-screen mode, so you need to use the correct hard-coded value. Another reason is that hard-coded values can speed up your application.

Listing 8-21 demonstrates the case when you want to use two-thirds of the available screen width for displaying something. When you use hard-coded values, the Java compiler calculates the correct result during the compile phase. Granted, this example won't speed up your application much, but it does demonstrate the principle. Take a look at the device database at *http://www.j2mepolish.org/devices-overview.html* to find out more about the available variables for your target devices.

Listing 8-21. *Using Preprocessing for Hard-Coding Variables*

```
//#ifdef polish.ScreenWidth:defined
   //#= final int myMessageWidth = ${polish.ScreenWidth} * 2 / 3;
//#else
   final int myMessageWidth = getWidth() * 2 / 3;
//#endif
```

Circumventing Known Issues

The device database (*http://www.j2mepolish.org/devices/issues.html*) not only contains the capabilities and features of most J2ME devices, but it also lists known issues associated with them. You can use this data for circumventing known issues.

As a random example, some devices have problems when you initialize a `DateField` with `null` instead of a `Date` instance. Specifically, the first Nokia Series 60 devices, like the 7650 and 3650, don't allow you to change the date when it has been initialized with `null`. Listing 8-22 shows how to check for this error and use the current date instead of `null`.

Listing 8-22. *Circumventing a Problem with an Uninitialized Date for a DateField*

```
DateField dateField = new DateField("Your Birthday:", DateField.DATE);
//#ifdef polish.Bugs.dateFieldAcceptsNoNullDate
   dateField.setDate( new Date() );
//#endif
```

Summary

This chapter explained how to make most of your application by using preprocessing. J2ME Polish makes device-specific adjustments quite easy by providing both a powerful preprocessor and an extensive device database.

The next chapter covers the logging framework, which is realized with preprocessing as well. It allows you to view logging messages on real devices, and can be configured or disabled just by setting some build variables.

CHAPTER 9

The Logging Framework

In this chapter:

- Log messages by using the #debug preprocessing directive, and print the messages with System.out.println().
- Specify the level of your message (debug, info, warn, error, fatal, or user-defined) in the #debug directive.
- Print stack traces automatically by adding an exception as the last parameter in the System.out.println() call.
- Use the <debug> element in the *build.xml* file to control the logging framework, including to specify different log levels for specific classes or packages (using nested <filter> elements).
- View logged messages on real devices—automatically when an error is logged and the J2ME Polish GUI is used, or manually with the de.enough.polish.util.Debug class in conjunction with the polish.debugEnabled preprocessing symbol.
- Use log handlers to process and forward log messages to other entities.

You use logging for determining the internal application state and to track errors. However, logging J2ME applications has some substantial disadvantages. Logging messages requires space and runtime resources. Therefore, logging slows down your application and increases the application size unnecessarily. You probably won't want to leave your logging statements in your final applications builds. Also, you can use System.out.println() statements for viewing log messages in the emulator, but these remain hidden on real devices. This chapter describes the logging framework of J2ME Polish and how it neutralizes these disadvantages.

With the logging framework, you can enable different log levels for specific classes and packages. When you deactivate the logging framework, no traces are left in your application, so you don't waste resources and space. Finally, you can view the logged messages on real devices as well as on emulators.

Logging Messages

You can log a message in your application by using the #debug preprocessing directive, followed by a normal System.out.println() statement, as shown in Listing 9-1. All logged messages are added to an internal log and printed on the System.out stream as well, so that you can view them on real devices and on the output of any emulator.

Listing 9-1. *Logging in an Application*

```
public Image getImage( String url ) {
   // try to get the image from the Hashtable cache:
   Image image = (Image) this.cache.get( url );
   if (image == null) {
      try {
         image = Image.createImage( url );
         this.cache.put( url, image );
         //#debug
         System.out.println("Loaded image [" + url + "]" );
      } catch (IOException e) {
         //#debug error
         System.out.println("Unable to load image [" + url + "]" + e );
      }
   }
   return image;
}
```

In this example, after successfully loading an image, we issue a simple statement that the image was loaded. You can specify the priority level of your message in the #debug directive. Predefined levels are debug, info, warn, error, and fatal. You can also define your own levels. The first #debug directive in Listing 9-1 does not specify a log level, so the debug level is used by default. The second #debug directive within the catch branch specifies the error level. You can activate specific log levels for classes or packages in your *build.xml* script, to filter out all log messages that have a lower priority, as explained in the "Controlling the Logging" section later in this chapter.

If you add an exception as the last parameter in the System.out.println() call, the logging framework will print its stack trace automatically. In Listing 9-1, an IOException is caught and used as the last parameter in the logged message:

```
System.out.println("Unable to load image [" + url + "]" + e);
```

The logging framework recognizes that the parameter is an exception, and the stack trace of the exception will be printed out along with the logged message in the emulator.

STACK TRACES OF EXCEPTIONS

Stack traces of exceptions are available only in emulators. In real devices, sadly, stack traces are not available. You can use the verbose debugging mode instead for tracking malfunctions. You activate this mode by setting the verbose attribute of the <debug> element to true.

Stack traces in emulators are resolved automatically when you install the Jad decompiler to *${polish.home}/bin*. Usually, only the instruction offset in the bytecode is specified by emulators; for example, at com.company.package.YourClass.doSomething(+20). When the Jad decompiler is installed, J2ME Polish shows you the corresponding position in the source code along with the original stack trace. You can download Jad for free from *http://www.kpdus.com/jad.html*.

Adding Debug Code for Specific Log Levels

You can include additional debugging code by checking the appropriate log level in the preprocessing step. You can test for a specific log level by checking the preprocessing symbol `polish.debug.[level-name]`. As with the `#debug` directive, a given log level includes all higher levels as well. So, when the `warn` level is activated for the current class, the preprocessing symbols `polish.debug.warn`, `polish.debug.error`, `polish.debug.fatal`, and `polish.debug.user-defined` are active.

Listing 9-2 demonstrates how to add information to your application when the `info` log level is active.

Listing 9-2. *Benchmarking Only When the info Log Level Is Active*

```
public void run() {
   //#if polish.debug.info
      int numberOfFrames = 0;
      int framesPerSecond = 0;
      long lastFpsTime = System.currentTimeMillis();
   //#endif
   while (gameIsRunning) {
      processUserInput();
      animateWorld();
      renderWorld();
      flushGraphics();
      //#if polish.debug.info
         numberOfFrames++;
         if (System.currentTimeMillis() - lastFpsTime >= 1000) {
            lastFpsTime = System.currentTimeMillis();
            framesPerSecond = numberOfFrames;
            numberOfFrames = 0;
         }
         this.graphics.drawString( "fps=" + framesPerSecond, 0, 0,
                        Graphics.TOP | Graphics.LEFT );
      //#endif
   }
}
```

Controlling the Logging

You can control the logging framework with the `<debug>` element in the *build.xml* file. You can enable different log levels for specific classes or packages by using nested `<filter>` elements, or deactivate the logging framework completely. For example, if you activate the `error` level for the corresponding class or package, any `debug`, `info`, or `warn` messages will not be shown. In that case, only messages with the levels `error` and `fatal` and user-defined levels will actually be logged. Inactive logging statements will be commented out in the source code, so that they don't use up any resources, as they are not compiled.

The <debug> element is nested inside the <build> section of the <j2mepolish> task, as shown in Listing 9-3. This listing also contains the test and init targets that are used to activate and deactivate the logging framework without changing the *build.xml* script.

Listing 9-3. *Controlling the Logging Framework with the* <debug> *Element in build.xml*

```
<project name="roadrunner" default="j2mepolish">
   <!-- define the installation folder of J2ME Polish -->
   <property name="polish.home" location="C:\programs\J2ME-Polish" />
   <!-- define the installation folder of the WTK -->
   <property name="wtk.home" location="C:\WTK22" />
   <!-- define the J2ME Polish task, classpath on one line please -->
   <taskdef name="j2mepolish"
      classname="de.enough.polish.ant.PolishTask"
      classpath="${polish.home}/import/enough-j2mepolish-build.jar:
      ${polish.home}/import/jdom.jar/>
   <!-- enable the test mode -->
   <target name="test">
      <property name="test" value="true" />
      <property name="dir.work" location="build/test" />
   </target>
   <!-- specify default settings -->
   <target name="init">
      <property name="test" value="false" />
      <property name="dir.work" location="build/real" />
   </target>
   <!-- start the build with J2ME Polish -->
   <target name="j2mepolish" depends="init" >
      <j2mepolish>
         <info
            license="GPL"
            name="Roadrunner"
            vendorName="A reader."
            version="0.0.1"
            jarName="${polish.vendor}-${polish.name}-roadrunner.jar"
         />
         <deviceRequirements>
            <requirement name="Identifier" value="Generic/midp1" />
         </deviceRequirements>
         <build
            usePolishGui="true"
            workDir="${dir.work}"
         >
           <midlet class="com.apress.roadrunner.Roadrunner" />
              <debug showLogOnError="true"
                  verbose="false"
                  level="error"
```

```
                if="test"
            >
                <filter
                    package="com.apress.roadrunner"
                    level="info"
                />
                <filter
                    class="com.apress.roadrunner.Roadrunner"
                    level="debug"
                />
            </debug>
        </build>
        <emulator />
    </j2mepolish>
  </target>
</project>
```

The `<debug>` element allows you to specify several options:

`showLogOnError`: This attribute determines whether J2ME Polish shows the log automatically when an error occurred. This setting is honored only when the J2ME Polish GUI is used and the error is forwarded to the logging framework. You can pass on any error to the logging framework by adding the exception as the last parameter to a logged message: `System.out.println("Unable to do something" + e );`.

`verbose`: When you activate the verbose logging mode with the `verbose` attribute, J2ME Polish will add the current time in milliseconds, the name of the corresponding source file, and the line within the source file in the logging statement. This feature helps you track bugs on real devices.

`level`: You specify the general log level with the `level` attribute. Predefined levels are `debug`, `info`, `warn`, `error`, and `fatal`. You can also define and use your own log levels. Custom log levels always have the highest possible priority; that is, a priority higher than the predefined `fatal` level. You can use custom levels just by adding them in the `#debug` directive and in the `<filter>` element, described next.

`<filter>`: You can fine-tune the level setting by using nested `<filter>` elements. In each `<filter>` element, you need to specify either the `package` or the `class` attribute along with the `level` attribute. This allows you to assign different log levels for specific classes or packages.

`if` and `unless`: You can activate and deactivate the logging framework completely by using the `if` or `unless` attributes. The `if` attribute specifies the Ant property that needs to be `true` or `yes` when the logging should be activated. The `unless` attribute names the Ant property that needs to be `false` or `no` when the logging framework should be activated. When you deactivate the logging, J2ME Polish comments out all logging statements before the application is compiled, so that no traces of the logging remain in your application.

You can use the if and unless attributes of the <debug> element, along with the write-once ability of Ant properties, to activate and deactivate the logging framework without changing your *build.xml* script. In Listing 9-3, the logging framework is activated only when the Ant property ${test} is true. You can set this property to true by calling the test target first on the command line:

```
ant test j2mepolish
```

Even though the init target is called subsequently by the j2mepolish target, the ${test} property is not changed, since Ant properties can be set only once. When the test target is not called, the ${test} property is set to false in the init target. The test and init targets also set different values for the ${dir.work} property. This property is then used for setting the workDir attribute of the <build> element.

■ **Tip** Use different working directories for builds with an activated logging framework, so that J2ME Polish does not need to preprocess and compile all files in each build.

Viewing the Log on Real Devices

You can view the log on real devices as well. The log contains all messages that have been added with the #debug directive. This is quite useful for tracking errors on real devices.

Figure 9-1 shows the log with an activated verbose mode on a Nokia Series 60 phone. In each logging message, the current time in milliseconds is shown first, followed by the name of the class and the line in the source file in which the logging message has been issued. After this verbose information, the real logging message appears. Just scroll down to view further messages.

Figure 9-1. *The log on a Nokia Series 60 phone*

The log is shown automatically when you set the showLogOnError attribute of the <debug> element to true and when an exception has been added as the last parameter, as shown in Listing 9-4. However, J2ME Polish can show the log automatically only when you use the J2ME Polish GUI.

Listing 9-4. *Logging an Exception*

```
try {
   image = Image.createImage( url );
} catch (IOException e) {
   //#debug error
   System.out.println("Unable to load image [" + url + "]" + e );
}
```

You can show the log manually at any time by calling the `de.enough.polish.util.Debug.showLog( Display display )` method. This class is located in the *${polish.home}/import/enough-j2mepolish-client.jar* file. You should add this file to the classpath of your project in your IDE.

You should show the log only when the logging framework is activated. Otherwise, you won't see many entries in your log. You can detect whether the logging framework is active by checking the `polish.debugEnabled` preprocessing symbol in your code. Listing 9-5 demonstrates how you can use a command to trigger the log.

Listing 9-5. *Showing the Log Manually*

```
import de.enough.polish.util.Debug;
import javax.microedition.lcdui.*;
import javax.microedition.midlet.*;

public class MyMIDlet extends MIDlet
implements CommandListener
{
   //#ifdef polish.debugEnabled
      private Command logCmd = new Command( "Show log",
                               Command.SCREEN, 10 );
   //#endif
   private Screen mainScreen;
   private Display display;

   public MyMIDlet() {
      this.mainScreen = new List( "Hello World", List.IMPLICIT );
      this.mainScreen.setCommandListener( this );
      //#ifdef polish.debugEnabled
         this.mainScreen.addCommand( this.logCmd );
      //#endif
   }

   public void startApp() {
      this.display = Display.getDisplay( this );
      this.display.setCurrent( this.mainScreen );
   }
```

```
    public void destroyApp( boolean unconditional ) {
        notifyDestroyed();
    }

    public void pauseApp() {
    }

    public void commandAction(Command cmd, Displayable screen ) {
        //#ifdef polish.debugEnabled
            if (cmd == logCmd) {
                Debug.showLog( this.display );
                return;
            }
        //#endif
    }
}
```

Forwarding Log Messages

You can use log handlers to process and forward log messages to other entities. At the time of writing this book, only the Record Management System (RMS) handler is available. So, currently, you could use the RMS log handler to store all log entries, and then view them later with the LogViewerMidlet.

You can activate the desired log handlers by using the <handler> element in your *build.xml* file. Listing 9-6 activates the RMS log handler for all Siemens devices.

Listing 9-6. *Activating the RMS Log Handler for Siemens Devices*

```
<debug level="warn" unless="test">
    <handler name="rms" if="polish.Vendor == Siemens" />
    <filter package="com.apress.application" level="debug" />
</debug>
```

The RMS log handler saves all log entries in the RMS, so that you can view them with the de.enough.polish.log.rms.LogViewerMidlet. You can find this MIDlet in *${polish.home}/samples/logviewer*. When you build it, make sure to set the following preprocessing variables in the <variables> section of the log viewer's *${polish.home}/samples/logviewer/build.xml* script:

- polish.log.MIDletSuite (corresponding to the name attribute in your <info> element)
- polish.log.Vendor (as in the vendorName attribute in your <info> section)

Without these variables, the log viewer will not be able to find the shared record store that contains the log messages.

After you have defined the necessary variables, you can then build the log viewer and install it on your device. Figure 9-2 shows the log viewer in action. You can filter the shown messages by typing in keywords.

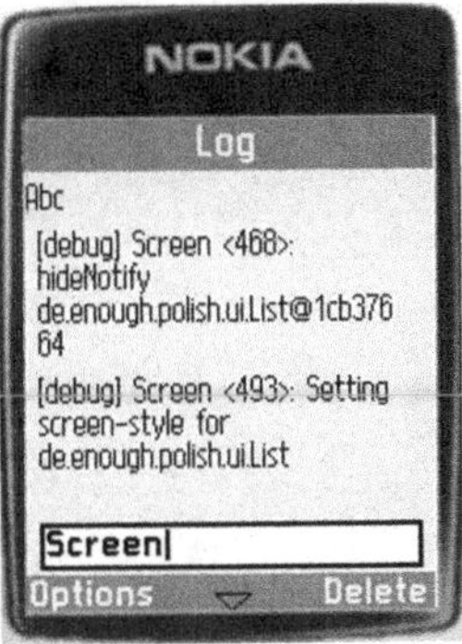

Figure 9-2. *The RMS log viewer allows you to filter messages easily.*

■ **Tip** You can easily create you own log handlers by extending the `de.enough.polish.log.LogHandler` class. This is described in detail in Chapter 13.

Summary

In this chapter, you learned how you can use J2ME Polish and simple `System.out.println()` statements for logging messages. The advantage of the logging framework is that it allows you to assign different log levels to different classes and packages. You can also deactivate the logging completely, so that no traces of the logging remain in your application. Last, but not least, you can use log handlers to store the messages into the RMS.

In the next chapter, you will learn how to use other J2ME Polish utilities, such as the Binary Editor and the `TextUtil` class.

CHAPTER 10

Using the Utilities

In this chapter:

- Use the ArrayList utility class as an alternative to the slow java.lang.Vector implementation.
- Fit your text within your display area with the TextUtil class.
- Customize fonts with the BitMapFont class.
- Convert any True Type font into a bitmap font with the Font Editor.
- Create and manipulate binary data files with the Binary Editor.
- Test the capabilities of your device with the MIDPSysInfo MIDlet.

J2ME Polish contains several handy utility classes and stand-alone utilities. In this chapter, we'll take a look at how to use them in developing your wireless Java applications.

Utility Classes

J2ME Polish's utility classes, de.enough.polish.util.*, equip you with advanced features not found in the MIDP standard. Make sure to add the *${polish.home}/import/enough-j2mepolish-client.jar* to the classpath, so that the Java runtime can find these additional classes. In most IDEs, you can set auxiliary libraries in the properties of your project.

Here, we will look at the following utility classes:

- The ArrayList class, which provides an alternative to the slow java.lang.Vector implementation
- The TextUtil class, which wraps your text so that it fits within your display area
- The BitMapFont class, which allows you to use custom fonts for displaying messages

Note If you take a look at the preprocessed code in the *build* folder of your project, you will notice that J2ME Polish adds all utility classes to your project, even if you don't want to use them. Don't worry about it—the obfuscator will remove all unused classes, so that no resources will be wasted.

The ArrayList Class

The de.enough.polish.util.ArrayList class implements a list that uses a dynamic array for storing its values. In contrast to java.util.Vector, ArrayList does not use synchronization and is, therefore, considerably faster. However, since the ArrayList is not synchronized, you need to make sure to implement your own synchronization when several threads access the ArrayList concurrently.

You can use all methods of java.util.ArrayList, which is available only for the Java 2 Standard Edition (J2SE).

Listing 10-1 demonstrates an example of using the ArrayList class for managing an arbitrary number of contacts in an address book.

Listing 10-1. *Using de.enough.polish.util.ArrayList*

```
package com.apress.adress;

import de.enough.polish.util.ArrayList;

public class AdressBook {

   ArrayList contactsList;

   public AdressBook() {
      super();
   }

   public void addContact( Contact contact ) {
      this.contactsList.add( contact );
   }

   public Contact[] searchContacts( String pattern ) {
      ArrayList matchingContacts = new ArrayList();
      for ( int i = this.contactsList.size(); --i >= 0;  ) {
         Contact contact = (Contact) this.contactsList.get( i );
         if ( contact.pattern.indexOf(pattern) != -1 ) {
            matchingContacts.add( contact );
         }
      }
      return (Contact[]) matchingContacts.toArray(
               new Contact[ matchingContacts.size() ]);
   }

}

package com.apress.adress;

public class Contact {
```

```
    public String firstName;
    public String lastName;
    public String chatAddress;
    public String emailAddress;
    public String pattern;

    public Contact(String firstName, String lastName,
          String chatAddress, String emailAddress)
    {
       this.firstName = firstName;
       this.lastName = lastName;
       this.chatAddress = chatAddress;
       this.emailAddress = emailAddress;
       this.pattern = firstName + lastName + chatAddress + emailAddress;
    }
}
```

The TextUtil Class

You can split text into a `String` array with the `de.enough.polish.util.TextUtil` class. This is useful for wrapping text so that it fits on the small screens found on handheld devices. Some split methods may take font metrics and preferred text widths into account, making it rather painless to display a lot of text in a small view. Listing 10-2 demonstrates using the `TextUtil` class for wrapping the text before it is painted on the screen.

Listing 10-2. *Using the de.enough.polish.util.TextUtil Class*

```
import de.enough.polish.util.TextUtil;
import javax.microedition.lcdui.Graphics;
import javax.microedition.lcdui.Font;

public final class TextViewer {
   private final String[] lines;
   private final Font font;
   private final int color;

   public TextViewer( String text ) {
      // splitting the text only at line breaks:
      this.lines = TextUtil.split( text, '\n' );
      this.font = Font.getDefaultFont();
      this.color = 0;
   }

   public TextViewer( String text, Font font, int color,
         int firstLineWidth, int lineWidth )
   {
```

```
        // wrapping the text for the specified font, so that
        // it fits on the screen:
        this.lines = TextUtil.split( text, font, firstLineWidth, lineWidth );
        this.font = font;
        this.color = color;
    }

    public void paint( int x, int y, Graphics g ) {
        g.setColor( this.color );
        g.setFont( this.font );
        int lineHeight = this.font.getHeight() + 2;
        for (int i = 0; i < this.lines.length; i++ ) {
            String line = this.lines[i];
            g.drawString( line, x, y, Graphics.TOP | Graphics.LEFT );
            y += lineHeight;
        }
    }
}
```

The BitMapFont Class

The J2ME standard isn't really overwhelming when it comes to font support. It provides for only the following:

- Three different font faces (proportional, monospace, and system), but often the system and the proportional fonts are the same.
- Three different sizes (small, medium, and large), with the actual size depending on the implementation. You can check the size with the `polish.Font.small`, `polish.Font.medium`, and `polish.Font.large` preprocessing variables.
- Font styles of bold, italic, underlined, and plain.

Fonts are very much implementation-specific, so you cannot expect them to look alike on different platforms. Some vendors, such as Motorola, provide only one font type in one size. Especially in games, you often need somewhat cooler fonts, and that's why J2ME Polish provides the `de.enough.polish.util.BitMapFont` class.

You can use any True Type font in your application with the `BitMapFont` class. Or, to be more precise, you can convert any True Type font into a bitmap font with the stand-alone Font Editor and use that bitmap font in your application. The Font Editor, located in the *${polish.home}/bin* folder, is described in detail later in this chapter.

If you want to display messages, you need to request a `BitMapFontViewer` from your `BitMapFont`. The viewer class manages particular text, whereas the bitmap font just holds the basic font information and glyphs. By splitting this functionality in two different classes, you can view text with custom fonts very efficiently.

Listing 10-3 shows how you can use the `BitMapFont` and `BitMapFontViewer` classes for displaying messages in a custom font.

Listing 10-3. *Displaying Messages with a Custom Bitmap Font*

```
import de.enough.polish.util.BitMapFont;
import de.enough.polish.util.BitMapFontViewer;
import javax.microedition.lcdui.CustomItem;
import javax.microedition.lcdui.Graphics;
import javax.microedition.lcdui.Font;

public final class BitMapTextViewer {
   private final BitMapFont bitMapFont;
   private BitMapFontViewer bitMapFontViewer;
   private final int verticalPadding;
   private final int firstLineWidth;
   private final int lineWidth;

   public BitMapTextViewer( String text, int verticalPadding,
          int firstLineWidth, int lineWidth )
   {
      this.bitMapFont = BitMapFont.getInstance("/china.bmf");
      this.verticalPadding = verticalPadding;
      this.firstLineWidth = firstLineWidth;
      this.lineWidth = lineWidth;
      setText( text );
   }

   public void setText( String text ) {
      this.bitMapFontViewer = this.bitMapFont.getViewer( text );
      this.bitMapFontViewer.layout( this.firstLineWidth, this.lineWidth,
             this.verticalPadding, Graphics.LEFT );
   }

   public void paint( int x, int y, Graphics g ) {
      this.bitMapFontViewer.paint( x, y, g );
   }
}
```

The `BitMapFontViewer` usually paints the text in one line from the top-left corner that is specified in the `paint( int x, int y, Graphics g )` method. You can, however, specify a different layout with the `layout( int firstLineWidth, int lineWidth, int horizontalPadding, int graphicsOrientation )` method. In that case, the viewer will wrap text lines automatically and arrange the lines according to the specified orientation (`Graphics.LEFT`, `Graphics.CENTER`, or `Graphics.RIGHT`). You need to take the orientation into account when you call the `paint()` method, just as when you use the `Font.drawString()` method. Figure 10-1 shows some centered text within a game display.

Figure 10-1. *Using a bitmap font in a game*

Other Utility Classes

J2ME Polish contains a few more utility classes, which are discussed in other chapters:

- The `de.enough.polish.util.Locale` class retrieves localized messages, provides additional information about the locale, and offers locale-specific methods like date formatting. Localization of mobile applications is discussed in Chapter 7.
- The `de.enough.polish.util.Debug` class allows you to log messages and is used by the `//#debug` preprocessing directive. Debugging is discussed in Chapter 9.
- J2ME Polish also contains some `CustomItems` that can be used independently of the J2ME Polish GUI, such as the `de.enough.polish.ui.SpriteItem`. These are discussed in Chapter 12.

■ **Tip** Some other classes are planned for future releases. For example, the upcoming `de.enough.polish.util.DeviceControl` class will allow you to control vibration and backlight settings. Check *http://www.j2mepolish.org* for the latest additions.

Stand-Alone Utilities

Apart from the utility classes, J2ME Polish also provides some stand-alone utilities that can help you during the development phase on the server side.

- The Binary Editor allows you to create and manipulate structured binary data files, like level files.
- The Font Editor converts any True Type font into a bitmap font that can be used by the `de.enough.polish.util.BitMapFont` class.
- The MIDPSysInfo MIDlet shows the capabilities of your device.

These applications reside in the *${polish.home}/bin* folder. Figure 10-2 shows how this folder looks on a Mac OS X system.

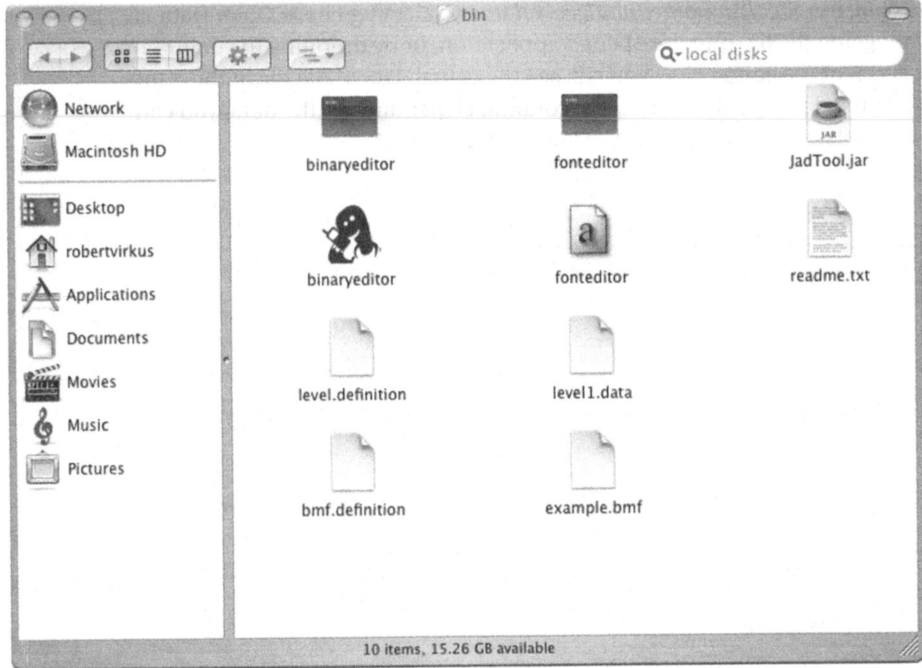

Figure 10-2. *The ${polish.home}/bin folder on Mac OS X systems*

The Binary Editor

You can use the Binary Editor for managing level files and other structured binary data files. Start it by double-clicking the Binary Editor executable in the *${polish.home}/bin* folder.

The Binary Editor stores the information about the setup of the data in `*.definition` files. A definition specifies which data types are used in what sequence in the actual data files. When you start the editor for the first time, you will start with a new blank definition file.

Let's take a tour through the editor. Open the *${polish.home}/bin/level.definition* file by selecting File ➤ Open Definition in the menu bar, by dragging the file into the opened application, or by dropping the definition file onto the start script of the editor, as shown in Figure 10-3.

Figure 10-3. *Opening a definition with drag-and-drop*

The structure of the corresponding data files is now shown in the editor. For each entry, you can specify how often the entry is repeated, the type of the entry (`byte`, `short`, and so on), and the actual data.

To load some data, use *${polish.home}/bin/level1.data* by selecting File ➤ Open Data in the menu bar, by dragging the file into the opened application, or by dropping the definition file onto the start script of the editor. Now you can see the actual data of the file in the right column. You can edit the data by clicking into the column. Depending on the data, you can edit it directly in the table or in a dialog box, as shown in Figure 10-4.

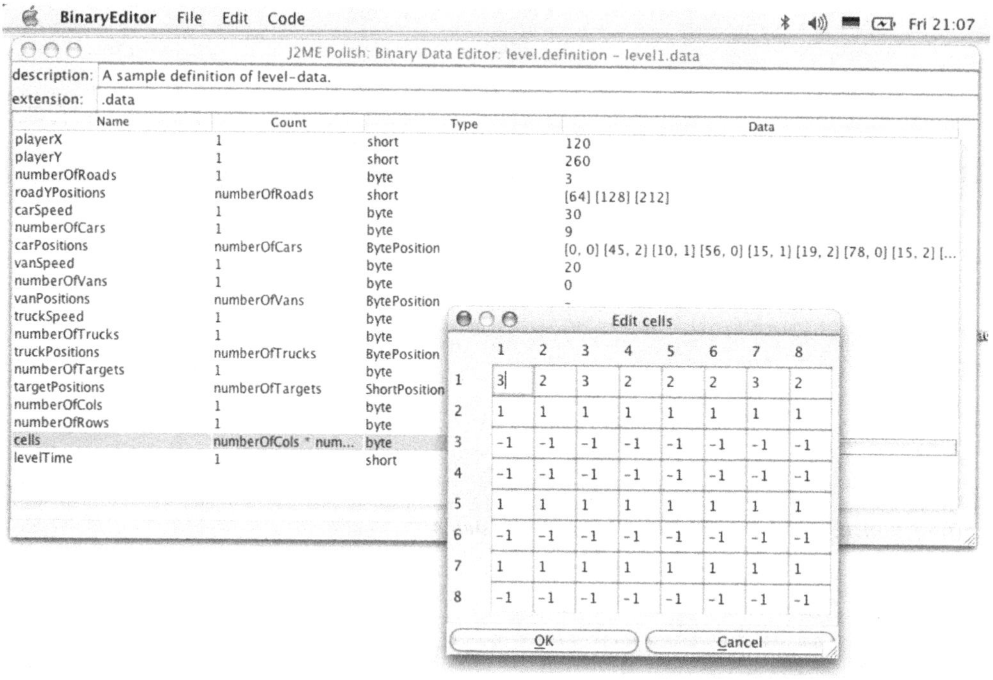

BinaryEditor File Edit Code Fri 21:07

J2ME Polish: Binary Data Editor: level.definition - level1.data

description: A sample definition of level-data.

extension: .data

Name	Count	Type	Data
playerX	1	short	120
playerY	1	short	260
numberOfRoads	1	byte	3
roadYPositions	numberOfRoads	short	[64] [128] [212]
carSpeed	1	byte	30
numberOfCars	1	byte	9
carPositions	numberOfCars	BytePosition	[0, 0] [45, 2] [10, 1] [56, 0] [15, 1] [19, 2] [78, 0] [15, 2] [...
vanSpeed	1	byte	20
numberOfVans	1	byte	0
vanPositions	numberOfVans	BytePosition	-
truckSpeed	1	byte	
numberOfTrucks	1	byte	
truckPositions	numberOfTrucks	BytePosition	
numberOfTargets	1	byte	
targetPositions	numberOfTargets	ShortPosition	
numberOfCols	1	byte	
numberOfRows	1	byte	
cells	numberOfCols * num...	byte	
levelTime	1	short	

Edit cells

	1	2	3	4	5	6	7	8
1	3	2	3	2	2	2	3	2
2	1	1	1	1	1	1	1	1
3	-1	-1	-1	-1	-1	-1	-1	-1
4	-1	-1	-1	-1	-1	-1	-1	-1
5	1	1	1	1	1	1	1	1
6	-1	-1	-1	-1	-1	-1	-1	-1
7	1	1	1	1	1	1	1	1
8	-1	-1	-1	-1	-1	-1	-1	-1

OK Cancel

Figure 10-4. *Editing data with the Binary Editor*

An entry can be repeated several times when you specify the Count value. You can define this number either directly by setting a static number or by using one or several other data entries. When you use another data entry for specifying the number, the numerical value of that entry is used. In Figure 10-4, the entry `roadYPositions` is repeated for `numberOfRoads` times, for example. Since the value of `numberOfRoads` is 3, the `roadYPosition` entry is repeated three times.

Apart from numerical values such as `byte` or `short`, you can also use `String` entries for the Count definition. When you use a `String` entry, the length of the data string is used to calculate its numerical value. You can also use several entries and add, multiply, subtract, or divide them for calculating the repetitions of the current entry. For example, in Figure 10-4, the `cells` entry is repeated for `numberOfCols * numberOfRows` times. Since data files are loaded sequentially you can only use entries that are already known; these are any entries that are defined above the entry for which you are specifying a Count value.

You can use several predefined types for your files; for example, you can specify byte, boolean, or PNG Image. You can change the type just by selecting the entry in the Type column. When the type has a fixed length, it is shown in parentheses after the type. Types with a variable length declare this by having "(-1)" at the end of their name. You can also define your own types by selecting Edit ➤ Add Custom Type. You can mix any already known types together. You could use two short values for creating a Position type, for example. The specifications of your custom types are saved in the corresponding **.definition* file. Table 10-1 describes the default types.

Table 10-1. *Predefined Types of the Binary Editor*

Type	Values	Explanation
byte	–128..+128	Standard Java byte value
unsigned byte	0..255	Positive 8-bit value
short	–32768..+32767	Standard Java short value (uses 2 bytes)
unsigned short	0..2^31–1 (2147483647)	Positive 16-bit value
int	–2^31..2^31-1	Standard Java int value (uses 4 bytes)
long	–2^63..2^63-1	Standard Java long value (uses 8 bytes)
boolean	true, false	One byte representing true (1) or false (0)
ASCII-String	Text	A string consisting of ASCII characters with a maximum length of 255 characters; uses length+1 bytes in the data file
UTF-String	Text	Standard Java String
PNG-Image	Image	A PNG image

Note PNG images should usually be the last entry in a definition file, unless you generate your own code for loading the images.

The Binary Editor can generate the Java code for loading the corresponding data files. Just select Code ➤ Generate Java Code to view the generated code. You can now save it or copy it to the clipboard.

You can save your definition files wherever you want to, but most often, you will save them along with the data files in the *resources* folder of your project. You then need to make sure that the **.definition* files are not included in your application bundles. You can do so by specifying the excludes attribute of the <resources> element in the *build.xml* file, as in this example:

```
<resources excludes="*.definition, readme.txt" />
```

This element is nested within the <build> section. Take a look at the *build.xml* file of the Menu sample application for a full example.

The Font Editor

You can use the Font Editor to create bitmap fonts out of any True Type fonts. Start the editor by double-clicking the Font Editor executable in the *${polish.home}/bin* folder.

You can open any True Type font **.ttf* file by selecting File ➤ Open True Type Font in the menu bar, by dragging the file into the opened application, or by dropping the font file onto the start script of the editor (see Figure 10-3 earlier in this chapter). As you can see in Figure 10-5, you can now change the size, color, and other attributes of the font in the editor.

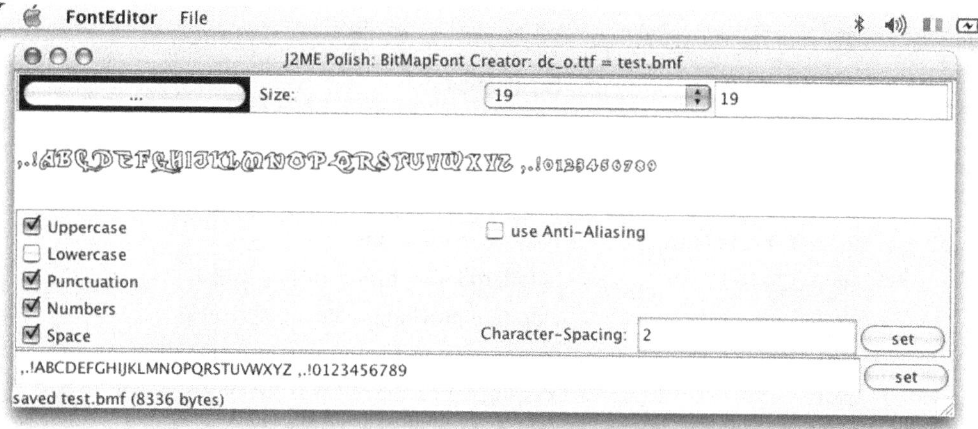

Figure 10-5. *Creating a bitmap font with the Font Editor*

You can specify which characters are supported by the bitmap font by setting the characters in the text field at the bottom. Since every additional character needs additional space, you should try to minimize the number of characters; just keep enough characters to display all the text that you are want to appear in this bitmap font. If your text contains a character that is not available in the corresponding bitmap font, that character cannot be displayed and is omitted from the screen.

You can use the character spacing to separate characters of dense or italic fonts. Remember that each character needs to be accessible individually, so a rectangle needs to fit around each character without overlapping other characters.

■ **Caution** Using anti-aliasing for bitmap fonts makes them look smoother, but also increases their size and reduces their readability. Anti-aliasing is, therefore, not recommended on devices with low resolutions.

You can optimize the bitmap font by manipulating the base PNG image in your favorite image editor, such as Photoshop or The Gimp. Save the corresponding PNG image of the font by selecting File ➤ Save PNG Image As. Then load it again by selecting File ➤ Open PNG Image. You can also fine-tune the bitmap font by selecting File ➤ Open in Binary Editor, or by starting the Binary Editor externally, loading the *${polish.home}/bin/bmf.definition*, and opening the bitmap font as the data. Use the `de.enough.polish.BitMapFont` class as described earlier in this chapter for displaying text with your bitmap fonts.

The SysInfo MIDlet

J2ME Polish also contains the MIDPSysInfo MIDlet, which allows you to check the capabilities of your device quickly. It is located in the *${polish.home}/samples/sysinfo* folder and needs to be built first, either by calling `ant` from the command line or by executing the *build.xml* script from within your IDE. You will then find the files *MIDPSysInfo.jar* and *MIDPSysInfo.jad* in the *dist* folder. Figure 10-6 shows the SysInfo application in action.

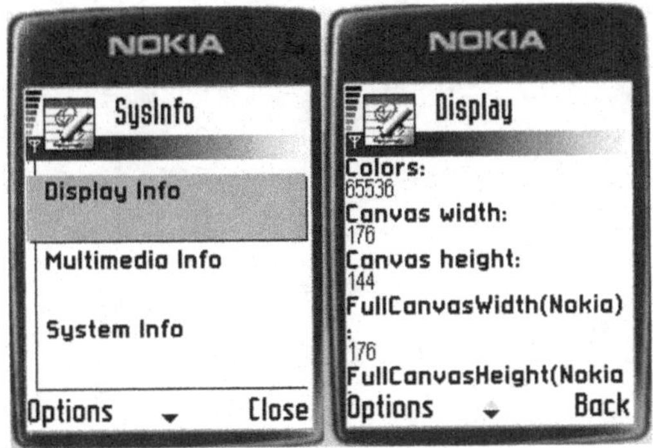

Figure 10-6. *Checking the capabilities of your device with the MIDPSysInfo MIDlet*

Summary

This chapter discussed the various utilities that come with J2ME Polish. Although they are not essential for developing J2ME applications, they are quite useful and might solve challenges that you encounter during application development.

In the next chapter, we'll take a look at the game engine of J2ME Polish and how it can help you to develop games for both MIDP 2.0 and MIDP 1.0 devices using a single-source base.

CHAPTER 11

Game Programming with J2ME Polish

In this chapter:

- The J2ME Polish game engine provides the complete MIDP 2.0 game API on MIDP 1.0 devices.
- Optimize the game engine by setting various preprocessing variables.
- Work around the game engine limitations on MIDP 1.0 platforms, which include the inability to detect collisions on the pixel level and that not all MIDP 1.0 platforms support the transformation of sprites.
- Port MIDP 2 games to MIDP 1.0 platforms by using vendor-specific libraries for low-level graphics operations, sound playback, and device control.

The games industry is the biggest player in the J2ME market. When you're programming J2ME applications, chances are that you are working on games. Gaming is a tremendous success story for mobile Java and belongs to the "3 Gs" that supposedly form the main revenues in the mobile arena: games, gambling, and girls. The gaming market is growing rapidly and has an estimated volume of $4 billion worldwide in 2005.

The industry has reacted by introducing great enhancements for game programming in the MIDP 2.0 standard through the Java Community Process web site (*http://jcp.org/en/jsr/detail?id=118*). Unfortunately, the majority of phones out there support only the MIDP 1.0 standard. This is where J2ME Polish's game engine comes to the rescue. As you'll learn in this chapter, you can use the game engine of J2ME Polish for quickly porting MIDP 2.0 games to MIDP 1.0 platforms.

Using the Game Engine

Programming games using the MIDP 2.0 game API is easy. You have sprites, a layer manager with a view window, and much more. These features are sorely missed when you develop your game for MIDP 1.0 platforms. This is why J2ME Polish includes a wrapper API that enables you to use the `javax.microedition.lcdui.game.*` API, even on MIDP 1.0 devices.

The game engine allows you to use the complete MIDP 2.0 game API on MIDP 1.0 devices. Usually, no source code changes are necessary when you use proper `import` statements. However, there are some principal restrictions that might require adjustments of your code, especially the inability to use the pixel-level collision detection. Also, not all MIDP 1.0 platforms support sprite transformations. Dealing with these limitations is discussed in the "Working Around the Limitations of the Game Engine" section later in this chapter.

Using the game engine is not difficult. J2ME Polish weaves the wrapper classes in your code automatically when you target MIDP 1.0 devices. This is done just by exchanging the `import` statements, so you must use proper `import` statements instead of fully qualified class names. Listing 11-1 demonstrates what you should *not* do.

Listing 11-1. *How **Not** to Use the Game Engine*

```
public class MyGameCanvas
extends javax.microedition.lcdui.game.GameCanvas
implements Runnable
{
   public MyGameCanvas(boolean supress) {
      super(supress);
   }

   public void run() {
      // main game-loop
   }
}
```

The code in Listing 11-1 won't work when you target an MIDP 1.0 device. Listing 11-2 shows a working example, which uses `import` statements properly.

Listing 11-2. *Proper Use of the Game Engine with import Statements*

```
import javax.microedition.lcdui.game.GameCanvas;
public class MyGameCanvas
extends GameCanvas
implements Runnable
{
   public MyGameCanvas(boolean supress) {
      super(supress);
   }

   public void run() {
      // main game-loop
   }
}
```

Optimizing the Game Engine

You can tweak the game engine by defining several preprocessing variables in the `<variables>` section of your *build.xml* script. The following optimizations are available:

- Enable the full-screen mode for your game
- Optimize the performance of the `TiledLayer` by using a back buffer and/or single tile images
- Increase the number of possible tiles
- Activate the game engine for MIDP 2.0 devices with a faulty or slow implementation of the game API

Running Your Game in Full-Screen Mode

Usually, you will want to use the full-screen mode for your game. To enable this mode, use the `fullscreen` attribute of the `<build>` element in your project's *build.xml* file. Possible values are `true`, `false`, or `menu`. The `menu` mode allows you to design the menu bar, but it is available only when you use the J2ME Polish GUI.

The `fullscreen` attribute of the `<build>` element enables the full-screen mode for the complete application. If you want to use a different setting for the actual game play, define a specific setting for the `GameCanvas` implementation by setting the `polish.GameCanvas.useFullScreen` preprocessing variable. Allowed values are again `true`, `false`, or `menu`. Listing 11-3 demonstrates how you can use the `menu` full-screen mode for your application, while using the regular full-screen mode for the `GameCanvas`.

Listing 11-3. *Enabling the Full-Screen Mode for the GameCanvas*

```
<j2mepolish>
   <info
      license="GPL"
      name="MazeRace"
      vendorName="A reader."
      version="0.0.1"
      jarName="${polish.vendor}-${polish.name}-${polish.locale}-mazerace.jar"
   />
   <deviceRequirements>
      <requirement name="Identifier" value="Nokia/Series60" />
   </deviceRequirements>
   <build
      usePolishGui="true"
      fullscreen="menu"
   >
      <midlet class="com.apress.mazerace.MazeRace" />
      <variables>
         <variable
          name="polish.GameCanvas.useFullScreen"
          value="true"
         />
      </variables>
   </build>
   <emulator />
</j2mepolish>
```

You need to enable the `menu` mode when you add commands to your `GameCanvas`. The `menu` mode requires the J2ME Polish GUI, which, in turn, requires that you do not implement the `paint( Graphics )` method, because this method is used by the J2ME Polish GUI internally. In such cases, you should use the `flushGraphics()` method instead. When this is not possible, you can use some preprocessing for implementing the `paintScreen( Graphics )` method instead of the `paint( Graphics )` method, as shown in Listing 11-4.

Listing 11-4. *Using the paintScreen() Method Instead of paint() in the Menu Full-Screen Mode*

```
import javax.microedition.lcdui.game.GameCanvas;
import javax.microedition.lcdui.Graphics;
public class MyGameCanvas
extends GameCanvas
implements Runnable
{

   public MyGameCanvas(boolean supress) {
      super(supress);
   }

   public void run() {
      // main game loop
   }
   //#if polish.usePolishGui && polish.classes.fullscreen:defined && !polish.midp2
      //# public void paintScreen( Graphics g )
   //#else
      public void paint( Graphics g )
   //#endif
   {
      // implement the paint method
   }
}
```

Using a Back Buffer in the TiledLayer

The `TiledLayer` paints several tiles on the screen and is often used to render the background of a game. The back buffer optimization uses an internal image buffer to which the tiles are painted only when they have changed. Instead of painting all tiles individually, the complete buffer will be painted to the screen. This can quite dramatically increase the speed of your game, especially in cases when the visible tiles are changed only occasionally.

The drawbacks of the back buffer optimization are that it uses more memory and that you can't use any transparent tiles. Therefore, you should not activate the back buffer optimization when any of the following apply:

- Memory is an issue.
- The `TiledLayer` is not used as the background.
- You use several `TiledLayers` simultaneously.

You can activate the back buffer optimization by setting the `polish.TiledLayer.useBackBuffer` preprocessing variable to `true`. You can also specify the background color by setting the `polish.TiledLayer.TransparentTileColor` variable to any integer color value, as shown in Listing 11-5. This color is then used for previously transparent tiles.

Listing 11-5. *Activating the Back Buffer Optimization for the TiledLayer*

```
<variables>
   <variable
      name="polish.TiledLayer.useBackBuffer"
      value="true"
   />
   <variable
      name="polish.TiledLayer.TransparentTileColor"
      value="0xCFCFCF"
   />
</variables>
```

Splitting an Image into Single Tiles

A `TiledLayer` can be drawn significantly faster when the base image is split into single tiles. This optimization needs a bit more memory compared with a basic `TiledLayer`. Also the transparency of the tiles is lost when the device does not support Nokia's UI API. You can activate this optimization by setting the `polish.TiledLayer.splitImage` preprocessing variable to `true`, as shown in Listing 11-6.

Listing 11-6. *Activating the Split Image Optimization for the TiledLayer*

```
<variables>
   <variable
      name="polish.TiledLayer.splitImage"
      value="true"
   />
</variables>
```

Defining the Grid Type of a TiledLayer

Each `TiledLayer` stores the information about the included tiles in an internal array called the *grid*. By default, J2ME Polish uses a byte grid that significantly decreases the memory footprint, but which limits the number of different tiles to 128. You can change the array type from the default `byte` to `int` or `short` by defining the preprocessing variable `polish.TiledLayer.GridType` accordingly. Listing 11-7 shows how to change to the `short` type, which allows you to use up to 32,767 different tiles—probably enough for even the most demanding mobile game.

Listing 11-7. *Supporting Up to 32,767 Different Tiles*

```
<variables>
   <variable
      name="polish.TiledLayer.GridType"
      value="short"
   />
</variables>
```

Using the Game Engine for MIDP 2.0 Devices

You can use the J2ME Polish implementation for MIDP 2.0 devices as well. You might want to do this because some vendor implementations are buggy or have sluggish performance. To use the game engine on MIDP 2.0 devices, set the preprocessing variable `polish.usePolishGameApi` to `true`, as shown in Listing 11-8.

Listing 11-8. *Using the J2ME Polish Game Engine for a Specific MIDP 2.0 Target Device*

```
<variables>
   <variable
      name="polish.usePolishGameApi"
      value="true"
      if="polish.identifier == VendorName/DeviceName"
   />
</variables>
```

Working Around the Limitations of the Game Engine

You can use any classes of the `javax.microedition.lcdui.game.*` API in your game, but you need to be aware of some technical limitations for the game engine:

- **Pixel-level collision detection:** On MIDP 1.0 platforms, you cannot use the pixel-level collision detection for sprites, so you need to set collision rectangles instead—preferably tight ones.

- **Evaluation of user input:** When you extend the `GameCanvas` class, you should call the super implementations when you override one of the methods `keyPressed(int)`, `keyReleased(int)`, or `keyRepeated(int)`, so that the game engine is informed about the events as well. I recommend using the `getKeyStates()` method in the main game loop for evaluating the user's input. This guarantees the best performance on both MIDP 2.0 and MIDP 1.0 platforms.

- **Sprite transformations:** At the time of writing this chapter, you can use `Sprite` transformations only for devices that support Nokia's UI API; otherwise, the transformations will be ignored. You can find out whether the current target device supports `Sprite` transformations by checking the preprocessing symbol `polish.supportSpriteTransformation` like shown in Listing 11-9. When no transformations are supported you can just add additional frames that are already transformed to your `Sprite` image. Instead of transforming the `Sprite`, you can achieve the same effect by setting another frame sequence that points to the transformed frames.

Listing 11-9. *Checking Whether the Device Supports Sprite Transformations*

```
import javax.microedition.lcdui.game.GameCanvas;
import javax.microedition.lcdui.game.Sprite;
public class MyGameCanvas
extends GameCanvas
implements Runnable
{
   //#if !( polish.midp2 || polish.supportSpriteTransformation )
      private static final int MIRROR_SEQUENCE = new int[]{ 2, 3 };
   //#endif
   Sprite player;

   public MyGameCanvas(boolean supress) {
      super(supress);
   }

   public void run() {
      // main game loop
   }

   public void mirrorPlayer() {
      //#if polish.midp2 || polish.supportSpriteTransformation
         this.player.setTransform( Sprite.TRANS_MIRROR );
      //#else
         // use an additional mirrored frame in the sprite:
         this.player.setFrameSequence( MIRROR_SEQUENCE );
      //#endif
   }
}
```

Porting an MIDP 2.0 Game to the MIDP 1.0 Platform

Thanks to the game engine and the GUI of J2ME Polish, you need to address only specific issues manually to allow an MIDP 2.0 game to run on an MIDP 1.0 platform. As usual, you can use preprocessing to detect the capabilities of your target device.

To port your MIDP 2.0 game to MIDP 1.0 devices, you first need to work around the restrictions of the J2ME Polish game engine, as outlined in the previous section. You might also need to adjust MIDP 2.0-specific code so that your application works on MIDP 1.0 devices.

In general, you cannot use any MIDP 2.0-only functionality in your game, but there are two important exceptions to this rule:

- You can use everything from the `javax.microedition.lcdui.game.*` API.
- You can use most MIDP 2.0 high-level GUI functions, like `CustomItem`, `POPUP` `ChoiceGroups`, or `Display.setCurrentItem()` when you use the J2ME Polish GUI.

So, for games, three porting issues commonly arise: usage of MIDP 2.0-only low-level graphics operations, sound playback, and device control (the vibration and display light). The solution is to use vendor-specific libraries.

■ **Tip** You will often need to integrate specific resources in your game depending on the capabilities of your target device. You can use the resource assembly feature of J2ME Polish to ensure that you include the correct files in your JAR file, as discussed in Chapter 7.

Porting Low-Level Graphics Operations

Porting low-level graphics operations is a challenging task. You can find low-level graphics operations in the `javax.microedition.lcdui.Graphics` and `javax.microedition.lcdui.Image` classes.

For example, the MIDP 2.0 platform allows you to draw raw RGB data directly with the `Graphics.drawRGB()` method. The `Image.createRGBImage()` method also processes raw RGB data. Whether you can port these functionalities depends on both your actual usage as well as the target device. All Nokia devices support the simple yet powerful Nokia UI API; other vendors often provide their own proprietary extensions.

Table 11-1 lists the proprietary libraries you can use for porting low-level graphics operations.

Table 11-1. *Proprietary APIs for Porting Low-Level Graphics Operations*

Functionality	MIDP 2.0	Nokia	Motorola	Siemens
RGB-Data	Graphics. drawRGB()	com.nokia.mid.ui. DirectGraphics. drawPixels()	com.motorola.game. ImageUtil.setPixels()	
Rotation and Reflection	Graphics. drawRegion()	com.nokia.mid.ui. DirectGraphics. drawImage()		com.siemens.mp.ui. Image.mirrorImage Horizontally() com.siemens.mp.ui. Image.mirrorImage Vertically()
Scaling	de.enough.polish. util.ImageUtil. scale()		com.motorola. game.ImageUtil. getScaleImage()	com.siemens. mp.ui.Image. createImageWith Scaling()

For example, if you use the `Graphics.drawRGB()` method for creating a translucent background, you can use the `com.nokia.mid.ui.DirectUtils` and `com.nokia.mid.ui.DirectGraphics` APIs for replicating the functionality when Nokia's UI API is supported by the target device.

Listing 11-10 shows how you can use preprocessing for determining which APIs can be used. It also demonstrates how the `drawRGB()` call is adjusted for devices that have the `drawRgbOrigin` bug, which is the case with some devices.

Listing 11-10. *Porting Translucent Backgrounds*

```
import javax.microedition.lcdui.Graphics;
import javax.microedition.lcdui.Image;
//#if polish.api.nokia-ui && !polish.midp2
   import com.nokia.mid.ui.DirectGraphics;
   import com.nokia.mid.ui.DirectUtils;
//#endif

import de.enough.polish.ui.Background;

public class TranslucentSimpleBackground extends Background {

   private final int argbColor;
   //#ifdef polish.midp2
      // int MIDP/2.0 the buffer is always used:
      private int[] buffer;
      private int lastWidth;
   //#elif polish.api.nokia-ui
      private Image imageBuffer;
      //# private int lastWidth;
      private int lastHeight;
   //#endif
```

```
    public TranslucentSimpleBackground( int argbColor ) {
        super();
        this.argbColor = argbColor;
    }

    public void paint(int x, int y, int width, int height, Graphics g) {
        //#ifdef polish.midp2
            //#ifdef polish.Bugs.drawRgbOrigin
                x += g.getTranslateX();
                y += g.getTranslateY();
            //#endif

            // check if the buffer needs to be created:
            if (width != this.lastWidth) {
                this.lastWidth = width;
                int[] newBuffer = new int[ width ];
                for (int i = newBuffer.length - 1; i >= 0 ; i--) {
                    newBuffer[i] = this.argbColor;
                }
                this.buffer = newBuffer;
            }
            if (x < 0) {
                width += x;
                if (width < 0) {
                    return;
                }
                x = 0;
            }
            if (y < 0) {
                height += y;
                if (height < 0) {
                    return;
                }
                y = 0;
            }
            g.drawRGB(this.buffer, 0, 0, x, y, width, height, true);
        //#elif polish.api.nokia-ui
            if (width != this.lastWidth || height != this.lastHeight) {
                this.lastWidth = width;
                this.lastHeight = height;
                this.imageBuffer = DirectUtils.createImage( width, height,
this.argbColor );
            }
            DirectGraphics dg = DirectUtils.getDirectGraphics(g);
            dg.drawImage(this.imageBuffer, x, y, Graphics.TOP | Graphics.LEFT, 0 );
        //#else
            // ignore alpha-value
```

```
            g.setColor( this.argbColor );
            g.fillRect(x, y, width, height);
        //#endif
    }
}
```

You can emulate other RGB functionalities as well, but be aware that Nokia devices use device-specific RGB data types. Check the Java documentation for more details.

Porting Sound Playback

Playing sounds is quite easy using the MMAPI playback functionalities on MIDP 2.0 devices. Some MIDP 1.0 devices also support the MMAPI, so you can just use the same code. Otherwise, you will need to use proprietary vendor-specific APIs, and very likely, you'll need different sound formats. Table 11-2 lists the available proprietary APIs for sound playback.

Table 11-2. *Proprietary APIs for Playing Sounds*

Platform	API
MIDP 2.0	`javax.microedition.media.Player`
Nokia	`com.nokia.mid.sound.Sound`

Motorola	`com.motorola.game.GameScreen`
	`com.motorola.game.BackgroundMusic`
	`com.motorola.game.SoundEffect`

Siemens	`com.siemens.mp.media.Player`
	`com.siemens.mp.game.Sound`
	`com.siemens.mp.game.Melody`

Listing 11-11 demonstrates how you can play back a TrueTones sound instead of a MIDI sound on Nokia devices.

Listing 11-11. *Porting the Playback of Sounds*

```
//#if polish.audio.midi && (polish.api.mmapi || polish.midp2)
   import javax.microedition.media.Manager;
   import javax.microedition.media.Player;
//#elif polish.api.nokia-ui
   import com.nokia.mid.sound.Sound;
   import java.io.ByteArrayOutputStream;
//#endif
...
public void playMusic() throws Exception {
   //#if polish.audio.midi && (polish.midp2 || polish.api.mmapi)
      Player musicPlayer =
         Manager.createPlayer(
            getClass().getResourceAsStream("/music.mid"), "audio/midi");
      musicPlayer.realize();
      musicPlayer.prefetch();
```

```
        musicPlayer.start();
    //#elif polish.api.nokia-ui
        InputStream is = getClass().getResourceAsStream("/music.tt");
        ByteArrayOutputStream out = new ByteArrayOutputStream();
        int read;
        byte[] buffer = new byte[ 1024 ];
        while( ( read = is.read( buffer, 0, 1024 )  ) != -1 ) {
           out.write( buffer, 0, read );
        }
        Sound sound = new Sound( out.getByteArray(), Sound.FORMAT_TONE );
        sound.play( 1 );
    //#endif
}
```

Controlling Vibration and the Display Light

Two other functionalities you might want to port are related to device control: controlling the vibration and display light. With MIDP 2.0, you can accomplish this control by using the `javax.microedition.lcdui.Display.vibrate()` and `flashBacklight()` methods. However, on MIDP 1.0 devices, you need to use the available proprietary libraries, which are listed in Table 11-3.

Table 11-3. *Proprietary APIs for Device Control*

Functionality	MIDP 2.0	Nokia	Motorola	Siemens

Vibrate	`Display.vibrate()`	`com.nokia.mid.ui.DeviceControl.startVibrate()`
		`com.nokia.mid.ui.DeviceControl.stopVibrate()`
				`com.siemens.mp.game.Vibrator.startVibrator()`
				`com.siemens.mp.game.Vibrator.stopVibrator()`
				`com.siemens.mp.game.Vibrator.triggerVibrator()`

Backlight	`Display.flashBacklight()`	`com.nokia.mid.ui.DeviceControl.flashLights()` `com.nokia.mid.ui.DeviceControl.setLights()`		`com.siemens.mp.game.Light.setLightOn()` `com.siemens.mp.game.Light.setLightOff()`

Listing 11-12 shows how you can use Nokia's `DeviceControl` class to allow for device vibration when the MIDP 2.0 standard is not supported.

Listing 11-12. *Allowing for Device Vibration*

```
//#if polish.midp2
   import javax.microedition.lcdui.Display;
//#elif polish.api.nokia-ui
   import com.nokia.mid.ui.DeviceControl;
//#endif
...
```

```
//#if polish.midp2
   private Display display;
//#endif
...
public void vibrate() {
   //#if polish.midp2
      this.display.vibrate( 500 );
   //#elif polish.api.nokia-ui
       try {
          DeviceControl.startVibra( 100, 500 );
       } catch (IllegalStateException e) {
          //#debug error
          System.out.println("Device does not support vibration" + e );
       }
   //#endif
}
```

Summary

In this chapter, you've looked at the game engine of J2ME Polish and how it helps you to port games to MIDP 1.0 platforms. When you use low-level graphics, sound playback, and device control functionalities of the MIDP 2.0 platform, you need to include some manual adjustments, but otherwise J2ME Polish takes care of everything for you. You can adjust the game engine to your needs by specifying various preprocessing variables.

In the next chapter, you'll learn how to use the enhanced GUI of J2ME Polish. This GUI allows you to use the MIDP 2.0 high-level UI on MIDP 1.0 devices. It also helps you to design your applications professionally and spectacularly.

CHAPTER 12

Working with the GUI

In this chapter:

- Learn the concepts of the GUI first, before delving into the configuration and programming.
- Configure and program with the J2ME Polish GUI, which is fully compatible with the MIDP 2.0 standard.
- Use MIDP 2.0 features such as `CustomItems` or `POPUP ChoiceGroups` even on MIDP 1.0 devices.
- Design the user interface outside your application code using simple CSS text files.

The graphical interface is the most important part of your application; in fact, it's crucial for people's perception of your application. It's simple: create a good-looking and responsive user interface, and your application will be perceived as being professional and good. Creating professional GUIs is, however, not that easy. You can use the so-called high-level GUI API of the `javax.microedition.lcdui` package for making your user interface fast and portable. Unfortunately, you have almost no chance to influence the presentation of this GUI. For MIDP 1.0 phones, the design cannot be changed at all, while MIDP 2.0 provides some hooks for changing the design; sadly, however, the implementations between the two versions differ a lot. So, traditionally, you would have needed to use the low-level GUI API for creating a good-looking user interface. Unfortunately, the implementation of the low-level API provides many surprises, so much manual porting is necessary when you want the interface to run on all or most J2ME devices.

In this chapter, you will learn how you can use the J2ME Polish GUI for your application. This GUI is compatible with the standard high-level GUI API but allows you to design every detail of your interface. So, the easy programming of the GUI remains, but all restrictions are blasted away!

Caution A word of warning: the GUI of J2ME Polish is powerful. Very powerful. You can let items fly around, use pulsating backgrounds, and more. Be advised, however, that not everything that's technically cool is also well suited for your user interface. A game can certainly use more funky stuff than banking software, but always keep the usability of your application in mind.

Introducing Interface Concepts

The J2ME Polish GUI provides a powerful and efficient way to design the user interface of wireless Java applications. In fact, the J2ME Polish GUI has several unique features:

- **Time to market**: The J2ME Polish GUI is compatible with the standard MIDP GUI, so you don't need to learn a new API and can turn on and off the J2ME Polish GUI selectively.
- **Automatic porting**: J2ME Polish weaves the necessary code "automagically" into your application so you don't need to modify your source code. The GUI circumvents known issues of your target devices automatically.
- **Innovative designs**: The GUI is designed using simple text files that reside outside the actual application source code. An extended version of the web standard CSS is used for the design, so web designers can now work on the design of J2ME applications without the help of programmers while the programmers concentrate on the business logic.
- **Customizable**: Another important advantage is that you can create extremely different designs for the same application code just by exchanging the *polish.css* file and other resources. This means you can adjust all designs easily to different devices, vendors, device groups, or even locales without changing the source code. Refer to the *resources/polish.css* file of one of the sample applications for an example.
- **Flexible**: You control the user interface with the *build.xml* file and `#style` preprocessing directives.
- **Extensible**: All elements of the MIDP 2.0 GUI are supported—even on MIDP 1.0 devices. So, you can use MIDP 2.0–specific items such as a `POPUP ChoiceGroup` or a `CustomItem` on MIDP 1.0 phones as well. When you extend the J2ME Polish GUI with `CustomItems`, you will find the same environment on every target device, even when the native implementation lacks important features like internal traversal.

The drawback of the J2ME Polish GUI is the increased size of the application package. You should calculate up to 30KB of additional space for the GUI, depending on what GUI elements and what designs you use. Modern devices such as Symbian-based devices (refer to Chapter 15) support application sizes up to several megabytes, so the additional size is most often no problem. The situation is, however, different on some older devices, such as Nokia's aged MIDP 1.0–based Series 40 models, which accept only applications with a size of up to 64KB. For such devices, the GUI is by default not used even when it is activated.

Figure 12-1 shows how you would use the J2ME Polish GUI for creating a "polished" application. For a complete and simple example that uses the *build.xml* and *polish.css* files, please refer to the "Creating a 'Hello, J2ME Polish World' Application" section of Chapter 7.

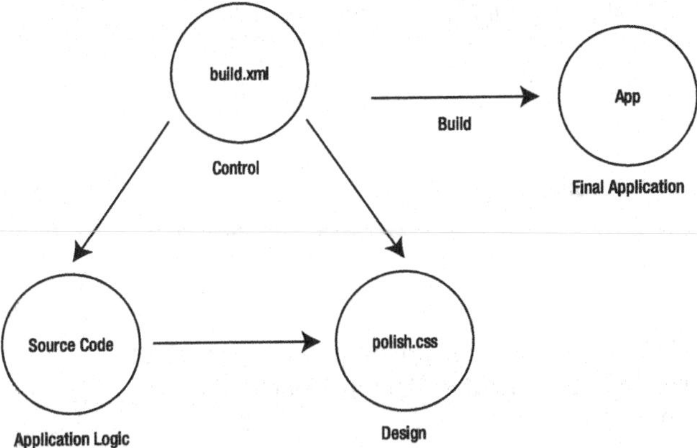

Figure 12-1. *Creating a "polished" application by using build.xml for controlling the process, using the source code for the business logic, and using the polish.css file for the design of your application*

Controlling the GUI

You control the J2ME Polish GUI with the *build.xml* file. You can also activate the J2ME Polish GUI selectively for specific devices and use several preprocessing variables for changing the behavior of the GUI.

Activating the GUI

Activate the GUI by setting the `usePolishGui` attribute of the `<build>` element in the *build.xml* file to `true`. J2ME Polish will then weave the necessary code automatically into the application.

The `usePolishGui` attribute accepts the values `yes`/`true`, `no`/`false`, and `always`. When `true` or `yes` is given, the GUI will be used, unless a target device does not have the recommended capabilities (that is, a maximum JAR size greater than 100KB and a color depth of at least 8 bits per color). For such devices, the normal MIDP GUI is then used instead. When the attribute is set to `always`, the J2ME Polish GUI will be used for all target devices, even when they do not have the recommended capabilities.

Listing 12-1 activates the GUI for most devices.

Listing 12-1. *Activating the GUI for Most Devices in the build.xml File*

```
<j2mepolish>
   <info
      license="GPL"
      name="Roadrunner"
      vendorName="A reader."
      version="0.0.1"
      jarName="${polish.vendor}-${polish.name}-roadrunner.jar"
   />
   <deviceRequirements>
```

```
      <requirement name="Identifier" value="Generic/midp1" />
   </deviceRequirements>
   <build
         usePolishGui="true"
      >
      <midlet class="com.apress.roadrunner.Roadrunner" />
   </build>
   <emulator />
</j2mepolish>
```

Alternatively, you can enable the J2ME Polish GUI by defining the preprocessing variable `polish.usePolishGui`. This is useful when you want to activate the GUI for selected devices only. Listing 12-2 activates the GUI for Series 60 devices only.

Listing 12-2. *Activating the GUI for Series 60 Phones Only*

```
<j2mepolish>
   <info
      license="GPL"
      name="Roadrunner"
      vendorName="A reader."
      version="0.0.1"
      jarName="${polish.vendor}-${polish.name}-roadrunner.jar"
   />
   <deviceRequirements>
      <requirement name="Identifier" value="Generic/midp1" />
   </deviceRequirements>
   <build
         usePolishGui="false"
      >
      <midlet class="com.apress.roadrunner.Roadrunner" />
            <variables>
               <!-- activate the GUI for Series 60 devices  -->
               <variable
                  name="polish.usePolishGui"
                  value="true"
                  if="polish.group.Series60" />
            </variables>
   </build>
   <emulator />
</j2mepolish>
```

Configuring the J2ME Polish GUI

You can configure the behavior of the GUI by modifying the *build.xml* file.

Using the GUI in Full-Screen Mode

The J2ME Polish GUI can use the complete screen on MIDP 2.0 devices as well as on MIDP 1.0 devices that provide proprietary methods for using a full-screen mode.

You can activate the full-screen mode with the `fullscreen` attribute of the `<build>` element, as shown in Listing 12-3. The attribute can have the values `yes/true`, `no/false`, or `menu`. When the application uses commands, you must use the `menu` mode. In that case, the menu bar will be rendered by J2ME Polish, and the menu can be designed with CSS (for example, by setting the `menubar-color` attribute or using the `menu` style).

Alternatively, you can set the `polish.FullScreen` preprocessing variable, which accepts the same values as the `fullscreen` attribute. With this mechanism, you can fine-tune the setting for different devices. Siemens devices, for example, accept commands even in the normal full-screen mode, so there is no need to use the `menu` mode for such devices. Listing 12-3 demonstrates this.

Listing 12-3. *Enabling the Full-Screen Mode*

```
<j2mepolish>
   <info
      license="GPL"
      name="Roadrunner"
      vendorName="A reader."
      version="0.0.1"
      jarName="${polish.vendor}-${polish.name}-roadrunner.jar"
   />
   <deviceRequirements>
      <requirement name="Identifier" value="Generic/midp1" />
   </deviceRequirements>
   <build
         usePolishGui="true"
         fullscreen="menu"
      >
      <midlet class="com.apress.roadrunner.Roadrunner" />
            <variables>
            <!-- Use the normal fullscreen for Siemens devices -->
               <variable
                  name="polish.FullScreen"
                  value="true"
                  if="polish.vendor == Siemens" />
            </variables>
   </build>
   <emulator />
</j2mepolish>
```

Some MIDP 2.0 devices do not support the `menu` mode, since they do not forward key events when a soft key is pressed. J2ME Polish determines whether a device supports the `menu` mode by evaluating the device database. When the `hasCommandKeyEvents` feature is set, the device supports the pure MIDP 2.0 `menu` mode. Additionally, you can set the capabilities key.LeftSoftKey and key.RightSoftKey to define the key codes for the soft keys (these are the values that are reported to the keyPressed() method of a Canvas). When no keys are defined, the value -6 is assumed for the left soft key and the value -7 for the right soft key. Listing 12-4 shows the definition of the Siemens/CX65 phone that includes these settings.

Listing 12-4. *Support of the Full-Screen Mode Depends on Events for the Soft Keys*

```
<device
   supportsPolishGui="true">
   <identifier>Siemens/CX65</identifier>
   <features>hasCommandKeyEvents</features>
   <capability name="ScreenSize" value="132x176"/>
   <capability name="key.LeftSoftKey" value="-1" />
   <capability name="key.RightSoftKey" value="-4" />
</device>
```

Configuring Commands, Labels, and Behavior of the GUI

You can use preprocessing variables and symbols for changing the appearance or logic of the J2ME Polish GUI. Tables 12-1 and 12-2 list the available configuration symbols and variables you can set in the *build.xml* file.

Table 12-1. *Available Preprocessing Symbols for Configuring the GUI*

Preprocessing Symbol	Explanation
polish.skipArgumentCheck	When this symbol is defined, method arguments will not be checked. This improves the runtime performance and the size of the application a bit.

Table 12-2. *Available Preprocessing Variables for Configuring the GUI*

Preprocessing Variable	Default	Explanation
polish.animationInterval	100	Defines the interval in milliseconds for animations.
polish.classes.ImageLoader		Usually, J2ME Polish loads all images from the JAR file using the Image.createImage(String url) method. This works fine for most situations, but sometimes images should be retrieved from the RMS or the Internet. In such cases, you can define the polish.classes.ImageLoader variable. The given class (or static field of a class) needs to implement the javax.microedition.lcdui.Image loadImage(String url) throws IOException method, which is responsible for retrieving the image. This option is discussed in detail in the "Loading Images Dynamically" section of Chapter 13.

Preprocessing Variable	Default	Explanation
polish.ChoiceGroup.suppressMarkCommands	false	A multiple List or ChoiceGroup adds the commands "Mark" and "Unmark" by default to the menu. The names of the commands can be changed easily; see the "Building Localized Applications" section in Chapter 7. If you want to suppress the commands completely, the polish.ChoiceGroup.suppressMarkCommands variable has to be set to true.
polish.ChoiceGroup.suppressSelectCommand	false	An implicit or pop-up ChoiceGroup or List does usually have a Select command that also can be deactivated.
polish.TextField.useDirectInput	false	Enables the direct input mode of all TextFields and TextBoxes in your application.
polish.TextField.suppressClearCommand	false	Set this variable to true to disable only the Clear command of TextFields.
polish.TextField.suppressDeleteCommand	false	Set this variable to true to disable only the Clear command of TextFields.
polish.TextField.suppressCommands	false	You can deactivate the Delete as well as the Clear commands by setting this variable to true.
polish.TextField.showInputInfo	true	When set to false, the indicator of the current input mode is not drawn in direct input mode TextFields.
polish.TextField.InputTimeout	1000	The timeout in milliseconds after which a chosen character is inserted into the text automatically.
polish.TextField.charactersKey1	".,!?:/@_-+1"	The characters that are available when the 1 key is pressed.
polish.TextField.charactersKey2	"abc2"	The characters that are available when the 2 key is pressed. It might be useful to add local, specific umlauts here.
polish.TextField.charactersKey3	"def3"	The characters that are available when the 3 key is pressed.
polish.TextField.charactersKey3	"ghi4"	The characters that are available when the 4 key is pressed.
polish.TextField.charactersKey5	"jkl5"	The characters that are available when the 5 key is pressed.
polish.TextField.charactersKey6	"mno6"	The characters that are available when the 6 key is pressed.
polish.TextField.charactersKey7	"pqrs7"	The characters that are available when the 7 key is pressed.
polish.TextField.charactersKey8	"tuv8"	The characters that are available when the 8 key is pressed.
polish.TextField.charactersKey9	"wxyz9"	The characters that are available when the 9 key is pressed.

Continued

Table 12-2. *Continued*

Preprocessing Variable	Default	Explanation
`polish.TextField.charactersKey0`	`" 0"`	The characters that are available when the 0 key is pressed. On Motorola devices, this key is used for switching the input mode.
`polish.TextField.charactersKeyStar`	`".,!?:/@_-+"`	The characters that are available when the key * is pressed. On Motorola devices, this key is used for entering spaces (" ").
`polish.TextField.charactersKeyPound`		The characters that are available when the key # is pressed. On Sony-Ericsson devices, this key is used for entering spaces (" ").
`polish.command.ok`	OK	The label for the OK command that is used when the `menu` full-screen mode is used.
`polish.command.cancel`	Cancel	The label for the Cancel command.
`polish.command.select`	Select	The label for the Select command that is used by an implicit or exclusive `List` or `ChoiceGroup`.
`polish.command.mark`	Mark	The label for the Mark command of a multiple `List` or `ChoiceGroup`.
`polish.command.unmark`	Unmark	The label for the Unmark command item of a multiple `List` or `ChoiceGroup`.
`polish.command.options`	Options	The label for the command that opens the list of available commands.
`polish.command.delete`	Delete	The label for the Delete command that is used by `TextFields`.
`polish.command.clear`	Clear	The label for the Clear command that is used by `TextFields`.
`polish.title.input`	Input	The title of the native `TextBox` that is normally used for the actual input of text. This title is used only when the corresponding `TextField` item has no label. When the `TextField` has a label, that label is used as a title instead.
`polish.usePolishGui`		Can be used for activating the Polish GUI for selected devices only.
`polish.FullScreen`		Can be used for selectively activating the full-screen mode. Possible values are `true`, `false`, and `menu`.

Listing 12-5 demonstrates how to use some of these options. Please refer to the "Building Localized Applications" section of Chapter 7 to learn more about the options for localizing your application. In the "Advanced Topics" section of Chapter 13, you will learn how you can load images dynamically with the help of the `polish.classes.ImageLoader` variable.

Listing 12-5. *Configuring the GUI with Preprocessing Variables and Symbols*

```
<j2mepolish>
   <info
      license="GPL"
      name="Roadrunner"
      vendorName="A reader."
      version="0.0.1"
      jarName="${polish.vendor}-${polish.name}-roadrunner.jar"
   />
   <deviceRequirements>
      <requirement name="Identifier" value="Generic/midp1" />
   </deviceRequirements>
      <!-- symbol: don't check method-parameters:  -->
   <build
         usePolishGui="true"
         fullscreen="menu"
         symbols="polish.skipArgumentCheck"
      >
            <midlet class="com.apress.roadrunner.Roadrunner" />
            <variables>
               <!-- suppress Mark/Unmark commands for ChoiceGroups and Lists:  -->
               <variable
                  name="polish.ChoiceGroup.suppressMarkCommands"
                  value="true" />
               <!-- suppress Delete/Clear commands for TextBoxes/TextFields:  -->
               <variable
                  name="polish.TextField.suppressCommands"
                  value="true" />
            </variables>
   </build>
   <emulator />
</j2mepolish>
```

Configuring the TextField

The J2ME Polish GUI version of the `TextField` can be programmed just like the standard `javax.microedition.lcdui.TextField`, but it offers two input modes: you can choose between the native and the direct inline input mode. You can also activate or deactivate the Delete and Clear commands that are attached to each `TextField` by default.

Configuring the Input Mode

The native input mode is used by default. When the user wants to edit the field, a native `TextField` is opened in another screen. The advantage of this approach is that the user can utilize all input helpers of the device, such as T9, handwriting recognition, and so on. You should always use the native input mode for stylus-based devices or when the user should edit long texts.

You can enable the direct input mode via the `textfield-direct-input` CSS attribute (see the following section for details) or by setting the `TextField.useDirectInput` preprocessing variable. Using the preprocessing variable improves the performance and size of your application a bit, but in that case the direct input mode is enabled for all `TextFields` as well as `TextBoxes`. You can limit the activation of the direct input mode to devices that have no stylus by using a condition in your variable definition: `<variable name="polish.TextField.useDirectInput" value="true" if="!polish.hasPointerEvents"/>`.

When you use the direct input mode, you might want to allow additional characters depending on your localization. You can define the variables `polish.TextField.charactersKey0`, `polish.TextField.charactersKey1`, and so on, for this task: `<variable name="polish.TextField. charactersKey2" value="abc2äåæ" />`. Please refer to Table 12-2 for the default values of these variables.

Tip If you use the direct input mode, you can allow any kind of input while setting the initial input mode to numbers by creating a `NUMERIC TextField` first and then changing the constraints to `ANY`: `field = new TextField( "password: ", null, 20, TextField.NUMERIC ); field.setConstraints ( TextField.ANY );`. This can improve the usability of your application drastically when you have fields that usually accept numbers but that are not limited to numbers only.

Configuring TextField Commands

Whenever a `TextField` is focused, the two additional commands Clear and Delete are added automatically. You can disable this by setting one of the following variables to `false`: `polish.TextField.suppressClearCommand`, `polish.TextField.suppressDeleteCommand`, or `polish.TextField.suppressCommands`. You should deactivate the Delete command only when the target device has a known clear key or when you don't use the direct input mode; otherwise, the user won't be able to delete wrong input. The following example removes both the Clear and Delete commands only when the device has a clear key: `<variable name="polish.TextField.suppressCommands" value="true" if="polish.key.ClearKey:defined"/>`.

Using Different Designs for Your Application

You can use completely different designs for your application just by using different resource folders. You can switch the used resources by specifying the folder in the `<resources>` element, as shown in Listing 12-6.

Listing 12-6. *Using Another Resources Folder*

```
<j2mepolish>
   <info
      license="GPL"
      name="Roadrunner"
      vendorName="A reader."
      version="0.0.1"
      jarName="${polish.vendor}-${polish.name}-roadrunner.jar"
```

```
    />
    <deviceRequirements>
       <requirement name="Identifier" value="Generic/midp1" />
    </deviceRequirements>
       <!-- symbol: don't check method-parameters:  -->
    <build
          usePolishGui="true"
          fullscreen="menu"
       >
       <midlet class="com.apress.roadrunner.Roadrunner" />
       <resources
          dir="resources2"
       />
    </build>
    <emulator />
</j2mepolish>
```

Figures 12-2, 12-3, and 12-4 show the Menu sample application with three designs. Note that the source code is not changed at all—all changes take place by providing different *polish.css* files and different images.

Figure 12-2. *The Menu sample application in the default design*

Figure 12-3. *The same application using a pop design*

Figure 12-4. *Yet again the same application using a dark design*

You can use this mechanism for customizing your application to different user groups or different corporate identities, for example. When you use the localization features (refer to the "Building Localized Applications" section in Chapter 7), you can also use different texts for your builds. So, you could use one application logic or game engine and create many different applications that look completely different but that differ only in their design and texts. This is a handy way to increase productivity, don't you think?

Programming the GUI

Using the J2ME Polish GUI is quite simple actually. Since the J2ME Polish GUI is compatible with the MIDP `javax.microedition.lcdui` classes, neither `import` statements nor the actual code usually needs to be changed. In addition, you can apply CSS styles to your items using the `#style` directive. J2ME Polish also contains some enhancements such as `TabbedForm`, `FramedForm`, and `SpriteItem`.

Using Correct import Statements

You need to use correct `import` statements and no fully qualified classnames in your application so that J2ME Polish can weave its GUI API into your application. Listing 12-7 shows you a nonworking example.

Listing 12-7. *How **Not** to Use the J2ME Polish GUI*

```
public class MyForm
extends javax.microedition.lcdui.Form
{
   private javax.microedition.lcdui.StringItem textItem;
   public MyForm( String title ) {
      //#style myForm, default
      super( title );
      this.textItem =
       new  javax.microedition.lcdui.StringItem( null, "Hello World" );
```

```
      append( this.textItem );
   }
}
```

The code in Listing 12-7 won't work because it does not use `import` statements correctly. Listing 12-8 demonstrates how to correctly use them.

Listing 12-8. *Use import Statements When You Want to Use the J2ME Polish GUI*

```
import javax.microedition.lcdui.Form;
import javax.microedition.lcdui.StringItem;
public class MyForm
extends Form
{
   private StringItem textItem;
   public MyForm( String title ) {
      //#style myForm, default
      super( title );
      this.textItem = new StringItem( null, "Hello World" );
      append( this.textItem );
   }
}
```

■ Tip You can use this `import` behavior of J2ME Polish for using native `lcdui` classes in your application even though you are using the J2ME Polish GUI. `TextBoxes` are a popular example that are used for getting a lot of text from the user. In such cases, you most likely don't want to use the direct text input mode provided by the J2ME Polish implementation, since the user cannot use T9 and other native input helpers. You can use the native `TextBoxes` directly just by using the fully qualified classname in your field declaration, for example, `javax.microedition.lcdui.TextBox nativeTextBox = new javax.microedition.lcdui.TextBox( "Message", null, 500, TextField.ANY )`.

Setting Styles

You should use the `#style` preprocessing directive for applying the desired design styles. This directive contains one or several style names that are separated by commas. When several style names are given, J2ME Polish will use the first available style. The preprocessor of J2ME Polish just selects the first available style and inserts it in the following line as the last parameter. For example, Listing 12-9 uses the `.mainMenu` or `default` style for the design of a `Form`.

Listing 12-9. *Applying a CSS Style to a Form*

```
import javax.microedition.lcdui.Form;
public class MainMenu extends Form {
   public MainMenu( String title ) {
      //#style mainMenu, default
```

```
        super( title );
        [...]
    }
}
```

You should also define the `.mainMenu` style in the *resources/polish.css* file, as shown in Listing 12-10. When none of the provided style definitions is found, J2ME Polish reports this error and aborts the processing. The `default` style is special because it is always defined, even when you don't specify it explicitly in the *polish.css* file.

Listing 12-10. *Defining the CSS Style in the resources/polish.css File*

```
.mainMenu {
   background-image: url( bg.png );
   columns: 2;
}
```

You can use the `#style` directive in front of any `Item` or `Screen` constructor and before some other methods, which are listed in Table 12-3.

Table 12-3. *Insertion Points for #style Directives*

Insertion Point	Example	Explanation

`Item` constructors	`//#style cool, frosty, default`
	`StringItem url = new StringItem`
	`( null, "http://192.168.101.101" );`
	`//#style cool`
	`ImageItem img = new ImageItem`
	`( null, iconImage,`
	`ImageItem.LAYOUT_DEFAULT, null );`
		The `#style` directive can be placed before any `Item` constructor.

`Item.setAppearanceMode()`	`//#style openLink`
	`url.setAppearanceMode`
	`( Item.HYPERLINK );`
		The `#style` directive can be placed before calling the `setAppearanceMode()` method of an `Item`. Please note that this method is available only in J2ME Polish.

`List.append()`	`//#style choice` `list.append( "Start", null );`	The `#style` directive can be placed before adding a list element.
`List.insert()`	`//#style choice` `list.insert( 2, "Start", null );`	The `#style` directive can be placed before inserting a list element.
`List.set()`	`//#style choice` `list.set( 2, "Start", null );`	The `#style` directive can be placed before setting a list element.
`Form.append()`	`//#style text` `form.append( textItem );`	The `#style` directive can be placed before adding any `Form` element.
`ChoiceGroup.append()`	`//#style choice` `group.append( "Choice 1", null );`	The `#style` directive can be placed before adding an element to a `ChoiceGroup`.

`ChoiceGroup.insert()`	`//#style choice`
	`group.insert( 2, "Choice 3",`
	`null );`
		The `#style` directive can be placed before inserting an element to a `ChoiceGroup`.

Insertion Point	Example	Explanation
`ChoiceGroup.set()`	`//#style choice` `group.set( 2, "Choice 3", null );`	The `#style` directive can be placed before setting an element of a `ChoiceGroup`.

`Screen` constructor	`//#style mainScreen`
	`Form form = new Form( "Menu" );`
	`// in subclasses of Screens:`
	`//#style mainScreen`
	`super( "Menu" );`
		The `#style` directive can be used before any `Screen` constructor or before calling `super()` in subclass constructors.

Using Dynamic and Predefined Styles

When you use dynamic styles, you do not even have to set the `#style` directives. In this case, the designs depend on the classes. All `Forms` can be designed with the `form` style, for example. Using dynamic styles can be a fast way to check out the GUI for existing applications, but this requires additional memory and runtime. You should, therefore, use normal "static" styles for the final application.

Some elements use predefined styles by default. The `title` style is responsible for the appearance of `Screen` titles, for example.

Please refer to the explanation in the following "Designing the GUI" section for more information about static, dynamic, and predefined styles.

Porting MIDP 2.0 Applications to MIDP 1.0 Platforms

When you use the J2ME Polish GUI, you can use MIDP 2.0 widgets like a `POPUP ChoiceGroup` or a `CustomItem` on MIDP 1.0 devices as well without any restrictions.

Source code adjustments are necessary only when MIDP 2.0–only features are used, which are outside the scope of the J2ME Polish GUI, for example, `Display.flashBacklight ( int )`.

The MIDP 2.0 call `Display.setCurrentItem( Item )` is supported by the J2ME Polish GUI for both MIDP 2.0 as well as MIDP 1.0 devices.

When a specific call is not supported by a target device, the build process will be aborted with a compile error. Usually that error then needs to be surrounded by an appropriate `#if` preprocessing directive, as shown in Listing 12-11.

Listing 12-11. *Circumventing MIDP 2.0–Only Calls with Preprocessing*

```
//#ifdef polish.midp2
   this.display.flashBacklight( 1000 );
//#endif
```

Please refer to the section "Writing Your Own Custom Items" in Chapter 13 for more information on designing custom items with CSS.

Programming Specific Items and Screens

In general, the J2ME Polish GUI is fully compatible with the MIDP 2.0 UI standard. However, some enhancements are not available in the MIDP 2.0 standard. The following sections discuss how to program `TabbedForm`, `FramedForm`, and `SpriteItem`. Please also refer to the JavaDoc documentation in *${polish.home}/doc/javadoc.html* for further details.

Programming the TabbedForm

The `de.enough.polish.ui.TabbedForm` is a `Form` that arranges the included GUI elements on several tabs. You can use any `Form` methods, such as `setItemStateListener()`, in the `TabbedForm` as well. Table 12-4 lists the additional methods for configuring the tabs of a `TabbedForm`.

Table 12-4. *Additional TabbedForm Methods*

Method	Example	Explanation
`TabbedForm( String title, String[] tabNames, Image[] tabImages )`	`//#style myTabbedForm TabbedForm form = new TabbedForm( "Hello", new String[] { "First Tab", "another tab" }, null );`	Creates a new `TabbedForm`.
`append( int tabIndex, Item item )`	`form.append ( 2, myStringItem );`	Adds the item to the specified tab. The first tab has the index 0.
`set( int tabIndex, int itemIndex, Item item )`	`form.set( 2, 1, myStringItem );`	Sets the item to the specified index on the given tab.
`delete( int tabIndex, Item item )`	`form.delete ( 2, myStringItem );`	Deletes the given item from the specified tab.
`getSelectedTab()`	`int tabIndex = getSelectedTab();`	Retrieves the currently used tab.
`setScreenStateListener ( ScreenStateListener listener )`	`form.setScreenStateListener ( this );`	Sets the `de.enough.polish.ScreenStateListener` that is notified whenever the active tab is changed. Use this feature for setting a tab-specific title, for example.

Listing 12-12 demonstrates how to use the `TabbedForm`.

Listing 12-12. *Using the TabbedForm*

```
package com.apress.ui;

import javax.microedition.lcdui.Choice;
import javax.microedition.lcdui.ChoiceGroup;
import javax.microedition.lcdui.Command;
import javax.microedition.lcdui.CommandListener;
import javax.microedition.lcdui.DateField;
import javax.microedition.lcdui.Display;
```

```
import javax.microedition.lcdui.StringItem;
import javax.microedition.lcdui.TextField;
import javax.microedition.lcdui.Item;
import javax.microedition.lcdui.ItemStateListener;

import de.enough.polish.ui.TabbedForm;

public class TabbedFormDemo implements ItemStateListener {


   private final TextField nameField;

   public TabbedFormDemo( CommandListener commandListener,
              Display display, Command returnCmd )
   {
      String[] tabNames = new String[]{ "Input", "Choice",
 "Connection" };
      //#style tabbedScreen
      TabbedForm form = new TabbedForm( "TabbedDemo", tabNames, null );
      //#style label
      StringItem label = new StringItem( null, "name:" );
      form.append( 0, label );
      //#style input
      this.nameField = new TextField( null, "Robert", 30,
                  TextField.ANY | TextField.INITIAL_CAPS_WORD );
      form.append( 0, this.nameField );
      //#style label
      label = new StringItem( null, "birthday:" );
      form.append( 0, label );
      //#style input
      DateField birthdate = new DateField( null, DateField.DATE );
      form.append( 0, birthdate );

      //#style label
      label = new StringItem( null, "What kind of animals do you like:" );
      form.append( 1, label );
      //#style multipleChoice
      ChoiceGroup choice = new ChoiceGroup( null, Choice.MULTIPLE );
      //#style choiceItem
      choice.append( "dogs", null );
      //#style choiceItem
      choice.append( "cats", null );
      //#style choiceItem
      choice.append( "birds", null );
      form.append( 1, choice );
```

```
        //#style label
        label = new StringItem( null, "Connection:" );
        form.append( 2, label );
        //#style multipleChoice
        choice = new ChoiceGroup( null, Choice.MULTIPLE );
        //#style choiceItem
        choice.append( "ISDN", null );
        //#style choiceItem
        choice.append( "DSL", null );
        //#style choiceItem
        choice.append( "Cable", null );
        form.append( 2, choice );

        form.addCommand( returnCmd );
        form.setCommandListener( commandListener );
        form.setItemStateListener( this );
        display.setCurrentItem( choice );
    }

    public void itemStateChanged( Item item ) {
        System.out.println( "Item State Changed: " + item );
    }
}
```

Figure 12-5 shows how TabbedForm looks.

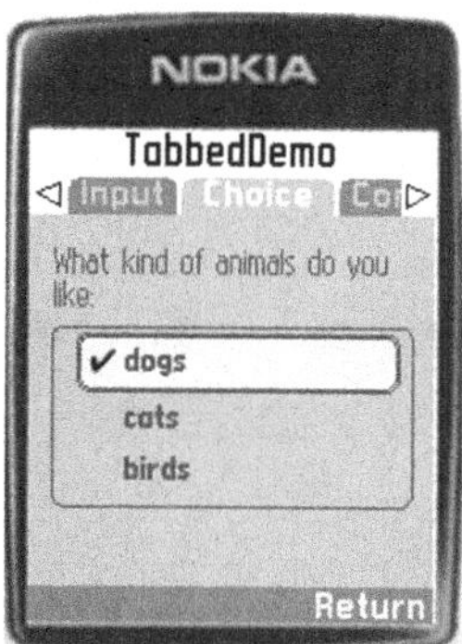

Figure 12-5. *The TabbedForm in action*

Programming the FramedForm

The de.enough.polish.ui.FramedForm splits the screen into a main area and four possible frames at the top, bottom, left, or right side of the screen. Only the main area is scrolled while the frames remain in their positions. You can use frames for positioning buttons at fixed positions or for including a TextField to filter the shown items, for example. Table 12-5 lists the additional methods of the FramedForm.

Table 12-5. *Additional FramedForm Methods*

Method	Example	Explanation
`append( int frameOrientation, Item item )`	`form.append ( Graphics.BOTTOM, myTextField );`	Adds the item to the specified frame. You can use either `Graphics.TOP`, `BOTTOM`, `LEFT`, or `RIGHT`.
`setScreenStateListener ( ScreenStateListener listener )`	`form.setScreenStateListener ( this );`	Sets the `de.enough.polish.ScreenStateListener` that is notified whenever the active frame is changed.

Listing 12-13 shows how you can use the `FramedForm` in your program for placing a non-scrollable `TextField` at the bottom of the screen.

Listing 12-13. *Using the FramedForm*

```
package com.apress.ui;

import javax.microedition.lcdui.Choice;
import javax.microedition.lcdui.ChoiceGroup;
import javax.microedition.lcdui.Command;
import javax.microedition.lcdui.CommandListener;
import javax.microedition.lcdui.DateField;
import javax.microedition.lcdui.Display;
import javax.microedition.lcdui.Graphics;
import javax.microedition.lcdui.TextField;
import javax.microedition.lcdui.Item;
import javax.microedition.lcdui.ItemStateListener;

import de.enough.polish.ui.FramedForm;

public class FramedFormDemo implements ItemStateListener {


   private final TextField inputField;
   private final Item[] items;

   public FramedFormDemo( CommandListener commandListener,
               Display display, Command returnCmd, Item[] items )
   {
      //#style framedScreen
      FramedForm form = new FramedForm( "TabbedDemo" );
      // add all normal items:
      for ( int i = 0; i < items.length; i ++ ) {
         form.append( items[i] );
      }
```

```
        //#style inputFilter
        this.inputField = new TextField( "Filter: ", "", 30, TextField.ANY );
        form.append( Graphics.BOTTOM, this.inputField );

        form.addCommand( returnCmd );
        form.setCommandListener( commandListener );
        display.setCurrentItem( this.inputField );
    }

    public void itemStateChanged( Item item ) {
        // the TextField has been changed, now filter
        // the item accordingly...
    }
}
```

Figure 12-6 shows an example of using a `FramedForm` in your program to create a nonscrollable `TextField` at the bottom of the screen.

Figure 12-6. *The FramedForm in action*

Programming the SpriteItem

Use the `de.enough.polish.ui.SpriteItem` for including animations in your menu `Form`. This item embeds a normal `javax.microedition.lcdui.game.Sprite` that is animated when the item is focused. Imagine a closed book that opens when the user focuses it, for example. Thanks to the J2ME Polish game engine (refer to Chapter 11), you can use `Sprites` on MIDP 1.0 devices as well. Table 12-6 lists the required arguments for creating a new `SpriteItem`. Depending on the state of your application, you can change the `Sprite`'s frame sequence for changing the animation by calling the `setFrameSequence( int[] )` method of the `Sprite`.

Table 12-6. *Arguments of the SpriteItem Constructor*

Argument	Explanation
`String label`	The item's label.
`Sprite sprite`	The embedded `Sprite`. The frame sequence of the `Sprite` displays during the animation.
`long animationInterval`	The interval between frame changes in milliseconds. This needs to be a multiple of 100, unless you set the `polish.animationInterval` preprocessing variable in your *build.xml* script.
`int defaultFrameIndex`	The frame index that is shown when the `SpriteItem` is not focused.
`boolean repeatAnimation`	Specifies whether the animation should be repeated when one circle has been completed.

Listing 12-14 demonstrates how to use the `SpriteItem` in your application.

Listing 12-14. *Programming the SpriteItem*

```
package com.apress.ui;

import java.io.IOException;

import javax.microedition.lcdui.Command;
import javax.microedition.lcdui.CommandListener;
import javax.microedition.lcdui.Display;
import javax.microedition.lcdui.Displayable;
import javax.microedition.lcdui.Form;
import javax.microedition.lcdui.Image;
import javax.microedition.lcdui.Item;
import javax.microedition.lcdui.ItemCommandListener;
import javax.microedition.lcdui.game.Sprite;
import javax.microedition.midlet.MIDlet;
import javax.microedition.midlet.MIDletStateChangeException;

import de.enough.polish.ui.SpriteItem;

public class AnimatedMenuMidlet
extends MIDlet
implements ItemCommandListener
{

   private Display display;
   private Form mainForm;
   private final Command startCmd;
   private final Command loadCmd;
   private final Command aboutCmd;
   private final Command exitCmd;
```

```
    public AnimatedMenuMidlet() {
        super();
        this.startCmd = new Command( "Start Game", Command.ITEM, 1 );
        this.loadCmd = new Command( "Load Game", Command.ITEM, 1 );
        this.aboutCmd = new Command( "About", Command.ITEM, 1 );
        this.exitCmd = new Command( "Exit", Command.ITEM, 1 );
        try {
            this.mainForm = new Form( "Main Menu" );
            int frameWidth = 30;
            int frameHeight = 30;
            // create the start game menu item:
            Image image = Image.createImage( "/player.png");
            Sprite sprite = new Sprite( image, frameWidth, frameHeight );
            sprite.setFrameSequence( new int[]{ 2, 5, 5, 6, 3, 7, 1 } );
            //#style mainScreenItem
            SpriteItem spriteItem = new SpriteItem( null, sprite, 200, 0, false );
            spriteItem.setDefaultCommand( this.startCmd );
            spriteItem.setItemCommandListener( this );
            this.mainForm.append( spriteItem );

            // create the load game menu item:
            image = Image.createImage( "/load.png");
            sprite = new Sprite( image, frameWidth, frameHeight );
            // use default frame sequence
            //#style mainScreenItem
            spriteItem = new SpriteItem( null, sprite, 200, 0, false );
            spriteItem.setDefaultCommand( this.loadCmd );
            spriteItem.setItemCommandListener( this );
            this.mainForm.append( spriteItem );

            // create the about menu item:
            image = Image.createImage( "/about.png");
            sprite = new Sprite( image, frameWidth, frameHeight );
            //#style mainScreenItem
            spriteItem = new SpriteItem( null, sprite, 200, 0, false );
            spriteItem.setDefaultCommand( this.aboutCmd );
            spriteItem.setItemCommandListener( this );
            this.mainForm.append( spriteItem );

            // create the exit menu item:
            image = Image.createImage( "/exit.png");
            sprite = new Sprite( image, frameWidth, frameHeight );
            //#style mainScreenItem
            spriteItem = new SpriteItem( null, sprite, 200, 0, false );
            spriteItem.setDefaultCommand( this.exitCmd );
            spriteItem.setItemCommandListener( this );
            this.mainForm.append( spriteItem );
```

```
        } catch ( IOException e ) {
            //#debug error
            System.out.println( "Unable to create menu screen" + e );
            this.mainForm = null;
        }
    }

    protected void startApp() throws MIDletStateChangeException {
        this.display = Display.getDisplay( this );
        if ( this.mainForm == null ) {
            throw new MIDletStateChangeException();
        }
        this.display.setCurrent( this.mainForm );
    }

    protected void pauseApp() {
        // just pause
    }

    protected void destroyApp( boolean unconditional )
    throws MIDletStateChangeException
    {
        // just quit
    }

    public void commandAction( Command cmd, Item item ) {
        if ( cmd == this.startCmd ) {
            // start game...
        } else if ( cmd == this.loadCmd ) {
            /// load game...
        } else if ( cmd == this.aboutCmd ) {
            // about this game...
        } else if ( cmd == this.exitCmd ) {
            notifyDestroyed();
        }
    }
}
```

Designing the GUI

You can design the J2ME Polish GUI with the web standard Cascading Style Sheets (CSS). So, every web designer can now design mobile applications with J2ME Polish! The following sections explain all the details of the design possibilities; no prior knowledge of CSS is required.

All design settings and files are stored in the *resources* directory of the project, unless another directory has been specified in the *build.xml* file. The most important file is *polish.css* in that directory. You can find all design definitions there. The design definitions are grouped in *styles*. You can assign a style to any GUI item, such as a title, a paragraph, or an input field. Within a style, several attributes and its values are usually defined, as shown in Listing 12-15.

Listing 12-15. *A Simple Style Definition*

```
.myStyle {
   font-color: white;
   font-style: bold;
   font-size: large;
   font-face: proportional;
   background-color: black;
}
```

In Listing 12-15, the style called `myStyle` defines some font values and the color of the background. Any style contains a selector as well as a number of attributes and its values, as shown in Figure 12-7.

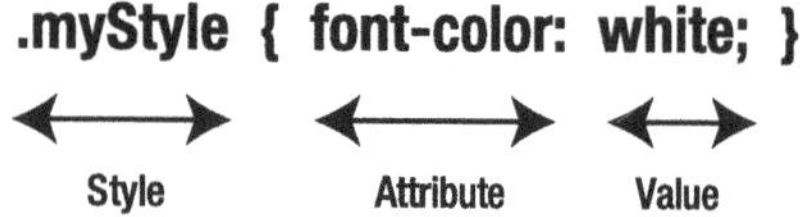

Figure 12-7. *The components of a CSS style*

You need to finish each attribute-value pair with a semicolon. The style declaration needs to end with a right curly parenthesis. The selector, or name, of a style is case-insensitive, so `.MySTYle` is the same as `.myStyle`.

You can adjust your design to different handsets easily by using subfolders in the *resources* folder. This mechanism uses the same features as the resource assembling described in Chapter 7. The relevant techniques are repeated in the "Designing for Specific Devices and Device Groups" section.

You can specify styles directly for GUI items with the `#style` preprocessing directive in the source code. Alternatively, you can use the dynamic names of the GUI items; for example, you can use `p` for text items, `a` for hyperlinks, or `form p` for all text items that are embedded in a `Form`. The possible combinations as well as the predefined styles are discussed in the section "Using Dynamic, Static, and Predefined Styles."

Styles can extend other styles with the `extends` keyword, such as `.myStyle extends baseStyle {}`. The section "Extending Styles" describes this process.

J2ME Polish supports the CSS box model with margins, paddings, and content. Other common design settings include the background, border, and font settings. The section "Common Design Attributes" describes these widespread settings. The possibilities for designing screens and items are discussed subsequently.

Designing for Specific Devices and Device Groups

Sometimes you need to adjust the design to a specific device, a group of devices, or a specific locale. You can easily use specific pictures, styles, and so on, by using the appropriate subfolders of the *resources* folder (as described in the "Resource Assembling" section of Chapter 7).

You adjust your design to a specific vendor, group, or device by adding a *polish.css* file to the appropriate folder, such as *resources/Series60/polish.css* or *resources/ScreenSize.240+x320+/polish.css*. Instead of repeating all styles and attributes from the more basic CSS files, you just need to identify the more specific setting. When you want to change the color of a font, you just need to specify the `font-color` attribute of that style, for example. You don't need to define any other attributes or styles. This is the cascading character of the Cascading Style Sheets of J2ME Polish.

Listings 12-16 and 12-17 illustrate the cascading character of *polish.css*. In Listing 12-16, you have a basic style definition that is situated in the *resources/polish.css* file.

Listing 12-16. *A Basic Style Definition in resources/polish.css*

```
.myStyle {
   padding: 5;
   font-color: white;
   font-style: bold;
   font-size: large;
   font-face: proportional;
   background-color: black;
   border-color: yellow;
}
```

Listing 12-17 shows the specialization of that style in the Nokia-specific file *resources/Nokia/polish.css*. In that case, only the `font-color` attribute is changed, and no background is used; all other settings remain the same. If you don't want to use an attribute even though that attribute has been defined in the parent style, you can use the `attribute-name: none` setting in most cases. In Listing 12-17, no background is used for the style by specifying `background: none`.

Listing 12-17. *A Nokia Specialization of the Style That Resides in resources/Nokia/polish.css*

```
.myStyle {
   font-color: gray;
   background: none;
}
```

Using Dynamic, Static, and Predefined Styles

J2ME Polish distinguishes between dynamic, static, and predefined styles:

- *Static* styles are defined in the source code of the application with the `#style` preprocessing directive.
- *Predefined* styles are used internally by J2ME Polish for some specific items such as screen titles, menu bars, or tabs in a `TabbedForm`.
- *Dynamic* styles are used for items according to their type.

Static Styles

Static styles are applied to specific `Items` or `Screens` using the `#style` preprocessing directive in the source code of the application. The programmer just needs to tell the designer the style names and what they are used for (that is, for what kind of items or screens), and the designer needs to define them in the *polish.css* file. Static styles always start with a dot in the CSS file, such as `.myStyle`, for example.

Static styles are faster and less resource intensive than dynamic styles. You should stick to static and predefined styles whenever possible.

Predefined Styles

The J2ME Polish GUI uses predefined styles internally. In contrast to the normal "user-defined" static styles, their names do not start with a dot, for example, `title` instead of `.title`.

Table 12-7 lists the available predefined styles. When you do not define a predefined style, the "default" style is used instead.

Table 12-7. *Supported Predefined Styles*

Style	Description
`title`	The style of screen titles. For MIDP 2.0 devices, the native implementation is used by default, unless the `menu` full-screen mode is used or the preprocessing variable `polish.usePolishTitle` is defined with `true`: `<variable name="polish.usePolishTitle" value="true" unless="polish.Vendor == Nokia" />`. You can also use custom styles for specific `Screens` or `ChoiceGroups` by using the `title-style` attribute.
`focused`	The style of a currently focused item. This style is used in `Lists`, in `Forms`, and for containers such as `ChoiceGroup`. You can also use custom styles for specific `Screens` or `ChoiceGroups` by using the `focused-style` attribute.
`menu`	This style is used for designing the menu bar in full-screen mode. The full-screen mode can be triggered by the `fullScreenMode` attribute of the `<build>` element in the *build.xml* (with `fullScreenMode="menu"`). In the menu style, you can also define which style is used for the currently focused command with the `focused-style` attribute, for example, `focused-style: menuFocused;`. In this case, you need to define the static style `.menuFocused` as well.
`menuItem`	The style used for the menu items (the commands) of a `screen`. When `menuItem` is not defined, the `menu` style is used instead.
`label`	This style is used for the menu label of any item. One can specify another label style by defining the CSS attribute `label-style` in the appropriate style, which refers to another style.
`info`	The style that is used for displaying additional information in a screen. Currently this is used only for showing the current input mode when the direct input mode of a `TextField` or a `TextBox` is enabled.
`default`	The style that is used by the J2ME Polish GUI when the desired predefined style is not defined. The default style is always defined, even when it is not explicitly defined in the *polish.css* file.
`tabbar`	This style designs the tab bar of a `TabbedForm`.
`activetab`	Designs the currently active tab of a `TabbedForm`.

Style	Description
inactivetab	Designs all tabs but the currently selected one of a TabbedForm.
topframe	Designs the upper frame of a FramedForm.
bottomframe	Designs the lower frame of a FramedForm.
leftframe	Designs the left frame of a FramedForm.
rightframe	Designs the right frame of a FramedForm.
frame	You can use the frame style for designing all frames of a FramedForm in one style, when you don't use a more specific style.

You are not allowed to use the names of predefined styles for static styles, so you must not use a static style with the name .title, and so on.

Dynamic Styles

Use dynamic styles to apply styles to items without using #style directives in the source code. With dynamic styles, the designer can work completely independently of the programmer and try new designs for GUI items that do not yet have an associated static style. You can also check out the power and possibilities of the J2ME Polish API without changing the source code of an existing application at all.

Dynamic styles need more memory and processing time than static and predefined styles. You should, therefore, use static styles if possible.

Dynamic styles do not start with a dot and use item- or screen-specific names for their selectors.

Texts use either p, a, button, or icon. Screens use the name of the screen, such as form, list, or textbox, as shown in Listing 12-18.

Listing 12-18. *Using Dynamic Styles in Your resources/polish.css File*

```
p {
   font-color: black;
   font-size: medium;
   background: none;
}
form {
   margin: 5;
   background-color: gray;
   border: none;
   font-size: medium;
}
```

You can also design items that are contained in other items or screens. The style form p selects all text items (of the class StringItem) that are embedded within a form, as shown in Listing 12-19.

Listing 12-19. *Selecting Texts Within a Form with the Dynamic form p Style*

```
form p {
   font-color: black;
   font-size: medium;
   background-color: white;
}
```

Table 12-8 shows the available dynamic styles for `Items` and `Screens`.

Table 12-8. *Available Dynamic Styles*

Class	Selector	Explanation
`StringItem`	`p`	`StringItem` shows text. The `p` selector is used when the item has the appearance mode `PLAIN`.
	`a`	The `a` selector is used when the item has the appearance mode `HYPERLINK`.
	`button`	The `button` selector is used when the item has the appearance mode `BUTTON`.
`ImageItem`	`img`	Shows an image.
`Gauge`	`gauge`	Shows a progress indicator.
`Spacer`	`spacer`	Is used for showing an empty space. Using the `Spacer` item is discouraged, since the spaces can be set for all items with the margin and padding attributes.
`IconItem`	`icon`	Shows an image together with text.
`TextField`	`textfield`	Allows textual input from the user.
`DateField`	`datefield`	Allows the input of dates or times from the user.
`ChoiceGroup`	`choicegroup`	Contains several choice items.
`ChoiceItem`	`listitem`	Shows a single choice. The selector `listitem` is used when this item is contained in an implicit list.
	`radiobox`	The selector `radiobox` is used when the list or choice group has the type `EXCLUSIVE`.
	`checkbox`	The selector `checkbox` is used when the list or choice group has the type `MULTIPLE`.
	`popup`	The selector `popup` is used when the choice group has the type `POPUP`.
`SpriteItem`	`spriteitem`	Contains an animated item.
`List`	`list`	Shows several choice items.
`Form`	`form`	Contains different GUI items.
`TextBox`	`textbox`	Contains a single text input field.
`TabbedForm`	`tabbedform`	A form with several tabs.
`FramedForm`	`framedform`	A form with several frames.

Extending Styles

You can also extend other styles. The child style then inherits all the attributes of the extended style. You can use this mechanism to keep the basic design in one or few style definitions while doing the actual design by extending the basic design. This saves you a lot of writing work and allows you to change the design more easily. In Listing 12-20, the `.highscoreScreen` style inherits all attributes of the `.mainStyle`, but the `font-color` and `background-color` attributes are specified differently.

Listing 12-20. *Extending Styles Saves Work and Allows You to Change the Basic Design in One Place*

```
.mainScreen {
   margin: 10;
   font-color: black;
   font-size: medium;
   font-style: italic;
   background-color: gray;
}

.highscoreScreen extends mainScreen {
   font-color: white;
   background-color: black;
}
```

Reviewing CSS Syntax

The CSS syntax of J2ME Polish is simple, but you need to obey some rules.

Structure of a CSS Declaration

Every style starts with the selector followed by an opening curved parenthesis, a number of attribute-value pairs, and a closing curved parenthesis.

The selector can consist of several item names and contain an `extends` clause.

Each attribute-value pair needs to end with a semicolon.

Naming

Styles can use any name, as long as it consists of alphanumeric and underline (_) characters only. Names are not case-sensitive. Static styles need to start with a dot. Static styles must not use the names of dynamic or predefined styles. All Java keywords, such as `class`, `int`, or `boolean`, are not allowed as style names.

Grouping of Attributes

You can group attributes for easier handling. The styles `.mainScreen` and `.helpScreen` in Listing 12-21 use the semantically equivalent font definition. The grouping does not change the meaning of the attributes, but it makes the declarations more readable for humans.

Listing 12-21. *Grouping CSS Attributes*

```
.mainScreen {
   padding: 5;
   font-color: black;
   font-size: medium;
   font-style: italic;
   font-face: system;
}

.helpScreen {
   margin: 5;
   background-color: yellow;
   font {
      color: black;
      size: medium;
      style: italic;
      face: system;
   }
}
```

Referring to Other Styles

When you refer to another style, you don't need to write the dots of static styles. You refer to other styles, for example, after the `extends` keyword or in attributes such as `title-style`, `focused-style`, and so on.

Comments

You can insert comments at any place by starting them with `/*` and stopping them with `*/`. Everything between these boundaries is ignored, as shown in Listing 12-22.

Listing 12-22. *Using Comments in the polish.css File*

```
/**
  * this style designs the main screen:
  **/
.mainScreen {
   /* defining the color of a font: */
   font-color: black;
   /* sizes are small, medium, and large: */
   font-size: medium;
   /* styles are plain, bold, italic, or underlined: */
   font-style: italic;
   /* the face can either be system, proportional, or monospace: */
   font-face: system;
}
```

Common Design Attributes

In each style, you can use some common attributes regardless of what item or screen you actually design with that style. In the following sections, you will learn how you can use these general attributes.

Structure of the polish.css File

The *polish.css* file can contain different sections:

- **The colors section**: The `colors` section contains the definition of colors.
- **The fonts section**: The `fonts` section contains font definitions that you can reference in several styles.
- **The backgrounds section**: The `backgrounds` section contains background definitions that can be used by several styles.
- **The borders section**: The `borders` section contains definition of borders for several styles.
- **The rest**: The rest of *polish.css* contains the actual style definitions.

You can reference the defined colors, fonts, backgrounds, and borders in the actual style definitions. This makes changes easy, since you need to change the value in only one place.

Structure of a Style Definition

Each style can contain several common attribute groups:

- **margin**: The gap between items
- **padding**: The gap between the border and the content of an item
- **font**: The used content font and its color
- **layout**: The layout of the items
- **background**: The definition of the `Item`'s or `Screen`'s background
- **border**: The definition of the `Item`'s or `Screen`'s border
- **before and after**: Elements that should be inserted before or after the items.
- **min-width and max-width**: The width of `Items`
- **focused-style**: The style that is used when the `Item` is focused
- **Specific attributes**: Any attributes for specific GUI items

Listing 12-23 demonstrates what a complete *polish.css* file can look like.

Listing 12-23. *A Complete polish.css File*

```
colors {
   bgColor:  rgb( 132,143,96 );
   highlightedBgColor:  rgb( 238,241,229 );
   highlightedFontColor: rgb( 238,241,229 );
   fontColor: rgb( 30, 85, 86 );
}

borders {
   thinBorder {
      type: round-rect;
      arc: 8;
      color: fontColor;
   }
}

backgrounds {
   imageBackground {
      color: highlightedBgColor;
      image: url( bg.png );
   }
}

/* The design of the title */
title {
   padding: 2;
   margin-top: 0;
   margin-bottom: 5;
   margin-left: 0;
   margin-right: 0;
   font-face: proportional;
   font-size: large;
   font-style: bold;
   font-color: highlightedFontColor;
   background-color: bgColor;
   border: thinBorder;
   layout: horizontal-center | horizontal-expand;
}

/* The design of the currently selected item */
focused {
   padding: 5;
   background {
      type: round-rect;
      arc: 8;
```

```
        color: highlightedBgColor;
        border-color: fontColor;
        border-width: 2;
    }
    font {
        style: bold;
        color: fontColor;
        size: small;
    }
    layout: expand | center;
    after: url( checked.png );
}

/* The design of the main menu screen */
.mainScreen {
    padding: 5;
    padding-left: 15;
    padding-right: 15;
    background: imageBackground;
    layout: horizontal-expand | horizontal-center | vertical-center;
    columns: 2;
    columns-width: equal;
    menubar-color: fontColor;
    show-text-in-title: true;
}
```

The CSS Box Model: Margins and Paddings

All GUI items support the standard CSS box model, as shown in Figure 12-8.

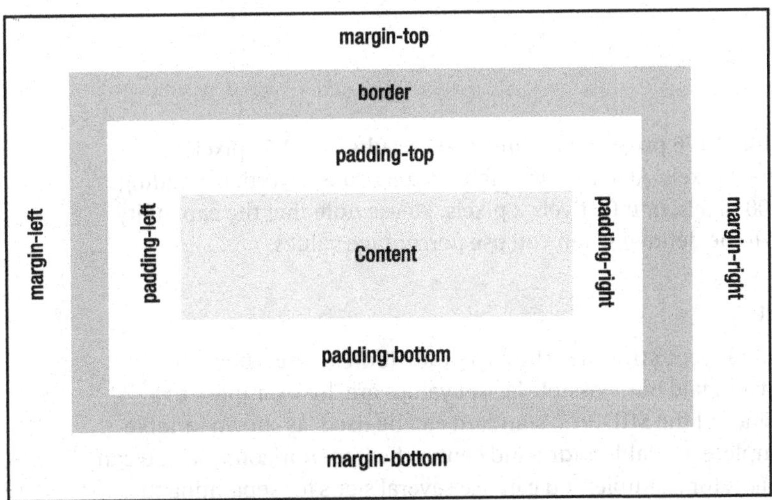

Figure 12-8. *The CSS box model of J2ME Polish*

The *margin* describes the gap to other GUI items. The *padding* describes the gap between the border of the item and the actual content of that item.

The `margin` and `padding` attributes define the default gaps for the left, right, top, and bottom elements. Any margin has the default value of 0 pixels, and any padding defaults to 1 pixel. Next to the left, right, top, and bottom padding, J2ME Polish also knows the vertical and horizontal paddings. These define the gaps between different content sections. The gap between the label of an item and the actual content is defined by the horizontal padding. Another example is the icon, which consists of an image and a text. Depending on the alignment of the image, either the vertical or the horizontal padding fills the space between the icon image and the icon text.

In Listing 12-24, the top, right, and bottom margins are 5 pixels, and the left margin is 10 pixels.

Listing 12-24. *Defining Simple Margins*

```
.myStyle {
   margin: 5;
   margin-left: 10;
   font-color: black;
}
```

You can also use percentage values. Percentage values for top, bottom, and vertical attributes relate to the height of the display. Percentage values for left, right, and horizontal attributes relate to the width of the display. Listing 12-25 demonstrates this.

Listing 12-25. *Defining Percentage Paddings*

```
.myStyle {
   padding-left: 2%;
   padding-right: 2%;
   padding-vertical: 1%;
   margin-left: 10;
   font-color: black;
}
```

When the device has a width of 176 pixels, a padding of 2% results into 3.52 pixels, meaning effectively a padding of 3 pixels. At a display height of 208 pixels, a vertical padding of 1% results in a padding of 2.08 pixels, or effectively 2 pixels. Please note that the capability `ScreenSize` of the device needs to be defined when you use percentage values.

Aligning the Items with Layout

You can align your items with the `layout` attribute. The `layout` attribute defines how the affected item should be aligned and laid out. Possible layout values are, for example, `left`, `right`, and `center`. All layout values of the MIDP 2.0 standard can be used, as shown in Table 12-9. If you want to use the complete available width and center the item horizontally, you can specify `layout: center | expand;`, for example. You can use several signs for separating the `layout` values: use the `||`, `|`, `or`, or `and` operator.

Table 12-9. *Available Layout Values*

Layout	Alternative Names	Explanation
`left`		The affected items should be left-aligned.
`right`		The affected items should be right-aligned.
`center`	`horizontal-center`, `hcenter`	The affected items should be centered horizontally.
`expand`	`horizontal-expand`, `hexpand`	The affected items should use the whole available width (that is, should fill the complete row).
`shrink`	`horizontal-shrink`, `hshrink`	The affected items should use the minimum width possible.
`top`		The affected items should be top-aligned.
`bottom`		The affected items should be bottom-aligned.
`vcenter`	`vertical-center`	The affected items should be centered vertically.
`vexpand`	`vertical-expand`	The affected items should use the whole available height (that is, should fill the complete column).
`vshrink`	`vertical-shrink`	The affected items should use the minimum height possible.
`newline-after`		Items following an item with a `newline-after` layout should be placed on the next line. Only relevant when you use the `midp2` view type.
`newline-before`		The affected items should always start on a new line (when there are any items in front of it). Only relevant when you use the `midp2` view type.
`plain`	`default`, `none`	No specific layout should be used; instead, the default behavior should be used. Such a layout does not need to be defined explicitly, but it can be useful to overwrite a basic setting when you extend another style.

Colors

You can define colors in the `colors` section and in each attribute that ends in `-color`, such as `font-color` and `border-color`, for example. You can use predefined colors, RGB definitions, and ARGB definitions.

Predefined Colors

You can use the standard Windows colors directly, such as `background-color: yellow;`, for example. Table 12-10 lists all the available predefined colors.

Table 12-10. *The Predefined Colors of J2ME Polish*

Color	Hex Value
`white`	#FFFFFF
`black`	#000000
`red`	#FF0000
`lime`	#00FF00
`blue`	#0000FF
`green`	#008000
`silver`	#C0C0C0
`gray`	#808080
`yellow`	#FFFF00
`maroon`	#800000
`purple`	#800080
`fuchsia`	#FF00FF
`olive`	#808000
`navy`	#000080
`teal`	#008080
`aqua`	#00FFFF

Another predefined color is `transparent`, which results in a transparent area. `transparent` is supported only by some GUI elements such as the menu bar of a full-screen menu or an image background.

The colors Section

You can define your own color in the `colors` section of the *polish.css* file. You can then reference these colors in your style definitions, as well as in the `fonts`, `border`, and `background` sections. Listing 12-23 already showed the `colors` section in action. By using the `colors` section, you can later change your colors globally in one place.

■ **Tip** You should try to use color names that describe their meaning, not their color. A bad name, for example, is `brightPink`. If you change this color at a later stage to a green tone, your CSS code will look a bit awkward, since it still references `brightPink`. A much better name would be `highlightedBackgroundColor`, for example. This allows you to change the color value without losing the meaning of the color's name.

How to Define Colors

You can define a color in many different ways, as demonstrated in Listing 12-26.

Listing 12-26. *Defining Colors in Different Ways*

```
.myStyle {
   /* the name of the color */
   font-color: white;
   /* an rgb hex value */
   border-color: #80FF80;
   /* a short rgb-hex-value - this is red */
   start-color: #F00;
   /* an alpha-rgb hex value */
   menu-color: #7F80FF80;
   /* a rrr,ggg,bbb value */
   background-color: rgb( 255, 50, 128 );
   /* an rgb-value with percentage */
   fill-color: rgb( 100%, 30%, 50% );
   /* a aaa, rrr, ggg, bbb value */
   label-color: argb( 128, 255, 50, 128 );
}
```

Color names refer to one of the predefined colors or to a color you have defined in the `colors` section: `color: black;` or `color: highlightedBackgroundColor;`.

The hex value defines a color with two hexadecimal digits for each color (RRGGBB). Additionally, the alpha blending component can be added (AARRGGBB): `color: #FF0000;` defines red. `color: #7FFF0000;` defines a half-translucent red.

The shortened hex value defines a color by an RGB value in hexadecimal. Every digit will be doubled to retrieve the full hex value: `color: #F00;` is equivalent to `color: #FF0000;`, `color: #0D2;` is equivalent with `color: #00DD22;`, and so on.

An RGB value starts with `rgb(` and then lists the decimal value of each color from 0 up to 255: `color: rgb( 255, 0, 0 );` defines red, `color: rbg( 0, 0, 255 );` defines blue, and so on. Alternatively, you can use percentage values for RGB colors: `color: rgb( 100%, 0%, 0% );` and `rgb( 100.00%, 0.00%, 0.00% );` both define red.

You can define alpha-RGB colors with the `argb()` construct: `color: argb( 128, 255, 0, 0 );` defines a half-transparent red. For the `argb()` construct, percentage values can be used as well.

Alpha Blending

You can define colors with alpha blending with hexadecimal or `argb()` definitions (see the previous section). An alpha value of 0 results in fully transparent pixels, whereas the value FF (or 255 or 100%) results in fully opaque pixels. Some devices such as Nokia phones and most MIDP 2.0 devices support values between 0 and FF, resulting in translucent colors. Colors with an alpha channel can be used only by specific GUI items. Please refer to the documentation of the specific design attributes. Not every component supports alpha-RGB values. You can use translucent colors for a simple background, for example, `focused { background-color: argb( 128, 255, 0, 0 ); }`.

Fonts

Many GUI items have text elements that you can design with the font attributes of the corresponding style. Table 12-11 explains the available attributes.

Table 12-11. *Available Font Attributes*

Attribute	Possible Values	Description
`color`	Reference to a color or direct declaration of the color.	Depending on the number of colors the device supports, colors can look differently on the actual device.
`face`	`system` (`default`, `normal`)	The default font face used when the `font-face` or `label-face` attribute is not set.
	`proportional`	A proportional face. This is on some devices actually the same font face as the system font.
	`monospace`	A font face in which each character has the same width.
`size`	`small`	The smallest possible font.
	`medium` (`default`, `normal`)	The default size for texts.
	`large` (`big`)	The largest possible font size.
`style`	`plain` (`default`, `normal`)	The default style.
	`bold`	A bold thick style.
	`italic` (`cursive`)	A cursive style.
	`underlined`	Not really a style, just an underlined text.
`bitmap`	The name of the bitmap font. The extension *.bmf* is not needed.	With the `bitmap` attribute, you can use a bitmap font rather than the standard system, proportional, and monospace fonts. Please note that bitmap fonts cannot be changed in size, color, or style. See Chapter 10 for a detailed discussion of bitmap fonts.

Listing 12-27 shows you how to specify font settings. In this listing, you could skip the `face` and `size` attributes, since they define the default behavior anyhow.

Listing 12-27. *Setting a Specific Font for the Currently Selected Item*

```
focused {
   font-color: white;
   font-face: default; /* same as system or normal */
   font-size: default; /* same as medium or normal */
   font-style: bold;
   background-color: highlightedBackgroundColor;
}
```

Bitmap Fonts

You can use bitmap fonts instead of the usual predefined fonts for any text elements such as titles, StringItems, and so on. Please refer to Chapter 10 to learn more about these fonts and how you can create them using the *${polish.home}/bin/fonteditor* tool.

You can integrate bitmap fonts with the font-bitmap attribute. You don't need to give the *.bmf* extension, by the way. Listing 12-28 uses the *china.bmf* font for the currently focused item.

Listing 12-28. *Using a Bitmap Font for the Currently Selected Item*

```
focused {
   font-bitmap: china;
   background-color: highlightedBackgroundColor;
}
```

Labels

All GUI items can have a label that is designed with the predefined style label. You can specify another style by using the label-style attribute, as shown in Listing 12-29. This also demonstrates how you can ensure that there is a line break after the focused label by specifying the newline-after layout in the label-style style.

Listing 12-29. *Using a Different Label Style*

```
focused {
   label-style: focusedLabelStyle;
   font-color: highlightedFontColor;
   background-color: highlightedBackgroundColor;
   border-width: 2;
}
.focusedLabelStyle {
   font-color: highlightedLabelColor;
   background-color: highlightedBackgroundColor;
   border-width: 2;
   layout: left | newline-after;
}
```

■ **Tip** You can use the max-width CSS attribute for limiting the widths or labels, as well as the actual items, so that both fit into a single line. Use this feature for creating clean designs without using a table.

---

before and after Attributes

You can insert images before and after any GUI items by using the before and after attributes. Listing 12-30 adds a heart picture after the currently focused item. You can view the result in Figure 12-9.

Listing 12-30. *Adding an Image After the Currently Focused Item*

```
focused {
   font-color: highlightedFontColor;
   background: none;
   border-type: round-rect;
   border-width: 2;
   border-color: highlightedBorderColor;
   after: url( heart.png );
}
```

Figure 12-9. *Using the after attribute for adding a heart to the currently focused item*

Backgrounds and Borders

You can use background and a border for every item or screen just by defining it in the appropriate style. Many types of backgrounds and borders are available, and some are even animated. Listing 12-31 uses a simple red background and black border for the title.

Listing 12-31. *Using a Simple Background for the Title*

```
title {
   font-color: highlightedFontColor;
   background-color: red;
   border-color: black;
   border-width: 2;
}
```

If you want to use more complex types, you need to define the `background-type` or `border-type` explicitly, for example, `background-type: pulsating;`.

Designing Borders

Many different border types use specific CSS attributes. When you want to use a border other than the default simple border, you need to specify the `border-type` attribute. Use the `border: none;` declaration when you extend another style that declares a border and you don't want any border for the child style.

Please refer to the appendix for learning the details of all available borders, such as the `round-rect`, `circle`, or `bottom` border.

Designing Backgrounds

You can choose between a great number of different backgrounds for your designs. When you deploy a background other than the default simple background or the image background, you need to declare the `background-type` attribute. When you extend another style and want to remove the background settings, you can use the `background: none;` declaration. The appendix describes details of all available backgrounds.

■ **Tip** Make sure to check out the online documentation at *http://www.j2mepolish.org/documentation.html* for learning about any new backgrounds that are now available.

Designing Screens

The MIDP user interface consists of screens such as `List` or `Form` that in turn contain GUI items such as `StringItem` or `TextField`. In the following sections, you will learn all the tricks for making the most out of your screens.

Designing the Screen Background

Designing the background of the screen is easy: just choose one of the available backgrounds and apply it to the screen style. A popular option is to use an image as the background. Since the background is always painted from the very top to the very bottom of the screen (regardless of whether there is a title or a commands menu present), you need to take this into account. Figure 12-10 shows the used background image, and Figure 12-11 shows the background in action in a `List` screen. You can even use animated backgrounds like the "pulsating-circles" background.

Figure 12-10. *The background image used for a screen*

Figure 12-11. *The background within a List screen*

Designing Titles

When you have activated the full-screen mode for your application, you need to design the title of your screen. In the title you can use all the common design attributes such as font and background settings. If you like, you can even use animated backgrounds for the title. You can move the title by setting the margins; refer to the forthcoming "Designing Lists" section for an example where the title is moved to a lower place.

Designing the Menu Bar and the Menu

Menu bars contain the commands of the screen. You can design the menu along with the menu bar when you have activated the full-screen mode for your application. J2ME Polish lets you choose between the standard menu bar and the extended menu bar. In contrast to the usual one, the extended menu bar allows you to design some additional details but requires about 2KB more JAR space.

Designing the Menu

When several commands are available, they will be grouped together into the Options menu. When you now press the left soft button, the menu will open.

You can design the opened menu with the `menu` style, whereas you design the items contained in the menu with the `menuitem` style by default—or with the `menu` style, in case you haven't defined the `menuitem` style at all.

You can design the currently focused element inside the opened menu with the `focused` style. Since the `focused` style is used for all focused elements anywhere by default, you might want to use a different style. You can do this by setting the `focused-style` attribute in the `menu` style.

Listing 12-32 illustrates how to use all these concepts.

Listing 12-32. *Designing the Menu*

```
menu {
   margin-left: 2;
   padding: 2;
   background {
```

```
        type: round-rect;
        color: highlightedBackgroundColor;
        border-width: 2;
        border-color: backgroundColor;
    }
    font-style: bold;
    font-color: highlightedFontColor;
    focused-style: .menuFocused;
    menubar-color: backgroundColor;
}

menuItem {
    margin-top: 2;
    padding: 2;
    padding-left: 5;
    font {
        color: black;
        size: medium;
        style: bold;
    }
    layout: left;
}

.menuFocused extends .menuItem {
    background-color: backgroundColor;
    font-color: highlightedFontColor;
    layout: left | horizontal-expand;
    after: url( dot.png );
}
```

Figure 12-12 shows you the opened menu of the application in action.

You can also change the names of the Options, Select, and Cancel commands, as explained in the "Building Localized Applications" section of Chapter 7.

Figure 12-12. *The opened menu in action*

Designing the Normal Menu Bar

You can design the normal bar using the predefined `menu` style. The font settings in this style render the actual commands, and the CSS attribute `menubar-color` defines the color of the menu bar. The color can have any setting including `transparent`, which is useful when the background of the corresponding screen should be shown instead of the menu bar. The `menubar-color` defaults to white, by the way. When this attribute is also defined in a screen style, it will override the setting in the `menu` style for the corresponding screen. Listing 12-33 shows you how you can use `black` for the normal screens while using a transparent menu bar for the screen with the `.mainScreen` style.

Listing 12-33. *Using Different Colors for the Menu Bar*

```
menu {
   margin-left: 2;
   padding: 2;
   background {
      type: round-rect;
      color: highlightedBackgroundColor;
      border-width: 2;
      border-color: bgColor;
   }
   font-style: bold;
   focused-style: .menuFocused;
   font-color: highlightedFontColor;
   menubar-color: black;
}

.mainScreen {
   background-image: url( bg.png );
   /* use a transparent menubar for screens with this style,
      so that the bg.png image is shown in the menubar as well: */
   menubar-color: transparent;
}
```

Figure 12-13 shows the main screen with the transparent menu bar on the left and another screen with the default black menu bar on the right.

Designing the Extended Menu Bar

You can use the extended menu bar in cases when the design possibilities of the normal menu bar are not sufficient for you. In contrast to the normal menu bar, the extended menu bar is a full-blown item and can, therefore, be designed just like any other item. The price for using the extended menu bar is to have an additional 2KB classfile in your JAR.

Figure 12-13. *The transparent menu bar (left) on the main screen and the black menu bar (right) on another screen*

For using the extended menu bar instead of the normal one, you need to set the `polish.MenuBar.useExtendedMenuBar` preprocessing variable to `true` in the `<variables>` section of the *build.xml* file, as shown in Listing 12-34.

Listing 12-34. *Activating the Extended Menu Bar*

```
<j2mepolish>
   <info
      license="GPL"
      name="Roadrunner"
      vendorName="A reader."
      version="0.0.1"
      jarName="${polish.vendor}-${polish.name}-roadrunner.jar"
   />
   <deviceRequirements>
      <requirement name="Identifier" value="Generic/midp1" />
   </deviceRequirements>
   <build
         usePolishGui="true"
      >
      <midlet class="com.apress.roadrunner.Roadrunner" />
            <variables>
               <!-- activate the GUI for Series 60 devices  -->
               <variable
                  name="polish.MenuBar.useExtendedMenuBar"
                  value="true" />
            </variables>
   </build>
   <emulator />
</j2mepolish>
```

You can design the extended menu bar with the predefined styles `menubar`, `leftcommand`, and `rightcommand`, as shown in Table 12-12. Table 12-13 lists the additional attributes supported by the `menubar` style.

Table 12-12. *Predefined Styles for the Extended Menu Bar*

Style	Description
`menubar`	Designs the menu bar itself.
`leftcommand`	Designs the left command (Options, Select, and user-defined commands). Accepts all attributes of the `IconItem`.
`rightcommand`	Designs the right command (Cancel and user-defined `Command.BACK` or `CANCEL` commands). Accepts all attributes of the `IconItem`.

Table 12-13. *Additional Attributes of the menubar Style*

Attribute	Required?	Description
`menubar-options-image`	No	Defines the image's URL for the Options image of the extended menu bar.
`menubar-select-image`	No	Defines the image's URL for the Select image of the extended menu bar.
`menubar-cancel-image`	No	Defines the image's URL for the Cancel image of the extended menu bar.
`menubar-show-image-and-text`	No	Determines whether the text should be shown as well in the menu bar when an image has been defined for the corresponding action. Defaults to `false`.

Listing 12-35 demonstrates the design of the extended menu bar.

Listing 12-35. *Designing the Extended Menu Bar*

```
menubar {
   margin-top: -10;
   margin-bottom: 0;
   margin-left: 2;
   margin-right: 2;
   padding: 1;
   background: none;
   menubar-options-image: url( options.png );
   menubar-select-image: url( checked.png );
   /*
   menubar-show-image-and-text: true;
   menubar-cancel-image: url( cancel.png );
   */
}
```

```
leftcommand {
   padding: 2;
   padding-left: 4;
   padding-right: 4;
   padding-horizontal: 4;
   padding-bottom: 0;
   font-color: fontColor;
   font-style: bold;
   background: none;
}

rightcommand {
   padding: 2;
   padding-left: 4;
   padding-right: 4;
   padding-horizontal: 4;
   padding-bottom: 0;
   font-color: fontColor;
   font-style: bold;
   background {
      type: round-rect;
      color: highlightedBgColor;
      border-color: fontColor;
      border-width: 1;
   }
}
```

Figure 12-14 shows the result of Listing 12-35. You can even use animations for the menu bar, the left command, and the right command.

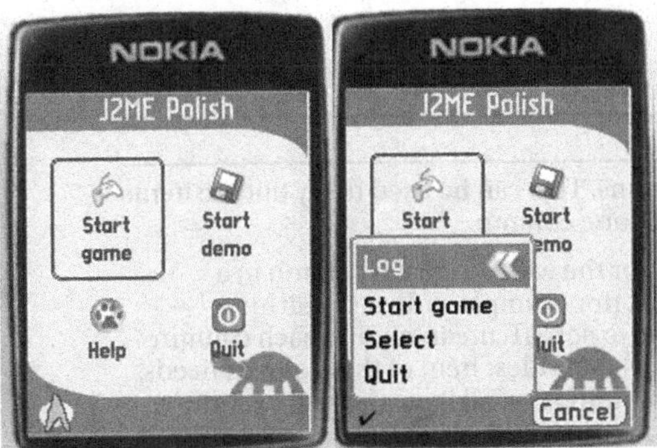

Figure 12-14. *The extended menu bar using images instead of the usual Option and Select commands*

Arranging Items on a Screen

Usually J2ME Polish arranges each GUI item on its own row, as shown in Figure 12-15. You can change the arrangement of the items either by using the `view-type` attribute or by using a tabular layout with the `columns` and `columns-width` attributes.

You can apply view types to any screens that contain items, for example, `Lists` or `Forms`. Several view types are available, which are usually defined in a screen style, for example, `.mainScreen { view-type: dropping; }`. You can use either a (predefined) name of the view type or the fully qualified classname of that type, which needs to extend the `de.enough.polish.ui.ContainerView` class. View types are responsible for the arrangement of items and can even animate the items.

Figure 12-15. *Unless told otherwise, J2ME Polish arranges each item on its own row.*

Using Tables

You can use tables for arranging all screen items neatly into cells by using the `columns` attribute in the screen's style. Table 12-14 explains the `columns` as well as `columns-width` attributes in detail.

Table 12-14. *Attributes for Table Arrangements*

Attribute	Required?	Description
`columns`	No	The number of columns. This can be used to lay out the items in a table. Defaults to one column.
`columns-width`	No	Either `normal`, `equal`, or the width for each column in a comma-separated list (for example, `columns-width: 60,60,100;`). Defaults to `normal`, meaning that each column uses as much space as the widest item of that column needs. The `equal` leads to columns that all have the same width. The explicit list of column widths results in the usage of those widths.

Listing 12-36 shows you an example of how to apply these attributes, and Figure 12-16 shows the result.

Listing 12-36. *Applying a Table Arrangement to the Input Screen*

```
.inputScreen {
   columns: 2;
   columns-width: 52,110;
}
```

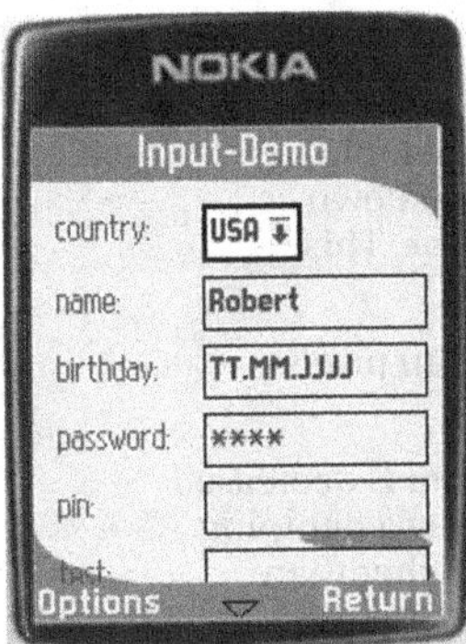

Figure 12-16. *Using a table arrangement with two columns*

Caution You cannot use the `columns` attribute along with a view type. When you use a view type, it is solely responsible for the arrangement of the items.

When you use explicit tables, you need to add labels and actual items separately to a form. This complicates the programming a bit and makes it harder to port existing applications to the J2ME Polish GUI. You can, therefore, alternatively use the `min-width` and `max-width` attributes for setting the exact width of labels and items. Listing 12-37 shows how you can achieve the same design as in Figure 12-16 by adjusting the label and the `.inputField` style (the latter being used for the input fields shown in Figure 12-16).

Listing 12-37. *Achieving a Tabular Arrangement with the min-width and max-width CSS Attributes*

```
.inputField {
   min-width: 110;
   max-width: 110;
}

label {
   min-width: 52;
   max-width: 52;
}
```

dropping View

The `dropping` view shows an animation of dropping and bouncing items. You can activate it by setting the `view-type` to `dropping`. Table 12-15 lists all additional attributes of this view.

Table 12-15. *Additional Attributes of the dropping View Type*

Attribute	Required?	Explanation
`droppingview-speed`	No	The speed in pixels per animation step. The default speed is 10.
`droppingview-repeat-animation`	No	Defines whether the animation should be repeated each time the screen is shown. Possible values are `true` and `false`. This defaults to `false`.
`droppingview-maximum`	No	The maximum bouncing height in pixels. This defaults to 30.
`droppingview-damping`	No	The value by which the maximum is decreased for each following item. By having a damping, the top items seem to bounce higher than lower ones. The default damping is 10.
`droppingview-maxperiode`	No	The maximum allowed number of bounces. This defaults to 5.

Listing 12-38 shows how to use the `dropping` view for your main screen, and Figure 12-17 shows it in action.

Listing 12-38. *Using the dropping View for Your Main Screen*

```
.mainScreen {
   padding-left: 5;
   padding-right: 5;
   view-type: dropping;
   droppingview-speed: 15;
   droppingview-damping: 5;
   droppingview-maxperiode: 2;
}
```

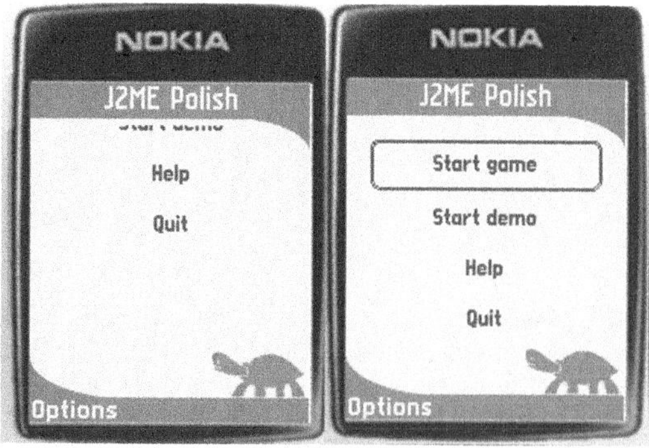

Figure 12-17. *The dropping view in action*

shuffle View

The `shuffle` view animates the items by moving them from the left and right side into their final target position. Activate it by setting the `view-type` attribute to `shuffle`. This view supports the additional attributes listed in Table 12-16.

Table 12-16. *Additional Attributes of the shuffle View Type*

Attribute	Required?	Explanation
`shuffleview-speed`	No	The speed in pixels per animation step. The default speed is 10.
`shuffleview-repeat-animation`	No	Defines whether the animation should be repeated each time the screen is shown. Possible values are `true` and `false`. This defaults to `false`.

Listing 12-39 shows how to use the `shuffle` view, and Figure 12-18 gives you an idea of what it looks like.

Listing 12-39. *Using the shuffle View Type for Your Main Screen*

```
.mainScreen {
   padding-left: 5;
   padding-right: 5;
   view-type: shuffle;
   shuffleview-speed: 15;
}
```

Figure 12-18. *The shuffle view in action*

midp2 View

The `midp2` view arranges the items just like the MIDP 2.0 standard encourages it: the items are all lined up into one row until there is not enough space anymore or until an item with a `newline-after` or `newline-before` layout is inserted. Since this often leads to cluttered and untidy interfaces, J2ME Polish usually puts each item on its own line (or cell when columns are used). The MIDP 2.0 arrangement has, however, one important advantage: you can view more content per screen. You can activate the `midp2` view by specifying the `midp2 view-type`. This view supports no additional attributes. Figure 12-19 shows it on a `Form`.

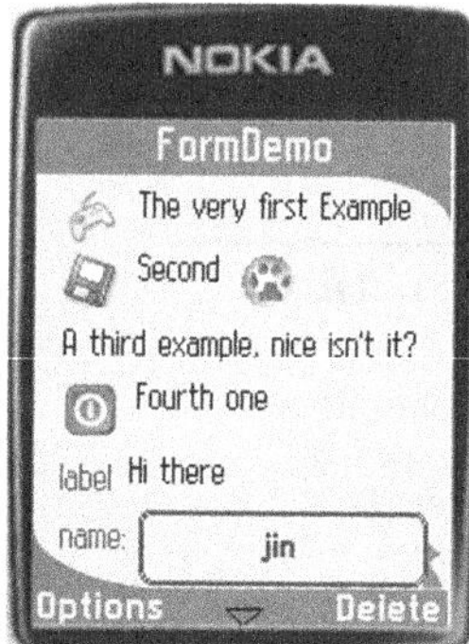

Figure 12-19. *The midp2 view in action*

Designing the Scroll Indicator

The scroll indicator displays at the bottom of a screen whenever there are more items on a screen than can be shown. You can set the color of the indicator with the `scrollindicator-color` attribute of the screen's style. The color defaults to black; see Figure 12-19 for an example.

■ **Tip** If you want to hide the scroll indicator for a specific screen, just set the color to the color of the menu bar.

Setting a Foreground Image

Each screen can have a so-called foreground image that is painted on top of all other elements. You can use this feature for displaying a figure that seems to hold the menu options, for example. Table 12-17 summarizes the relevant attributes for setting a foreground image.

Table 12-17. *Additional Attributes for Setting a Foreground Image*

Attribute	Required?	Explanation
`foreground-image`	No	The URL of a image that should be painted at the front of the screen, for example, `foreground-image: url( mascot.png );`.
`foreground-x`	No	The x-position of the foreground image in pixels from the left border.
`foreground-y`	No	The y-position of the foreground image in pixels from the top border.

Listing 12-40 sets the turtle to the very front. The attributes `foreground-x` and `foreground-y` position the image exactly. When you now focus the item on the bottom-right position, the turtle is drawn above the focused element, as shown in Figure 12-20.

Listing 12-40. *Using a Foreground Image on the Main Screen*

```
.mainScreen {
   padding-left: 5;
   padding-right: 5;
   foreground-image: url( turtle.png );
   foreground-x: 112;
   foreground-y: 162;
}
```

Figure 12-20. *The turtle is displayed on top of all other elements, even the focused item.*

Designing Lists

`Lists` contain several items that can be selected. Each list item can contain a text string and an image. You can use an implicit list for your main menu. Exclusive lists allow you to select only one element, whereas multiple lists allow you to select several items.

An interesting option for lists is to show only the image of the embedded items and to use the text of the currently focused item for the title. Listing 12-41 and Figure 12-21 demonstrate this option. In this case, a background image is used for the list, and the actual title is moved downward by setting the appropriate margins. You can set the image for list items with the `icon-image` attribute.

Listing 12-41. *Using the Text of the Currently Focused Item As a Title*

```
title {
   padding: 2;
   margin-top: 32;
   margin-bottom: 2;
   margin-left: 16;
   margin-right: 0;
   font-face: proportional;
```

```
    font-size: large;
    font-style: bold;
    font-color: highlightedFontColor;
    background: none;
    border: none;
    layout: left | horizontal-expand;
}

.mainScreen {
    padding: 5;
    padding-left: 15;
    padding-right: 15;
    background-image: url( bg.png );
    show-text-in-title: true;
    layout: horizontal-expand | horizontal-center | vertical-center;
    columns: 2;
}

.mainCommand {
    padding: 5;
    icon-image: url( %INDEX%.png );
    icon-image-align: center;
}
```

Figure 12-21. *Using the text of the currently focused list item as a title*

Table 12-18 lists the allowed attributes for implicit list items. When you have either a multiple or an exclusive list, you have some additional attributes; refer to the discussion of `ChoiceItems` in Chapter 13.

Table 12-18. *Additional Attributes for List Items*

Attribute	Required?	Explanation
`icon-image`	No	The URL of the image, for example, `icon-image: url(icon.png);`. The keyword `%INDEX%` can be used for adding the position of the icon to the name, for example, `icon-image: url(icon%INDEX%.png);`. The image used for the first icon will be *icon0.png*, the second icon will use the image *icon1.png*, and so on. Defaults to `none`.
`icon-image-align`	No	The position of the image relative to the text. Either `top`, `bottom`, `left`, or `right`. Defaults to `left`, meaning that the image will be drawn left of the text.
`scale-factor`	No	The factor in percent by which the icon image should be scaled when it is focused on a MIDP 2.0 device; for example, `150` for enlarging the image to 1.5 times its size.
`scale-steps`	No	The number of steps used for scaling the icon image, applicable only when the `scale-factor` attribute is used.

Designing Forms

`Forms` can contain any kind of items, even `CustomItems` that you can create for yourself. They support all the common screen attributes, such as `foreground-image`, `view-type`, and so on, so please refer to the previous discussion about the common screen features for learning more about these options.

Designing TabbedForms

`TabbedForms` are just like `Forms`, but they are able to split the screen into several tabs. You can design tabbed forms like a normal form, but you can use the predefined styles `tabbar`, `activetab`, and `inactivetab` to design the additional elements of a tabbed form. The `tabbar` style is responsible for the bar containing the tabs at a whole; the `activetab` style designs the currently active tab, and the `inactivetab` style designs all remaining tabs. You can set the color of the scrolling indicator within the `tabbar` style with the `tabbar-scrolling-indicator-color` attribute, as demonstrated in Listing 12-42. You can see the results in Figure 12-22.

Listing 12-42. *Designing a TabbedForm*

```
tabbar {
   background-color: white;
   layout: expand;
   padding-bottom: 0;
   tabbar-scrolling-indicator-color: black;
}

activetab {
   background-type: round-tab;
   background-color: silver;
   background-arc: 8;
```

```
    font-color: white;
    padding-left: 10;
    padding-right: 8;
}

inactivetab {
    padding-left: 6;
    padding-right: 4;
    margin-left: 2;
    margin-right: 2;
    background-type: round-tab;
    background-color: gray;
    background-arc: 8;
    font-color: silver;
}
```

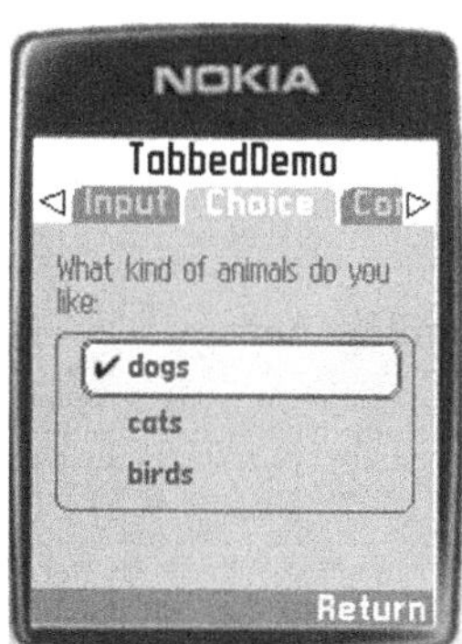

Figure 12-22. *A TabbedForm in action*

Designing FramedForms

FramedForms have a scrollable content area along with the nonscrollable top, bottom, left, and right frames. You can design each frame using the predefined styles topframe, bottomframe, leftframe, and rightframe. Alternatively, you can use the frame style for defining all frames in one style. The right and left frames are one of the few elements that do actually use the vertical-expand and vertical-center layout settings. Listing 12-43 demonstrates the design of a FramedForm with a bottom frame. You can see the FramedForm in action in Figure 12-23.

Listing 12-43. *Designing the Lower Frame in a FramedForm*

```
bottomframe {
    padding: 3;
    background-color: silver;
    layout: expand;
    padding-bottom: 0;
}
```

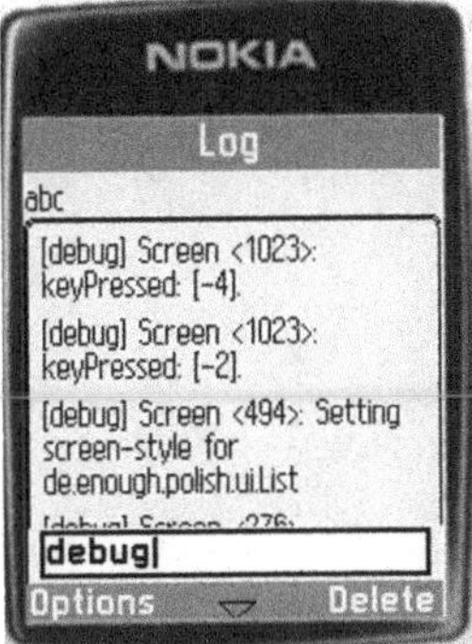

Figure 12-23. *A FramedForm in action*

Designing TextBoxes

`TextBoxes` are used for getting text input from the user. They support all the additional attributes of `TextFields`, so please refer to the following discussions of these fields.

Designing Items

Apart from the common design attributes, some GUI items support additional CSS attributes. With the help of these advanced settings, you can influence the design even more.

Designing String Items

`StringItems` are used quite often and form the basis for many other items such as `TextField`, `DateField`, and `IconItem` (the latter is used internally by J2ME Polish for `Lists`). Apart from the already discussed common attributes, no further attributes are supported by `StringItems`. The most important CSS attributes are the `font` ones. You can even use bitmap fonts for `StringItems`; please refer to the earlier "Fonts" section. If you want to change the line spacing within one `StringItem`, you can use the `padding-vertical` attribute.

Designing Image Items

You can use `ImageItems` for displaying an image within a `Form`. `ImageItems` do not support additional CSS attributes. Since images can also be added by using various backgrounds or using `before` and `after` attributes, you often don't need to use `ImageItems` directly in your application.

Designing Choice Groups

`ChoiceGroups` hold several items of which one or several can be selected. You have access to three kinds of `ChoiceGroups`: exclusive groups in which only one item can be selected, multiple groups in which you can select several items, and pop-up groups that display the currently selected item only when inactive but that "pop up" and show all possibilities when they are activated.

When you design ChoiceGroups, you need to differentiate between the group and the actual items. Listing 12-44 demonstrates how you can use the #style directive and the append() method for applying different styles to the group and the actual item.

Listing 12-44. *Applying Different Styles for the ChoiceGroup and Its Embedded Items*

```
public ChoiceGroup createChoiceGroup( String label, String[] choices ) {
   //#style exclusiveChoiceGroup
   ChoiceGroup group = new ChoiceGroup( label, Choice.EXCLUSIVE );
   for ( int i = 0; i < choices.length; i++ ) {
      String choice = choices[i];
      //#style exclusiveChoiceItem
      group.append( choice, null );
   }
   return group;
}
```

You can set the style of the currently focused item with the focused-style attribute. When you don't specify it, the usual focused style is used instead. Listing 12-45 demonstrates how to set a custom focused style (see the next section). You can also set the number of columns for displaying the ChoiceGroup and even the view-type, which allows you to use animations and other arrangements of the items contained in the group. Table 12-19 lists the available options. For a discussion of the focused-style, view-type, and columns attributes, please refer to the earlier "Designing Screens" section.

Table 12-19. *General Attributes for ChoiceGroups*

Attribute	Required?	Explanation
columns	No	The number of columns. This can be used to lay out the items in a table. Defaults to one column.
columns-width	No	Either normal, equal, or the width for each column in a comma-separated list (for example, columns-width: 60,60,100;). Defaults to normal, meaning that each column uses as much space as the widest item of that column needs. The equal width leads to columns that all have the same width. The explicit list of column widths results in the usage of those widths.
view-type	No	The view type used for this choice group. Please refer to the discussion of view types in the "Designing Screens" section.

Designing Exclusive Choice Groups

Exclusive ChoiceGroups are like radio boxes encountered on web pages: you can select only one item at a time. You can use several additional attributes, which are listed in Table 12-20.

Table 12-20. *Additional Attributes for Items in Exclusive ChoiceGroups*

Attribute	Required	Explanation
icon-image	No	The URL of the image, for example, `icon-image: url( icon.png );`. The keyword `%INDEX%` can be used for adding the position of the item to the name, for example, `icon-image: url( icon%INDEX%.png );`. The image used for the first item will be *icon0.png*, the second item will use the image *icon1.png*, and so on.
icon-image-align	No	The position of the image relative to the text. Either `top`, `bottom`, `left`, or `right`. Defaults to `left`, meaning that the image will be drawn left of the text.
choice-color	No	The color in which the radio box will be painted. Defaults to black.
radiobox-selected	No	The URL of the image for a selected item. Default is a simple image drawn in the defined choice color.
radiobox-plain	No	The URL of the image for a not-selected item. Default is a simple image drawn in the defined choice color. When `none` is given, no image will be drawn for not-selected items. Only the image for selected items will be drawn in that case.
view-type	No	The exclusive `ChoiceGroup` additionally supports the `exclusive` view type that shows only the currently selected item while allowing the user to scroll right and left.

Listing 12-45 shows you a style definition for designing an exclusive `ChoiceGroup`, and Figure 12-24 shows the result.

Listing 12-45. *Designing an Exclusive ChoiceGroup*

```
/* Designing the ChoiceGroup */
.exclusiveChoiceGroup {
   focused-style: choiceGroupFocused;
}

/* Designing the items contained in the ChoiceGroup */
.exclusiveChoiceItem {
   margin: 1; /* compensation for the border of the focused style */
   padding: 3;
   padding-horizontal: 5;
   font-color: fontColor;
   font-style: plain;
   radiobox-selected: url( checked.png );
   radiobox-plain: none;
}
```

```
/* Designing the currently focused item of the ChoiceGroup */
.choiceGroupFocused {
   padding: 3;
   padding-horizontal: 5;
   font-color: fontColor;
   font-style: bold;
   border {
      type: round-rect;
      color: fontColor;
      arc: 8;
   }
   layout: left | expand;
}
```

Figure 12-24. *The exclusive ChoiceGroup with a custom "radio box–selected" image in action*

When you replace the `radiobox` attributes with the setting `choice-color: fontColor;`, you get the design shown in Figure 12-25.

Figure 12-25. *The exclusive ChoiceGroup with the standard selection marker*

Exclusive ChoiceGroups do also support the specialized exclusive view-type. When this view is activated, only the currently selected item is shown. The user can change the selection by scrolling left or right. Listing 12-46 shows how you can apply and adjust this view type with the exclusiveview-arrow-color attribute, and Figure 12-26 shows it in action.

Listing 12-46. *Using the Exclusive View Type*

```
.exclusiveChoiceGroup {
   padding: 2;
   padding-horizontal: 5;
   background: none;
   font-color: fontColor;
   view-type: exclusive;
   exclusiveview-arrow-color: fontColor;
}
```

Figure 12-26. *The exclusive ChoiceGroup with the exclusive view type*

Designing Multiple Choice Groups

Multiple ChoiceGroups allow you to select several items at once. You can design multiple ChoiceGroups just like exclusive ones, with the difference that you need to use checkbox attributes rather than radiobox ones, as Table 12-21 shows.

Table 12-21. *Additional Attributes for Items in Multiple Choice Groups*

Attribute	Required?	Explanation
icon-image	No	The URL of the image, for example, icon-image: url(icon.png);. The keyword %INDEX% can be used for adding the position of the item to the name, for example, icon-image: url(icon%INDEX%.png);. The image used for the first item will be *icon0.png*, the second item will use the image *icon1.png*, and so on.
icon-image-align	No	The position of the image relative to the text. Either top, bottom, left, or right. Defaults to left, meaning that the image will be drawn left of the text.

Continued

Table 12-21. *Continued*

Attribute	Required?	Explanation
`choice-color`	No	The color in which the check box will be painted. Defaults to `black`.
`check box-selected`	No	The URL of the image for a selected item. Default is a simple image drawn in the defined choice color.
`checkbox-plain`	No	The URL of the image for a not-selected item. Default is a simple image drawn in the defined choice color. When `none` is given, no image will be drawn for not-selected items. Only the image for selected items will be drawn in that case.

Listing 12-47 demonstrates how you can select multiple choices, and Figure 12-27 shows you the result.

Listing 12-47. *Designing a Multiple ChoiceGroup*

```
/* Designing the ChoiceGroup */
.multipleChoiceGroup {
   focused-style: choiceGroupFocused;
}

/* Designing the items contained in the ChoiceGroup */
.multipleChoiceItem {
   margin: 1; /* compensation for the border of the focused style */
   padding: 3;
   padding-horizontal: 5;
   font-color: fontColor;
   font-style: plain;
   choice-color: fontColor;
}

/* Designing the currently focused item of the ChoiceGroup */
.choiceGroupFocused {
   padding: 3;
   padding-horizontal: 5;
   font-color: fontColor;
   font-style: bold;
   border {
      type: round-rect;
      color: fontColor;
      arc: 8;
   }
   layout: left | expand;
}
```

Figure 12-27. *The multiple ChoiceGroup with the standard selection marker in action*

Designing Pop-up Choice Groups

Pop-up ChoiceGroups normally show you only the currently selected item. Only when you activate the group by either pressing the fire button or invoking the Select command will all available options be shown. After you have selected an item, the group closes again. Table 12-22 lists the available attributes. In contrast to the multiple and exclusive ChoiceGroups, these attributes apply only to the actual ChoiceGroup style, not to the style of the items contained within the ChoiceGroup.

Table 12-22. *Additional Attributes for Items in Multiple ChoiceGroups*

Attribute	Required?	Explanation
popup-image	No	The URL to the image that should be shown in the closed pop-up group. Per default a simple drop-down image will be used.
popup-color	No	The color for the arrow in the drop-down image of a closed pop-up group. Defaults to black and makes sense only when no pop-up image has been specified.
popup-background-color	No	The color for the background in the drop-down image of a closed pop-up group. Defaults to white and makes sense only when no pop-up image has been specified.

Listing 12-48 shows how to design a pop-up ChoiceGroup, and Figure 12-28 shows it in action.

Listing 12-48. *Designing a Pop-up ChoiceGroup*

```
/* Designing the ChoiceGroup */
.popupChoiceGroup {
   popup-color: fontColor;
   popup-background-color: backgroundColor;
   focused-style: choiceGroupFocused;
}
```

```
/* Designing the items contained in the ChoiceGroup */
.popupChoiceItem {
   margin: 1; /* compensation for the border of the focused style */
   padding: 3;
   padding-horizontal: 5;
   font-color: fontColor;
   font-style: plain;
}

/* Designing the currently focused item of the opened ChoiceGroup */
.choiceGroupFocused {
   padding: 3;
   padding-horizontal: 5;
   font-color: fontColor;
   font-style: bold;
   border {
      type: round-rect;
      color: fontColor;
      arc: 8;
   }
   layout: left | expand;
}
```

Figure 12-28. *The pop-up ChoiceGroup in the closed state (left) and in the opened mode (right)*

Designing Gauge Items

A Gauge shows a progress indicator or can be used to enter a fixed range of numbers. It supports quite a few additional attributes, listed in Table 12-23.

Table 12-23. *Additional Attributes for Gauge Items*

Attribute	Required?	Explanation
`gauge-image`	No	The URL of the image, for example, `gauge-image: url(progress.png);`. When no gauge width is defined, the width of this image will be used instead.
`gauge-color`	No	The color of the progress bar. Defaults to `blue`.
`gauge-width`	No	The width of the gauge element in pixels. When no width is defined, either the available width or the width of the provided image will be used.
`gauge-height`	No	The height of the gauge element in pixels. Defaults to 10. When an image is provided, the height of the image will be used.
`gauge-mode`	No	Either `chunked` or `continuous`. In the continuous mode, only the gauge color will be used, whereas the chunked mode intersects the indicator in chunks. The setting is ignored when an image is provided. Default value is `chunked`.
`gauge-gap-color`	No	The color of gaps between single chunks. Only used in the chunked gauge mode or when a gauge with an indefinite range is used. In the latter case, the provided color will be used to indicate the idle state. Default gap color is `white`.
`gauge-gap-width`	No	The width of gaps in pixels between single chunks. Only used in the chunked gauge mode. Defaults to 3.
`gauge-chunk-width`	No	The width of the single chunks in the chunked gauge mode.
`gauge-show-value`	No	Either `true` or `false`. Determines whether the current value should be shown. This defaults to `true` for all definite gauge items.
`gauge-value-align`	No	Either `left` or `right`. Defines where the current value of the gauge should be displayed. Defaults to `left`, which is left of the actual gauge item.

When the `Gauge` item is used with an indefinite range, the `gauge-gap-color` indicates the idle state. When the "continuous running" state is entered and an image has been specified, the image will "fly" from the left to the right of the indicator. Listing 12-49 shows you how you can apply some of the supported items. Figure 12-29 shows the result.

Listing 12-49. *Designing a Gauge Item*

```
.gaugeItem {
   margin: 0;
   margin-right: 10;
   padding-left: 16;
   border: thinBorder;
   font-size: small;
   font-color: fontColor;
   layout: left | expand;
   gauge-width: 60;
```

```
    gauge-mode: chunked;
    gauge-color: rgb( 86, 165, 255 );
    gauge-gap-color: rgb( 38, 95, 158 );
    gauge-value-align: right;
    gauge-show-value: true;
}
```

Figure 12-29. *The Gauge in action*

Designing Text Fields

You can use a TextField to get user input. You can choose whether the native input methods or a direct input mode should be used. When the native mode is activated, a new input screen will pop up for the user and special input modes such as T9 or handwriting recognition can be used if available on the device. When the direct input mode is used instead, no extra screen will be shown, and J2ME Polish accepts the entered character directly. Table 12-24 lists the additional CSS attributes that are supported by TextFields.

Table 12-24. *Additional Attributes for TextField Items*

Attribute	Required?	Explanation
textfield-width	No	The minimum width of the textfield element in pixels.
textfield-height	No	The minimum height of the textfield element in pixels. Defaults to the height of the used font.
textfield-direct-input	No	Defines whether the direct input mode should be activated. Possible values are either false or true. By default the direct input mode is deactivated (false). You can set the preprocessing variable polish.TextField.useDirectInput for activating the direct input for all TextFields.

Attribute	Required?	Explanation
`textfield-caret-color`	No	The color of the caret that indicates the editing position. This defaults to the color of the used font.
`textfield-caret-char`	No	The character that indicates the editing position. This defaults to the pipe symbol, |.
`textfield-show-length`	No	Determines whether the length of the entered text should be shown during the editing of this field. This has an effect only when the direct input mode is used.

Listing 12-50 shows you how to design a `TextField` item, and Figure 12-30 shows you the result of Listing 12-49.

Listing 12-50. *Designing a TextField Item*

```
.textInput {
   margin: 1;
   padding: 4;
   padding-left: 2;
   padding-right: 2;
   padding-horizontal: 4;
   textfield-direct-input: true;
   font-style: bold;
   font-size: small;
   font-color: fontColor;
   background-color: highlightedBgColor;
   border-color: black;
   layout: left;
   textfield-width: 90;
   datefield-width: 90;
   textfield-caret-color: red;
   textfield-caret-char: >;
   textfield-show-length: true;
   textfield-direct-input: true;
   focused-style: .focusedInput;
}
```

Figure 12-30. *The TextField with direct input in action*

■ **Tip** You can even use bitmap fonts for your `TextField`. Just use the `font-bitmap` attribute for setting the font.

Designing Date Fields

You use `DateFields` for entering dates or times in your application. Currently, the input is done with the use of the native functions so that special input modes can be used (such as T9 or handwriting recognition). The `DateField` supports the additional attributes listed in Table 12-25.

Table 12-25. *Additional Attributes for DateField Items*

Attribute	Required?	Explanation
`datefield-width`	No	The minimum width of the `datefield` element in pixels.
`datefield-height`	No	The minimum height of the `datefield` element in pixels. Defaults to the height of the used font.

Listing 12-51 shows how to design a `DateField` item, and Figure 12-31 demonstrates the design.

Listing 12-51. *Designing a DateField Item*

```
.dateInput {
   margin: 1;
   padding: 4;
   padding-left: 2;
   padding-right: 2;
   padding-horizontal: 4;
   textfield-direct-input: true;
```

```
    font-style: bold;
    font-size: small;
    font-color: fontColor;
    background-color: highlightedBgColor;
    border-color: black;
    layout: left;
    textfield-width: 90;
    datefield-width: 90;
    textfield-caret-color: red;
    textfield-caret-char: >;
    textfield-show-length: true;
    textfield-direct-input: true;
    focused-style: .focusedInput;
}
```

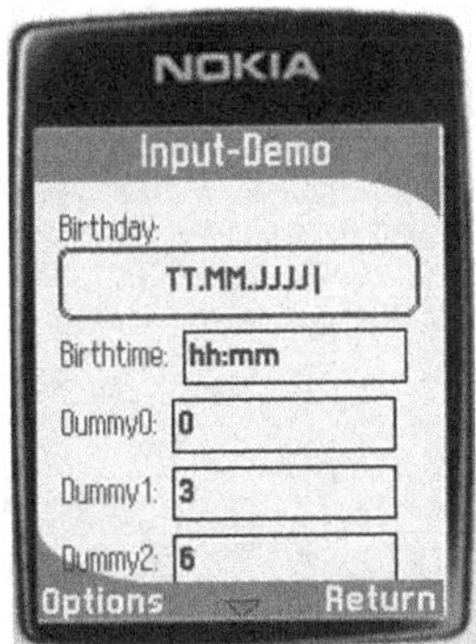

Figure 12-31. *The DateField in action*

Designing Tickers

`Tickers` are the animated texts that scroll through the screen. They are often used for displaying advertisements and, of course, are fully configurable with J2ME Polish. Table 12-26 lists the attributes for `Ticker` items.

Table 12-26. *Additional Attribute for Ticker Items*

Attribute	Required?	Explanation
`ticker-step`	No	The number of pixels by which the ticker is shifted at each update. Defaults to 2 pixels.

Listing 12-52 shows how to design a `Ticker` item, and Figure 12-32 demonstrates it in action.

Listing 12-52. *Designing a Ticker Item*

```
.tickerStyle {
   font-color: fontColor;
   font-size: small;
   border-color: backgroundColor;
   background-color: yellow;
   ticker-step: 4;
}
```

Figure 12-32. *The Ticker in action. The turtle has been moved to the front with the* `foreground-image` *attribute of the screen's style.*

Designing the Focused Item

You can design the currently focused item by using the predefined `focused` style. But you can choose to highlight the focused item in different ways.

Often you will use another background or border setting for indicating that an item has been focused, but you can use other attributes as well. When you have a `List` or a `ChoiceGroup`, for example, you can set the `icon-image` attribute in the normal as well as in the focused style and switch the image to a highlighted version in the focused style.

You can also use the `after` and `before` attributes for inserting an image after or before the currently focused item.

For each `Screen` or `Item`, you can set a different focused style by using the `focused-style` attribute, for example, `focused-style: .myExtraFocusedStyle;`. This mechanism allows you to use different styles, but make sure you don't confuse your users by having too many different ways of showing that an item is focused. Use this mechanism to distinguish between input fields and buttons in one `Form`, for example.

Using Animations

You can use animated background and animated items at several positions in your application. The most important place is the currently focused item, but you can also use animated backgrounds for your screen or use animated view types for your screen or your menu. Other possible places are the title as well as the extended menu bar of the current screen. Please use animations sparsely so that the usability of your application is not harmed. Depending on your application, you will be able to use different levels of animated and "crazy" designs—whether you create mobile banking software or the latest games can make a difference in the users' expectations. Your mileage may vary.

You can include an animation whenever you show a different screen in your application by specifying the `screen-change-animation` attribute. Such animations help you to create a very lively application. Table 12-27 lists all available values along with a brief description.

Table 12-27. *Possible Screen Change Animations*

Animation	Explanation
`left`	Moves the new screen from the left to the right. You can specify the speed in pixels per animation phase with the `left-screen-change-animation-speed` attribute.
`right`	Moves the screen from the right to the left. Set the speed in pixels per animation phase with the `right-screen-change-animation-speed` attribute.
`top`	Moves the new screen from the top to the bottom. You can specify the speed in pixels per animation phase with the `top-screen-change-animation-speed` attribute.
`bottom`	Moves the new screen from the bottom to the top. You can specify the speed with the `bottom-screen-change-animation-speed` attribute.
`zoomOut`	Starts with a magnified and almost transparent screen and zooms out of it gradually.
`zoomInAndHide`	Magnifies the previously shown screen and makes it more transparent in each animation phase.

Summary

Well done! You have mastered the most complex part of J2ME Polish—the user interface. You have now learned how you can program, control, and design the GUI for creating truly professional applications. Just to repeat the main lessons: you program the GUI just like the normal `javax.microedition.lcdui` API, but you need to ensure that you use proper `import` statements. For controlling the GUI, you can set various preprocessing variables in your project's *build.xml* file. Last but not least, you can design the user interface outside the application code with the *resources/polish.css* file.

In the next chapter, you will finish the J2ME Polish part of this book by learning how you can extend this framework. J2ME Polish contains various hooks so that you can extend it quite easily, whether you want to add your own preprocessor or your own GUI background.

CHAPTER 13

Extending J2ME Polish

In this chapter:

- Discover how to integrate your own tools for each phase of the development cycle: preprocessing, compiling, postcompiling, obfuscating, and packaging.
- Learn how to extend the J2ME Polish GUI by providing your own backgrounds, borders, custom items, and image loader.
- Learn how to extend the logging framework by providing your own log handlers.

J2ME Polish is powerful, but sometimes you may encounter a situation that requires specific adjustments. In this chapter, you will learn how you can extend J2ME Polish to realize your own build solutions and your own user interface extensions.

Extending the Build Tools

In the following sections, you will learn how you can extend the build phases of J2ME Polish. By extending the build process, you can satisfy your specific company needs such as using a specific compiler, your own preprocessing directives, or your own resource assembling strategies. You can also use this mechanism to create (and sell) extensions of J2ME Polish for other developers.

Understanding the Extension Mechanism

All build extensions share some capabilities, such as a common superclass and the possibility to accept parameters. Also, the registration of extensions works the same way for all kinds of build extensions. I will discuss these common characteristics in the following sections.

Recapitulating the Build Phases

During the build process, J2ME Polish goes through various build phases, as discussed in Chapter 7. You can extend each phase by implementing your own extension or by providing and calling another Ant target in your *build.xml* script.

Table 13-1 summarizes the build phases along with their extension points. One extension that is not tied to a specific build phase is the property function, which can be used not only in the preprocessing phase but also in various elements of your *build.xml* script.

Table 13-1. *Extension Points of Build Phases*

Phase	Element	Description
Preprocess	`<preprocessor>`	This changes the source code of the application according to preprocessing directives.
Compile	`<compiler>`	This compiles the preprocessed source code.
Postcompile	`<postcompiler>`	In the postcompile step, the binary bytecode can be processed and changed.
Obfuscate	`<obfuscator>`	The obfuscation step removes unnecessary code and shrinks the remaining code.
Preverify	`<preverifier>`	The bytecode of MIDP applications needs to be preverified before the application can be installed.
Package	`<resourcecopier>`	The resource copier copies all device- and locale-specific resources to a temporary directory before these are compressed into a JAR file.
Package	`<packager>`	The packager is responsible for creating a JAR file from all resources and classes.
Finalize	`<finalizer>`	You can use the finalizer for processing the finished JAR and JAD files.
Emulate	`<emulator>`	You can test your application in a simulator in this phase.
Property function		You can define and use your own property functions.

Using the Extension Superclass

All build extensions have a common superclass; they extend the `de.enough.polish.Extension` class.

The `Extension` class contains references to `org.apache.tools.ant.Project`, which represents your Ant *build.xml* script; `de.enough.polish.Environment`, which holds all settings of the current target device as well as user-defined variables; and references to the definition and settings of the extension, which you can use to parameterize your extension.

All extensions need to implement the `public void execute( de.enough.polish.Device, java.util.Locale, de.enough.polish.Environment )` method, which is invoked when the build phase is reached (for example, during the preprocessing, postcompiling, or obfuscation phase). Most subclasses map this call to a more specialized call; the `PostCompiler` forwards the call to the `postCompile( java.io.File classesDir, Device device )` method, for example.

Each extension can influence other build phases by overriding the `public void initialize( Device, Locale, Environment )` and `public void finalize( Device, Locale, Environment )` methods. During the initialization, you can set preprocessing variables and symbols by calling the `setVariable( String, String )`, `setSymbol( String )`, or `set( Object )` method of the `Environment` instance. You can evaluate and use these settings in the preprocessing phase, or you can use them to influence other build phases.

Configuring Build Extensions

You can configure most extensions in your *build.xml* script by setting nested `<parameter>` elements. Listing 13-1 shows how to configure a custom preprocessor with the parameters `logfile` and `enableLogging`.

Listing 13-1. *Configuring a Preprocessor Extension*

```
<preprocessor class="com.apress.preprocess.FullScreenPreprocessor">
   <parameter name="logfile" value="fullscreen.log" />
   <parameter name="enableLogging" value="true" />
</preprocessor>
```

The `<parameter>` element accepts the attributes `name`, `value`, `file`, `if`, and `unless`, as listed in Table 13-2.

Table 13-2. *Attributes of <parameter> Elements*

<parameter> Attribute	Required?	Explanation
`name`	Yes, unless `file` is used	The name of the variable.
`value`	Yes, unless `file` is used	The value of the variable.
`file`	No	The file that contains several parameters. In the file, the `name` and `value` parameters need to be separated by equals characters (=). Empty lines and lines starting with a hash mark (#) are ignored.
`if`	No	The Ant property that needs to be `true` or the preprocessing term that needs the result `true` for this parameter to be included.
`unless`	No	The Ant property that needs to be `false` or the preprocessing term that needs the result `false` for this parameter to be included.

When you want to accept parameters in your extension, you have two options:

- You can implement the `public void setParameters( de.enough.polish.Variable[] parameters, java.io.File baseDir )` method.
- You can implement the method `set[parameter-name]` for each supported parameter. This method can accept either a `String`, a `boolean`, or a `File` as input. For the parameters in Listing 13-1, a good choice is to implement the methods `setLogfile( File logfile )` and `setEnableLogging( boolean enable )`, for example. Note that the method names are case-sensitive, so you need use the same case as in the `name` attribute of the `<parameter>` element. The exception to this rule is the first character after the "set" part of the method name, which always needs to be an uppercase character.

The difference between these two configuration options is that you can use conditional parameters (the ones that use `if` or `unless` attributes) only when you implement the `setParameters( Variable[], File )` method. You can determine whether the condition of a parameter is fulfilled by calling `isConditionFulfilled( Environment )` on that parameter. Listing 13-2 demonstrates how you can use conditional parameters in a preprocessor extension. This example uses the `configure( Variable[] )` convenience method, which in turn calls the `set[param-name]` method for each parameter that has no condition or has a fulfilled condition. If you want to use variables with dynamic names, you need to implement your own processing in the `setParameters( Variable[], File )` method.

Listing 13-2. *Configuring an Extension with Conditional Parameters*

```
package com.apress.preprocess;

import java.io.File;
import java.io.IOException;

import de.enough.polish.Device;
import de.enough.polish.preprocess.CustomPreprocessor;
import de.enough.polish.Variable;
import de.enough.polish.util.FileUtil;
import de.enough.polish.util.StringList;

public class FullScreenPreprocessor extends CustomPreprocessor {

   private Variable[] parameters;
   private File logfile;
   private boolean enabledLogging;

   public FullScreenPreprocessor() {
      super();
   }

   public void notifyDevice(Device device, boolean usePolishGui) {
      super.notifyDevice(device, usePolishGui);
      // set default values:
      this.logfile = null;
      // configure this extension:
      configure( this.parameters );
   }

   public void processClass( StringList lines, String className ) {
      // now preprocess class...
      System.out.println( "FullScreenPrepocessor: processing class "
         + className );
   }
```

```
    public void setParameters( Variable[] parameters, File baseDir ) {
        this.parameters = parameters;
    }

    public void setLogfile( File logfile ) {
        this.logfile = logfile;
    }

    public void setEnableLogging( boolean enabledLogging ) {
        this.enabledLogging = enabledLogging;
    }

}
```

Using Build Extensions

You need to register your build extensions before you can use them. You have two options for this: either you define them in your *build.xml* script or you register them in *${polish.home}/ custom-extensions.xml*. You can also use extensions conditionally.

Using Extensions Directly

You can define your extension directly in the *build.xml* file by using the `class` and `classpath` attributes that every extension provides. Listing 13-3 shows how you can use this mechanism to define the `FullScreenPreprocessor` of Listing 13-2.

Listing 13-3. *Defining an Extension in build.xml*

```
<j2mepolish>
    <info
        license="GPL"
        name="Roadrunner"
        vendorName="A reader."
        version="0.0.1"
        jarName="${polish.vendor}-${polish.name}-roadrunner.jar"
    />
    <deviceRequirements>
        <requirement name="Identifier" value="Generic/midp1" />
    </deviceRequirements>
    <build
        usePolishGui="true"
    >
        <midlet class="com.apress.roadrunner.Roadrunner" />
        <preprocessor
            class="com.apress.preprocess.FullScreenPreprocessor"
            classPath="../apress-preprocessor/bin/classes"
        >
            <parameter name="logfile" value="log.txt" />
```

```
    </preprocessor>
  </build>
  <emulator />
</j2mepolish>
```

Registering Extensions for Several Projects

When you want to use your extension in more than one project, you can register the extension in *${polish.home}/custom-extensions.xml*. Listing 13-4 registers the `FullScreenPreprocessor` extension under the name `fullscreen`.

Listing 13-4. *Registering an Extension in ${polish.home}/custom-extensions.xml*

```
<extension>
  <type>preprocessor</type>
  <name>fullscreen</name>
  <class>com.apress.preprocess.FullScreenPreprocessor</class>
  <classpath>../apress-preprocessor/bin/classes:
            ${polish.home}/import/apress.jar</classpath>
</extension>
```

The `<type>` element depends on the kind of extension; examples include `preprocessor`, `propertyfunction`, `packager`, and `finalizer`. You also need to provide the `<class>` element and usually the `<classpath>` element as well, unless your extensions are on the classpath of your system anyway. Note that you can use several classpaths when you separate them with colons (`:`) or semicolons (`;`). In Listing 13-4, J2ME Polish tries to load the `FullScreenPreprocessor` class from the *../apress-preprocessor/bin/classes* directory first, before using the *${polish.home}/import/apress.jar* file. In this way, you will always use the latest version on your development system, while coworkers can use the same *custom-extensions.xml* file when they have the *apress.jar* file in *${polish.home}/import*. Last but not least, you need to set a `<name>` element, which has to be unique for the type of extension.

Listing 13-5 uses the registered extension in the *build.xml* script. Instead of defining the `class` and `classpath` attributes, you simply need to provide the `name` attribute.

Listing 13-5. *Using a Registered Extension in build.xml*

```
<preprocessor name="fullscreen" >
  <parameter name="logfile" value="log.txt" />
</preprocessor>
```

Using Extensions Conditionally

You can implement extensions conditionally by using the `if` and `unless` attributes of the extension in your *build.xml* script. You can use any Ant properties or preprocessing terms in these attributes, as demonstrated in Listing 13-6. The code uses the `fullscreen` preprocessor only when the current target device has a known native `fullscreen` class.

Listing 13-6. *Using an Extension Conditionally*

```
<preprocessor
   name="fullscreen"
   if="polish.classes.fullscreen:defined"
>
   <parameter name="logfile" value="log.txt" />
</preprocessor>
```

Invoking Ant Targets

Most build extensions allow you to call Ant targets instead of implementing your own extension. J2ME Polish makes all capabilities and features of the current target device available as Ant properties so that you can evaluate and use them within the specified target. For calling an Ant target, set the name of the extension to `antcall` and specify the Ant target with the `target` attribute. Listing 13-7 demonstrates how you can use the `yguard` Ant task for obfuscating your application. Using the `yguard` Ant task instead of the built-in integration of J2ME Polish allows you to further tweak the yGuard obfuscator, since the Ant task exposes some additional configuration options.

Listing 13-7. *Invoking Ant Targets from Within J2ME Polish*

```
<project name="roadrunner" default="j2mepolish">
   <property name="polish.home" location="C:\programs\J2ME-Polish" />
   <property name="wtk.home" location="C:\WTK22" />
   <taskdef name="j2mepolish"
      classname="de.enough.polish.ant.PolishTask"
      classpath="${polish.home}/import/enough-j2mepolish-build.jar:
      ${polish.home}/import/jdom.jar"/>
   <target name="j2mepolish">
      <j2mepolish>
         <info
            license="GPL"
            name="Roadrunner"
            vendorName="A reader."
            version="0.0.1"
            jarName="${polish.vendor}-${polish.name}-roadrunner.jar"
         />
         <deviceRequirements>
            <requirement name="Identifier" value="Generic/midp1" />
         </deviceRequirements>
         <build
            usePolishGui="true"
         >
            <midlet class="com.apress.roadrunner.Roadrunner" />
            <obfuscator name="antcall" target="yguard" />
         </build>
         <emulator />
```

```
        </j2mepolish>
    </target>

    <target name="yguard" >
        <taskdef name="yguard"
                classname="com.yworks.yguard.ObfuscatorTask"
                classpath="import/yguard.jar"
        />
        <echo message="obfuscating for ${polish.identifier}." />
        <yguard>
            <property name="error-checking" value="pedantic"/>
            <inoutpair in="${polish.obfuscate.source}" ➥
            out="${polish.obfuscate.target}"/>
             <externalclasses
              path="${polish.obfuscate.bootclasspath}:${polish.obfuscate.classpath}"
             />
              <expose>
               <class name="com.apress.roadrunner.Roadrunner" />
               </expose>
          </yguard>
    </target>
</project>
```

As already mentioned, you can use J2ME Polish properties in your Ant target. Some extensions, such as the `<obfuscator>` one, additionally provide extension-specific properties. Listing 13-7 uses, for example, the properties `${polish.obfuscate.bootclasspath}` and `${polish.obfuscate.classpath}`, which point to the supported libraries of the current target device. Refer to the following sections for learning whether an extension sets additional properties for the `antcall`.

Note When you refer to J2ME Polish properties outside the J2ME Polish task, you need to use lowercase letters only. J2ME Polish stores all capability names in lowercase internally and converts queries to lowercase to make preprocessing terms, and so on, case-insensitive.

You can also set your own properties by using nested `<parameter>` elements. In contrast to the usual Ant properties that can be set only once, such properties can also change with each target device. Of course, you can also use J2ME Polish–specific variables and property functions inside your `<parameter>` elements, as demonstrated in Listing 13-8.

Listing 13-8. *Setting Your Own Ant Properties*

```
<finalizer name="antcall" target="deploy">
   <parameter name="dir.ftp" value="${ nospace( polish.Vendor ) }" />
</finalizer>
```

Creating Your Own Preprocessor

The preprocessor is responsible for changing the source codes before they are compiled. You can add your own custom preprocessor to J2ME Polish by extending the `de.enough.polish.preprocessor.CustomPreprocessor` class and integrating it with the `<preprocessor>` element in *build.xml*.

Preparing

Create a new project in your IDE, and set the classpath so it includes *enough-j2mepolish-build.jar*, which you can find in the *${polish.home}/import* folder. Also, include the *ant.jar* file from your Ant installation in the classpath.

Implementing the Preprocessor Class

Create a new class that extends `de.enough.polish.preprocess.CustomPreprocessor`, and call it `com.apress.preprocess.UserAgentPreprocessor`. You have two options for creating the actual functionality: either you can choose the easy way and register a preprocessing directive or you can parse all source codes yourself.

Registering Directives

I will now show how to implement the `UserAgentPreprocessor` that inserts the user agent for the current device and locale whenever it encounters the `//#useragent` directive. This is useful when your application connects to HTTP servers, as Listing 13-9 demonstrates.

Listing 13-9. *Using the #useragent Preprocessing Directive*

```
public byte[] openHttpConnection( String url )
throws IOException, SecurityException
{
   HttpConnection connection = (HttpConnection)
   Connector.open( url,Connector.READ_WRITE, true );
   connection.setRequestMethod( HttpConnection.GET );
   connection.setRequestProperty("Connection", "close");
   //#useragent connection.setRequestProperty( "UserAgent", "${useragent}" );
   int responseCode = connection.getResponseCode();
   if ( responseCode == HttpConnection.HTTP_OK ) {
      InputStream in = connection.openInputStream();
      ByteArrayOutputStream out = new ByteArrayOutputStream();
      byte[] buffer = new byte[ 5 * 1024 ];
      int read;
      while ( ( read = in.read( buffer, 0, buffer.length ) ) != -1 ) {
         out.write( buffer, 0, read );
      }
      return out.toByteArray();
   } else {
      throw new IOException( "Got invalid response code: " + responseCode );
   }
}
```

The CustomPreprocessor class provides the registerDirective(String) method, which makes preprocessing quite comfortable. In this case, you want to process only those lines that start with the //#useragent directive, so you can register this directive by calling registerDirective("//#useragent"). For each registered directive, you need to implement the method process[directive-name], so implement processUseragent() as shown in Listing 13-10. This method is responsible for the actual preprocessing and replaces the term ${useragent} with the actual user agent in this example. Please note that the spelling of the method name must be the same as the directive name, with the exception that the first letter after "process" is capitalized in the method name.

Listing 13-10. *Registering Directives in the UserAgentPreprocessor*

```
package com.apress.preprocess;

import org.apache.tools.ant.BuildException;

import de.enough.polish.preprocess.CustomPreprocessor;
import de.enough.polish.util.StringList;

public class UserAgentPreprocessor extends CustomPreprocessor {

   public UserAgentPreprocessor() {
      super();
      registerDirective( "//#useragent" );
   }

   public void processUseragent( String line, StringList lines, String className ) {
      int directiveStart = line.indexOf( "//#useragent" );
      String argument = line.substring( directiveStart
                  + "//#useragent".length() ).trim();
      int replacePos = argument.indexOf( "${useragent}" );
      if ( replacePos == -1 ) {
         throw new BuildException( getErrorStart( className, lines )
               + "Unable to process #useragent-directive: "
               + "found no ${useragent} sequence in line ["
               + line + "]." );
      }
      String userAgent = this.currentDevice.getCapability( "polish.UserAgent" );
      if ( userAgent == null ) {
         userAgent = this.currentDevice.getIdentifier();
      }
      if ( this.currentLocale != null ) {
         userAgent += "<" + this.currentLocale.toString() + ">";
      }
```

```
        String result = argument.substring( 0, replacePos )
            + userAgent
            + argument.substring( replacePos + "${useragent}".length() );
        lines.setCurrent( result );
    }
}
```

You can use various instance fields in your preprocessing methods:

- `de.enough.polish.Environment environment` queries any preprocessing variables or symbols.
- `de.enough.polish.BooleanEvaluator booleanEvaluator` evaluates complex terms that can be used in `#if` directives.
- `de.enough.polish.Device currentDevice` contains device settings (these can also be queried from the preprocessor).
- `java.util.Locale currentLocale` represents the current localization; this is the only variable that can be `null`.

The example used the device to get the applicable user agent. When you use the localization, you also add the localization setting to the user agent. If you have the English locale and target the Nokia 6600 device, the user agent would be `Nokia/6600<en>`, for example. This user agent can then be queried by a server application, which in turn can generate content specifically for that device and the used localization.

After preprocessing the given line, you can persist your changes by calling `lines.setCurrent( line )`. When you encounter a fatal error, you can abort the build by throwing an `org.apache.tools.ant.BuildException` that explains the situation.

Taking Full Control

For more complex situations, you can override the `processClass()` method, which allows you to process the complete source files. This requires you to do the parsing yourself, but it gives you greater flexibility as well. Listing 13-11 creates another preprocessor called `FullScreenPreprocessor`. This preprocessor just looks for classes that extend the `javax.microedition.lcdui.Canvas` class and changes the `extends` statement so that these classes extend the native `fullscreen` class of the current target devices, for example, Nokia's `com.nokia.mid.FullCanvas`. This allows you to always use any available `fullscreen` class without using extra preprocessing directives in your application.

Caution Remember that `fullscreen` classes may not support all normal `Canvas` operations. Nokia's `com.nokia.mid.FullCanvas` does not support commands, for example, so use this preprocessor with care.

Listing 13-11. *Parsing the Complete Source Code in the FullScreenPreprocessor*

```
package com.apress.preprocess;

import de.enough.polish.Device;
import de.enough.polish.preprocess.CustomPreprocessor;
import de.enough.polish.util.StringList;

public class FullScreenPreprocessor extends CustomPreprocessor {

   private boolean doProcessClass;
   private String fullScreenClass;

   public FullScreenPreprocessor() {
      super();
   }

   public void notifyDevice( Device device, boolean usesPolishGui ) {
      super.notifyDevice( device, usesPolishGui );
      this.fullScreenClass = device.getCapability( "polish.classes.fullscreen" );
      this.doProcessClass = ( this.fullScreenClass != null );
   }

   public void notifyPolishPackageStart() {
      super.notifyPolishPackageStart();
      this.doProcessClass = false;
   }

   public void processClass( StringList lines, String className ) {
      if ( !this.doProcessClass ) {
         return;
      }
      while ( lines.next() ) {
         String line = lines.getCurrent();
         int extendsIndex = line.indexOf( "extends Canvas" );
         if ( extendsIndex != -1 ) {
            line = line.substring( 0, extendsIndex )
                 + "extends " + this.fullScreenClass
                 + line.substring( extendsIndex + "extends Canvas".length() );
            lines.setCurrent( line );
         }
      }

   }
}
```

In the `FullScreenPreprocessor`, you are searching for `extends Canvas` terms in the complete source code. For making this efficient, you start the parsing only when the current target device has a `fullscreen` class defined. You check this in the overridden `notifyDevice()` method that is called by J2ME Polish whenever a new target device is processed. Thanks to the device database, you need to check only whether the current target device has a defined `polish.classes.fullscreen` capability that contains the name of the native `fullscreen` class, if the device has one.

Another important feature is that you do not change any of the J2ME Polish core classes, since these adhere to the `fullscreen` settings in *build.xml* anyway. Whenever the J2ME Polish core classes are processed, the `notifyPolishPackageStart()` method is called automatically. Handily enough, these core classes are always processed last, so you can wait for the next `notifyDevice()` call for starting all over again.

■ **Note** In cases when you have your own preprocessing directives but choose to parse the complete source yourself with the `processClass()` method, you must still register your directives so that J2ME Polish knows about them. When you implement the `processClass()` method, you do not need to implement the `process[directive-name]` methods. Whenever J2ME Polish encounters an unknown preprocessing directive, it will abort the build process.

Using Your Preprocessor

Use the nested `<preprocessor>` element of the `<build>` section in your *build.xml* for using your preprocessor. Please refer to the previous discussion of using build extensions for learning how to do this.

You can also call any Ant target in the preprocessing phase by using the `antcall` preprocessor. In that case, you have two additional Ant properties at your disposal: `${polish.classname}` contains the name of the currently processed class, and `${polish.source}` points to the directory that contains the source code.

Setting the Compiler

You can use another compiler or configure the compiler by using the `<compiler>` element, as shown in Listing 13-12. Ant supports the following compilers: `classic`, `modern`, `jikes`, `jvc`, `kjc`, `gcj`, `sj`, and `extJavac`. You can use any attributes and nested elements that are supported by Ant's `<javac>` task. Usually, debugging information is included only when you activate the logging framework with the `<debug>` element, but with the settings of Listing 13-12 you will always include debugging information.

Listing 13-12. *Using a Specific Compiler*

```
<j2mepolish>
   <info
      license="GPL"
      name="Roadrunner"
      vendorName="A reader."
      version="0.0.1"
      jarName="${polish.vendor}-${polish.name}-roadrunner.jar"
```

```
    />
    <deviceRequirements>
       <requirement name="Identifier" value="Generic/midp1" />
    </deviceRequirements>
    <build
        usePolishGui="true"
    >
       <midlet class="com.apress.roadrunner.Roadrunner" />
       <compiler compiler="gcj" debug="true" debuglevel="lines,vars,source" />
    </build>
    <emulator />
</j2mepolish>
```

Using a Postcompiler

A postcompiler is called after the sources have been successfully compiled. You can use it to modify the bytecode of your application, which is a source of never-ending fun—if you happen to like this sort of humor, that is.

Several bytecode modification libraries are available, most notably BCEL (`http://jakarta.apache.org/bcel`) and ASM (`http://asm.objectweb.org`). When you are at home with the bytecode level, you can gain some amazing benefits. The Floater tool of Enough Software uses this mechanism for allowing floating-point calculations on CLDC 1.0 devices, for example.

You can integrate your postcompiler by extending the `de.enough.polish.postcompile.PostCompiler` class and implementing the `postcompile( File classesDir, Device device )` method. Integrate your postcompiler with the `<postcompiler>` element inside the `<build>` element in your *build.xml* script. You can register your postcompiler in *${polish.home}/custom-extensions.xml* by using the `postcompiler` type.

Call any Ant targets within your *build.xml* script by using the `antcall` postcompiler: `<postcompiler name="antcall" target="mytarget" />`. Next to the usual J2ME Polish properties, you can use the `polish.postcompile.dir` property that points to the directory containing the compiled classfiles.

Integrating Your Own Obfuscator

You can easily integrate your own or an unsupported third-party obfuscator by extending the `de.enough.polish.obfuscate.Obfuscator` class and implementing the `obfuscate( Device device, File sourceFile, File targetFile, String[] preserve, Path bootClassPath )` method. Integrate your obfuscator with the `<obfuscator>` element, and register it with the `obfuscator` type in the *custom-extensions.xml* file.

Most obfuscators provide their own Ant tasks as well. Sometimes you might improve the obfuscation by using such specialized tasks because they may offer more detailed settings than J2ME Polish. You can call any Ant target by using the `antcall` obfuscator: `<obfuscator name="antcall" target="myobfuscator" />`. The `antcall` obfuscator provides the additional properties listed in Table 13-3 that you can use in your Ant target. Since you are providing your own Ant target, you will probably not need the `keep` properties but instead use the necessary classnames of your MIDlet directly. Refer to Listing 13-7, which invokes the yGuard obfuscator as an Ant target.

Table 13-3. *Additional Ant Properties for the antcall Obfuscator*

Property	Description
polish.obfuscate.source	The JAR file containing the unobfuscated classes
polish.obfuscate.target	The JAR file that should be created
polish.obfuscate.bootclasspath	The boot classpath for the target device
polish.obfuscate.classpath	The classpath for the current target device
polish.obfuscate.keepcount	The number of classes that should not be obfuscated
polish.obfuscate.keep	All classes separated by a comma that should not be obfuscated
polish.obfuscate.keep.0	The first class that should not be obfuscated
polish.obfuscate.keep.n	The *n*th class that should not be obfuscated

Integrating a Preverifier

MIDP applications need preverification for allowing fast verification on the resource-constrained devices. You can call different preverifiers by using the `<preverifier>` element, which is nested inside the `<build>` element in your *build.xml* script.

You can implement your own preverifier by extending the `de.enough.polish.preverify.Preverifier` class and implementing the `preverify( Device device, File sourceDir, File targetDir, Path bootClassPath, Path classPath )` method. You can register your implementation in *${polish.home}/custom-extensions.xml* using the type `preverifier`.

You can call any Ant target for preverifying your application with the `antcall` preverifier: `<preverifier name="antcall" target="mypreverify" />`. Along with the usual J2ME Polish properties, you can use `polish.preverify.source`, which points to the directory containing the unpreverified classes; `polish.preverify.target`, which contains the folder to which the preverified classes should be written; and `polish.preverify.bootclasspath` and `polish.preverify.classpath`, which contain the classpaths for the current target device.

Use the `none` preverifier for skipping the obfuscation step: `<preverifier name="none" />`. This is useful for devices that do not need preverification, such as cell phones compliant to the Korean WIPI standard.

If you want to always use a specific preverifier (or `none`, for that matter) for a specific device, vendor, or platform, you can define the `build.Preverifier` capability in the device database. J2ME Polish defines the `none` preverifier for the WIPI profiles in *${polish.home}/platforms.xml*, such as `<capability name="build.Preverifier" value="none" />`.

Copying and Transforming Resources

Use the `<copier>` element for copying the device- and locale-specific resources to a temporary directory. Along the way, you could rename resources or even merge them to save some bytes in your JAR file.

The `<copier>` element is nested inside the `<resources>` element, which in turn can be used in the `<build>` section of your *build.xml* file. J2ME Polish provides the standard `renamer` extension that can rename your resources while copying them. Use the parameters `searchPattern` and `replacement` for configuring this process. In Listing 13-13, all parts in resource names that are surrounded by curly braces are removed. You can use this mechanism for adding verbose information to resource names without wasting space. A file called *m0{first icon of main command}.png* would be renamed to *m0.png*, for example.

Listing 13-13. *Renaming Resources on the Fly*

```
<resources
   dir="resources/default"
   defaultexcludes="yes"
   excludes="*.db"
>
   <copier name="renamer">
      <parameter name="searchPattern" value="\{.*\}" />
      <parameter name="replacement" value="" />
   </copier>
   <localization locales="en" />
</resources>
```

You can also call any Ant target for copying the resources: `<copier name="antcall" target="copy" />`. Use the additional Ant properties `polish.resources.target` (which points to the directory to which all resources should be copied) and `polish.resources.files` (which contains a list of comma-separated paths of the resources that need to be copied). You can also use the Ant property `polish.resources.filePaths`, which contains the paths of the files separated by semicolons (Windows) or colons (Unix).

Extend the `de.enough.polish.resources.ResourceCopier` class, and implement its `copyResources( Device device, Locale locale, File[] resources, File targetDir )` method for taking full control. You can register your extension in the *${polish.home}/custom-extensions.xml* file using the `resourcecopier` type.

Using Different Packagers

The packager is responsible for creating the final JAR bundles from the application classes and the resources. You can integrate your own packager by defining the `<packager>` element inside the `<build>` element in your *build.xml* script.

If you call an Ant target with `<packager name="antcall" target="package" />`, you can use the additional Ant properties `polish.package.source` (in which all resources, classes, and the manifest reside) and `polish.package.target` (which points to the file in which the application should be packaged).

Create your own packager by extending the `de.enough.polish.jar.Packager` class. In this class, you need to provide the method `createPackage( File sourceDir, File targetFile, Device device, BooleanEvaluator evaluator, Map variables, Project project ) throws IOException, BuildException`. You can register your packager implementation in *${polish.home}/custom-extensions* with the `packager` type.

Integrating Finalizers

After a project has been preprocessed, compiled, postcompiled, obfuscated, and packaged, it is finalized. Examples for the finalizers are the signing of the application bundles or the automatic transformation into COD files for BlackBerry devices.

Use the `<finalizer>` element inside the `<build>` section of your *build.xml* script to invoke a finalizer. You can invoke any Ant target in this step with the `antcall` finalizer: `<finalizer name="antcall" target="finalizeme" />`. Use the additional Ant properties `polish.finalize.jad` and `polish.finalize.jar` for accessing the paths of the created JAD and JAR files.

You can also implement your own finalizer by extending the `de.enough.polish.finalize.Finalizer` class and implementing its `finalize( File jadFile, File jarFile, Device device, Locale locale, Environment env )` method. Register your finalizer using the `finalizer` type in *${polish.home}/custom-extensions.xml.*

You can automatically trigger a finalizer by specifying the `build.Finalizer` capability in the device database. J2ME Polish uses this feature for automatically invoking the COD transformation for all BlackBerry devices, for example, `<capability name="build.Finalizer" value="jar2cod" />`.

Integrating Emulators

Invoking emulators automatically after a successful build can speed up your development time. As discussed in Chapter 7, J2ME Polish can already invoke various emulators automatically. If you want to extend these mechanisms, you can specify command-line options in the device database.

You can invoke any emulator that can be started via the command line by specifying the `Emulator.Executable` and `Emulator.Arguments` capabilities. Listing 13-14 shows you how to invoke a Motorola emulator by specifying these capabilities in the *${polish.home}/devices.xml* file.

Listing 13-14. *Defining Emulator Arguments in devices.xml*

```
<device>
   <identifier>Motorola/V550</identifier>
   <features>doubleBuffering, hasCamera</features>
   <capability name="OS" value="Motorola" />
   <capability name="JavaPlatform" value="MIDP/2.0" />
   <capability name="JavaConfiguration" value="CLDC/1.0" />
   <capability name="JavaPackage" value="mmapi, wmapi, phonebook" />
   <capability name="ScreenSize" value="176x220" />
   <capability name="ClosedFlipScreenSize" value="96x80" />
   <capability name="BitsPerPixel" value="16" />
   <capability name="HeapSize" value="800 kb" />
   <capability name="MaxJarSize" value="100 kb" />
   <capability name="MaxRecordStoreSize" value="64 kb" />
```

```
    <capability name="JavaProtocol" value="udp, http, https, socket, tcp" />
    <capability name="SoundFormat" value="midi, wav, amr, mp3" />
    <capability name="Emulator.Executable"
      value="${motorola.home}/EmulatorA.1/bin/emujava.exe" />
    <capability name="Emulator.Arguments"
       value="${polish.jadPath};;-deviceFile;;${motorola.home}/
              EmulatorA.1/bin/Resources/V550_V545.props" />
</device>
```

You can separate several command parameters by using two semicolons sequentially in the `Emulator.Arguments` capability. You can also use any Ant properties as well as J2ME Polish properties. Often needed are the `polish.jadPath` and `polish.jarPath` variables that point to the JAD and JAR files.

After you have defined such an emulator in the device database, you can use the `<emulator>` section inside the `<j2mepolish>` task of your *build.xml* script to invoke the correct emulator automatically.

Adding Property Functions

Property functions are somewhat different from the rest of the build extensions since they can be used in various elements of your `<j2mepolish>` task and inside preprocessing code.

Create your own property function by extending `de.enough.polish.propertyfunctions.PropertyFunction` and implementing the `public String process( String input, String[] arguments, Environment env )` method. After you have registered your function in *${polish.home}/custom-extension.xml* with the `propertyfunction` type, you can use your function like any other property function under the registered name, for example, in the #= directive: `//#= private String vendor = "${ nospace( polish.vendor ) }";`.

Extending the J2ME Polish GUI

Extending the J2ME Polish GUI allows you to use unique design elements that are not found anywhere else. In the following sections, you will learn how to implement your own custom item, backgrounds, and borders. You can also provide your own image-loading mechanism for changing the user interface of your application dynamically.

Writing Your Own Custom Items

You can use custom items for implementing your own form of widgets. You just need to extend the `javax.microedition.lcdui.CustomItem` class and implement its `paint( Graphics g, int width, int height )` method.

Creating a Scrollable List Item

Programming a `CustomItem` is not too difficult once you have digested the MIDP documentation. In this section, I will show how to implement the `com.apress.ui.StringListItem` class, which contains a list of strings. Figure 13-1 shows the final version.

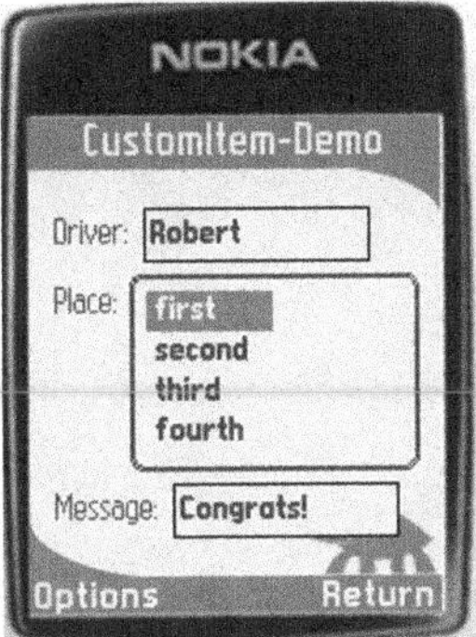

Figure 13-1. *The StringListItem in action*

Without further ado, please refer to Listing 13-15, which shows how to implement `StringListItem`. Do not worry—I will explain the details in the following sections.

Listing 13-15. *Implementing the StringListItem*

```
//#condition polish.midp2 || polish.usePolishGui
package com.apress.ui;

import javax.microedition.lcdui.Canvas;
import javax.microedition.lcdui.CustomItem;
import javax.microedition.lcdui.Display;
import javax.microedition.lcdui.Font;
import javax.microedition.lcdui.Graphics;

//#ifdef polish.usePolishGui
   import de.enough.polish.ui.Style;
//#endif

public class StringListItem extends CustomItem {

   private final Display  display;
   private final String[] entries;
   private final String shortestEntry;
   private final String longestEntry;
   private final int numberOfVisibleItems;
   private Font font;
   private int linePadding = 2;
   private boolean inTraversal;
   private int focusedIndex = -1;
   private int topIndex;
   private int lineHeight;
   private int highlightedBackgroundColor;
   private int backgroundColor;
```

```
	private int highlightedForegroundColor;
	private int foregroundColor;
	private boolean isInitialized;


	public StringListItem( String label,
			String[] entries, int numberOfVisibleItems,
			Display display ) {
		//#style customListStyle, default
		super( label );
		this.display = display;
		this.entries = entries;
		this.numberOfVisibleItems = numberOfVisibleItems;
		String longest = null;
		String shortest = null;
		int shortestLength = -1;
		int longestLength = -1;
		for ( int i = 0; i < entries.length; i++ ) {
			String entry = entries[i];
			int length = entry.length();
			if ( length < shortestLength || shortest == null ) {
				shortest = entry;
				shortestLength = length;
			}
			if ( length > longestLength ) {
				longest = entry;
				longestLength = length;
			}
		}
		this.longestEntry = longest;
		this.shortestEntry = shortest;
	}

	private void init() {
		this.isInitialized = true;
		if ( this.font == null ) {
			this.font = Font.getDefaultFont();
		}
		this.lineHeight = this.font.getHeight() + this.linePadding;
		if ( this.backgroundColor == this.highlightedBackgroundColor ) {
			// the colors haven't been set so far:
			//#if polish.midp2
				this.highlightedBackgroundColor =
					this.display.getColor( Display.COLOR_HIGHLIGHTED_BACKGROUND );
				this.backgroundColor =
					this.display.getColor( Display.COLOR_BACKGROUND );
				this.highlightedForegroundColor =
```

```
            this.display.getColor( Display.COLOR_HIGHLIGHTED_FOREGROUND );
         this.foregroundColor =
            this.display.getColor( Display.COLOR_FOREGROUND );
      //#else
         this.highlightedBackgroundColor = 0;
         this.backgroundColor = 0xFFFFFF;
         this.highlightedForegroundColor = 0xFFFFFF;
         this.foregroundColor = 0;
      //#endif
   }
}

public int getMinContentHeight() {
   if ( !this.isInitialized ) {
      init();
   }
   return this.lineHeight;
}

public int getMinContentWidth() {
   if ( !this.isInitialized ) {
      init();
   }
   return this.font.stringWidth( this.shortestEntry );
}

public int getPrefContentHeight( int width ) {
   if ( !this.isInitialized ) {
      init();
   }
   return this.lineHeight * this.numberOfVisibleItems;
}

public int getPrefContentWidth( int height ) {
   if ( !this.isInitialized ) {
      init();
   }
   return this.font.stringWidth( this.longestEntry );
}

public int getFocusedIndex() {
   return this.focusedIndex;
}

private void showFocusedEntry() {
   if ( this.focusedIndex < this.topIndex ) {
```

```
            this.topIndex = this.focusedIndex;
        } else if ( this.focusedIndex - this.topIndex + 1
          > this.numberOfVisibleItems ) {
            this.topIndex = this.focusedIndex - this.numberOfVisibleItems + 1;
        }
    }

    protected void paint( Graphics g, int width, int height ) {
        int numberOfLines = height / this.lineHeight;
        int lastLineIndex = this.topIndex + numberOfLines;
        if ( lastLineIndex > this.entries.length ) {
            lastLineIndex = this.entries.length;
        }
        int y = 0;
        g.setFont( this.font );
        for ( int i = this.topIndex; i < lastLineIndex; i++ ) {
            String entry = this.entries[i];
            boolean isSel = ( i == this.focusedIndex );
            g.setColor( isSel ?
            this.highlightedBackgroundColor : this.backgroundColor );
            g.fillRect( 0, y, width, this.lineHeight );
            g.setColor( isSel ?
            this.highlightedForegroundColor : this.foregroundColor );
            g.drawString( entry, 0, y + this.linePadding/2,
                Graphics.TOP | Graphics.LEFT );
            y += this.lineHeight;
        }

        if ( y < height ) {
            g.setColor( this.backgroundColor );
            g.fillRect( 0, y, width, height - y );
        }
    }

    public boolean traverse( int direction, int viewportWidth,
                    int viewportHeight, int[] visRectInOut ) {
        if ( !this.inTraversal ) {
            // this user entered the ListItem
            this.inTraversal = true;
            if ( this.focusedIndex == -1  ) {
                if ( direction == Canvas.UP || direction == Canvas.LEFT ) {
                    if ( this.topIndex + this.numberOfVisibleItems
                        < this.entries.length )
{
                        this.focusedIndex =
                            this.topIndex + this.numberOfVisibleItems;
                        } else {
```

```
                this.focusedIndex = this.entries.length - 1;
            }
        } else {
            this.focusedIndex = 0;
        }
        showFocusedEntry();
        repaint();
        notifyStateChanged();
    }
    visRectInOut[0] = 0;
    visRectInOut[1] = 0;
    visRectInOut[2] = viewportWidth;
    visRectInOut[3] = viewportHeight;
    return true;
}

if ( direction == Canvas.DOWN ) {
    if ( this.focusedIndex < this.entries.length - 1 ) {
            this.focusedIndex++;
    } else {
        return false;
    }
} else if ( direction == Canvas.UP ) {
    if ( this.focusedIndex > 0 ) {
        this.focusedIndex--;
    } else {
        return false;
    }
} else if ( direction != NONE ) {
    return false;
}

showFocusedEntry();
repaint();
visRectInOut[0] = 0;
visRectInOut[1] = ( this.focusedIndex - this.topIndex )
                * this.lineHeight;
visRectInOut[2] = viewportWidth;
visRectInOut[3] = this.lineHeight;

notifyStateChanged();
return true;
}

public void traverseOut() {
    this.inTraversal = false;
}
```

```
 //#ifdef polish.hasPointerEvents
protected void pointerPressed( int x, int y ) {
   int row = y / this.lineHeight + this.topIndex;
   if ( row != this.focusedIndex ) {
      this.focusedIndex = row;
      showFocusedEntry();
   }
}
//#endif

//#ifdef polish.usePolishGui
public void setStyle( Style style ) {
   //#if true
      // the super-call needs to be hidden:
      //# super.setStyle( style );
   //#endif
   this.font = style.font;
   //#ifdef polish.css.stringlistitem-foreground-color
        Integer foregroundColorInt =
         style.getIntProperty( "stringlistitem-foreground-color" );
        if ( foregroundColorInt != null ) {
           this.foregroundColor = foregroundColorInt.intValue();
        }
     //#endif
     //#ifdef polish.css.stringlistitem-highlighted-foreground-color
        Integer highlightedForegroundColorInt =
         style.getIntProperty( "stringlistitem-highlighted-foreground-color" );
        if ( highlightedForegroundColorInt != null ) {
           System.out.println( "setting highlighted foreground color to ["
           + Integer.toHexString( highlightedForegroundColorInt.intValue() )
           + "]" );
           this.highlightedForegroundColor =
              highlightedForegroundColorInt.intValue();
        }
     //#endif
     //#ifdef polish.css.stringlistitem-background-color
        Integer backgroundColorInt =
         style.getIntProperty( "stringlistitem-background-color" );
        if ( backgroundColorInt != null ) {
           this.backgroundColor = backgroundColorInt.intValue();
        }
     //#endif
     //#ifdef polish.css.stringlistitem-highlighted-background-color
        Integer highlightedBackgroundColorInt =
         style.getIntProperty( "stringlistitem-highlighted-background-color" );
        if ( highlightedBackgroundColorInt != null ) {
           this.highlightedBackgroundColor =
```

```
                highlightedBackgroundColorInt.intValue();
            }
        //#endif
        this.linePadding = style.paddingVertical;
        init();
        invalidate();
    }
    //#endif
}
```

You start the implementation with the `#condition` preprocessing directive for ensuring that the `StringListItem` is included only when the current target device supports the MIDP 2.0 platform or when the J2ME Polish GUI is used for the target device.

The list implementation itself is quite basic. The `String[] entries` field contains the list items, `int focusedIndex` marks the currently selected entry, and `int topIndex` marks the first shown entry. The `traverse()` method is responsible for navigating through the list, while the `paint()` method displays the visible entries on the screen. The `pointerPressed()` method is added only when the current target device supports pointer events and can also navigate through the list. I will explain the design of the list in the following sections.

Understanding J2ME Polish's Handling of Custom Items

The MIDP 2.0 specification provides some room for which features a custom item actually supports. When you use the J2ME Polish GUI, you can be sure that your custom item behaves the same on each target device, regardless of the native implementation. So, there will be a porting effort only when you use low-level graphics operations that are erroneously implemented on your target device. Please refer to the known issues list of your target devices at *http://www.j2mepolish.org/devices-overview.html*. Another possible porting issue is the usage of MIDP 2.0–only features when you want to use your item on MIDP 1.0 phones as well.

Initialization

J2ME Polish calls the `getPrefContentWidth( allowedHeight )` method first, providing an undefined `allowedHeight ( -1 )`. This is followed by a call of the `getPrefContentHeight( allowedWidth )` method, which retrieves the actual granted width. When the width has to be adjusted by J2ME Polish, your custom item will be notified again with the `setSize(width, height)` method. The maximum possible width is the screen width of the device; depending on the design of your application, you might have less space.

Please note that the `Display.getColor( int )` and `Font.getFont( int )` methods are available only on MIDP 2.0 devices. Such calls can, therefore, be used only when the current target device supports the MIDP 2.0 platform. Please refer to the `init()` method of Listing 13-15 for an example that uses the `#if` preprocessing directive for distinguishing the different cases.

Interaction Modes

J2ME Polish supports the interaction modes `CustomItem.KEY_PRESS`, `CustomItem.TRAVERSE_HORIZONTAL`, and `CustomItem.TRAVERSE_VERTICAL` on every platform. Additionally, the `CustomItem.POINTER_PRESS` mode is supported on all devices that support pointer events.

Traversal

When your custom item gains the focus for the first time, the `traverse()` method will be called with the `CustomItem.NONE` direction. Subsequent calls will include the direction (either `Canvas.UP`, `Canvas.DOWN`, `Canvas.LEFT`, or `Canvas.RIGHT`).

Designing the CustomItem

When you want to use CSS styles for designing your `CustomItem`, make sure the project classpath contains *enough-j2mepolish-client.jar*. You will find it in the *import* folder of the J2ME Polish installation directory.

Applying a Style When the J2ME Polish GUI is used, the preprocessing symbol `polish.usePolishGui` is defined. You can extend `CustomItems` only in MIDP 2.0 environments or when you use the J2ME Polish GUI. Use the `#if` preprocessing directive to distinguish these cases when you want to use your `CustomItem` in the J2ME Polish GUI as well as in a plain MIDP 2.0–based UI. The `StringListItem` of Listing 13-15 implements the `setStyle()` method only when the J2ME Polish GUI is used, for example.

You can integrate a CSS style into your `CustomItem` in several ways:

- You can define a static style before the `super` constructor is called.
- You can use the `Form.append()` method.
- You can create an additional constructor that accepts a `Style` as the last parameter.
- You can use dynamic styles.

I will explain each of these choices now. First, defining a static style in your constructor is easy—just use the `#style` directive:

```
//#style stringListItem, default
super( label );
```

You should always allow the `default` style when you use this construct so that the build is not aborted when your first style is not defined. Do this by adding it as the last possible style in your `#style` directive.

Second, using the `Form.append()` method is more flexible, because you can use different styles for your `CustomItem` in your application. Listing 13-16 shows you how you can apply the `winnerStringListStyle` for the `StringListItem`.

Listing 13-16. *Using the Form.append() Method for Setting a Style*

```
String[] entries = new String[] { " first ", " second ",
   " third ", " fourth ", " fifth ", " sixth ", " seventh " };
StringListItem customListItem = new StringListItem( "Place:",
   entries, 4, this.display );
//#style winnerStringListStyle
this.inputForm.append( customListItem );
```

Third, using an additional constructor that accepts a `Style` as the last parameter is just as flexible as using the `Form.append()` method, but it is more complex to implement. Listing 13-17 demonstrates how you can implement this strategy. Since your IDE does not know about the J2ME Polish `CustomItem` implementation, you need to hide the call of the `super` constructor that contains the `Style` parameter. As you can see in the `getHighscoreInstance()` method, you can now define the desired style just by adding a `#style` directive before creating a new instance of the `MyCustomItem` class.

Listing 13-17. *Using an Additional Constructor for Setting a Style*

```
public class MyCustomItem extends CustomItem {

   public MyCustomItem( String label ) {
      //#style myCustomItemStyle, default
      super( label );
   }


   //#ifdef polish.usePolishGui
   public MyCustomItem( String label, Style style ) {
      //#if true
         //# super( label, style );
      //#else
         super( label );
      //#endif
   }
   //#endif

   public static MyCustomItem getDefaultInstance( String label ) {
      // use either the myCustomItemStyle or the default style:
      return new MyCustomItem( label );
   }

   public static MyCustomItem getHighscoreInstance( String label ) {
      // use the highscore style:
      //#style highscore
      return new MyCustomItem( label );
   }

   protected int getMinContentWidth() {
      return 50;
   }

   protected int getMinContentHeight() {
      return 10;
   }

   protected int getPrefContentWidth( int allowedWidth ) {
      return 100;
   }
```

```
    protected int getPrefContentHeight( int allowedHeight ) {
        return 20;
    }

    protected void paint( Graphics g, int width, int height ) {
        // paint the item...
    }
}
```

The fourth and last option is to use dynamic styles. You need to override the `createCssSelector()` method in that case, as shown in Listing 13-18. The returned style name needs to be in lowercase. You can use a mixed case notation in your *polish.css* file, however.

Listing 13-18. *Using Dynamic Styles*

```
public class MyCustomItem extends CustomItem {

    public MyCustomItem( String label ) {
        super( label );
    }

    //#ifdef polish.useDynamicStyles
        protected String createCssSelector() {
            return "mycustomitem";
        }
    //#endif

    protected int getMinContentWidth() {
        return 50;
    }

    protected int getMinContentHeight() {
        return 10;
    }

    protected int getPrefContentWidth( int allowedWidth ) {
        return 100;
    }

    protected int getPrefContentHeight( int allowedHeight ) {
        return 20;
    }

    protected void paint( Graphics g, int width, int height ) {
        // paint the item...
    }
}
```

For reading the specific style settings, you need to implement the `setStyle( Style )` method. The implementation of the `StringListItem` shown in Listing 13-15 demonstrates this. Again, you need to hide the `super.setStyle( Style )` call with preprocessing so that your IDE is not confused.

J2ME Polish will call the `setStyle()` method before the preferred content width and height is requested so that your `CustomItem` has a style when the dimensions are requested.

Please note that the variable needs to be called `style`, or it needs to end with a lowercase `style`, so that J2ME Polish can process all styles correctly. This is required because the `String`-based attribute names are replaced by numerical `short` values during the preprocessing step. This approach significantly improves the runtime performance and minimizes the heap usage.

You have four possible ways to retrieve a property from a style:

- `style.getProperty( String name )` returns either a `String` representing that value or `null` when the property is not defined.
- `style.getIntProperty( String name )` returns either an `Integer` representing that value or `null` when the property is not defined.
- `style.getBooleanProperty( String name )` returns either a `Boolean` representing that value or `null` when the property is not defined.
- `style.getObjectProperty( String name )` returns either the value as an `Object` or `null` when the property is not defined.

Please note that you can use the last three methods only when you have registered the corresponding attribute in the file *custom-css-attributes.xml*. The attribute types are `string`, `integer/color`, `boolean`, and `object/style`, respectively. If you do not specify the type, the attribute will be treated as a `string` attribute. For each set CSS attribute, the preprocessing symbol `polish.css.[attribute-name]` will be defined. You can use this mechanism for requesting the attribute values only when they are used at least once. Again, Listing 13-15 of the `StringListItem`'s `setStyle()` method demonstrates how you can save some precious bytes with this mechanism.

Registering Custom CSS Attributes You will find the *custom-css-attributes.xml* file in the installation directory of J2ME Polish. You can use this file to register CSS attributes that are used in your `CustomItems`.

Registering these attributes is required only when you use the `style.getIntProperty( String name )`, `style.getBooleanProperty( String name)`, or `style.getObjectProperty( String name )` method in the `setStyle( Style )` method of your `CustomItem`. The registration is encouraged nevertheless, since future versions of J2ME Polish might use this information for an Eclipse CSS plug-in.

Each attribute is represented by an `<attribute>` element, with the attributes listed in Table 13-4.

Table 13-4. *Definition of Custom Attributes*

Attribute	Required?	Explanation
name	Yes	The name of the attribute, for example, icon-image.
description	No	A description of this attribute.
type	No	The type of the attribute. Either string, integer, color, boolean, object, or style. Defaults to string. When the getIntProperty() method is used, the type needs to be either integer or color. When the getBooleanProperty() method is used, the type needs to be boolean. When the getObjectProperty() method is used, the type needs to be either object or style.
appliesTo	No	A comma-separated list of classnames for which this attribute can be applied.
default	No	The default value of this item.
values	No	A comma-separated list of allowed values for this attribute.

Listing 13-19 shows the definition of the color attributes that are used by the StringListItem.

Listing 13-19. *Defining Custom CSS Attributes in custom-css-attributes.xml*

```
<attributes>
   <attribute
      name="stringlistitem-highlighted-foreground-color"
      type="color"
      appliesTo="StringListItem"
      description="The text color of the currently focused entry."
   />
   <attribute
      name="stringlistitem-foreground-color"
      type="color"
      appliesTo="StringListItem"
      description="The text color of a normal non-focused entry."
   />
   <attribute
      name="stringlistitem-highlighted-background-color"
      type="color"
      appliesTo="StringListItem"
      description="The background color of the currently focused entry."
   />
   <attribute
      name="stringlistitem-background-color"
      type="color"
      appliesTo="StringListItem"
      description="The background color of a normal non-focused entry."
   />
</attributes>
```

Designing Your Custom Item At last you can now design your custom item in the *resources/polish.css* file. Listing 13-20 shows the design of the StringListItem already shown in Figure 13-1.

Listing 13-20. *Designing the StringListItem*

```
colors {
   bgColor: rgb( 132, 143, 96 );
   highlightedBgColor: rgb( 238, 241, 229 );
   highlightedFontColor: rgb( 238, 241, 229 );
   fontColor: rgb( 30, 85, 86 );
}
.winnerStringListStyle {
   font-size: medium;
   font-style: bold;
   stringlistitem-foreground-color: fontColor;
   stringlistitem-highlighted-foreground-color: highlightedFontColor;
   stringlistitem-background-color: highlightedBgColor;
   stringlistitem-highlighted-background-color: bgColor;
}
```

Background and border settings will be enforced by J2ME Polish, so your CustomItem merely needs to paint its contents. You need to paint a background only when the J2ME Polish GUI is not used, as shown in Listing 13-21.

Listing 13-21. *Painting the CustomItem's Background Only When the J2ME Polish GUI Is Not Used*

```
protected void paint( Graphics g, int width, int height ) {
   //#ifndef polish.usePolishGui
      // draw default background:
      g.setColor( this.backgroundColor );
      g.fillRect( 0, 0, this.width, this.height );
   //#endif
}
```

Loading Images Dynamically

Pictures are used quite often in user interfaces. Normally you just put all images into the *resources* folder or one of its subfolders so that these images are then included in the JAR application bundle (refer to the "Resource Assembling" section in the Chapter 7). In some circumstances, however, you may want to load the images from another source. You could load all images from a web server, for example, so that your JAR file does not include these files and is, therefore, much smaller. Or you could change the appearance of your application dynamically by exchanging the images depending on the state of your application.

J2ME Polish supports dynamic image loading by setting the preprocessing variable polish.classes.ImageLoader. You need to provide a class (or static field of a class) that implements the `javax.microedition.lcdui.Image loadImage( String url )` method. When no image loader is defined, J2ME Polish just calls `Image.createImage( url )` for loading the picture.

In Listing 13-22, the `com.apress.ui.ImageLoader` class loads images from a web server and stores them in a `RecordStore`. You can also influence which server is used by setting the preprocessing variable `ImageLoader.server.url`.

■ **Note** Please note that the code in Listing 13-22 needs some optimizations: normally you would load and store all images in one pass instead of creating a new HTTP connection for each new requested image. Because the image data is retrieved and stored *after* a request, you will see the images only after restarting the application.

Listing 13-22. *Implementing an Image Loader for Getting the Images from a Web Server*

```
package com.apress.ui;

import java.io.ByteArrayOutputStream;
import java.io.IOException;
import java.io.InputStream;

import javax.microedition.io.Connector;
import javax.microedition.io.HttpConnection;
import javax.microedition.lcdui.Image;
import javax.microedition.rms.RecordStore;
import javax.microedition.rms.RecordStoreException;
import javax.microedition.rms.RecordStoreNotFoundException;


public final class ImageLoader
implements Runnable {
   //#if ImageLoader.server.url:defined
      //#= private final static String WEBSERVER_URL = "${ImageLoader.server.url}";
   //#else
      private final static String WEBSERVER_URL =
         "http://www.company.com/servlet/ImageProvider?img=";
   //#endif

   private final String imageUrl;
   private final String recordStoreName;

   private ImageLoader( String recordStoreName, String imageUrl ) {
      this.imageUrl = imageUrl;
      this.recordStoreName = recordStoreName;
   }
```

```
public static Image loadImage( String url )
throws IOException
{
   String recordStoreName = url.substring( 1, url.length() - ".png".length() );
   try {
      RecordStore store = RecordStore.openRecordStore( recordStoreName, false );
      byte[] imageData = store.getRecord( store.getNextRecordID() - 1 );
      return Image.createImage( imageData, 0, imageData.length );
   } catch ( RecordStoreNotFoundException e ) {
      // load image in background:
      Thread thread = new Thread(
         new  ImageLoader( recordStoreName, url ) );
      thread.start();
      return null;
   } catch ( RecordStoreException e ) {
      //#debug error
      System.out.println( "Unable to load image from recordstore" + e );
      throw new IOException( e.toString() );
   }
}

private byte[] loadImageFromHttpServer()
throws IOException
{
   try {
      HttpConnection connection = (HttpConnection)
               Connector.open(
                    WEBSERVER_URL + this.imageUrl,
                  Connector.READ_WRITE, true );
      connection.setRequestMethod( HttpConnection.GET );
      connection.setRequestProperty( "Connection", "close" );
      int responseCode = connection.getResponseCode();
      if ( responseCode == HttpConnection.HTTP_OK ) {
         InputStream in = connection.openInputStream();
         ByteArrayOutputStream out = new ByteArrayOutputStream();
         byte[] buffer = new byte[ 5 * 1024 ];
         int read;
         while ( (read = in.read( buffer, 0, buffer.length ) ) != -1 ) {
            out.write( buffer, 0, read );
         }
         return out.toByteArray();
      } else {
         throw new IOException( "Got invalid response code: " + responseCode );
      }
   } catch ( SecurityException e ) {
      //#debug error
      System.out.println( "Not allowed to open connection" + e );
```

```
            throw new IOException( e.toString() );
        }
    }

    private void storeImageInRms( byte[] data ) {
        try {
            RecordStore store = RecordStore.openRecordStore(
                                    this.recordStoreName, true );
            store.addRecord( data, 0,  data.length );
        } catch ( RecordStoreException e ) {
            //#debug error
            System.out.println( "Unable to store image in record-store ["
                + this.recordStoreName + "]" + e );
        }
    }

    public void run() {
        System.out.println( "running image loader..." );
        try {
            byte[] data = loadImageFromHttpServer();
            storeImageInRms( data );
        } catch ( IOException e ) {
            //#debug error
            System.out.println( "Unable to load image from server ["
                + WEBSERVER_URL + "]" + e );
        }
    }

}
```

Listing 13-23 integrates the `com.apress.dynamic.ImageLoader` class in the *build.xml* script by specifying the `polish.classes.ImageLoader` variable.

Listing 13-23. *Integrating Your Own Image Loader*

```
<j2mepolish>
    <info
        license="GPL"
        name="Roadrunner"
        vendorName="A reader."
        version="0.0.1"
        jarName="${polish.vendor}-${polish.name}-roadrunner.jar"
    />
    <deviceRequirements>
        <requirement name="Identifier" value="Generic/midp1" />
    </deviceRequirements>
        <!-- symbol: don't check method-parameters:  -->
    <build
```

```
        usePolishGui="true"
        fullscreen="menu"
     >
     <midlet class="com.apress.roadrunner.Roadrunner" />
         <variables>
         <!-- use own image loader implementation:  -->
         <variable
            name="polish.classes.ImageLoader"
            value="com.apress.ui.ImageLoader" />
         <variable
            name="ImageLoader.server.url"
            value="http://www.j2mepolish.org/images" />
       </variables>
     </build>
   <emulator />
</j2mepolish>
```

Creating Your Own Background

For adding a new background, make sure your classpath includes the files *enough-j2mepolish-build.jar*, *enough-j2mepolish-client.jar*, and *midp2.jar* from the *${polish.home}/import* folder.

Each background needs two implementation classes: one client-side class paints the background on the actual handheld, and the server-side class is responsible for creating and configuring the client class during the build phase.

In the following sections, you will create and integrate an animated background for focused items. It smoothly follows the current selection whenever the user changes the focused item.

Creating the Client-Side Background Class

You can create the client-side background by extending the `de.enough.polish.ui.Background` class and implementing its `paint( int x, int y, int width, int height, Graphics g )` method. For animating the background, you can also override the `animate()` method. Whenever the user focuses another item, the background is painted at a different position (if used in the `focused` style). You use these position changes for detecting such focus changes. Within the `animate()` method, you then move the background until you reach the new destination position. Listing 13-24 demonstrates this.

Listing 13-24. *Implementing a Moving Background*

```
//#condition polish.usePolishGui
package com.apress.ui;

import javax.microedition.lcdui.Graphics;
import de.enough.polish.ui.Background;

public class MovingBackground extends Background {
   private final int color;
```

```
    private final int speed;
    private int nextX;
    private int nextY;
    private int currentX;
    private int currentY;

    public MovingBackground( int color, int speed ) {
       this.color = color;
       this.speed = speed;
    }

    public void paint( int x, int y, int width, int height, Graphics g ) {
       if ( x != this.nextX || y != this.nextY ) {
          this.nextX = x;
          this.nextY = y;
       }
       g.setColor( this.color );
       g.fillRect( this.currentX, this.currentY, width, height );
    }

    public boolean animate() {
       if ( this.currentX == this.nextX && this.currentY == this.nextY ) {
          return false;
       }
       if ( this.currentX < this.nextX ) {
          this.currentX += this.speed;
          if ( this.currentX > this.nextX ) {
             this.currentX = this.nextX;
          }
       } else if ( this.currentX > this.nextX ) {
          this.currentX -= this.speed;
          if ( this.currentX < this.nextX ) {
             this.currentX = this.nextX;
          }
       }
       if ( this.currentY < this.nextY ) {
          this.currentY += this.speed;
          if ( this.currentY > this.nextY ) {
             this.currentY = this.nextY;
          }
       } else if ( this.currentY > this.nextY ) {
          this.currentY -= this.speed;
          if ( this.currentY < this.nextY ) {
             this.currentY = this.nextY;
          }
       }
```

```
        return true;
    }
}
```

Creating the Server-Side Background Class

For converting the design settings from the *polish.css* file correctly, you need to implement a converter class that extends `de.enough.polish.preprocess.BackgroundConverter` and that implements its `createNewStatement( HashMap background, Style style, StyleSheet styleSheet )` method. This method parses the provided CSS settings and creates the necessary source code for creating a new instance of the client-side background class. Listing 13-25 implements the converter that creates the `MovingBackground`.

Listing 13-25. *Implementing the Background Converter*

```
//#condition false
package com.apress.ui;

import java.util.HashMap;
import org.apache.tools.ant.BuildException;
import de.enough.polish.preprocess.BackgroundConverter;
import de.enough.polish.preprocess.Style;
import de.enough.polish.preprocess.StyleSheet;

public class MovingBackgroundConverter extends BackgroundConverter {

   public MovingBackgroundConverter() {
   }

   protected String createNewStatement(
         HashMap background,
         Style style,
         StyleSheet styleSheet )
   throws BuildException
   {
      String speedStr = (String) background.get( "speed" );
      if ( speedStr != null ) {
         super.parseInt( "speed", speedStr );
      } else {
         speedStr = "5";
      }
      return "new com.apress.ui.MovingBackground( "
         + this.color + ", " + speedStr + " )";
   }

}
```

In the method `createNewStatement()`, you can read the design settings from the provided `background HashMap`. To parse these values, you can utilize the helper methods `parseInt()`, `parseFloat()`, `parseBoolean()`, `parseColor()`, `getUrl()`, and `parseAnchor()`. Each helper method requires the name and the value of the attribute as parameters.

In this example, use the attributes `color` and `speed`. The `color` value is parsed by the superclass already and can be accessed with `this.color`. In case no color has been defined, the background color defaults to white. When a required value is missing or a value is set incorrectly, you can throw a `BuildException` explaining the details of what went wrong. When everything is okay, just return a `String` containing the source code for creating a new instance of your background.

Integrating the Custom Background

For integrating your custom background, you need to add the converter class to the classpath of the `<j2mepolish>` task and adjust the source paths of your project so that your client-side background class is included, too.

First, add your background converter class to the `<j2mepolish>` task by adjusting the `<taskdef>` element in your *build.xml* file. Add the path for the *classes* directory of your converter project to the classpath attribute of the `<taskdef>` element, as demonstrated in Listing 13-26.

Listing 13-26. *Adjusting the Classpath of J2ME Polish*

```
<taskdef
   name="j2mepolish"
   classname="de.enough.polish.ant.PolishTask"
   classpath="${polish.home}/bin/classes:
     ${polish.home}/import/jdom.jar:
     ../apress-j2mepolish/bin/classes"
/>
```

Second, you need to inform J2ME Polish about the additional background. You can do this with the `srcDir` attribute of the `<build>` element in *build.xml*. Separate several directories with colons; for example, use `srcDir="source/src:../apress-j2mepolish/source/src"`. You can also use the nested `<source>` element, which additionally allows you to include source conditionally with its `if` and `unless` attributes.

Finally, you need to use the new background in the *resources/polish.css* file of your application. As the `background-type`, specify the server-side converting class, as demonstrated in Listing 13-27.

Listing 13-27. *Using the Moving Background in the polish.css File*

```
focused {
   padding: 5;
   background {
      type: com.apress.ui.MovingBackgroundConverter;
      color: white;
      speed: 10;
```

```
    }
    font {
        style: bold;
        color: fontColor;
        size: small;
    }
    layout: expand | center;
}
```

Now build your application, and enjoy the background shown in Figure 13-2.

Figure 13-2. *Your very own background class in action. On the right side, it is just about to move up.*

Adding a Custom Border

Adding a custom border requires the same steps as creating a custom background. Instead of extending the `Background` class, though, you need to extend the `de.enough.polish.ui.Border` class. For the server side, you need to extend `de.enough.polish.preprocess.BorderConverter`. Please refer to the JavaDoc documentation and the previous background description for further information.

■ Note Please note that borders do not support the `animate()` method, so if you want to use animated borders, you need to implement them with a `Background` class.

Extending the Logging Framework

You can extend the logging framework of J2ME Polish by providing your own log handler. A log handler extends the `de.enough.polish.log.LogHandler` class and implements the `handleLog( LogEntry entry )` method. Use this mechanism for creating your own logging features such as forwarding logged messages to an HTTP server, for example.

After you have implemented your log handler, you need to register and integrate it. You register your log handler by adding it to *${polish.home}/custom-extensions.xml*, as shown in Listing 13-28.

Listing 13-28. *Registering a Log Handler in custom-extensions.xml*

```
<extension>
   <type>loghandler</type>
   <name>http</name>
   <clientClass>com.apress.log.HttpLogHandler</clientClass>
</extension>
```

After the registration, you can integrate your log handler by adding a `<handler>` element to the `<debug>` element in your *build.xml* file. In the `<handler>` element, you need to repeat only the name that was used for the registration. When your log handler is located in a different project, you also need to include the source directory of that project by modifying your `<source>` element or the `sourceDir` attribute of the `<build>` section. Listing 13-29 demonstrates how you can include a log handler. You can include any number of log handlers just by providing several `<handler>` elements.

Listing 13-29. *Including Several Log Handlers*

```
<debug level="error" showLogOnError="true" verbose="false" >
   <handler name="rms">
      <parameter name="useBackgroundThread" value="false" />
   </handler>
   <handler name="http" />
</debug>
```

Summary

This chapter concludes the J2ME Polish part of this book. In this chapter, I discussed the various ways you can extend J2ME Polish—including integrating your own preprocessor and other build tools, creating your own GUI elements, and extending the logging framework.

In the following part, you will take a close look at the real world of J2ME programming. Sadly, a difference always exists between the theoretical standard and the actual implementations of the J2ME environments on real phones. In the next part, you will learn how you can adjust your application to the various real-world issues while still delivering a top-notch application.

PART 3

Programming in the Real World

The J2ME standard is tight and simple, yet in the real world there is a surprisingly high number of challenges waiting for you. In this part you will learn how to identify and overcome these obstacles.

CHAPTER 14

Overview of the Wireless Market

In this chapter:

- Learn how J2ME devices differ in many aspects, such as in hardware and software.
- Consider the wireless market and how it relates to your applications, including your business model and the technical positioning of your applications.

This chapter introduces you to the challenges of developing wireless applications in the real world. You need to deal with a highly fragmented device base, in which devices range from simple black-and-white screens with JAR sizes up to 30KB to state-of-the-art UMTS devices with 80MB of storage space. The wireless market is rapidly evolving and introduces new opportunities each day. In this chapter, you will learn what device differences you can expect in the real world. You will also learn how the market is evolving and what consequences this has for your business model.

Introducing Device Differences

Sun's chief software architect, Jonathan Schwartz, estimates that 500 million J2ME devices are currently in use in the market worldwide.[1] This is great, but you have to keep in mind that many devices differ quite a lot. In the following sections, I will discuss how and why J2ME devices differentiate.

Hardware

The hardware of J2ME devices varies greatly: memory, screen resolutions, color depth, network technologies, inclusion of cameras . . . you name it.

If you need specific hardware features, you can use the device selection mechanism of J2ME Polish. Listing 14-1 demonstrates how you can select all phones that have an integrated camera in your *build.xml* file. Your application is then built only for devices that meet your requirements. I discussed this in detail in the "Building for Multiple Devices" section of Chapter 7.

1. *http://blogs.sun.com/roller/page/jonathan/20050219#back_from_3gsm*

Listing 14-1. *Selecting All Devices That Include a Camera and Support Image Capturing*

```
<j2mepolish>
   <info
      license="GPL"
      name="Roadrunner"
      vendorName="A reader."
      version="0.0.1"
      jarName="${polish.vendor}-${polish.name}-roadrunner.jar"
   />
   <deviceRequirements>
      <requirement name="Term" value="polish.hasCamera and polish.Capture.image" />
   </deviceRequirements>
   <build
      usePolishGui="true"
   >
      <midlet class="com.apress.roadrunner.Roadrunner" />
   </build>
   <emulator />
</j2mepolish>
```

Furthermore, you can use the resource assembling mechanism when dealing with different screen sizes. Current device screens range from 128×128 pixels in Nokia Series 40 phones to 640×320 pixels in high-end devices. Often you will want to use adjusted graphics for the best perception. You can use device groups, vendor devices, and even canvas sizes in full-screen mode for assembling the best-suited resources. For example, you can put your general resources into the *resources* folder and put the images for devices with big screens into the *resources/ScreenSize.150+x200+* directory. Please refer to the "Resource Assembling" section in Chapter 7 for more information about this option.

Profiles and Configurations

J2ME devices can support different profiles and configurations, as shown in Figure 14-1. A distinct line is drawn between the Connected Device Configuration (CDC) and the Connected Limited Device Configuration (CLDC). The CDC standard is build upon the Java 2 Standard Edition and the Java Virtual Machine, so it is very powerful. But support for the CDC standard has dropped significantly in past years, so you can choose to ignore this configuration along with its personal and foundation profiles when you are targeting mobile phones. The CLDC standard, on the other hand, contains only some core classes of the Java 2 Standard Editions and contains further restrictions such as the inability to process floating-point calculations on CLDC 1.0 devices.

Configurationwise, the importance of the CLDC 1.1 configuration, which allows floating-point arithmetic, is increasing; however, most of today's devices support the CLDC 1.0 configuration only. Table 14-1 lists the available configurations.

Again, you can use preprocessing for distinguishing the configurations in your source code. CLDC 1.1 devices define the `polish.cldc1.1` preprocessing symbol, and CLDC 1.0 devices define the `polish.cldc1.0` symbol.

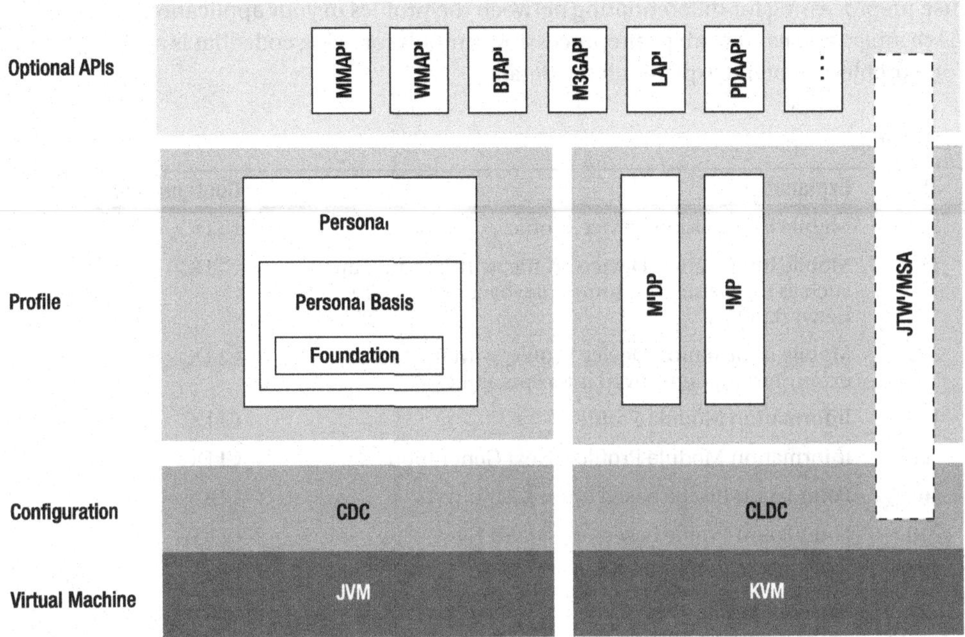

Figure 14-1. *The J2ME architecture*

Table 14-1. *J2ME Configurations*

Name	JSR	Explanation
CLDC 1.0	30	Connected Limited Device Configuration
CLDC 1.1	139	Connected Limited Device Configuration, allows floating-point arithmetic
CDC 1.0	36	Connected Device Configuration

Most J2ME devices support the MIDP 1.0 profile, and support for MIDP 2.0 is growing rapidly today. The MIDP 1.0 standard extends the CLDC 1.0 or 1.1 configuration and introduces the notion of MIDlets, the LCDUI user interface, and the record store persisting mechanism. Depending on your time frame, you can even consider using the forthcoming MIDP 3.0 standard (see JSR 271 at *http://jcp.org/en/jsr/detail?id=271*), but this standard will need a couple of years before it will be adopted on a broad device base. IMP is used for devices without a user interface and allows you to create solutions for machine-to-machine communications. Table 14-2 lists all available profiles for the J2ME world.

You can use preprocessing for differentiating between the profiles in your application. Check the `polish.midp1` and `polish.midp2` preprocessing symbols for using code that is available for only one profile. Chapter 8 explains all the details.

Table 14-2. *J2ME Profiles*

Name	JSR	Explanation	Configuration
MIDP 1.0	37	Mobile Information Device Profile	CLDC
MIDP 2.0	118	Mobile Information Device Profile, with enhancements such as the Game API, sound playback, and secure networking	CLDC
MIDP 3.0	271	Mobile Information Device Profile, with further extensions and improved interoperability	CLDC
IMP 1.0	195	Information Module Profile	CLDC
IMP 2.0	228	Information Module Profile—Next Generation	CLDC
FP 1.0	46	Foundation Profile based upon J2SE 1.3	CDC
FP 1.1	219	Foundation Profile based upon J2SE 1.4	CDC
PBP 1.0	129	Personal Basis Profile	CDC
PP 1.0	62	Personal Profile	CDC

■ **Note** Also, J2ME-compatible platforms exist that are not standardized by the Java Community Process, such as the Korean WIPI and Japanese DoJa platforms. Chapter 15 discusses these platforms in more detail. From J2ME Polish 1.3 onward, you will be able to define additional platforms in the *${polish.home}/platforms.xml* file.

Optional Packages

Many libraries are available that extend the basic functionality of MIDP devices. Some libraries are vendor- or carrier-specific; others are standardized by the Java Community Process (JCP).

Most MIDP 1.0 devices contain only vendor-specific API enhancements such as Nokia's UI API, Samsung's device control classes, and Motorola's Phonebook API. Some carriers such as Vodafone provide additional extensions. For compatibility reasons, these libraries continue to exist even in modern devices, but their usage is mostly deprecated and superseded either by the MIDP 2.0 profile or by optional packages.

Many MIDP 2.0 devices support standardized optional APIs, such as the Mobile Media API or the Wireless Messaging API. You can use them without locking yourself into a specific vendor or carrier. Table 14-3 contains the most popular optional packages, and you can find their specifications on the Java Community Process home page (*http://www.jcp.org*). If you want to deploy an optional library, refer to J2ME Polish's device database at *http://www.j2mepolish.org/devices/apis.html* for getting an idea of how widely your library has been adopted. Also, read the specification carefully, since often some parts are optional, such as the OBEX transfer of the Bluetooth API.

You can use preprocessing for detecting whether a library is available for the current target device. For each supported API, the symbol `polish.api.[api-name]` is defined (for example, `polish.api.mmapi`). You can also use resource assembling for including content for only those devices that support a specific library. Use, for example, the *resources/mmapi* folder when your application contains content that depends on the Mobile Media API. Please refer to Chapters 7 and 8 for detailed information about these options.

Table 14-3. *Optional Packages for MIDP Devices*

Name	JSR	Stage	Explanation
MMAPI	135	Available	The Mobile Media API allows you to play and record sounds, images, and videos.
WMAPI 1.1	120	Available	The Wireless Messaging API allows you to send and receive text messages (SMS).
WMAPI 2.0	205	Final	The 2.0 version allows you to send and receive multimedia messages (MMS).
M3GAPI	184	Available	The Mobile 3D Graphics API provides 3D capabilities.
SIMPLEAPI	165	Early	This extends the JAIN SIP API (JSR 32) to provide instant messaging on J2ME devices.
PDAPI	75	Available	The PDA optional packages actually define two independent APIs: the Personal Information Management (PIM) API allows you to access the address book, organizer, and so on; the File Connection (FC) API allows you to read and write files that reside outside the application (for example, on a memory card). In practice, devices always support either both libraries or none.
SIPAPI	180	Final	The Session Initiation API for J2ME extends the Generic Connection Framework to allow secure multimedia IP sessions.
LAPI	179	Available	The Location API allows you to pinpoint the position of the user.
WAAPI	172	Available	The Web Services API provides XML-parsing APIs and allows you to access web services as a SOAP client.
IMAPI	187	Early	Provides a protocol-agnostic way to send and receive instant messages.
CHAPI	211	Final	The Content Handler API allows applications to register themselves as handlers for specific MIME types.
SVGAPI	226	Available	The Scalable 2D Vector Graphics API allows you to render vector images in the SVG format, a format similar to Macromedia's proprietary Flash format.
PAPI	229	Final	The Payment API allows you to initiate microbillings from within your application.
DSAPI	230	Early	The Data Sync API enables you to access native data synchronization implementations.
MIAPI	238	Final	The Mobile Internationalization API allows you to use localized content in your application.

Continued

Table 14-3. *Continued*

Name	JSR	Stage	Explanation
MTA	253	Early	The Mobile Telephony API allows you to initiate and accept voice calls, receive network notifications and IDs, and so on.
MSAPI	256	Early	The Mobile Sensor API allows you to discover and sample data from sensors independent from the underlying transport protocol.
MUICAPI	258	Early	The Mobile User Interface Customization API allows you to query user interface settings of the device.
AHNAPI	259	Early	The Ad Hoc Networking API eases the development of peer-to-peer applications.
UMBAAPI	266	Early	The Unified Message Box Access API allows you to read, write, copy, and move any kind of messages on the device.
MBSAPI	272	Early	The Mobile Broadcast Service API for Handheld Terminals allows you to receive and interact with broadcast media.

The JTWI Specification and Mobile Service Architecture

JSR 185, Java Technology for the Wireless Industry (JTWI), is a combined effort of several manufacturers to create a more predictable environment for Java application developers. JSR 248, Mobile Service Architecture (MSA), continues the work started by JTWI and enhances the definition with new technologies.

JTWI is based upon the MIDP 2.0 profile and mandates that compatible devices at least support the Wireless Messaging API (WMAPI 1.1) and—where applicable but optionally—the Mobile Media API (MMAPI 1.1). JTWI also clarifies some parts of the CLDC and MIDP specifications that are open to interpretation, including the following:

- Compliant implementations support at least ten parallel threads.
- The clock resolution for `System.currentTimeMillis()` is 40 milliseconds or less.
- Basic Latin and Latin-1 characters are supported.
- Custom GMT-compatible time zones are possible.
- JAR files are supported up to at least 64KB, and JAD files can be at least 5KB.
- MIDlets can at least occupy 30KB of data in the record management system of JTWI-compliant phones.
- A heap size of at least 256KB is available for the MIDlets.
- A screen size of at least 125×125 pixels and a color depth of at least 12 bits per pixel (4,096 colors) is required.
- JPEG and PNG images are supported.
- HTTP 1.1 needs to be supported for retrieving multimedia content.

- Devices need to be able to execute MIDlets at specific timings (using the `PushRegistry.registerAlarm()` mechanism).
- Phones need to be able to execute MIDlets upon incoming messages, when this has been registered, either by using the JAD attribute `MIDlet-Push-n` or by calling `PushRegistry.registerConnection()`.
- When multimedia functionality is made available through Java libraries, JTWI-compliant devices need to expose the functionality through the Mobile Media API.
- Devices with MMAPI support need to be able to play back at least MIDI and tone-sequence files. They also need to allow the capture of JPEG images and WAV audio when the device contains the corresponding capabilities.

The Mobile Service Architecture specification is still in an early phase, but minimum requirements of compliant phones will be the CLDC 1.1 configuration and the MIDP 2.0 profile.

You can check whether a device complies with the JTWI standard by testing the preprocessing symbol `polish.jtwi`.

Supported Formats

Devices support a wide range of audio, video, and image formats, but only a few formats are generally accepted. In general, you should stick to MIDI, tone-sequence, and AMR sounds and PNG images. The device database of J2ME Polish contains information of the supported formats, so you can use resource assembling for including the correct resources and use preprocessing for integrating the correct code for that format. Chapter 15 discusses the playback of sounds in more detail.

Device Modifications

A device can change its behavior and capabilities thanks to different firmware versions and carrier modifications.

Firmware can be very interesting. A quite drastic example is the Motorola E398 that changes its key events for the soft keys from one firmware version to another. New firmware can resolve issues, but they can also introduce new bugs. Unfortunately, you cannot hope that users will update their firmware, even when the latest version resolves mission-critical issues. A common strategy is to support only the most widely adopted firmware, even if this often means not supporting early adopters.

Some carriers modify devices, too. Vodafone, for example, adds its Vodafone Service Class Library, which includes some 3D and other functionality. You need to become a certified Vodafone partner to get the full information about these libraries. A more serious modification is the disabling of certain functionality. A carrier can choose to open specific APIs to certified partners only, such as the Location API, for example. Such carrier modifications have ramifications not only for the technical feasibility but also for the business model of your projects, so take them into account.

Device Issues

Device issues are the main reason why it is so difficult to create compelling yet flawlessly working applications for mobile phones. Chapter 15 discusses these issues in detail, but I mention them here to complete the collection of device differences.

The Emulator Trap

Emulators are great for testing your application directly on your development system, but unfortunately you cannot trust them. A commonly heard excuse on mailing lists and discussion boards is "but it works on the emulator!"

Many emulators are based on Sun's original Wireless Toolkit, while the actual Java implementations are created by different companies. So, often the real behavior differs from the simulation on the PC. Common problems include how colors and images render, performance, and device-specific issues. Often emulators do not reproduce issues that the actual device has. More serious, however, is the fact that emulators can contain errors that are not present on the actual device.

The bottom line is that you should use emulators for speeding up the implementation phase, but you should not trust emulators when you are trying to solve device-specific issues. An emulation is never perfect, so testing on the real device is crucial for your application's success.

Examining the Current Market

The growth of the mobile market is legendary, and sales of mobile phones have outnumbered the predictions of market researchers several times. In the following sections, I will discuss how the market has evolved and what this means for your business.

Telecom Market

There are 1.5 billion[2] telecom users, which constitutes a quarter of the population worldwide. Specifically, 78% of these users connect with GSM, 14% with CDMA, and 6% with TDMA network technologies, according to Forrester Research.[3] The same study concludes that about 80% of the population is covered by network access, so a further 3.5 billion potential users exist, but most of them do not have much money to spend. The 3G network technologies UMTS and WDCMA have gained in importance, but in 2004 only 4% of all sold handsets supported 3G technologies, according to ARC Group.[4] However, IDC estimates that in Western Europe 16% of all handsets sold in 2005 do support 3G technologies.[5]

---

2. U.S. numbers are used, so one billion is one milliard in continental Europe.
3. *http://www.moneyplans.net/frontend1-verify-7139.html*
4. *http://www.itfacts.biz/index.php?id=P2011*
5. *http://www.idc.com/getdoc.jsp?pid=23571113&containerId=pr2005_03_07_134916*

Worldwide, the most important manufacturers of mobile devices are Nokia with a market share of about 31%, Motorola with 16%, Samsung with 13%, and Siemens and LG with about 7% each.[6] Sony Ericsson is trailing them closely and is expected to enter the top five again in 2005.[7] In Western Europe, Siemens still holds second place with an estimated market share of about 16%,[8] according to IDC. Table 14-4 summarizes the vendor market worldwide, and Table 14-5 highlights Western Europe.

Table 14-4. *Worldwide Mobile Phone Sales in 2004*

Vendor	Number of Phones (in millions)	Share
Nokia	207.6	31.2%
Motorola	104.5	15.7%
Samsung	86.5	13.0%
Siemens	49.4	7.4%
LG Electronics	44.4	6.7%
Others	172.0	25.9%
Total	664.5	99.9%

Table 14-5. *Western European Mobile Phones Sales in 2004*

Vendor	Number of Phones (in millions)	Share
Nokia	50.2	34.8%
Siemens	22.5	15.6%
Motorola	17.5	12.1%
Sony Ericsson	15.9	11.0%
Samsung	14.7	10.2%
Others	23.3	16.2%
Total	144.1	99.9%

According to iSupply, 68% of all phones sold in 2004 had color screens with 16 bits per pixel being the norm (65,000 colors) and had an average screen size of 128×160.[9]

6. *http://www.theinquirer.net/?article=21668*
7. *http://www.idc.com/getdoc.jsp?containerId=pr2005_01_27_112549*
8. *http://www.idc.com/getdoc.jsp?pid=23571113&containerId=pr2005_03_07_134916*
9. *http://www.isuppli.com/marketwatch/default.asp?id=283*

J2ME Market

The wireless gaming market is playing a dominant role in the J2ME market with an estimated $350 million generated in 2004 in the United States alone.[10] IDC expects that sales of J2ME games in the United States will overtake ring tones in 2005 and continue to grow to up to $1.5 billion in 2008.[11] Compared with the competing BREW technology that generated a worldwide revenue of $200 million in 2004 for application developers, according to Qualcomm,[12] it is clear that the future belongs to the J2ME standard.

About 40% of all wireless developers use J2ME, with another 26% evaluating its usage, according to the Evans Data Corporation.[13] In 2006 ARC Group expects that around 90% of all shipped mobile phones will support the Java standard.[14] Symbian as the main platform now supports the MIDP 2.0 standard for all Series phones, even in the lower Series 40 segment.

Promising competitors for J2ME will be Flash for mobile devices and maybe Microsoft, even though Microsoft phones do not enjoy good ratings so far. Flash has the potential to become a major player in the mobile market, but this does not need to be a threat to the J2ME market. More likely, Flash will be used for marketing games and business applications, while the applications themselves will continue to be implemented in Java.

Summary

In this chapter, you learned how J2ME devices differ from each other and how the J2ME market has evolved. In the following chapter, you will look at some aspects you will commonly encounter in practice, such as detecting interruptions, establishing network connections, and accessing native functionality.

---

10. *http://msnbc.msn.com/id/7130108/site/newsweek/*
11. *http://www.idc.com/getdoc.jsp?containerId=prUS00043705*
12. *http://www.itfacts.biz/index.php?id=P1869*
13. *http://www.3g.co.uk/PR/Sept2004/8356.htm*
14. See *Programming Java 2 Micro Edition on Symbian OS*, by Martin de Jode (John Wiley & Sons, 2004).

CHAPTER 15

Dancing Around Device Limitations

In this chapter:

- Learn the actual differences among the devices on the market today.
- Learn how to write portable applications.
- Solve frequently encountered problems with some easy-to-follow strategies.
- Find out where you can get help when you are stuck.

The J2ME implementations that are used in devices on the market today behave differently. In the previous chapter, you learned what differences you should expect because of the different profiles and configurations; in this chapter, you will get to know the practical differences and difficulties that you are will encounter when programming J2ME applications. You will also learn how to avoid some frequently encountered problems and where to get help if you get stuck.

Identifying Vendor Characteristics

In the following sections, you will learn how to deal with the devices of the most popular vendors, including Nokia, Motorola, Samsung, and so on.

Tip Some vendors support specific JAD attributes. Please refer to the "Managing JAD and Manifest Attributes" section in the appendix for a complete discussion of such attributes.

Nokia

Nokia is the world's biggest player in the mobile phone market with a share of about 31% in 2004.

Nokia is pushing new devices into the market with amazing speed: in 2004 Nokia released more than 30 new models, and for 2005 Nokia has announced it will release more than 40. Fortunately, you can group the Nokia devices into different series that in turn are separated by different versions. From the point of view of the number of sold devices, the most important series are the low-cost Series 40 for the mass market and the Series 60 for smart phones.

Nokia manufactures high-quality devices and provides one of the best-maintained developer sites at *http://forum.nokia.com*; it hosts forums, provides tools, and contains documentation for the devices. Nokia also maintains "known issues" papers that list problems and how you can circumvent these problems. Table 15-1 lists the available series and their main features.

Series 40

Series 40 devices are manufactured for the mass market; they feature small sizes and low prices but also are more resource restrained than other Nokia devices. All Series 40 models are based on Nokia's proprietary operating system. The screen size is usually 128×128 pixels and can be used fully by either using Nokia's `FullCanvas` class or setting the `Canvas` to full-screen mode on MIDP 2.0–based devices. Few Series 40 devices have screens with 128×160 pixels, and some even have screens with 96×65 pixels. In general, you can expect a color depth of at least 12 bits per pixels (4,096 colors).

The Series 40 Developer Platform 1.0 features phones based on MIDP 1.0 and CLDC 1.0 that accept Java applications with a size of up to 64KB and a heap size of about 200KB. You can use the record store (RMS) up to 20KB only. You need to use the Nokia UI API for playing sounds, using the full-screen mode, controlling the vibration and backlight of the device, and performing some advanced image manipulations such as rotating images or manipulating pixel data. One of the big drawbacks for manipulating image data buffers with the Nokia UI API is that the devices have different internal formats, so sometimes you need to use `TYPE_USHORT_4444_ARGB` and other times `TYPE_INT_888_RGB`. The main challenge for the old Series 40 phones is to keep the application size smaller than 64KB. The Chinese models accept only 59KB JARs. Some devices of the Developer Platform 1.0 also support the Wireless Messaging API. On Series 40 Development Platform 1.0 phones, the `pauseApp()` method of your MIDlet will never be called, so you can detect whether your application is paused only by using the `hideNotify()` method of `Canvas`. This does not work when you use high-level GUI screens such as `Form` or `List`, unfortunately. When an uncaught exception occurs, the Application Management System will close the application by calling `destroyApp( false )`.

You can build your application for this platform by using the device identifier "Nokia/Series40DP1" in your device requirements:

```
<requirement name="Identifier" value="Nokia/Series40DP1" />
```

The Series 40 Development Platform 2.0 uses the MIDP 2.0 profile and the CLCDC 1.1 configuration as the base technology. It also supports all additional elements specified by the JTWI standard, so the Wireless Messaging API is available on all Series 40 Development Platform 2.0 devices. The Mobile Media API is also supported and allows the playback of True Tone and MIDI files. Some devices support additional APIs such as the Bluetooth API or the Mobile 3D Graphics API. Usually, you should not use the Nokia UI API on Development Platform 2.0 devices, since most functionality is now superseded by the MIDP 2.0 platform.

Development Platform 2.0 devices support applications with a JAR size up to 128KB. When an application launches a platform request on the Development Platform 2.0, the user needs to quit the application before the request is actually launched. Requests for starting voice calls are, however, processed immediately.

Table 15-1. *Main Features of Nokia Devices*

Series	Version	OS	Profile	Configuration	Libraries	Screen Size
Series 40	Development Platform 1.0	Nokia OS	MIDP 1.0	CLDC 1.0	Nokia UI API	128X128
Series 40	Development Platform 2.0	Nokia OS	MIDP 2.0, JTWI 1.0	CLDC 1.1	WMAPI, MMAPI, Nokia UI API	128X128
Series 40	Development Platform 3.0	Nokia OS	MIDP 2.0, JTWI 1.0	CLDC 1.1	Nokia UI API, MMAPI (+capture support), BTAPI, PDAAPI, M3GAPI	240X320
Series 60	First Edition	Symbian OS 6.1	MIDP 1.0	CLDC 1.0	Nokia UI API, MMAPI, WMAPI	176X208
Series 60	Second Edition Feature Pack 1	Symbian OS 7.0s	MIDP 2.0	CLDC 1.1	MMAPI, WMAPI (+Push), Nokia UI API, BTAPI	176X208
Series 60	Second Edition Feature Pack 2	Symbian OS 8.0a	MIDP 2.0, JTWI 1.0	CLDC 1.1	MMAPI 1.1, WMAPI (+Push), Nokia UI API, BTAPI, M3GAPI, PDAAPI	176X208
Series 60	Second Edition Feature Pack 3	Symbian OS 8.1a	MIDP 2.0	CLDC 1.1	MMAPI, WMAPI (+Push), Nokia UI API, BTAPI (including OBEX), Web Services API	176X208
Series 60	Third Edition	Symbian OS 9.1	MIDP 2.0	CLDC 1.1	MMAPI, WMAPI 2.0, Nokia UI API, BTAPI (including OBEX), Web Services API, SIPAPI, Security API, SVGAPI, Location API	176X208
Series 80	Developer Platform 2.0	Symbian OS 7.0s	MIDP 2.0 + Personal Profile	CLDC 1.0 + CDC	MMAPI, WMAPI, Nokia UI API, BTAPI, PDAAPI	128X128 (external), 640X200 (internal)
Series 90	Developer Platform 2.0	Symbian OS 7.0s	MIDP 2.0	CLDC 1.0	MMAPI, WMAPI, Nokia UI API, BTAPI, PDAAPI	320X200

You can build your application for this platform by targeting the "Nokia/Series40DP2" device.

If you want to deploy your applications on Series 40 devices via Bluetooth, you need to use the Nokia Development Suite. The optional OBEX transfers are not supported by the Nokia Bluetooth API.

Series 60

The Series 60 platform provides the basis for smart phones not only from Nokia but also from many other vendors, such as Sendo, Siemens, and Panasonic. The Series 60 platform is based on the Symbian OS 6 and higher. The screen size is 176×208 pixels with a color depth of 16 bits per pixel (65,536 colors). You can find general information about Series 60 at *http://www.series60.com*. Series 60 phones are divided into different editions that reflect improvements of the underlying Symbian OS. Each edition can also have feature packs that provide enhancements and bug fixes.

The first Series 60 edition is based on the MIDP 1.0 platform and supports the Nokia UI API, the Mobile Media API, and the Wireless Messaging API. A notable exception is the Nokia 7600 phone, which supports only the Nokia UI API. You can build for this edition by targeting the virtual "Nokia/Series60E1" phone:

```
<requirement name="Identifier" value="Nokia/Series60E1" />
```

The second Series 60 edition is separated in the Feature Packs 1, 2, and 3.

Feature Pack 1 uses the MIDP 2.0 platform along with the CLDC 1.0 configuration. Also, the Mobile Media API 1.1 and the Wireless Messaging API are supported. Use the "Nokia/Series60E2" or "Nokia/Series60E2FP1" phone for building your application for this feature pack:

```
<requirement name="Identifier" value="Nokia/Series60E2FP1" />
```

Feature Pack 2 uses the CLDC 1.1 configuration that supports floating-point calculations and is JTWI compliant. Additional features include the PDAAPI (the FileConnection and PIM API), the support of Bluetooth connections for the push registry, and the Mobile 3D Graphics API for OpenGL-compatible devices. You can use the "Nokia/Series60E2FP2" device to build your application for this feature pack.

Feature Pack 3 additionally supports the Web Services API. Also, the Bluetooth implementation provides the optional OBEX part for exchanging data. Use the "Nokia/Series60E2FP3" device for targeting devices that support this feature pack.

The third edition of Series 60 brings some exciting new Java technology into play. It supports the Security and Trust API, the Session Initialization API, the Scalable 2D Vector Graphics API, the Location API, and the Wireless Messaging API 2.0. Use the virtual "Nokia/Series60E3" device to build your application for this edition.

Difficulties with Series 60 vary between different editions and feature packs. Some devices have problems with reading Bluetooth `InputStreams`, some older second-edition devices lack the root certificate that is used by the Java Verified program, and some have UI issues such as a nonworking `setCurrentItem()` method. Most Series 60 devices flicker whenever you show a new `Canvas`. When a previously shown `Canvas` is displayed, an internal buffer is shown first before the `paint()` method of that `Canvas` is called again. In case you do not use the J2ME Polish GUI, which handles this issue automatically, you should consider using only one `Canvas` for displaying all screens of your application. Please refer to the issues database at *http://www.j2mepolish.org/devices/issues.html* for an up-to-date overview. Most Series 60 phones support applications of any size when the required space is available. The available heap is mostly 4MB or greater.

Series 80

Nokia's Series 80 platform consists of devices that combine PDAs and mobile phones. They target enterprise users quite successfully. The Nokia Communicator phones are the market leaders for these phone types.

A typical Series 80 device looks like a normal phone, but opening it reveals a screen size of 640×200 pixels and a QWERTY keyboard. Along with the MIDP 2.0 and CLDC 1.0 standards, Series 80 devices also support the Personal Java profile and CDC. Optional APIs are the Bluetooth API, the Wireless Messaging API, the Mobile Media API, the PDAAPI, and the Nokia UI API.

You can build for a typical Series 80 device by targeting the "Nokia/Series80" device:

```
<requirement name="Identifier" value="Nokia/Series80" />
```

Series 90

Series 90 devices are optimized to display media with their 320×200 screens and their pen-based input methods. As of April 2005, the Nokia 7710 is the only available Series 90 device.

Series 90 devices support the MIDP 2.0 profile along with the CLDC 1.1 configuration. Optional APIs are the Bluetooth API (JSR 82), the Wireless Messaging API, the Mobile Media API, the PDAAPI, and Nokia's UI API.

Use the "Nokia/Series90" device for targeting a typical device of this series:

```
<requirement name="Identifier" value="Nokia/Series90" />
```

Motorola

Motorola is the second biggest vendor with a share of about 16% worldwide in 2004. Motorola is unique in using not one, two, or three different operating systems but four: its own proprietary Motorola OS, Symbian OS, Microsoft Smartphone, and Linux.

Motorola provides excellent developer resources on *http://motocoder.com*. You can query the somewhat hidden known issues database by selecting Knowledge & Support and then Bug Submission.

Motorola MIDP 2.0 phones support only one font size (20) and one font style (plain). Motorola recommends a JAR size of 100KB for the J2ME applications, but there is no hard limit. On modern devices you can expect a heap size of 800KB and higher.

You can normally prefetch only one sound at a time on older MIDP 2.0 devices. Exceptions to this rule are MIDI, iMelody, and the Motorola-specific mix and basetrack formats, of which you can prefetch two sounds simultaneously. You can also prefetch one MIDI first and then one WAV file. You need to stop and deallocate the previous sound before playing the next one. In general, you can use up to four simultaneous TCP connections on Motorola phones. The icons of your MIDlets need to be 15×15 pixels; otherwise, only a generic icon will be displayed. If you want to use more than 16KB in your RMS, you need to set the `MIDlet-Data-Size`

JAD attribute, which defines the needed space in bytes. The maximum possible value is 524288 (512KB), but of course you can use only the space that is available. When the requested space is not available, the device will abort the application's installation.

Motorola offers some additional libraries such as the Phonebook API. These APIs are accessible only for licensees. If you want to use them, you need to build a business relationship with Motorola.

Samsung

Samsung is the third biggest player with a market share of about 13% worldwide in 2004. Samsung also maintains a good developer community at *http://developer.samsungmobile.com*. For some weird reason, you either need Microsoft Internet Explorer or KDE Konqueror to access the site. Mozilla-based browsers are not supported. Still, make sure to check out the developer tips for the phones. You can find them in the site's Resources section.

Typical problems with Samsung phones include the JAD attributes that need to be in a specific order and should be trimmed to the absolute necessary. You can use the `<jadFilter>` and `<manifestFilter>` elements in your *build.xml* file, as shown in Listing 15-1. Also, you should use only a relative URL in the `jarName` and `jarUrl` attributes of the `<info>` element. It's a challenge to get network connections to work on Samsung phones. In general, you need to stick to one connection and make sure to use an Internet Access Point Name (APN) rather than a WAP access point. It also helps to use static IP addresses instead of domain names. Icon sizes vary from not supported at all, to 24×24, and up to 40×35 pixels.

Listing 15-1. *Filtering JAD Attributes on Samsung Devices*

```
<j2mepolish>
   <info
      license="GPL"
      name="Roadrunner"
      vendorName="A reader."
      version="0.0.1"
      jarName="${polish.vendor}-${polish.name}-roadrunner.jar"
   />
   <deviceRequirements>
      <requirement name="JavaPlatform" value="MIDP/2.0" />
   </deviceRequirements>
   <build>
      <midlet class="com.apress.roadrunner.Roadrunner" />
      <jad>
         <jadFilter if="polish.Vendor == Samsung">
         MIDlet-1, MIDlet-2?, MIDlet-3?, MIDlet-4?, MIDlet-5?,
         MIDlet-JarSize, MIDlet-Jar-URL,
         MIDlet-Name, MIDlet-Vendor, MIDlet-Version
         </jadFilter>
      </jad>
      <manifestFilter>
```

```
        Manifest-Version, MIDlet-Name,
        MIDlet-1, MIDlet-2?, MIDlet-3?, MIDlet-4?, MIDlet-5?,
        MIDlet-Version, MIDlet-Vendor,
        MicroEdition-Configuration, MicroEdition-Profile
        </manifestFilter>
    </build>
    <emulator />
</j2mepolish>
```

Samsung is famous for its secret menus that can be enabled by pressing some key combination, such as #*536963# for enabling the serial Java transfer on the D500. Just search the Web for "Samsung secret codes" to find many menus.

Siemens

Siemens is still the fourth biggest player in the mobile device market with a share of about 7% worldwide in 2004. All Siemens handsets except the Series 60–based SX1 device use a proprietary Siemens operating system. The Siemens brand belongs to BenQ now.

Siemens provides emulators and information at *https://communication-market.siemens.de/portal/main.aspx?pid=1*. You will find the community by selecting Device Based Applications, Community, and then Forum.

You can separate Siemens devices into the 55, 65, and 75 groups. The 75 generation is expected to be shipped in the third quarter of 2005. The currently available 65 generation supports the MIDP 2.0 profile along with the CLDC 1.1 configuration. Along with being JTWI compliant, the devices support many optional APIs: the Wireless Messaging API, the Mobile Media API, the Bluetooth API, the Mobile 3D Graphics API, and the Location API. Please note that some low-cost devices support only some, if any, of these APIs. Also, the entry model, A65, still features only the former standard MIDP 1.0 with CLDC 1.0. The recommended JAR size is now up to 350KB, and the available heap size is 1.5MB. Table 15-2 lists the main features of the Siemens groups.

Table 15-2. *Main Features of Siemens Devices*

Group	OS	Profile	Configuration	Libraries	Screen Size
55	Siemens OS	MIDP 1.0	CLDC 1.0	Siemens-Color-Game-API	101×64, 101×80
65	Siemens OS	MIDP 2.0, JTWI 1.0	CLDC 1.1	WMAPI, MMAPI, BTAPI (optional), M3GAPI (optional), Location API (optional), Siemens-Color-Game-API	132×176
75	Siemens OS	MIDP 2.0, JTWI 1.0	CLDC 1.1	WMAPI, MMAPI, BTAPI (optional), M3GAPI (optional), Location API (optional)	132×176–240×320
SX1 (single device)	Symbian OS	MIDP 1.0	CLDC 1.0	WMAPI, MMAPI, BTAPI, Nokia UI API, Siemens-Color-Game-API	176×220

You can target a group by using the "Siemens/x55," "Siemens/x65," and "Siemens/x75" virtual devices:

```
<requirement name="Identifier" value="Siemens/x65" />
```

Typical problems with Siemens handsets include the `javax.microedition.lcdui.game` API, because this is based on the Siemens former game API that sometimes behaves differently from the MIDP 2.0 standard. For example, you cannot set the view window in `LayerManager.setViewWindow()`. Instead, you need to adjust the `paint()` call in your code: `layerManager.paint( g, x - viewX, y - viewY );`. When you set an alarm using `PushRegistry`, your application does not start automatically. Instead, an icon displays to indicate that an application is waiting to be launched. In addition, when you handle sounds, you should prefetch and play only one sound at a time.

LG Electronics

The Korean manufacturer LG Electronics (LGE) is the fifth biggest player with a market share of about 6% worldwide in 2004.

LGE is selling its phones only through operators who in turn can change the phone details, which is why LGE seems to be of the opinion that it does not need to release detailed phone information or provide a developer community. You must depend on external forums when you encounter problems. I discuss these in the "Getting Help" section toward the end of this chapter.

Sony Ericsson

Sony Ericsson is sixth biggest player with a market share of about 6% worldwide in 2004.

Sony Ericsson maintains an excellent developer community at *http://developer.sonyericsson.com*. Select Tech Support to reach the forums. The mass-market phones use a proprietary Sony Ericsson OS, whereas the high-class smart phones are based on the Symbian UIQ platform (a pen-based user interface). Table 15-3 lists the available groups, called *Java platforms*, by Sony Ericsson.

You can target a specific group by using the virtual devices "SonyEricsson/JavaPlatform1," "SonyEricsson/JavaPlatform2," "SonyEricsson/JavaPlatform1Symbian," and so on:

```
<requirement name="Identifier" value="SonyEricsson/JavaPlatform5" />
```

The MIDP 1.0 phones have a limit of 30KB for the RMS, but you can use the complete available file space on Sony Ericsson's MIDP 2.0 phones. You can use up to 256KB on MIDP 1.0 and about 1.5MB on MIDP 2.0 phones on the heap.

Table 15-3. *Main Features of Sony Ericsson Devices*

Java Platform	OS	Profile	Configuration	Libraries	Screen Size
1	SE OS	MIDP 1.0	CLDC 1.0	MMAPI, WMAPI (optional)	128×160
2	SE OS	MIDP 2.0, JTWI 1.0	CLDC 1.1	WMAPI, MMAPI, Nokia UI API	176×220
3	SE OS	MIDP 2.0, JTWI 1.0	CLDC 1.1	WMAPI, MMAPI, Nokia UI API, M3GAPI, Mascot-Capsule 3.0	128×128, 128×160, 176×220, 240×320
4	SE OS	MIDP 2.0, JTWI 1.0	CLDC 1.1	WMAPI, MMAPI, Nokia UI API, M3GAPI, Mascot-Capsule 3.0, VSCL (optional)	176×220
5	SE OS	MIDP 2.0, JTWI 1.0	CLDC 1.1	WMAPI, MMAPI, Nokia UI API, M3GAPI, Mascot-Capsule 3.0, PDAAPI, BTAPI (optional)	176×220
1-Symbian	Symbian UIQ OS	MIDP 1.0	CLDC 1.0		208×320
2-Symbian	Symbian UIQ OS	MIDP 2.0	CLDC 1.0	WMAPI, MMAPI, BTAPI	208×320

Typical problems include MIDP 2.0 graphics features such as transforming sprites (the reference point is sometimes not taken into account) and drawing RGB data (the translation origin is not taken into account). Support for `CustomItems` is limited to viewing purposes only, since key events are not forwarded to the item. Another problematic area is the full-screen mode on the Java platform 2-Symbian devices: the first screen that uses the full-screen mode needs to enable it in the `paint()` method and not in the constructor. A more difficult issue to overcome is the full-screen mode on the K700. It works just fine, but it does not show system alerts correctly, for example, when you are establishing an HTTP connection. You can circumvent this by using the `com.nokia.mid.ui.FullCanvas` class instead. Most user interface bugs, such as the previously mentioned one, are resolved by the J2ME Polish GUI automatically. The good thing about Sony Ericsson platforms is that they behave consistently, so your chances are quite good that your application works fine on all Sony Ericsson devices once it works flawlessly on one device.

RIM BlackBerry

The BlackBerry series from Research in Motion (RIM) has become quite popular for business solutions with its integrated e-mail push functionality. You can find quite extensive information at *http://www.blackberry.com/developers*. RIM also maintains a community at *http://www.blackberry.com/developers/forum*.

BlackBerry extends the CLDC and MIDP standards with its own proprietary API that allows you to integrate your application tightly into the handset. You can use the provided Java Development Environment (JDE) for developing BlackBerry applications under Windows. This is not a requirement; you can also use any other IDE. BlackBerry devices do not accept JAR files but only proprietary COD files. J2ME Polish converts the JAR files automatically for BlackBerry devices when you have defined the `blackberry.home` Ant property, which points to the location of the JDE.

Other Vendors

Many other device manufacturers exist, including Sanyo, Sharp, and Palm. Judging from their worldwide market share, they don't play a big role, but you should consider supporting them depending on your target market. Please refer to the device database of J2ME Polish at *http://www.j2mepolish.org/devices-overview.html* to get to know the specifics of such phones.

Identifying Carriers

Carriers such as Vodafone, Sprint, and T-Mobile can modify devices by including or deactivating additional libraries and by adding or changing root certificates.

Vodafone (*http://via.vodafone.com*) is quite active by providing its own Vodafone Service Class Library (VSCL) that includes 3D and multimedia features. You need to sign a nondisclosure agreement and start a business relationship with Vodafone before you can get more information about these opportunities.

Sprint (*http://developer.sprintpcs.com*) provides many resources and forums for their phones.

Nextel (*http://developer.nextel.com*) even provides its own open-source UI API (*http://nextel.sourceforge.net*), but this hasn't been updated since 2001.

AT&T Wireless (*http://developer.cingular.com/developer*) provides a developer community and J2ME documentation.

O2 (*http://www.sourceo2.com*) publishes information and provides forums on its developer site.

Some carriers expect that your application has been verified by the Java Verified program (*http://www.javaverified.com*) when you want to market your applications on their portals.

Identifying Platforms

In addition to the MIDP platforms, several similar mobile Java platforms are available that are partly compatible with the J2ME standard. Table 15-4 lists the most important platforms.

Tip From J2ME Polish 1.3 onward, you can build for any of these platforms and even define additional platforms in the *${polish.home}/custom-platforms.xml* file.

Table 15-4. *Important Mobile Java Platforms*

Platform	Region	Specialties
MIDP	Worldwide	Leading standard for creating mobile Java applications.
JTWI	Worldwide	Additional libraries and clarification of the MIDP 2.0 standard.
IMP	Worldwide	Standard for creating embedded Java applications without user interface.
Personal Java	Worldwide	For enterprise applications, based on J2SE.
DoJa	Japan	NTT DoCoMo's (*http://www.nttdocomo.co.jp/english*) mobile Java platform. Similar but not compatible with the MIDP standard.
WIPI	Korea	WIPI 1.0 is 90% compatible with MIDP 1.0, and WIPI 1.2 is 100% compatible with the MIDP 2.0 standard. Neither platform requires preverification.

MIDP Platforms

MIDP-compatible platforms (based on JSRs 37, 118, and 271) form the vast majority of available mobile Java implementations.

Symbian (*http://www.symbian.com/developer*) provides the most widely used operating system and with it the MIDP profile. The UIQ 2.*x* version from Symbian additionally supports the Personal Java profile. The current Symbian OS uses Sun's CLDC HI 1.1 implementation, which features a dynamic adaptive compiler. This DAC compiler can compile selected bytecode on demand and hotswap it in the middle of a method.

Aplix's JBlend JVM (*http://www.aplix.co.jp/en/jblend*) is the leading virtual machine implementation in Japan and is used worldwide. Manufacturers such as Sharp, Sanyo, and Motorola deploy JBlend in several devices. Operators such as Vodafone, NTT DoCoMo, and Sprint also use JBlend. The platform supports the MIDP 1.0, MIDP 2.0, and DoJa profiles along with the CLDC 1.1 and CLDC 1.0 configurations. Optional APIs such as the Mobile Media API, the Wireless Messaging API, and the Mobile 3D Graphics API are supported. Additionally, JBlend supports some carrier extensions such as Vodafone's Service Class Library and the Common Java Service Platform.

Other common virtual machines include IBM's WEME virtual machine (also called J9, *http://www-306.ibm.com/software/wireless/weme*), which is used on Palm platforms. Esmertec's Jbed platform (*http://www.esmertec.com*) is often used for BREW devices. BREW, Binary Runtime Environment for Wireless, is the North American competing standard to J2ME. Tao Group's Intent platform (*http://withintent.biz*) targets mainly Windows smart phone devices.

Not really a platform but an interesting technology is AMR's Jazelle (*http://www.arm.com/products/solutions/Jazelle.html*). The idea is to have hardware that interprets and executes the Java bytecode directly. AMR offers processor designs that include the Jazelle technology. Since the hardware is directly embedded in the main processor, Jazelle offers high performance.

DoJa Platforms

DoJa (also called iAppli, *http://www.doja-developer.net*) is the de facto Japanese Java standard made by NTT DoCoMo. Initial versions allowed applications with JAR sizes up to only 10KB in DoJa 1.0 and then 30KB in DoJa 2.5. The current DoJa 4.0 version supports JAR sizes up to 100KB and allows up to 400KB for the persistent data.

DoJa is built upon the CLDC 1.0 configuration and offers a similar feature set as MIDP. Main differences are the persistence mechanism (DoJa can store only one large byte array in the so-called scratchpad), the application life cycle and threading model (it's recommend to use only a single thread in DoJa applications), and the event handling (DoJa offers functions similar to the MIDP 2.0 `GameCanvas` class). You can find porting instructions at *http://www.doja-developer.net*.

■ **Note** J2ME Polish will support building DoJa applications from version 1.3 onward. You can use either preprocessing or different source folders (using the `<source>` elements in your *build.xml*) for targeting DoJa and MIDP platforms in the same project.

WIPI Platforms

The Wireless Internet Platform for Interoperability (WIPI, *http://wipi.or.kr/English*) is the Korean standard for mobile Java applications. Previously the BREW standard was strong in Korea, but now all operators have embraced the WIPI 1.2 standards, with WIPI 2.0 waiting just around the corner.

Java applications don't need to be preverified, because the bytecode is transcoded into C source code first and subsequently compiled to the native binary code on WIPI platforms. Otherwise, the deployment is compatible with the MIDP standard: the JAR file contains resources and classes, and the JAD file contains the description.

WIPI 1.2 applications are based on CLDC 1.0 and have a similar feature set as the MIDP 1.0 profile.

WIPI 2.0 is fully compatible with the CLDC 1.1 and MIDP 2.0 standards.

■ **Note** You can build your application for WIPI platforms beginning with the J2ME Polish 1.3 release.

Writing Portable Code

Writing portable code is one of the main challenges of creating wireless Java applications. But writing portable code is a Good Thing, because you want to support as many devices as possible for maximum revenue. Basically, four strategies are available for writing portable code:

- Use the lowest common denominator.
- Use dynamic code that adjusts itself during the runtime.
- Use different source files depending on the target device.
- Use preprocessing.

In the following sections, I will discuss the advantages and caveats of each approach. The J2ME Polish GUI uses preprocessing for adjusting itself to the various environments.

Using the Lowest Common Denominator

Using the lowest common denominator makes things quite simple; you just need to stick to the MIDP 1.0 profile and the CLDC 1.0 profile. Unfortunately, this is not the whole truth. Besides the need for professional user interfaces and the limited functionality, you still have to circumvent device bugs somehow. But since you deal only with a small fraction of the available possibilities, you might get away lucky.

A similar strategy is to target only MIDP 2.0 devices, which is becoming more and more feasible, even though new devices with MIDP 1.0 support are still released into the market. The MIDP 2.0 technology is, however, young and therefore behaves quite differently and unexpectedly on different existing devices. Problems with device issues are inevitable.

The advantage of using a common denominator is that you have only one application bundle, so deploying the application is much easier. But this strategy does not relieve you of the testing burden, since you still need to test your application on every target device. Business relationships can be seriously jeopardized when you say that your application is running on a specific handset but in reality it isn't.

■ **Caution** Using the lowest common denominator is a valid approach, but you should consider the business aspects of this decision as well. Users might be disappointed about "old" or "lame" applications, so they will choose another vendor the next time. Also, you will have difficulties finding marketing partners unless you have come up with a revolutionary new concept.

Using Dynamic Code

Dynamic coding is one of the main benefits of Java platforms. Since there is no real reflection support on the CLDC/MIDP platforms, you can use only `Class.forName()`, parameters, and flexible functions for implementing this approach.

An example for using dynamic class loading is the obligatory splash screen. Listing 15-2 demonstrates how Nokia's `FullCanvas` implementation is used when the Nokia UI API is present and the `setFullScreenMode()` method is called when the MIDP 2.0 API is available.

Listing 15-2. *Implementing a Full Screen Dynamically*

```
package com.apress.dynamic;
import javax.microedition.lcdui.*;
import javax.microedition.midlet.*;

public class GameMidlet extends MIDlet {
   private Display display;
   public GameMidlet() {
   }
   public void startApp() {
      this.display = Display.getDisplay( this );
      Canvas splash;
      // check if this device supports the MIDP 2.0 standard:
      try {
         Class.forName("javax.microedition.io.PushRegistry");
         // okay, MIDP 2.0 standard is supported:
         splash = (Canvas) Class.forName
                  ("com.apress.dynamic.Midp2Splash").newInstance();
      } catch (Exception e) {
         // the MIDP 2.0 standard is not supported
         // check if this device supports the Nokia-UI-API:
         try {
            Class.forName("com.nokia.mid.ui.FullCanvas");
            splash = (Canvas) Class.forName
                     ("com.apress.dynamic.NokiaUiSplash").newInstance();
         } catch (Exception e2) {
            // okay, neither MIDP 2.0 nor Nokia UI API is supported:
            splash = new Midp1Splash();
         }
      }
      // show the splash screen:
      this.display.setCurrent( splash );
   }
   public void destroyApp( boolean unconditional ) {
   }
   public void pauseApp() {
   }
}

// the normal MIDP 1.0 splash screen:
package com.apress.dynamic;
import javax.microedition.lcdui.*;
public class Midp1Splash extends Canvas {
   public void paint( Graphics g ) {
      g.drawString("Starting!", getWidth()/2, getHeight()/2,
         Graphics.HCENTER | Graphics.BASELINE );
```

```
   }
}

// the MIDP 2.0 splash screen:
package com.apress.dynamic;
import javax.microedition.lcdui.*;
public class Midp2Splash extends Canvas {
   public void paint( Graphics g ) {
      setFullScreenMode( true );
      g.drawString("Starting!", getWidth()/2, getHeight()/2,
         Graphics.HCENTER | Graphics.BASELINE );
   }
}

// the Nokia UI API splash screen:
package com.apress.dynamic;
import javax.microedition.lcdui.*;
import com.nokia.mid.ui.FullCanvas;
public class NokiaSplash extends FullCanvas {
   public void paint( Graphics g ) {
      g.drawString("Starting!", getWidth()/2, getHeight()/2,
         Graphics.HCENTER | Graphics.BASELINE );
   }
}
```

The dynamic code of Listing 15-2 has only one problem: Nokia's `FullCanvas` implementation often does not report the correct height in the `getHeight()` method. This is not a real problem, since the only effect is that the "Starting" `String` is drawn not really vertically centered. The case is different, however, when you also paint a background. In that case, a blank area would remain when you call `g.fillRect( 0, 0, getWidth(), getHeight() )` or similar.

The previous code has already circumvented one issue of Sony Ericsson's P910 phone, though. This phone reacts quite irritated whenever you enable the MIDP 2.0 full-screen mode anywhere other than the `paint()` method—at least for the first shown screen. Of course, the whole approach also fails when you want to target other platforms than the MIDP ones.

Another possible problem is the associated code bloat when you use dynamic code. This is not most likely a real problem on modern devices, but the whole purpose of using dynamic programming is to provide one application code for all devices. In fact, the performance might be affected quite badly. In Listing 15-2, two exceptions will be thrown when neither the MIDP 2.0 profile nor the Nokia UI API is present on the device. Exceptions are very costly in regard to the performance of an application, so you lose quite a lot potential here.

Dynamic programming can be quite powerful, though; you can even check for keycodes of nonstandardized keys, such as the soft keys, dynamically by using the `Canvas.getKeyName()` method, for example. In general, you need to provide one solution for any possible combination. So, this makes dynamic programming quite difficult.

You also need to notify J2ME Polish about each dynamically loaded class by specifying the appropriate `<keep>` element inside the `<obfuscator>` element in your *build.xml* file, for example, `<obfuscator name="ProGuard"> <keep name="com.apress.dynamic.Midp2Splash" /> </obfuscator>`.

Again, I should point out that dynamic programming does not relieve you of the testing burden: you still need to test your application on every target device you want to support. The benefit is to have only one JAR file, which eases the application's deployment.

■ **Tip** When you're deploying dynamic code, you should consider separating your code according to the Model-View-Control pattern so that you can exchange views more easily. The common practice on wireless Java platforms is to merge the controller and the model to minimize class usage (and therefore JAR space).

Using Preprocessing

Preprocessing changes your source code before it is actually compiled. This approach provides an unmatched flexibility. Listing 15-3 shows how to get the same functionality as in the dynamic code example in Listing 15-2 with only a fraction of code. In more complex scenarios, you will profit even more by using preprocessing.

Listing 15-3. *Implementing a Full Screen with Preprocessing*

```
package com.apress.preprocessing;
import javax.microedition.lcdui.*;
import javax.microedition.midlet.*;

public class GameMidlet extends MIDlet {
   private Display display;
   public GameMidlet() {
   }
   public void startApp() {
      this.display = Display.getDisplay( this );
      Splash splash = new Splash();
      this.display.setCurrent( splash );
   }
   public void destroyApp( boolean unconditional ) {
   }
   public void pauseApp() {
   }
}

// the splash screen:
package com.apress.preprocessing;
import javax.microedition.lcdui.*;
public class Splash
```

```
//#if polish.midp2
   extends Canvas
//#elif polish.classes.fullscreen:defined
   //#= extends ${polish.classes.fullscreen}
//#else
   // hide extends clause from the IDE:
   //# extends Canvas
//#endif
{
   public void paint( Graphics g ) {
      //#if polish.midp2
         setFullScreenMode( true );
      //#endif
      //#if polish.FullCanvasSize:defined
         //#= g.drawString("Starting!",
         //#=  ${polish.FullCanvasWidth}/2,
         //#=  ${polish.FullCanvasHeight}/2,
         //#=  Graphics.HCENTER | Graphics.BASELINE );
      //#else
         g.drawString("Starting!", getWidth()/2, getHeight()/2,
            Graphics.HCENTER | Graphics.BASELINE );
      //#endif
   }
}
```

The simple preprocessing code needs two fewer classes than the dynamic code, which is a reduction of 50%! It also solves the problem of Nokia's `getHeight()` method in full-screen mode, since it uses hard-coded values.

Another benefit of preprocessing is that you can check for known issues by testing the `polish.Bugs` capability, for example, `//#if polish.Bugs.drawRgbOrigin`. This allows you to circumvent most bugs; please refer to the known issues database at *http://www.j2mepolish.org/devices/issues.html* and Chapter 8 for more details.

Tip The J2ME Polish client APIs, like the user interface, make heavy use of preprocessing so that they can adapt to the target device. This is a kind of fully automatic adjustment, since no further manual intervention is needed from your side. Since you can find most errors in the user interface classes, you can save a lot of effort and sweat here.

A disadvantage of preprocessing is the little or nonexisting support for it by the common IDEs. That's why J2ME Polish includes a preprocessing-aware Java editor for the Eclipse IDE from version 1.3 onward, as shown in Figure 15-1.

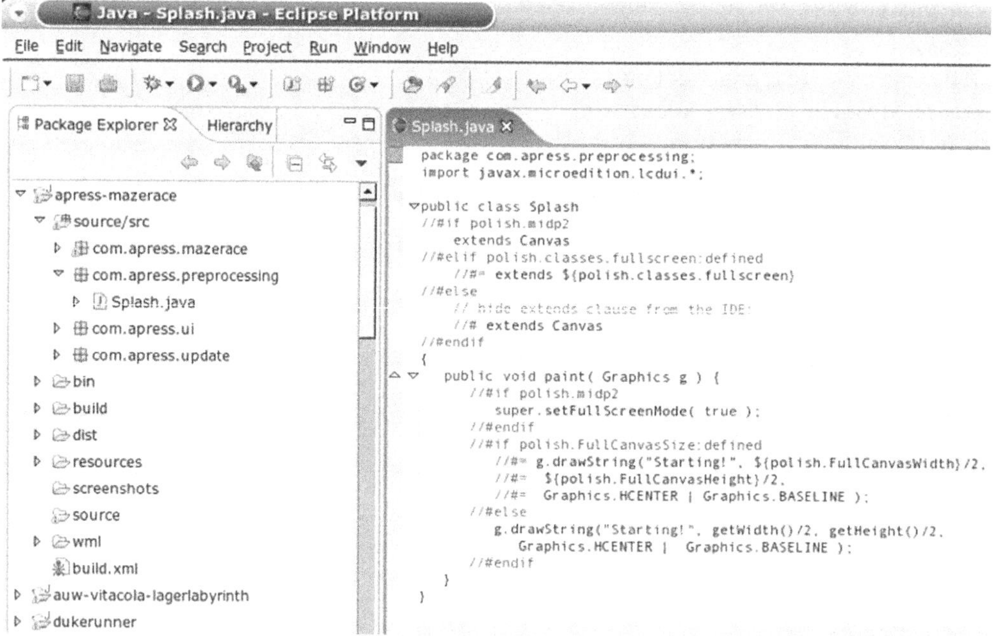

Figure 15-1. *The preprocessing-aware Eclipse editor in action*

■ **Note** Aspect-oriented programming provides a similar flexibility to preprocessing. It is, however, quite difficult to manage. The available solutions also depend on reflection and add their own dispatcher core, which needs additional JAR space of around 40KB.

Using Different Source Files

A similar approach to preprocessing is to use different source folders. You use different source files and folders by implementing conditional `<source>` elements in your *build.xml* file. Listing 15-4 shows you how you can use different source files depending on the current target device.

Listing 15-4. *Using Different Source Files with the <source> Elements*

```
<j2mepolish>
  <info
    license="GPL"
    name="Roadrunner"
    vendorName="A reader."
    version="0.0.1"
    jarName="${polish.vendor}-${polish.name}-roadrunner.jar"
  />
```

```
  <deviceRequirements>
    <requirement name="Identifier"
                 value="Nokia/Series60, Siemens/x75" />
  </deviceRequirements>
  <build
    usePolishGui="true"
  >
    <midlet class="com.apress.roadrunner.Roadrunner" />
    <sources>
      <source dir="source/src" />
      <source dir="source/midp2"
              if="polish.midp2" />
      <source dir="source/nokiaui"
              if="polish.api.nokia-ui and not polish.midp2" />
      <source dir="source/midp1"
              if="not (polish.api.nokia-ui or polish.midp2)" />
    </sources>
  </build>
  <emulator />
</j2mepolish>
```

The code is actual quite similar to dynamic Java source code, as you can see in Listing 15-5. The main difference is, however, that you don't waste JAR and memory space by including unused classes in your application. Also, the code itself is easier to understand for developers who don't know J2ME Polish.

Listing 15-5. *Implementing a Full-Screen Splash Screen by Using Different Source Folders*

```
package com.apress.folders;
import javax.microedition.lcdui.*;
import javax.microedition.midlet.*;

public class GameMidlet extends MIDlet {
  private Display display;
  public GameMidlet() {
  }
  public void startApp() {
    this.display = Display.getDisplay( this );
    Splash splash = new Splash();
    this.display.setCurrent( splash );
  }
  public void destroyApp( boolean unconditional ) {
  }
  public void pauseApp() {
  }
}
```

```
// the normal MIDP 1.0 splash screen,
// this class resides in source/midp1:
package com.apress.folders;
import javax.microedition.lcdui.*;
public class Splash extends Canvas {
   public void paint( Graphics g ) {
      g.drawString("Starting!", getWidth()/2, getHeight()/2,
         Graphics.HCENTER | Graphics.BASELINE );
   }
}

// the MIDP 2.0 splash screen,
// this class resides in source/midp2:
package com.apress.folders;
import javax.microedition.lcdui.*;
public class Splash extends Canvas {
   public void paint( Graphics g ) {
      setFullScreenMode( true );
      g.drawString("Starting!", getWidth()/2, getHeight()/2,
         Graphics.HCENTER | Graphics.BASELINE );
   }
}

// the Nokia UI API splash screen,
// this class resides in source/nokiaui:
package com.apress.folders;
import javax.microedition.lcdui.*;
import com.nokia.mid.ui.FullCanvas;
public class Splash extends FullCanvas {
   public void paint( Graphics g ) {
      g.drawString("Starting!", getWidth()/2, getHeight()/2,
         Graphics.HCENTER | Graphics.BASELINE );
   }
}
```

Every serious Java IDE supports several source folders for one project. In Eclipse you can add source folders by right-clicking the project, selecting Properties, and then selecting Java Build Path, as shown in Figure 15-2. On the Source tab, click Add Folder to add another source folder. You should, however, not do this when you want to implement the same classes several times. In that case, your IDE would (correctly) complain about duplicate class definitions. Just use one main source folder (such as *source/src*), and add the other source folders to the parent directory, such as *source/midp2*, *source/nokiaui*, and so on. Another strategy is to use different projects in your IDE that contain the different sources.

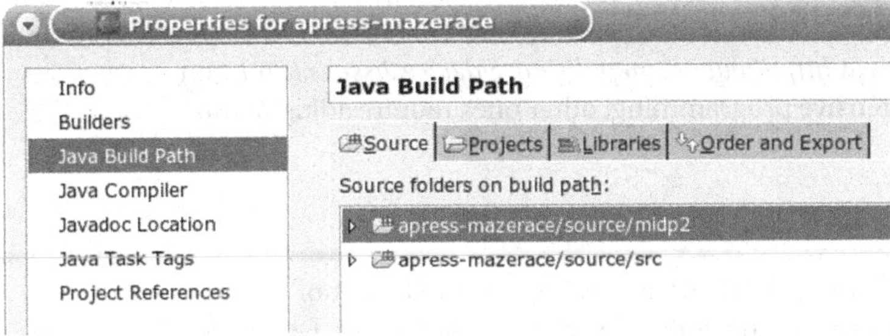

Figure 15-2. *Adding a new source folder to an Eclipse project*

The main drawback of using different source files is the additional work that is needed for each change. Depending on the business requirements, you might need to create loads of different Java source files. When you now need to include an additional feature or bug fix, you need to implement the change in every affected source file.

Solving Common Problems

Typically, you will encounter similar problems in your projects. In the following sections, I will discuss how you can resolve common difficulties.

Using the Appropriate Resources

The main difference between different devices is the screen size, so you will often need to adjust images for the best results. Also, you will often need different multimedia resources, for example, different types of sound files.

Using J2ME Polish's automatic resource assembling, this task is quite easy to accomplish. Just put all common resources into the *resources* folder of your project and use subfolders for specific resources, such as *resources/Nokia* for Nokia resources, *resources/mmapi* for devices that support the Mobile Media API, and *resources/Motorola/A1000* for Motorola's A1000 phone.

Another nice feature is that you can use flexible folders as well: resources from the *resources/BitsPerPixel.12+* folder will be used for all devices that have a color depth of at least 12 bits per color (4,096 colors), for example. Another example is the *resources/ScreenSize.150+x200+* folder. Resources from this folder will be used when the device has a screen that is at least 150 pixels wide and 200 pixel high. When you use several of these flexible resource folders, the closest match will be used.

You can also specify conditions for resources using the `<resources>` element and its nested `<fileset>` elements in your *build.xml* script.

Please refer to the "Packaging Your Application" section in Chapter 7 for learning the full details of the resource assembling options with J2ME Polish.

Circumventing Known Issues

You can see the many known issues at *http://www.j2mepolish.org/devices/issues.html*. You can circumvent some issues by defensive programming; other ones require adjustments of your code.

Defensive Programming

One issue that you can circumvent by defensive programming is the behavior of the `InputStream.available()` implementation on Symbian and Motorola devices. On these devices the `available()` method returns `0` when you read a resource from your JAR file. Please note that this behavior is perfectly allowed by the CLDC specification, which states that the default `available()` implementation always returns `0` but that subclasses *should* override this method. It is just somewhat unexpected.

Listing 15-6 shows an implementation that reads a resource and returns its contents as a byte array. Next to the `available()` call is another problem in that code: you probably just assume that the whole buffer will be read in one go when you call `InputStream.read( byte[] )`. This is not the case, as the JavaDoc of the CLDC mentions. Rather than filling the buffer completely, the number of read bytes is returned by the `read()` method. When you know the exact size of the input, you should use the `DataInputStream.readFully( byte[] )` method instead. A third problem is that you do not close the input stream when the `read()` method throws an exception. This could lead to memory leaks in your application.

Listing 15-6. *Reading a Resource Incorrectly*

```
public byte[] readResource( String url )
throws IOException
{
   InputStream in = getClass().getResourceAsStream( url );
   // the following always returns 0 on Symbian and Motorola:
   int available = in.available();
   byte[] buffer = new byte[ available ];
   // this is not guaranteed to work either:
   in.read( buffer );
   // the input stream is not guaranteed to be closed,
   // since in.read() may throw an exception.
   in.close();
   return buffer;
}
```

Listing 15-7 shows a defensive implementation of the same method that works on Motorola and Symbian devices as well. You read the resource as long as the `read()` method signals the end of the stream by returning `-1`. You also use a `ByteArrayOutputStream` for buffering the read bytes. Last but not least, you surround the actual reading of the resource with a `try {...} finally` block. The `finally` block executes even when an exception occurs in the surrounded code. The resulting application is much more complicated than the original one, but, hey, it works!

Listing 15-7. *Reading a Resource Correctly Using Some Defensive Techniques*

```
public byte[] readResource( String url )
throws IOException
{
   InputStream in = getClass().getResourceAsStream( url );
   byte[] buffer;
   // the following always returns 0 on Symbian and Motorola:
   int available = in.available();
   if ( available == 0 ) {
      available = 4 * 1024; // 4 kb
   }
   buffer = new byte[ available ];
   ByteArrayOutputStream out = new ByteArrayOutputStream( available );
   int read;
   try {
      while ( (read = in.read( buffer ) ) != -1 ) {
         out.write( buffer, 0, read );
      }
   } finally {
      in.close();
   }
   return out.toByteArray();
}
```

■ **Tip** Always read the documentation carefully. Whenever it says *might*, *may*, or *should*, you cannot assume that the behavior is the same on all devices. You are, however, most likely on the safe side when the documentation states that a feature *must* be present.

Code Adjustments

Often, defensive programming in itself is not sufficient to circumvent issues. In such cases you need to adjust your code either on the source code level or on the bytecode level.

Using Preprocessing

You can use preprocessing for circumventing known issues in your source code.

An example for an issue that requires code changes is the implementation of the full-screen mode on the Sony Ericsson K700 device. When the MIDP 2.0 full-screen mode has been activated by calling `Canvas.setFullScreenMode( true )`, system alerts are no longer displayed. System alerts are shown whenever you access a restricted resource, for example, when you want to start an HTTP connection. A possible workaround is to use the `com.nokia.mid.ui.FullCanvas` class of the Nokia UI API that is present on the K700 device as well. Please note that the `FullCanvas` class does not allow you to add any commands. J2ME Polish sets the preprocessing symbol `polish.Bugs.needsNokiaUiForSystemAlerts` when this issue is present. Using the `polish.Bugs.[name]` symbols allows you to abstract your code from specific devices so that you can later use the same workarounds for any device that has the corresponding issue. You can add issues in the device database by setting the `Bugs` capability in *devices.xml, custom-devices.xml, groups.xml,* and so on: `<capability name="Bugs" value="issueName1, issueName2" />`.

Listing 15-8 shows how to check if this issue is present on the current target device. When this is the case and the Nokia UI API is available, you extend the `FullCanvas` class instead of the normal `Canvas` class. In this case, you use the `polish.classes.fullscreen` preprocessing variable, which contains the value `com.nokia.mid.ui.FullCanvas` for devices that support the Nokia UI API. This is a bit more flexible compared to extending the `FullCanvas` directly. You do not call `setFullScreenMode()` when this bug is present or when the MIDP 2.0 profile is not supported by the target device.

Listing 15-8. *Using the FullCanvas When the needsNokiaUiForSystemAlerts Bug Is Present*

```
package com.apress.preprocessing;
import javax.microedition.lcdui.*;
public class Splash
//#if polish.midp2 && !polish.Bugs.needsNokiaUiForSystemAlerts
   extends Canvas
//#elif polish.classes.fullscreen:defined
   //#= extends ${polish.classes.fullscreen}
//#else
   // hide extends clause from the IDE:
   //# extends Canvas
//#endif
{
   public void paint( Graphics g ) {
      //#if polish.midp2 && !polish.Bugs.needsNokiaUiForSystemAlerts
         setFullScreenMode( true );
      //#endif
      g.drawString( "Starting!", getWidth() / 2, getHeight() / 2,
            Graphics.HCENTER | Graphics.BASELINE );
   }
}
```

The `Graphics.drawRGB()` implementation is problematic on many MIDP 2.0 devices, such as Nokia Series 60 and Sony Ericsson K700. You can use the `drawRGB()` method for painting integer arrays that contain pixel information in the RGB format. A cool thing about this method is that you can use translucent data as well so your background shines through. On the K700 device, the `drawRGB()` implementation does not take the translation origin into account—instead, the `(0, 0)` origin is always used. So, when you translate the origin of `Graphics` by calling `Graphics.translate( x, y )`, the drawn RGB data will be misaligned when this bug is present. A possible solution is not to use `translate()` at all, but on some devices this is called anyway by the native implementation, for example, when the title is painted. When you use a bit of preprocessing, you are on the safe side. Listing 15-9 shows how to circumvent this bug by adjusting the `x` and `y` values before calling `drawRGB()`.

Listing 15-9. *Circumventing the drawRgbOrigin Issue*

```
public void paintArgbColor( int argbColor, int x, int y,
                            int width, int height, Graphics g )
{
   // circumvent the drawRgbOrigin issue when it is present:
   //#ifdef polish.Bugs.drawRgbOrigin
      x += g.getTranslateX();
      y += g.getTranslateY();
   //#endif
   // in reality you need to buffer this:
   int[] rgbBuffer = new int[ width ];
   for ( int i = rgbBuffer.length - 1; i >= 0 ; i-- ) {
      rgbBuffer[ i ] = argbColor;
   }
   // defensive programming: some implementations
   // don't accept negative coordinates:
   if ( x < 0 ) {
      width += x;
      if ( width < 0 ) {
         return;
      }
      x = 0;
   }
   if ( y < 0 ) {
      height += y;
      if ( height < 0 ) {
         return;
      }
      y = 0;
   }
   // now paint the RGB data:
   g.drawRGB( rgbBuffer, 0, 0, x, y, width, height, true );
}
```

Using preprocessing is sometimes tedious work for circumventing bugs, but often there is no alternative. All J2ME Polish libraries use preprocessing for adapting themselves to the target devices, so you can just use the libraries without needing to be too concerned about device issues. You should, however, build your application to specific target devices when these have known issues. J2ME Polish has no chance to circumvent device-specific bugs when you use generic target devices such as “Generic/midp2.”

Manipulating Bytecode

Another option for circumventing bugs is to alter the application on the bytecode level.

This approach has several advantages because the programmer does not need to circumvent issues herself during the application development phase. Also, certain aspects of programs can be tracked on the bytecode level easier than on the source code level, such as the usage of floating-point calculations. A third advantage is that you can circumvent a new known issue in an existing application just by rebuilding it. The disadvantage is, of course, the complexity of bytecode manipulations. If you are up to the task, you can create a postcompiler that extends the `de.enough.polish.postcompile.PostCompiler` class. You can integrate it into the processing chain using the `<postcompiler>` element in the *build.xml* file. Postcompilers are invoked after the compilation phase and can change a lot of things. An example includes the Floater tool of Enough Software, which allows you to implement floating-point calculations using the primitive types `float` and `double` on CLDC 1.0 devices. Please refer to the "Using a Postcompiler" section in Chapter 13 for more details about this option.

■ **Tip** For manipulating bytecode, refer to the ASM (*http://asm.objectweb.org*) and BCEL (*http://jakarta.apache.org/bcel*) libraries.

Implementing the User Interface

The user interface is often the most problematic area when you target different devices. For implementing the user interface in MIDP devices, you can choose between the so-called high-level GUI, which offers `Forms`, `Lists`, and so forth, and the low-level GUI, which allows you to paint your own widgets.

A common source for errors is the event handling. You must never block the event handling thread, for example, in the `commandAction()` method of a `CommandListener` or in the `keyPressed()` method of a `Canvas`. When you have a long-running calculation, a network connection, and so on, you need to do this in a separate `Thread`.

Using the High-Level GUI

Using the high-level GUI has several advantages:

- Your application is smaller, since you do not need so much code for creating the user interface.
- Your application can be ported easier, because many low-level GUI implementations contain issues.
- Development is easier, because the low-level GUI is quite complex.

The main disadvantage is that the look and feel of your application depends on the vendor's implementation. Some implementations have a pleasant appearance, but others provide a somewhat awkward-looking user interface. The MIDP 2.0 profile offers some great new features, such as the `CustomItem`, the ability to focus items by calling `Display.setCurrentItem()`, and pop-up `ChoiceGroups`.

With the J2ME Polish GUI, you can use the high-level GUI in your application code and take full control at the same time by specifying designs outside the application code with CSS text files. The J2ME Polish GUI also supports the new MIDP 2.0 high-level GUI features on MIDP 1.0 devices. The J2ME Polish GUI internally uses preprocessing for adapting itself to various handsets. You can activate and deactivate the usage of the J2ME Polish GUI depending on conditions. Please refer to Chapter 12 for a detailed discussion of the possibilities.

Using the Low-Level GUI

The low-level GUI API allows you to control every detail of the user interface but brings along the burden of having to manage every detail yourself, including scrolling, handling events, and, most of all, painting the user interface.

Custom Items

On MIDP 2.0 devices you can also mix the low- and high-level GUI API with the `javax.microedition.lcdui.CustomItem` class. Depending on the target device, you can even receive key events for complex interactions with your `CustomItem`. The only mandatory functionality is, however, to display the contents of your `CustomItem`, so you cannot rely on any advanced interaction modes. You are not restricted, however, when you use the J2ME Polish GUI, which supports the same interaction modes and forwards key- and pointer-pressed events on every target device.

Soft Keys

Soft keys are not standardized, so you will encounter different keycodes between different vendors. The device database contains the keycodes for most devices; Listing 15-10 demonstrates how to use the information with a bit of preprocessing. When `polish.key.LeftSoftKey` is not defined, assume that the appropriate keycode is `-6`. The default keycode for the right soft key is `-7`. In the `keyPressed()` method, you first check whether one of the soft keys has been pressed, before you get the game action. This is a defensive programming technique because some devices throw `IllegalArgumentExceptions` when a soft key value is given to the `getGameAction()` method.

Listing 15-10. *Using the Correct Keycodes for the Soft Keys*

```
package com.apress.preprocessing;
import javax.microedition.lcdui.*;

public class MyCanvas extends Canvas {
   //#ifdef polish.key.LeftSoftKey:defined
      //#= private static final int LEFT_SOFT_KEY = ${polish.key.LeftSoftKey};
   //#else
      private static final int LEFT_SOFT_KEY = -6;
   //#endif
   //#ifdef polish.key.RightSoftKey:defined
      //#= private static final int RIGHT_SOFT_KEY = ${polish.key.RightSoftKey};
   //#else
      private static final int RIGHT_SOFT_KEY = -7;
   //#endif

   public void keyPressed( int keyCode ) {
      if ( keyCode == LEFT_SOFT_KEY ) {
         // process left soft key
      } else if ( keyCode == RIGHT_SOFT_KEY ) {
         // process right soft key
```

```
        } else {
            int gameAction = getGameAction( keyCode );
            // process key pressed event...
        }
    }

    protected void paint( javax.microedition.lcdui.Graphics graphics ) {
    }

}
```

Some devices do not produce any key events when soft keys are pressed. In that case, you can sometimes add empty and thus invisible commands, mostly one `Command.BACK` type and one `Command.SCREEN` type, so that both keys have an associated command. You can then process these commands in the `commandAction()` method of the `CommandListener`.

Networking

Networking allows you to interact with the outside world. On MIDP platforms, you have a different range of possible techniques, such as text messaging (SMS), Bluetooth, and HTTP.

Short Message Service

The short message service (SMS) allows you to send text messages up to a length of 160 characters from your mobile device. You can use the Wireless Messaging API (WMAPI, JSR 120) for sending and receiving text messages. The WMAPI 2.0 (JSR 205) also supports multimedia messages (MMS).

A potential problem for wireless messages is the running time, which can vary greatly. Also, you have no guarantee that the message is really delivered. In general, SMS is, however, an easy and reliable communication protocol.

Bluetoothing

Bluetooth allows you to connect other Bluetooth-enabled devices directly. This kind of connection is great for exchanging information ad hoc. Using the so-called pico networks, you can also connect to several other devices at once. Not every device that supports Bluetooth connections makes them available through the optional Bluetooth API (JSR 82), but the support is constantly growing.

A common problem with Bluetooth is that only few devices have implemented the optional OBEX part in the Bluetooth API. You can create your own protocol or use the Avetana OBEX library (*http://sourceforge.net/projects/avetanaobex*) for exchanging data.

For security reasons, most Bluetooth devices keep their ID hidden, unless the user requests to be "visible" explicitly. When you already know your communication partners, this is not a problem, but this can have serious implications when your application depends on discovering new devices. An example of such an application is a dating service that matches interests whenever it discovers another device that also runs this service.

Finally, another problem is the latency of creating connections. When you have only a short time for making connections—for example, when users pass by each other—you might not be able to discover the device and establish a connection.

HTTP Networking

The Hypertext Transfer Protocol (HTTP) is the only guaranteed way to make connections on all devices. MIDP 2.0 devices additionally need to support HTTPS connections for secure communication.

HTTP is a network-agnostic protocol, so in principle your application does not need to care whether the device uses WAP, TCP, GSM, GPRS, UMTS, or other network technology.

When you have problems establishing a connection on a device, you should first check whether you are using an Internet access point or a connection through the WAP gateway of the carrier. Connecting through a WAP gateway often causes trouble when you try to connect to nonstandard ports. You should, therefore, try to use port 80, 8080, or 443 for your server application. In case you still encounter problems, make sure to use an Internet access point on your device. Resolving domain names slows down network connections and can also cause problems, so try to use a static IP address instead in your J2ME application. You can configure your application by providing the server IP address as a JAD attribute or as a preprocessing variable.

The latency for network connections is quite high, often several seconds. This rules out complex real-time applications, such as multiplayer action games. Again, you might speed up latency a bit by using an IP address instead of a domain name. This can cause problems, however, when your sever application is relocated in the future.

Since connections cost money, the device is required to ask the user for permission when an HTTP connection is about to be established. When the user does not allow the connection, a `SecurityException` is thrown. When you sign your application, you can use the `MIDlet-Permissions` JAD attribute for stating that your application needs HTTP connections to function. In that case, the user is asked only once during the installation. When the user declines the required resource, the application is not installed at all. In J2ME Polish you can use the `permissions` attribute of the `<info>` element for setting this JAD attribute: `<info permissions="javax.microedition.io.Connector.http" [...] />`.

Data Protocols

You should think twice before using XML or SOAP for exchanging data with a server. XML is a syntactically verbose protocol that carries a lot of overhead compared to the actual data. You also need to parse and construct the XML messages in your J2ME application, which can be quite costly in terms of performance and heap memory usage. Often it is better to use your own proprietary binary protocol instead. You can use `DataInputStream` and `DataOutputStream` for reading and writing binary data comfortably.

Anyway, if you can't resist using an XML protocol for communication, you can use kXML (*http://kxml.sourceforge.net*) for parsing the data.

Authentication

When the J2ME application needs to authenticate the user, you can use several approaches for transmitting the data securely. On MIDP 2.0 devices you can just use an HTTPS connection. On MIDP 1.0 devices you can calculate the hash value of the password and send this value over HTTP. You should also add a timestamp to each authentication request and use this timestamp in your hashing function as well for preventing replay attacks. In a replay attack a malicious intruder intercepts the communication, copies the authentication request, and resends it onward later. You can use the Bouncy Castle encryption API for calculating hash values (*http://www.bouncycastle.org*).

Sessions and Cookies

You can use sessions for maintaining the state of an HTTP connection over several requests. This is useful whenever you deal with user data, because otherwise the J2ME application would need to send authentication data in each request. You can use URL rewriting or cookies for keeping track of the used session. You can retrieve cookies by cycling through all headers of a connection. When you start a new request, you need to set the cookie as a request property. Listing 15-11 shows a possible solution for this.

Listing 15-11. *Receiving and Setting Cookies*

```
import javax.microedition.io.HttpConnection;
import java.io.IOException;

public class CookieStore {
   private String cookie;

   public void readCookie( HttpConnection con ) throws IOException {
      this.cookie = con.getHeaderField( "Set-Cookie" );
      if ( this.cookie == null ) {
         this.cookie = con.getHeaderField( "Set-Cookie2" );
      }
   }
   public void setCookie( HttpConnection con )
   throws IOException {
      if ( this.cookie != null ) {
         con.setRequestProperty( "Cookie", this.cookie );
      }
   }
}
```

Playing Sounds

Playing sounds and music has become quite easy nowadays thanks to the Mobile Media API (MMAPI, JSR 135). In practice you need to be aware of some limitations.

Specifically, you need to be careful when you want to play several sounds at the same time. On many devices this is not possible. The `supports.mixing` system property is `true` when the device can play back several sounds simultaneously:

```
if ( "true".equals( System.getProperty( "supports.mixing" ) ) { ...
```

Likewise, you can check the preprocessing variable `polish.Property.supports.mixing` in your source code:

```
//#if  polish.Property.supports.mixing == true
```

The safest way is to use only one player at a time and dispose all resources when you are done with one sound. Prefetching several sounds at once is also not always possible. Listing 15-12 shows you how to play one sound over and over again, at least as long as the `playMusic` field is `true`. Please also note that the `PlayerListener` uses the `equals()` method for comparing incoming events. This works on all devices, whereas using the `==` comparator that is used by the JavaDoc documentation of the MMAPI does not work on all devices.

Listing 15-12. *Playing Background Music with the MMAPI*

```
//#condition polish.api.mmapi || polish.midp2
package com.apress.multimedia;
import java.io.IOException;
import javax.microedition.media.*;
public class MusicPlayer
implements PlayerListener {
   public boolean playMusic = true;
   private Player player;

   public void playMusic( String url, String contentType )
   throws MediaException, IOException {
      boolean registerListener = ( this.player == null );
      if ( !registerListener ) {
         this.player.stop();
         this.player.deallocate();
      }
      this.player = Manager.createPlayer(
         getClass().getResourceAsStream( url ), contentType );
      if ( registerListener ) {
         player.addPlayerListener( this );
      }
      player.realize();
      player.prefetch();
      player.start();
   }
```

```
   public void playerUpdate( Player p, String event, Object data )
   throws MediaException {
      if ( this.playMusic && event.equals( END_OF_MEDIA ) ) {
         p.start();
      }
   }
}
```

Using Floating-Point Arithmetic

Java offers the `float` and `double` primitives and advanced mathematical functions in the `java.lang.Math` class. Unfortunately, you can use floating-point calculations on CLDC 1.1 platforms only. Most J2ME devices are still based on the CLDC 1.0 configuration, for which several solutions exist: you can use integer calculations instead, use a floating-point emulation library, or use the Floater program (*http://www.enough.de/floater*) for converting floating-point calculations automatically.

Using Integer Instead of Floating-Point Calculations

Often floating-point calculations are not really necessary. In such cases you can emulate the floating-point calculations yourself with `int` and `long` primitives.

You can use your own fixed-point calculation just by multiplying every number with a fixed factor such as `100` or `1000`. To get the real value, you just need to divide the result by your chosen factor. Consider, for example, the simple fraction calculation shown in Listing 15-13. You can use the `Mover` class to calculate the traveled distance of an object. Each call of `moveForward()` will return the traveled distance. You can use such a calculation in animations, for example.

Listing 15-13. *A Simple Floating-Point Calculation*

```
public class Mover {
   private int step;
   private final int steps;
   private final float distancePerStep;

   public Mover( int distance, int steps ) {
      this.steps = steps;
      this.distancePerStep = (float) distance / (float) steps;
   }

   public int moveForward() {
      this.step++;
      if ( step > this.steps ) {
         this.step = 0;
```

```
        }
        return (int) ( this.step * this.distancePerStep );
    }
}
```

When you don't need high precision, you can use `int` variables instead of `float` ones. For higher prevision, use `long` variables instead of `double` ones. Listing 15-14 shows a `Mover` implementation that simulates two decimal places by multiplying the `distancePerStep` variable with `100`.

Listing 15-14. *A Solution That Uses Only Integers for a Simple Floating-Point Calculation*

```
public class Mover {
    private int step;
    private final int steps;
    private final int distancePerStep;

    public Mover( int distance, int steps ) {
        this.steps = steps;
        this.distancePerStep = ( distance * 100 ) / steps;
    }

    public int moveForward() {
        this.step++;
        if ( step > this.steps ) {
            this.step = 0;
        }
        return ( this.step * this.distancePerStep ) / 100;
    }
}
```

Using Floating-Point Emulation Libraries

Floating-point emulation libraries allow you to realize complex calculations involving trigonometrical functions and more. Popular libraries are MathFP for fast calculations and the MicroFloat library for high-precision calculations. Table 15-5 lists some available floating-point libraries for the CLDC 1.0 configuration.

Table 15-5. *Floating-Point Emulation Libraries*

Name	License	Home Page
MathFP	Liberal Source License	*http://home.rochester.rr.com/ohommes/MathFP*
MicroFloat	GPL	*http://www.dclausen.net/projects/microfloat*
JMFP	LGPL	*http://sourceforge.net/projects/jmfp*
FPLib	Artistic License	*http://bearlib.sourceforge.net*

MathFP

The MathFP library by Onno Hommes offers fast calculations and is licensed under the Liberal Source License. You can download it from *http://home.rochester.rr.com/ohommes/MathFP*.

You can use the MathFP library either in the `long` mode for higher precision (using the `net.jscience.math.MathFP` class) or in the less resource `int` mode (using the `net.jscience.math.kvm.MathFP` class). Instead of using `float` or `double` values, you need to convert `Strings` into the internal MathFP format first. After the conversion you will get an internal integer representation of your value. You can also convert an internal MathFP integer value back to the corresponding `int` or `long` value without the fraction. Listing 15-15 shows you how to calculate the space of a circle with MathFP.

Listing 15-15. *Calculating the Space Occupied by a Circle with MathFP*

```
public int calculateCircleSpace( String radiusStr ) {
   int radius = MathFP.toFP( radiusStr );
   int exponent = MathFP.toFP( 2 );
   int result = MathFP.mul( MathFP.PI,
                MathFP.pow( radius, exponent ) );
   return MathFP.toInt( result );
}
```

MicroFloat

The MicroFloat library by Dave Clausen is known for its high precision. Calculations with MicroFloat yield the results similar to native Java floating-point calculations, since MircoFloat follows the international IEEE 754 standard (*http://grouper.ieee.org/groups/754*). You can download MicroFloat at *http://www.dclausen.net/projects/microfloat*.

The usage of MicroFloat is similar to MathFP. You can use either the `net.dclausen.microfloat.MicroFloat` class for emulating `float` or the `net.dclausen.microfloat.MicroDouble` class for emulating `double` values. Listing 15-16 shows you how you can calculate the used space of a circle with MicroFloat.

Listing 15-16. *Calculating the Space Occupied by a Circle with MicroFloat*

```
public int calculateCircleSpace( String radiusStr ) {
   int radius = MicroFloat.parseFloat( radiusStr );
   int result = MicroFloat.mul( MicroFloat.PI,
                MicroFloat.mul( radius, radius ) );
   return MicroFloat.intValue( result );
}
```

Automatic Conversion

You can also use Enough Software's Floater tool for automatically converting any floating-point calculations. J2ME Polish includes an evaluation version of this converter. You can find more information about Floater at *http://www.enough.de/floater*.

With Floater you can use all functions of the CLDC 1.1 `java.lang.Math` implementation along with using `floats` and `doubles` normally. Floater does this by processing the bytecode after the compilation phase. The J2ME Polish integration processes the bytecode automatically for all CLDC 1.0 target devices. An additional benefit is that Floater does not need to use `String` for converting floating-point values in the internal format, so applications processed by Floater are leaner and faster compared to a manual conversion on the source code level. Also, you do not need to distinguish between any internal formats and real integer variables, since Floater takes care of this transparently.

Using Trusted MIDlets

The possibility of signing J2ME applications has caused a lot of confusion and frustration in the developer community, since most devices do not recognize the popular VeriSign and Thawte code-signing certificates.

The MIDP 2.0 profile introduced the notion of trusted MIDlets. A MIDlet is regarded as trusted when the following conditions are fulfilled:

- The MIDlet has been signed.
- The signature has been authenticated by the device.
- The integrity of the signed MIDlet has been verified by the device.

Permissions

Signing MIDlets is required when your application needs to access security-sensitive resources such as Internet connections. You can state your required permissions in the `MIDlet-Permissions` JAD attribute. In J2ME Polish you can use the `permissions` attribute of the `<info>` element for defining the necessary permissions, for example, `<info permissions= "javax.microedition.io.Connector.http" [...] />`. Likewise, you can define optional permissions using the `optionalPermissions` attribute.

Possible values for permissions include `javax.microedition.ui.Connector.http`, `javax.microedition.ui.Connector.socket`, and `javax.microedition.io.PushRegistry`. Please check the appendix for all possible permissions.

When you want to access so-called closed resources such as the low-level networking API (datagram, socket, serial), you usually need a valid signature; otherwise, a `SecurityException` will be thrown immediately.

Signing MIDlets

When the application is signed, the SHA1 hash value of the JAR file is calculated and added to the JAD file. The certificate that is used for the calculation is added to the JAD file, too. The JAR file itself is not changed and must not be modified later. The user is asked once if she gives the signed MIDlet the requested permission. When a required permission is denied, the installation is aborted. When the user denies an optional permission, the installation proceeds. In such cases the user is asked again during the runtime of the application just like an unsigned MIDlet.

Note Please refer to the "Signing MIDlets" section of Chapter 7 for learning how to automatically sign your application with J2ME Polish.

Root Certificates and Java Verified

You need a certificate for signing your application. The device also needs to recognize and trust the used certificate; otherwise, the installation is aborted. All devices contain so-called root certificates for this purpose.

Root certificates are separated in three categories:

- Vendor certificates are used to sign preinstalled J2ME applications. Such applications enjoy the highest possible trust level and can access everything. Obviously, you need a business relationship with the vendor for getting signed with vendor certificates.
- Carriers can also add their own root certificates to their phones. Again, you need a business relationship with the corresponding vendor for signing your application with a carrier certificate.
- The Java Verified/GEO Trust certificate is also present on most MIDP 2.0–compliant devices.

Java Verified (*http://www.javaverified.com*) is a initiative that provides testing and signing services. When your application passes the tests and you have paid the necessary fee, your application will be signed by Java Verified using the GEO Trust certificate (*http://www.geotrust.com*) and then returned to you via e-mail. So, there is in general no chance for you to sign your MIDlets yourself. This is especially annoying if you depend on a valid signature because you access closed resources such as the low-level networking API. Some devices might support importing new certificates, so in that case you can create and use your own certificate for the development phase.

A possible strategy to minimize the number of required verifications is to split the application into the application itself and the data it operates on. In this scenario the application itself would stay the same and download the data that is needed for its operation on the first run. In reality, however, few applications can remain constant.

When your application needs to be signed, you should try to limit the number of target devices, because you have to pay for each application version that is tested and signed. You can use the virtual devices such as "Nokia/Series40DP2" or "Generic/midp2." They group the functions of their respective device class.

Identifying Devices

Every device has a globally unique identification number called International Mobile Equipment Identity (IMEI). A similar identification is the International Mobile Subscription Identity (IMSI) that is tied to the Subscriber Identification Module (SIM) card of a user. On some devices you can access these values from within your J2ME application by querying a system property; on others you need to run your own identification program.

You can access the IMSI on Motorola devices by requesting the `IMSI` system property. Siemens makes the IMEI with the system property `com.siemens.mp.imei` available. On Sony

Ericsson devices you need either `com.sonyericsson.imei` or `com.sonyericsson.IMEI`. RIM BlackBerry devices make the IMEI accessible by calling `GPRSInfo.getIMEI()`. The J2ME Polish device database contains the required keys for accessing these identities in the `polish.Property.imei` and `polish.Property.imsi` variables.

On Nokia devices you cannot access the IMSI or EMEI from within your J2ME application. In such cases you need to create your own identification solution.

Often, the user's mobile phone number (MSISDN) is used for identification purposes. The MSISDN can be added dynamically to the application bundle when the user requests the application at your over-the-air (OTA) server. When the user is accessing your OTA server via WAP, you can extract the MSISDN from the HTTP headers of the WAP request when the carrier is adding this information. Carriers usually add MSISDN headers or similar identification headers only when you have a business relationship with that carrier. Of course, you can also ask the user to provide his mobile phone number. Once you have the MSISDN, you can insert it into the JAD file that is used for the installation. You can then access the JAD attribute by calling `MIDlet.getAppProperty( String attributeName )` in your application. JAD files can be changed easily; a more secure option is to rebuild the application on request and provide the MSISDN as a preprocessing variable.

On devices that support the Bluetooth API, you could also use the Bluetooth address of the device as a globally unique identification by calling `LocalDevice.getLocalDevice().getBluetoothAddress()`.

Listing 15-17 demonstrates how you can use the different identification options in one method. When the preprocessing variable `user.msisdn` is defined, the corresponding value is returned. Then it is checked whether the IMEI or IMSI can be retrieved. When this is also not possible, the Bluetooth address is returned on devices supporting the Bluetooth API. Last but not least, the application property `user.msisdn` is retrieved from the MIDlet when all other methods fail. To allow you to distinguish between the identifications method, each returned ID starts with a header, like `msisdn:+4916012345678`.

Listing 15-17. *Retrieving a Globally Unique Identification ID*

```
public String getIdentification( MIDlet midlet ) {
   //#if user.msisdn:defined
      //#= return "msisdn:${user.msisdn}";
   //#elif polish.Property.imei:defined
      //#= return "imei:" + System.getProperty( "${polish.Property.imei}" );
   //#elif polish.Property.imsi:defined
      //#= return "imsi:" + System.getProperty( "${polish.Property.imsi}" );
   //#elif polish.api.btapi
      return "bluetooth:" + LocalDevice.getLocalDevice().getBluetoothAddress();
   //#else
      String msisdn = midlet.getAppProperty( "user.msisdn" );
      if ( msisdn != null ) {
         return "misdn:" + msisdn;
      } else {
         return null;
      }
   //#endif
}
```

Accessing Native Functionality

Thanks to optional APIs, applications can now access many phone features that were previously available only for native applications. However, J2ME applications still cannot access some areas. When you require native functions for your application, you have one of two options: developing a native application or accessing native functions from within your J2ME application. Creating native applications is outside the scope of this book, but you should be aware that different operating systems with partly incompatible versions exist. So, if you want to reach a broad user base, you should try to stick to pure Java whenever it's possible.

When your target device supports the Personal Java profile, you can just use the Java Native Interface (JNI) technology for accessing native functions. JNI provides a comfortable and standardized way for calling functions and receiving their return values. In that case, you need to port your native functions only when you want to support a new platform, since the Java code can remain the same. You need to be aware that the Personal Java profile is supported only by a few J2ME devices, for example, the Nokia Communicator series or Sony Ericsson's UIQ devices such as the P910.

Some KVMs also support JNI or similar technologies. The JBlend platform provides this possibility, for example (*http://www.aplix.co.jp/en/jblend/jblend/practical04.html*). In general, you need to have a business relationship with the corresponding vendor or carrier to be allowed to use JNI.

A third possibility is to implement a native application that uses a server connection and waits for incoming requests by listening on a specific port, like `4242`. In this scenario, you could open a socket connection and access the local server, for example, `SocketConnection mySocket = (SocketConnection) Connector.open( "socket://127.0.0.1:4242" );`.

Finally, it is theoretically possible to use the `MIDlet.platformRequest()` mechanism for launching native applications. Usually you can initialize telephone calls when the request starts with the `tel:<number>` scheme and launch the browser using the `http:<url>` scheming. Manufacturers can add their own request schemes in the future.

Detecting Interruptions

MIDlets can be interrupted at any time by incoming phone calls and similar events. The Application Management System (AMS) should call the `MIDlet.pauseApp()` in such cases, but on some devices this does not happen. With some defensive programming techniques you can detect interruption on all phones.

A typical scenario is a game that should be paused whenever it is interrupted. For best portability you should tackle this problem from three different angles: using `MIDlet.pauseApp()`, using `Canvas.hideNotify()`, and detecting unusual time gaps.

Using the `MIDlet.pauseApp()` mechanism is straightforward. You can enter the `PAUSED` state after the `pauseApp()` has been called and can resume the application when the `MIDlet.startApp()` is called again.

Some devices, most notably the Nokia Series 40, never call `pauseApp()`. Instead, you are notified when your current (low-level GUI) screen is not shown anymore. You can override the `Canvas.hideNotify()` method in your game for pausing it and can override the `Canvas.showNotify()` method for resuming the game.

Finally, some devices seem to stop the whole Java Virtual Machine without calling any notification methods when an interruption occurs. Your only chance is then to remember the last time your application thread was executed and compare this with the current time on the next run. When you see an unusual long gap between the two runs, you can assume there has been an interruption. Use the `System.currentTimeMillis()` method for getting the current time.

■ Caution When devices support both `MIDlet.pauseApp()/startApp()` and `Canvas.hideNotify()/showNotify()`, the order of the calls might be unexpected. One implementation can call `hideNotify()`, `pauseApp()`, `<interruption>`, `showNotify()`, and `startApp()`, while another one might call `pauseApp()`, `<interruption>`, `startApp()`, `hideNotify()`, and `showNotify()`. Be prepared for different call orders in your application.

Getting Help

In the following sections, you will learn in which forums and mailing lists you can ask your questions.

Honoring Netiquette

You should honor certain rules when you post any questions or statements. These rules make everyone's life easier, so please stick to this netiquette if possible. Netiquette is really just common sense, but you may be surprised how many people do not care about it.

Before asking a question, you should search for an answer. Start with a normal search engine such as Google, and then check out specialized forums and portals. Most forums provide a search function and compile a list of frequently asked questions that you should consult first.

When you cannot find the answer to your problem, post your question to an appropriate forum and try to describe your problem in as much detail as possible. Name the exact phone or emulator that produces the error, name any third-party software and version you are using, describe the problem as concretely as possible, and provide stack traces or exception names when applicable. You should also add the relevant parts of the source code so that other users can track down coding errors. On many forums you can surround the source code with `[code]..[/code]` so that it is formatted correctly. Do not forget to describe what you want to achieve; sometimes there are alternative ways to solve a problem. Finally, you should mention whether the same program works on other devices or emulators without the problem occurring.

When you are frustrated about a problem, it is easy to lose your temper, so make sure you ask your questions in a polite way. You cannot expect to get a useful answer if you are swearing or aggressively demanding in any way.

Last but not least, you should be careful with advertising your products in forums. Some forums provide specific boards for such items. In general, you should post news about your products only when they are of real interest to J2ME developers.

Exploring J2ME Polish Forums

English and German forums exist for discussing J2ME Polish–related problems. You can also join the J2ME Polish user mailing list. On *http://www.j2mepolish.org*, select Discussion for accessing the forums. Or get directly in touch with other J2ME Polish users by joining the *irc://irc.synyx.de#j2mepolish* Internet Relay Chat.

Exploring Vendor Forums

Many vendors also provide forums for discussions about their J2ME devices. Table 15-6 summarizes the most important vendor-specific forums.

Table 15-6. *Vendor-Specific Forums*

Vendor	URL
Nokia	*http://discussion.forum.nokia.com/forum/forumdisplay.php?forumid=3*
Siemens	*http://agathonisi.erlm.siemens.de:8080/jive3*
Samsung	*http://developer.samsungmobile.com*
Sony Ericsson	*http://developer.sonyericsson.com/show_forums.do*
DoJa	*http://www.doja-developer.net/forums*
BlackBerry	*http://www.blackberry.com/developers/forum/index.jsp*

Exploring General J2ME Forums and Mailing Lists

Many independent J2ME Forums and mailing lists are available. Table 15-7 lists some of the best forums.

Table 15-7. *General J2ME Forums*

Name	URL
J2me.org	*http://www.j2me.org/yabbse*
Java Forums: CLCD and MIDP	*http://forum.java.sun.com/forum.jspa?forumID=76*
JavaRanch	*http://saloon.javaranch.com/cgi-bin/ubb/ultimatebb.cgi?ubb=forum&f=41*
Mobile Game Developer	*http://www.mobilegd.com/modules.php?name=Forums*
J2MeForum (German)	*http://www.j2meforum.com*
KVM-INTEREST mailing list	*http://archives.java.sun.com/cgi-bin/wa?SUBED1=kvm-interest&A=1*
KEITAI-L mailing list	*http://www.appelsiini.net/keitai-l*

Summary

Programming in the real world is different from the theory. Sadly, Java's promise of "code once, run everywhere" is not yet fulfilled. In this chapter, you learned about the difficulties you will encounter in the real world and how to overcome the most common dilemmas. Also, you now know where to ask for help when you cannot solve specific problems.

In the forthcoming chapter, you will learn how to optimize the performance, the size, and the memory usage of your application.

CHAPTER 16

Optimizing Applications

In this chapter:

- Understand that optimizing is the last step for creating a successful application for the resource constrained J2ME world.
- Learn to optimize in the following three areas: performance, memory consumption, and JAR size.
- Discover that some optimizations improve all areas, while others constitute tradeoffs.
- Plan possible high-level optimizations during the architecture phase but postpone low-level optimizations until your application works correctly.

Since J2ME devices are resource constrained, you need to optimize your application for execution speed, memory consumption, and JAR file size. In this chapter, you'll learn tips and tricks for getting the very best out of your application.

Optimization Overview

Optimizing your application is not a trivial task. As discussed in this section, you need to consider unintentional side effects, different levels of optimizations, and how you want to structure your efforts.

One unintentional side effect of optimization is increased usage of heap memory when optimizing for performance. For example, painting different parts of an image using the `Graphics.setClip()` method is quite slow compared to splitting the image into the different parts and painting each part directly. But the splitting process requires additional heap memory—at least double the original memory required for the base image.

Also, low-level optimizations often decrease the readability and maintainability of your source code. Modulo operations can be implemented using the `&` operator, when the argument is a power of two; for example, `int round = i % 8;` can be rewritten as `int round = i & 7;`. Whereas the first term is easy to understand, the second one is not so obvious. You can also change the argument `8` in the first term to any number without changing the logic of the program. In contrast, you can use only numbers that are one less than a power of two (x^2 `- 1`) in the second term.

A general piece of advice about optimization is to ensure the correctness of your application first before moving into the optimization phase. This is not entirely true for the J2ME world, however. You need to take the constraints of your target devices into account in the architecture phase and possibly even in the idea phase. Some high-level architecture decisions such as the class model or the used protocols have a direct impact on the runtime behavior of your application. So in the J2ME world, the advice to postpone optimizations applies only to low-level optimizations.

You can optimize your application in two different ways.

One approach is to come up with some ideas about why your application is slow, and then change all the code pieces that can be improved in one way or another, throw away working but possibly slow parts, and introduce new features along the way.

The other, more rational approach is to measure the performance on your actual target devices. This helps you to identify the bottlenecks in your application. Set realistic goals such as "Part X should complete in under two seconds in 80% of cases." Then hypothesize why a specific part is too slow. Prove your hypothesis by implementing one change at a time, repeating the measurement, and then asking yourself, "Has this particular change improved the situation?" Always choose to eliminate the easiest bottleneck first, because removing one bottleneck can alter the measurements of the complete application.

Improving Performance

To improve the performance of your application, you first need to know what parts of the application need to be improved. You can first identify the bottlenecks in your application by measuring performance, both in the emulator as well as on the actual device. Then you can tune the performance through high-level architectural strategies and low-level optimizations. You can also improve the perceived performance of your application. In the sections that follow, you'll explore all four aspects of performance tuning.

Measuring Performance

Measuring the performance of an application is important for two reasons. First, most applications spend 80% of their time within 20% of their code, so it's crucial to find out what's happening in that 20%. Otherwise, you end up wasting your time and effort on parts of your application that don't have any impact at all on performance. Second, you need to measure the performance to find out whether your changes are really improving the situation.

In this section, you'll learn how to measure an application's performance both in the WTK emulator and on the target device.

Measuring Performance in the WTK Emulator

You can measure an application's performance in the WTK-compliant emulator by setting the `enableProfiler` attribute of the `<emulator>` element to `true`, as shown in Listing 16-1. The profiler collects information during the run of your application and then displays it after you close the emulator. Figure 16-1 shows typical profiler output.

Listing 16-1. *Enabling the WTK Profiler*

```
<j2mepolish>
   <info
      license="GPL"
      name="Roadrunner"
```

```
        vendorName="A reader."
        version="0.0.1"
        jarName="${polish.vendor}-${polish.name}-roadrunner.jar"
    />
    <deviceRequirements>
        <requirement name="Identifier"
                value="Generic/midp2" />
    </deviceRequirements>
    <build
        usePolishGui="true"
    >
        <midlet class="com.apress.roadrunner.Roadrunner" />
    </build>
    <emulator enableProfiler="true" />
</j2mepolish>
```

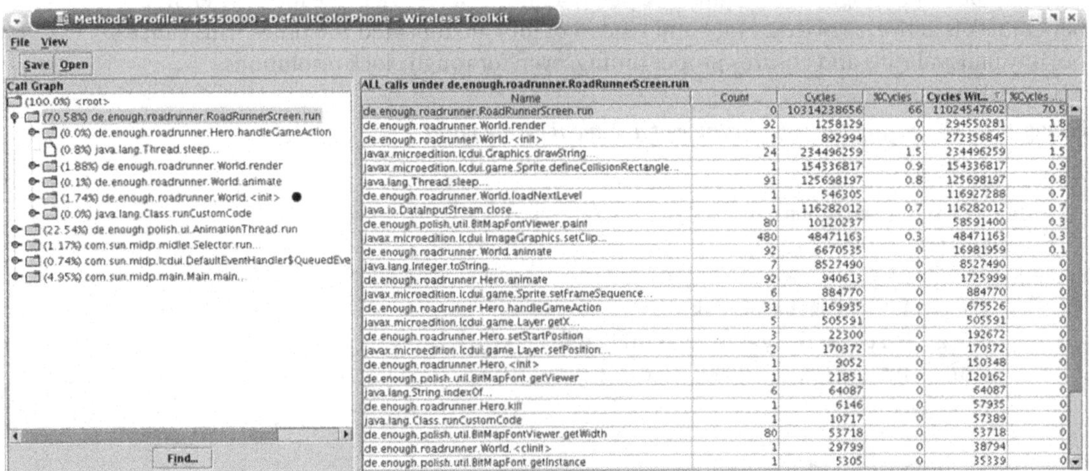

Figure 16-1. *Measuring performance with the WTK profiler*

Note The profiler is included in WTK versions starting with 1.0.4, but you can successfully invoke it from external programs such as J2ME Polish only from version 2.2 onward. Make sure you're using a recent version of WTK.

Measuring Performance on the Actual Target Device

The WTK profiler is great for finding bottlenecks in your application, but it may unfortunately provide misleading information. Measuring performance on your 3GHz machine with 1GB RAM does not necessarily yield the same results as on your 200MHz phone with 600KB of heap memory. Typical counter examples are network operations and persisting data in record stores. These are blindingly fast on your development machine, but on the real device you may encounter quite different processing times. You can configure some performance-related settings on some emulators, but this is not a replacement for measuring performance on the actual device. To make matters worse, devices themselves vary greatly in their performance. A good strategy is to ensure that your application runs adequately on the lower range of your target devices.

To measure the performance on real devices, you can use the logging framework of J2ME Polish along with the `System.currentTimeMilis()` method. The logging framework is not really needed, but it allows you to turn on and off your benchmarking tests without changing the code. Alternatively, you can use normal preprocessing for activating or deactivating your benchmark, but in that case you also need to provide your own means for displaying the measured values.

When you benchmark your code, try to test typical real-world scenarios. Also, you should repeat the measurements enough to rule out differences between single runs. Keep in mind that the resolution of the `System.currentTimeMilis()` method can differ between devices. On JTWI (JSR 185)-compliant devices, you have a clock resolution of 40 milliseconds or lower, so you should run your tests for a couple of seconds if possible.

The code in Listing 16-2 measures the performance of a typical game loop. When the benchmark is active, `animateWorld()` and `renderWorld()` are repeated 100 times. This cancels out any unusual runs and ensures proper timing, even for rough clock resolutions.

Listing 16-2. *Measuring the Performance of a Typical Game Loop*

```
public void run() {
   while ( this.gameIsRunning ) {
      evaluateUserInput();

      //#if polish.debug.benchmark
         long startTime = System.currentTimeMillis();
         for ( int i = 0; i < 100; i++ ) {
      //#endif

            animateWorld();

      //#if polish.debug.benchmark
         }
         long timeAnimate = System.currentTimeMillis() - startTime;
      //#endif

      //#if polish.debug.benchmark
         startTime = System.currentTimeMillis();
         for ( int i = 0; i < 100; i++ ) {
      //#endif

            renderWorld();

      //#if polish.debug.benchmark
         }
```

```
            long timeRender = System.currentTimeMillis() - startTime;
            //#debug benchmark
            System.out.println( "animateWorld: " +  timeAnimate
                                + "renderWorld: " +  timeRender );
        //#endif
    }
}
```

The benchmark log level used in Listing 16-2 is a user-defined level, but you can enable it just like any other log level in the <debug> element in your *build.xml* script, as shown in Listing 16-3. All user-defined levels have the highest possible priority, so you can alternatively activate a lower level such as error or info instead.

Listing 16-3. *Enabling the benchmark Log Level*

```
<j2mepolish>
   <info
      license="GPL"
      name="Roadrunner"
      vendorName="A reader."
      version="0.0.1"
      jarName="${polish.vendor}-${polish.name}-roadrunner.jar"
   />
   <deviceRequirements>
      <requirement name="Identifier"
                   value="Nokia/Series60, Siemens/x75" />
   </deviceRequirements>
   <build
      usePolishGui="true"
   >
      <midlet class="com.apress.roadrunner.Roadrunner" />
      <debug level="benchmark" />
   </build>
</j2mepolish>
```

Performance Tuning

You can improve the performance of your application in various ways, as discussed in this section. High-level optimizations involve the architecture and used protocols of your application, while low-level optimizations involve the used algorithms or data structures. You should do such low-level changes as a last step, when further high-level optimizations are not possible anymore.

High-Level Performance Tuning

Many performance problems can be resolved by changing the architecture, the used protocols, or the used algorithms. Usually high-level changes can improve (or decrease, for that matter) the performance of your application drastically.

Tweaking the Architecture

The architecture provides the foundation for your application and allows you to tune the application in the design phase already. You should aim to reduce the abstraction and to strengthen the grouping of functionalities.

Reducing Abstraction Abstraction is good for reusing components in different environments. But each abstraction layer not only increases the application size, but also decreases the execution speed, since the virtual machine needs to resolve the inheritance structure during runtime. Calling a method that is implemented by only one concrete class is much faster than calling an interface method that is implemented by an abstract class and overridden by a concrete class.

You can avoid and use interfaces at the same time by using a bit of preprocessing. Listing 16-4 demonstrates how you can use an interface only for cases when a concrete implementation is not known.

Listing 16-4. *Using and Avoiding Interfaces at the Same Time with Preprocessing*

```
public interface SelectionListener {
   public void selectionChanged( StringListItem item );
}

public class StringListItem extends CustomItem {
   //#if SelectionListenerImplementation:defined
      //#= ${classname( SelectionListenerImplementation )} selectionListener;
   //#else
      SelectionListener selectionListener;
   //#endif

   //#if SelectionListenerImplementation:defined
      //#= public void setSelectionListener(
      //#= ${classname( SelectionListenerImplementation )} selectionListener
      //#= ) {
   //#else
      public void setSelectionListener(
      SelectionListener selectionListener
      ) {
   //#endif
      this.selectionListener = selectionListener;
   }
   [...]
}

public class Controller
//#if SelectionListenerImplementation:defined
   //# implements CommandListener
//#else
   implements CommandListener, SelectionListener
```

```
//#endif
{
   public void selectionChanged( StringListItem item ) {
      //#debug info
      System.out.println( "selection changed: " + item );
   }
   [...]
}
```

You can "publish" a concrete implementation by setting a preprocessing variable in your *build.xml* script. Listing 16-4 doesn't use the interface when the variable `SelectionListenerImplementation` is defined:

```
<variable name="SelectionListenerImplementation" value="Controller" />
```

In the code, you additionally use the `classname` property function for cases when all classes are moved into the default package by J2ME Polish (this is enabled by the `useDefaultPackage` attribute of the `<obfuscator>` element in the *build.xml* file). The `classname` function returns the fully qualified name like `com.apress.performance.Controller` when the default package is not used, but only the class name itself—`Controller` in this case—when the default package is used. This is necessary because the `useDefaultPackage` option moves all source files into the default package before they are compiled.

Note Eliminating interfaces that are implemented by only one class is a potential target for automatic optimizations. Enough Software currently works on the Juicer optimizer (*http://www.enough.de/juicer*), which will do just that, along with several other improvements at the bytecode level.

Threading Threads are expensive resources and should be used with care in your application. Try to design your architecture with as many single-threaded areas as possible. This also reduces the need for `synchronized` methods, which slow down your application.

Reusing and Caching Objects Object creation can be expensive, even though the cost of creating objects is much lower on the current HotSpot virtual machines than on the first generation KVMs. Design your architecture so that reusing objects is possible.

Reusing objects sometimes involves caching the objects. In many cases, caching complicates the usage and also increases the required heap memory, so you might be better off not reusing those objects. Caching is useful when the retrieval of the data is expensive, the data is accessed frequently, and the data itself is small enough to fit into the heap. You also need to consider how to maintain integrity between the cache and the data source. If you have large data sets, you might be able to identify the parts that are needed most often, so that you don't need to cache everything.

Protocols and Network Operations

The protocols that you choose for storing and transmitting data influence both the memory consumption as well as the performance of your application.

Using XML-based protocols for transmitting data is quite fashionable, but it requires additional resources for parsing the data. Also, a lot of redundant data is transmitted. The same is true when using SOAP or web services. When your application should talk only to your own proprietary server application, it is often better to use a binary protocol instead. You can use the `DataInputStream` and `DataOutputStream` classes for such protocols. When you have a multichannel server application or need to access servers from different companies, using web services is, however, often the better option.

To improve the network throughput, you can also consider transmitting only the changed data, especially in conjunction with caching the data. Keep in mind that this complicates the interpretation of the data. A similar option is to compress the data. Unfortunately, the MIDP standard does not provide the means for reading and writing ZIP streams. Alternatively, you can use the `GZIPInputStream` implementation of the TinyLine project (*http://www.tinyline.com*), for example.

To improve performance, you can also minimize the use of encryption, for example by authenticating only once per session. When you have a security-sensitive application, however, you should be very careful about not using all available means to secure the data. See the "Improving Perceived Performance" section for some ideas on how to increase the usability of your application while maintaining a high level of security.

Network operations are very slow compared to almost anything else. Apart from decreasing the transmitted data and using IP addresses instead of server names, there is not much you can do to speed up network operations. Caching the data might help, and you might even want try storing the received data in the record store so that you have at least some (but possibly outdated) data when you restart your application.

Record Stores

Record stores are required for persisting data. You read them by calling the `RecordStore.enumerateRecords()` method, which allows you to use a comparator and a filter for the enumeration.

The problem with the interfaces `RecordFilter` and `RecordComparator` is that they only get the `byte[]` data of the single recordsets. Usually you will need to restore the original object for comparing the single recordsets, so when you have both a filter and a comparator, you need to create and discard each recordset object at least four times: twice in the comparator, once in the filter, and once in your application. This not only degrades the performance, but also greatly increases the memory footprint of your application. Listing 16-5 demonstrates the usage of these elements.

Listing 16-5. *Creating Many Temporary Objects by Filtering and Sorting a Record Store*

```
import javax.microedition.rms.*;
import de.enough.polish.util.ArrayList;

public class RecordStoreReader
implements RecordFilter, RecordComparator
{
   private final ArrayList list;
   private final Object condition;
```

```
   public RecordStoreReader( Object condition )
   throws RecordStoreException
   {
      this.condition = condition;
      this.list = new ArrayList();
      // open record store:
      RecordStore store = RecordStore.openRecordStore( "store", false );
      // enumerate the record sets:
      RecordEnumeration enumeration =
         store.enumerateRecords( this, this, false );
      while ( enumeration.hasNextElement() ) {
         MyRecordData data = new MyRecordData( ennumeration.nextRecord() );
         this.list.add( data );
      }
      store.closeRecordStore();
   }

   public ArrayList getRecords() {
      return this.list;
   }

   public int compare( byte[] rec1, byte[] rec2 ) {
      MyRecordData data1 = new MyRecordData( rec1 );
      MyRecordData data2 = new MyRecordData( rec2 );
      return data1.compare( data2 );
   }

   public boolean matches( byte[] candidate ) {
      MyRecordData data = new MyRecordData( candidate );
      return data.conditionFulfilled( this.condition );
   }
}
```

A possible solution is to cleverly store the required data for sorting and filtering so that you can use single bytes instead of creating temporary objects out of the recordsets. Another approach is not to use `RecordFilter` and `RecordComparator`, but instead use your own filtering and sorting mechanism during the reading of the enumeration. Listing 16-6 filters and sorts the entries all at once. It also uses a local `ArrayList` for accessing the data slightly faster. In contrast to the previous example, each recordset object is created only once.

Listing 16-6. *Filtering and Sorting a Record Store Simultaneously*

```
import javax.microedition.rms.*;
import de.enough.polish.util.ArrayList;

public class RecordStoreReader {
   private final ArrayList list;
```

```
    public RecordStoreReader( Object condition )
    throws RecordStoreException
    {
        // open record store:
        RecordStore store = RecordStore.openRecordStore( "store", false );
        // enumerate the record sets the fastest possible way:
        RecordEnumeration enumeration =
            store.enumerateRecords( null, null, false );
        ArrayList recordList = new ArrayList( enumeration.numRecords() );
        while ( enumeration.hasNextElement() ) {
            MyRecordData data = new MyRecordData( enumeration.nextRecord() );
            if ( !data.conditionFulfilled( condition ) ) {
                continue;
            }
            boolean notInserted = true;
            for ( int i = recordList.size(); --i >= 0; ) {
                MyRecordData compare = (MyRecordData) recordList.get( i );
                if ( data.compare( compare ) != RecordComparator.PRECEDES ) {
                    recordList.add( i + 1, data );
                    notInserted = false;
                    break;
                }
            }
            if ( notInserted ) {
                recordList.add( 0, data );
            }
        }
        store.closeRecordStore();
        this.list = recordList;
    }

    public ArrayList getRecords() {
        return this.list;
    }

}
```

When you need to sort and filter vast amounts of data from the record store regularly, consider using index recordsets that contain pointers to the actual data. To retrieve a particular recordset, you look up its position in the index set before loading it directly. This technique can improve data reading a great deal, but it makes persisting new entries much more complex. Your mileage may vary.

Selecting Algorithms

If you have an application that needs to perform many calculations and do a lot of data processing, consider the used algorithms carefully. Since algorithms are very much specific to your application, discussion of the merits and disadvantages of different algorithms are outside of the scope of this book.

Low-Level Performance Tuning

After you have implemented high-level optimizations, you can continue to the exciting area of low-level tuning. Before we move on to cover these optimizations, a word of warning is in order: low-level optimizations can easily introduce new bugs, often decrease the readability and maintainability of your application, and might improve the performance only on specific target devices.

Improving Graphic Operations

Rendering graphics or text on the screen is quite complex and therefore takes some time to complete. The best you can do is avoid painting altogether, for example by rendering data only after it has changed, or by using and evaluating clipping regions. In addition, you can use image buffers for complex backgrounds that don't change often. Splitting an image into single tiles also improves performance greatly when you need to paint an animation, for example.

Using Appropriate Containers

Containers are used to hold several elements. MIDP platforms provide the `Vector`, `Hashtable`, and `Stack` implementations for this purpose. Alternatively, you can implement your own solution, use simple arrays, or deploy J2ME Polish's `de.enough.polish.util.ArrayList`.

The main disadvantage of the standard MIDP containers is that they are synchronized and thus slow.

The `ArrayList` provided by J2ME Polish is not synchronized, so it is faster compared to the standard containers.

If you know or can guess the needed capacity of the containers, you should set it in the constructor (for example, `new Vector( 20 )`).

The fastest way to store several elements is, however, to use arrays instead of containers. The drawback is that you are responsible for ensuring a sufficient capacity. Use the `System.arrayCopy()` method to copy elements when you need to increase your array. It is faster to use one-dimensional arrays instead of two-dimensional ones, because the JVM needs to check twice whether a requested element is inside the allowed bounds of a two-dimensional array. Usually you can use some calculations for simulating an array of more than one dimension. Instead of accessing the two-dimensional array element `data[ row ][ column ]`, you could use the one-dimensional array element `data[ row * numberOfColumns + column ]`.

In cases when you frequently need to access a specific element from your array or from your container, you should consider adding an instance field to hold that element. In that case, you save the repeated checking of the array bounds.

■ **Note** Storing configuration values such as level data in arrays can increase your application's size, since Java bytecode cannot store such data directly. Refer to the "Decreasing the Size of JAR Files" section of this chapter to learn more about the alternatives.

Precalculating Data

When you do performance-intensive calculations, you should do them only once whenever possible. Typical examples include the calculation of random data with `Random.nextInt()` or calls to trigonometric functions such as `Math.sin()`. Simple calculations that involve only constants are already resolved by the compiler, so you shouldn't waste space using extra fields in class such as `defaultAnchor = Graphics.TOP | Graphics.LEFT`.

Using Optimized Arithmetic Operations

For specific arithmetic operations, you can use much faster bit-shifting operators. Whenever possible, use multiplication instead of division. Last but not least, integer operations are faster than float operations.

Divisions by a power of two can be done faster using the shift right operator `>>`. Instead of dividing a number x by 2^y, you can just use `x >> y`, so `x >> 3` yields the same result as `x / 8`.

Modulo operations can be done by bit operators, when the modulo argument is a power of two. Instead of calculating `int round = i % 8;` you can use the faster bit operation `int round = i & 7;`.

Using switch Statements

Instead of using several `if` blocks, you can use the `switch` statement. When you use a contiguous value range, the `switch` statement uses a constant processing time regardless of which case does match. So it might be even worth it to add dummy cases to create a contiguous test range. Listing 16-7 demonstrates a slow and a fast usage of the `switch` statement.

Listing 16-7. *Accelerating the switch Statement*

```
public char slowSwitch( int keyEvent ) {
   switch ( keyEvent ) {
      case Canvas.KEY_NUM6: return '6';
      case Canvas.KEY_NUM3: return '3';
      case Canvas.KEY_NUM8: return '8';
      case Canvas.KEY_NUM9: return '9';
      case Canvas.KEY_NUM2: return '2';
      case Canvas.KEY_NUM1: return '1';
      case Canvas.KEY_NUM5: return '5';
   }
}

public char fastSwitch( int keyEvent ) {
   switch ( keyEvent ) {
      case Canvas.KEY_NUM1: return '1';
      case Canvas.KEY_NUM2: return '2';
      case Canvas.KEY_NUM3: return '3';
      case Canvas.KEY_NUM4: return '4';
      case Canvas.KEY_NUM5: return '5';
      case Canvas.KEY_NUM6: return '6';
      case Canvas.KEY_NUM7: return '7';
```

```
        case Canvas.KEY_NUM8: return '8';
        case Canvas.KEY_NUM9: return '9';
    }
}
```

Accelerating Loops

Loops can be improved in several ways. You can move method calls and calculations outside of the loop, use better termination conditions, and unroll loops.

A typical loop header is `for ( int i = 0; i < list.size(); i++ )`. A simple yet effective improvement is to run the list from top to bottom instead: `for ( int i = list.size(); --i >= 0; )`. In this case, the `list.size()` call is done only once at the start of the loop. You have also improved the termination condition by checking against the value `0`, which is slightly faster than comparing a variable against a different number.

If you do any calculations inside the loop, check whether you can do them outside of the loop as well. The same applies to the creation of temporary objects, which not only decreases the available memory, but also requires more frequent garbage collection.

A very low-level optimization is to unroll loops. To successfully unroll a loop, you need to know the number of possible invocations in advance. When your loop is always executed a multiple of four times, for example, you can repeat the loop body four times, reducing the number of needed jumps and termination checking by a factor of four. Listing 16-8 shows an example in which an array that contains either four elements or a multiple of four elements is filled with integer values. The `slowFill()` method uses a traditional loop, whereas the `fastFill()` method unrolls the loop.

Listing 16-8. *Accelerating Loops by Unrolling*

```
public void slowFill( int[] numbers ) {
    for ( int i = numbers.length; --i >= 0; ) {
        numbers[ i ] = i;
    }
}

public void fastFill( int[] numbers ) {
    // warning: this will crash if numbers.length != x * 4
    for ( int i = numbers.length; --i >= 0; ) {
        numbers[ i ] = i;
        numbers[ --i ] = i;
        numbers[ --i ] = i;
        numbers[ --i ] = i;
    }
}
```

Setting Default Values of Instance Fields

All instance fields have default values that you don't need to set again. Primitive numbers such as `int`, `long`, and `float` are all `0` by default; `boolean` fields are `false`; and objects are `null`. This is a rare example of a low-level optimization that you should always apply. To be more precise, don't waste time by setting default values for instance fields.

Using Access Modifiers

Methods and fields can have different modifiers that may influence performance. For J2ME applications, you can choose one or several of the following modifiers: `synchronized`, `private`, `protected`, `public`, `static`, and `final`.

Using `synchronized` methods ensures that only one thread at a time can run through these methods. This is costly because a lock needs to be acquired for the method and because only one thread can run through it a time. You don't need synchronization when you have stateless objects or when you only read data. When you write data, you can sometimes minimize the impact by using a `synchronized` block instead of synchronizing the complete method. Also remember that accessing instance fields is atomic, so in some cases you might not need synchronization at all.

A popular myth is that using `static` fields and methods improves performance greatly. The `static` modifier allows the access without instantiating the corresponding class. The truth about the performance of the `static` access is, however, that it depends on your target platform. The first virtual machines did indeed penalize the usage of normal instance fields, while modern HotSpot JVMs access instance fields and methods even faster than `static` ones. As always, you should measure the performance on your target devices. Using the `static` modifier excessively most certainly degrades the architecture of your application and makes subsequent changes harder.

The `final` modifier prevents subclasses from overriding a method and allows you to set a variable only once. This eases the interpretation and optimization of the inheritance structure and simplifies the access of field values for the compiler and the virtual machine, thus increasing performance.

A special issue are `static final` constants. These are directly embedded by the compiler. Simple calculations such as `Graphics.TOP | Graphics.LEFT` are also done during the compilation phase, so using constants is a good thing.

Much faster than `static` and instance fields are local variables. Local variables are stored on the stack of the virtual machine, whereas other variables are stored in the heap memory. The JVM is a stack-based machine, so accessing data from the stack is faster than reading from and writing data to the heap.

When you use the `public` access modifier for fields, you can access them directly from within other classes instead of using getter and setter methods. This is again only faster on old KVM devices, whereas the differences are negligible on HotSpot machines. Also keep in mind that accessing fields directly complicates adjustments at a later stage. Take, for example, the setting of a date field. When you use a setter method, you can easily include the calculation of the remaining time until the date inside of the `setDate()` method; this is not possible if you modify the field directly.

Improving Perceived Performance

In many cases, you cannot further improve the actual performance of an application. In this situation, you should concentrate on improving the *perceived* performance instead. Do this by giving feedback to the user about the progress of an ongoing process and ensuring the responsiveness of your application, as discussed in the following sections.

Improving the perceived performance objectively often increases the time needed to accomplish a task, but to the user your application feels more responsive, and the user's impression is what counts.

Giving Feedback About Progress

Letting users know about the progress of your application is a good investment, because it increases your users' patience dramatically.

During application startup, it is often necessary to do some initialization work such as reading data from the record store. The standard solution is to provide a splash screen and do the necessary initialization in a background thread. J2ME Polish provides the `de.enough.polish.ui.splash.InitializerSplashScreen` for this task. This splash screen shows an image along with an optional message and initializes the actual application in a background thread. As shown in Listing 16-9, you need to implement the `initApp()` method of the `de.enough.polish.ui.splash.ApplicationInitializer` interface for the actual initialization. The `InitializerSplashScreen` can also have different views; please refer to the JavaDoc documentation for more information.

Listing 16-9. *Showing a Splash Screen and Doing the Initialization in a Background Thread*

```
import de.enough.polish.ui.splash.InitializerSplashScreen;
import de.enough.polish.ui.splash.ApplicationInitializer;
import javax.microedition.lcdui.*;
import javax.microedition.midlet.*;

public class QuickStartupMidlet extends MIDlet
//#if ! polish.clases.ApplicationInitializer:defined
implements ApplicationInitializer
//#endif
{
   private Screen mainScreen;
   private Display display;

   public  QuickStartupMidlet() {
      // do the initialization in the initApp() method
   }

   public void startApp()
   throws MIDletStateChangeException
   {
      this.display = Display.getDisplay( this );
      if ( this.mainScreen != null ) {
         // the MIDlet has been paused:
         this.display.setCurrent( this.mainScreen );
      } else {
         // the MIDlet is started for this first time:
         try {
            Image image = Image.createImage( "/splash.png" );
            int backgroundColor = 0xFFFFFF;
            String readyMessage = "Press any key to continue...";
            // set readyMessage = null to forward to the next
            // displayable as soon as it's available.
```

```
            int messageColor = 0xFF0000;
            InitializerSplashScreen splashScreen = new InitializerSplashScreen (
               this.display, image, backgroundColor, readyMessage,
               messageColor, this );
            this.display.setCurrent( splashScreen );
         } catch ( IOException e ) {
            throw new MIDletStateChangeException(
                        "Unable to load splash image" );
         }
      }
   }

   public Displayable initApp() {
      // initialize the application,
      // e.g., read data from the record store, etc.
      [...]
      // now create the main menu screen:
      // e.g., this.mainScreen = new Form( "Main Menu" );
      [...]
      return this.mainScreen;
   }

   public void pauseApp() {}

   public void destroyApp( boolean unconditional ) {}
}
```

For long operations such as loading data over the network or searching for data in record stores, you should give some thought to how you can measure and visualize the progress.

The best case is when you know in advance how long the operation lasts and how many steps it involves. In such a case, you can just show a progress meter starting at 0% and ending at 100%, for example, by using a Gauge with a definite range. Please try to make an equally distributed progress, as it is quite annoying when the meter quickly advances to 90% and then crawls the rest of the way to 100%. In network operations, you can transmit the length of the data. When searching through record stores, you can query the number of recordsets in advance.

Sometimes you can split the operation into several steps, even though you don't know the exact number of needed steps. In such cases, you can use an incrementally updating Gauge for displaying progress.

In cases when you can't determine the required time and can't split up the operation into single steps, you should give at least some feedback to the user that an operation is in progress. Use a continuously running Gauge or an animation for this purpose.

Ensuring Responsiveness

When you are notified about events such as the pressing of a key or the invocation of a command, you need to return control as quickly as possible back to the System thread. When you set a current screen by calling Display.setCurrent(), the screen will not be shown until your method returns, for example. So you are required to use background threads for ongoing operations like network access or storing large amounts of data in the record store. When you do CPU-intensive tasks, you should pause the background thread between different steps, so that the operating system thread has a chance to deliver events to your application.

Reducing Memory Consumption

Depending on your target devices, you can have a heap size between 200KB and several megabytes available for your application. But even several megabytes may not be enough when your application is experiencing memory leaks. Also, reducing the memory footprint may increase the performance of your application, because garbage collection does not need to kick in as frequently.

In this section, you'll first learn how to measure your application's memory consumption, and then you'll examine how to improve the memory footprint by reducing the number of objects, using recursion, and avoiding memory leaks.

Measuring Memory Consumption

You can measure the memory footprint of your application in the WTK emulator by enabling the `enableMemoryMonitor` option of the `<emulator>` element, as shown in Listing 16-10. Figure 16-2 shows the memory monitor in action.

Listing 16-10. *Enabling the Memory Monitor in the WTK Emulator*

```
<j2mepolish>
   <info
      license="GPL"
      name="Roadrunner"
      vendorName="A reader."
      version="0.0.1"
      jarName="${polish.vendor}-${polish.name}-roadrunner.jar"
   />
   <deviceRequirements>
      <requirement name="Identifier"
                   value="Generic/midp2" />
   </deviceRequirements>
   <build
      usePolishGui="true"
   >
      <midlet class="com.apress.roadrunner.Roadrunner" />
   </build>
   <emulator enableMemoryMonitor="true" />
</j2mepolish>
```

Again, the memory consumption on your development machine might differ from that on the actual device. For some operating systems, you can get native applications that control the memory when your MIDlet runs. On Symbian devices, you can use TaskSpy (*http://www.pushl.com*), for example.

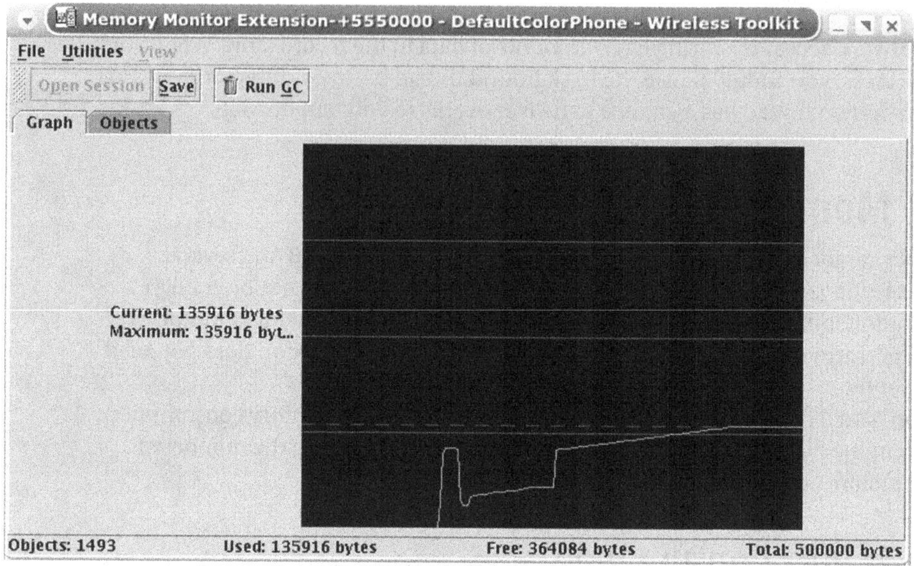

Figure 16-2. *Measuring the memory footprint with the WTK emulator*

You can also use `Runtime.freeMemory()` and `Runtime.totalMemory()` in your application, but these values depend on the memory strategy of the virtual machine. Use the difference between the return values for detecting the approximately used memory: `long usedMemory = runtime.totalMemory() - runtime.freeMemory()`.

Improving the Memory Footprint

You can improve the memory footprint in a couple of ways: reducing the number of objects and using recursion. You should also take preventative measures to guard against memory leaks that you might accidentally produce.

Reducing the Number of Objects

Each created object reduces the available memory, so you should aim to reduce the number of the needed objects in your application. Isn't that simple?

One strategy is to reuse existing objects. Reusing objects can, however, introduce new problems such as caches that are held in memory even though the cached objects are no longer needed. So consider the implications carefully before adopting this strategy widely.

Another strategy involves reducing the number of temporary objects. These objects are often created in loops; `String` operations are a prime example. `String`s are immutable, so a new `String` needs to be instantiated at each change. Consider, for example, the creation of a `String` that contains a consecutive range of numbers like `01234`. When you need to concatenate several `String`s, it's often better to use `StringBuffer`s instead of the + operator. Listing 16-11 shows a bad example and a good example of creating a `String` containing such numbers.

Listing 16-11. *Reducing the Number of Temporary Objects by Using StringBuffer Instead of String*

```
public String getSlowNumberString( int top ) {
   String number = "";
   for ( int i = 0; i <= top; i++ ) {
      number += i;
   }
   return number;
}

public String getFastNumberString( int top ) {
   // we assume that top is less than 10 here:
   StringBuffer number = new StringBuffer( top );
   for ( int i = 0; i <= top; i++ ) {
      number.append( i );
   }
   return number.toString();
}
```

Another popular place for creating unnecessary `String`s is the `Graphics.drawString()` method. When you call `g.drawString( "Points: " + this.points, x, y, Graphics.TOP | Graphics.LEFT )` in your `paint()` method, you create a new temporary `String` object every time the method is called. It might be better to create the `String` containing the points only when the number of points is actually changed.

In some cases, it's worthwhile to postpone the creation of objects until they are really needed. This so-called lazy initialization helps to reduce the memory usage but also complicates your application logic, so use this strategy with care.

Using Recursion

Using recursive methods yields good-looking and easy-to-understand algorithms, but unfortunately it introduces memory and performance overhead. This is due to the parameters and the state, which needs to be pushed on the stack of the virtual machine for each invocation of the method. In most cases, you can use equivalent iterative algorithms instead.

Avoiding Memory Leaks

You can create undesirable memory leaks in Java by not dereferencing unused objects. This is especially easy when you use containers such as `Vector` or `Hashtable` for storing objects.

To avoid creating leaks, when using containers always try to guess and set the appropriate size, so that the internal array does not need to be increased. Increasing the internal array often includes copying all elements from the old array into a new array, so it not only takes time, but also increases the memory usage. Don't forget to remove elements from containers when they are not needed anymore. You should also consider dereferencing variables as soon as possible by explicitly setting them to `null`. This helps the garbage collector to figure out which objects are not used and reachable anymore.

Sometimes devices have different types of memory. Old Sony Ericsson devices such as the T610 differentiate between the normal Java heap, the native UI heap, and the Video RAM, for example. Images are loaded into the Video RAM, which offers faster access but is also limited compared to the Java heap. Garbage collecting images from the Video RAM is different than from the normal Java heap memory, so you should try to load images that are used all the time first.

Using large `StringBuffers` can also be problematic when you call `toString()` frequently. The retrieved `Strings` use the complete internal array of the `StringBuffer`, so when you later change the buffer, the internal array may need to be copied to a new one. In those cases, you end up with having the complete internal array as often as you have called `toString()` on the `StringBuffer`.

Many optional APIs use native calls for accomplishing their work. Due to device bugs, this can be difficult, so you exercise caution when using Bluetooth connections, playing music, or viewing three-dimensional graphics. Make sure to study known issues of your target devices with respect to memory handling.

Decreasing the Size of JAR Files

Minimizing the size of JAR files not only improves download times, but it's often necessary to meet the restrictions of your target devices. MIDP 1.0-based devices of Nokia's Series 40 only accept JAR files up to 64KB, for example.

In this section, you'll learn how to decrease the size of your JAR bundle by simplifying the class model, reducing the size of resources, removing resources altogether, and by using third-party packagers and obfuscators.

Improving the Class Model

You can improve your class model by minimizing the number of classes and interfaces in your application. You can do so by grouping similar functionalities and by removing unnecessary classes, as described in the sections that follow.

Grouping Functionalities

Each class adds overhead to your JAR files, because it needs an additional entry in your JAR file as well as some Java-specific data such as class constants. Grouping functionalities allows you to minimize the number of needed classes.

A good example is to implement a `CommandListener` only in one class. Often it seems to be easier to provide specialized `Screens` that handle their commands and events autonomously. However, this undermines the model view control principle, because the view (`Screen`) provides also the control (`CommandListener`). When you process events in only one controller class like the main `MIDlet`, you gain several advantages at once:

- You decouple the control from the view.
- You implement the `CommandListener` interface only once, saving precious space.
- Often you can remove the specialized classes completely, since using and populating standard `Forms`, `Lists`, and so on is sufficient in many cases.

Look out for one-to-one class relations, which are classes that are used by only one other class. Often you can merge the functionality of such classes without jeopardizing your architecture.

■ **Caution** Too much grouping severely decreases the maintainability and extensibility of your application. Also, some devices enforce a maximum size for classes. On Siemens devices, a class must not exceed 16KB, for example.

Removing Unnecessary Classes and Methods

Sometimes you can remove classes or methods altogether. This is often true for redundant abstraction and for some helper classes.

Somehow, many developers tend to abstract the event handling in MIDlets, for example. While abstracting the event handling might be good idea for J2SE and J2EE applications, it is usually redundant for J2ME applications. In the end, such event handling abstractions mirror the behavior of the `javax.microedition.lcdui.CommandListener` interface in one way or another. Avoid abstractions that provide functions similar to the ones offered by the MIDP standard.

Helper classes are great for easing complex interactions, but over time they tend to bloat and mirror the same functionality as the underlying ones.

A typical example is a helper class for the MMAPI audio playback. At first the helper classes are much easier to handle than the complex MMAPI itself. But over time, you encounter cases that need special treatment, so you add functionality to your helper class. Need a feedback system? Add a new interface for event handling. Need to handle different audio sources? Add additional constructors. You will end up reimplementing most of the MMAPI functionality in your helper class. This might be easier to handle for yourself, but what happens when another programmer needs to change your code? Always assess the need for helper classes critically. If your helper classes are merely there to reduce the complexity of other APIs, try to get rid of them.

In addition, unnecessary helper methods are often seen in the wild. Take, for example, a `Form` that provides some methods for adding special items to it, such as `public void addChoiceGroup( String label, String[] elements )`. This might seem to be easier than creating a new `ChoiceGroup` and adding it to the `Form`. But sooner or later, you will find yourself adding the helper methods `addMultipleChoiceGroup()` and `addPopupChoiceGroup()`, too. In most cases, the effort is not really worth it. If anything looks like a duplication of code, try to get rid of it.

Storing Array Data

Long array definitions inside class files take up considerable space, because Java's bytecode cannot store array data directly. Instead, each array element is first pushed on the stack and then stored at the correct array position, as shown in Listing 16-12. At first, the virtual machine is instructed to allocate a new array with the `newarray` instruction. For each element, the array position is then pushed on the stack, for example, with `iconst_0` (push the integer constant `0`) for the first element, or with `bipush 6` (push a 1-byte signed integer) for the seventh element.

Then the actual value of the array element is pushed on the stack with either `bipush` (1-byte integer values), `sipush` (2-byte integer values), or `ldc` (load value from the constant pool). Finally, the element is stored inside the allocated array with `iastore`.

Listing 16-12. *Bytecode Instruction for Storing a Simple Integer Array*

```
// Java source-code instruction:
int[] values = new int[]{ 23, 57, 23453, 2342, 232, 213, 345, 56, 6767 };
// Resulting bytecode instructions:
bipush          9
newarray        int[]
dup
iconst_0
bipush          23
iastore
dup
iconst_1
bipush          57
iastore
dup
iconst_2
sipush          23453
iastore
dup
iconst_3
sipush          2342
iastore
dup
iconst_4
sipush          232
iastore
dup
iconst_5
sipush          213
iastore
dup
bipush          6
sipush          345
iastore
dup
bipush          7
bipush          56
iastore
dup
bipush          8
sipush          6767
iastore
```

Arrays are often used to store configuration values such as the setup of levels in games. Instead of using arrays that need long chains of bytecode instructions, you can either use other variables or store the data outside of your classes.

When you store your data inside a `String` instead of an `int[]` array, you might be able to save space even if you have to unpackage the single values and parse them. Listing 16-13 makes use of the J2ME Polish `de.enough.polish.util.TextUtil` helper class to split the `String` that contains the values. In cases when your application uses this helper class anyhow, you can minimize the JAR size in this way. You need only 22 instructions to unpack and to parse the integer array, compared with the 38 instructions you need for the directly specified example `int[]` array with 9 elements.

Listing 16-13. *Saving Space by Storing Array Data in Strings*

```
// Java source code instructions:
String value = "23,57,23453,2342,232,213,345,56,6767";
String[] valueChunks = TextUtil.split( value, ',' );
int[] values = new int[ valueChunks.length ];
for ( int i = 0; i < values.length; i++ ) {
   values[ i ] = Integer.parseInt( valueChunks[ i ] );
}

// resulting Java bytecode instructions:
ldc1            #75  <String "23,57,23453,2342,232,213,345,56,6767">
astore          4
aload           4
bipush          44
invokestatic    #81  <Method String[] TextUtil.split( String, char )>
astore          5
aload           5
arraylength
newarray        int[]
astore          6
iconst_0
istore          7
goto            208
aload           6
iload           7
aload           5
iload           7
aaload
invokestatic    #87  <Method int Integer.parseInt( String )>
iastore
iinc            7  1
```

Another option to save space while gaining flexibility is to store the data outside of the actual classes and load it using a `DataInputStream`. You can use the Binary Editor in *${polish.home}/bin* to manage such data files comfortably (see Chapter 10). Listing 16-14 shows loading an integer array from a resource file. In this example, you assume that the first short value in the file includes the length of the following integer array. In this way, you need only 22 instructions to load the integer array compared with 38 instructions for defining the example `int[]` array directly in the class. Of course, additional space is needed for every resource file, so storing each moderately long array in an external file will do more harm than good. But as soon as the data gets complex, you will almost certainly profit from this approach.

Listing 16-14. *Loading Array Data from a Resource File*

```
// Java source-code instructions:
InputStream is = getClass().getResourceAsStream( "/l1.data" );
DataInputStream in = new DataInputStream( is );
short arrayLength = in.readShort();
int[] values = new int[ arrayLength ];
for ( int i = 0; i < values.length; i++ ) {
   values[ i ] = in.readInt();
}

// resulting Java byte-code instructions:
aload_0
invokevirtual   #97  <Method Class Object.getClass()>
ldc1            #99  <String "/l1.data">
invokevirtual   #105 <Method java.io.InputStream Class.getResourceAsStream(String)>
astore          7
new             #107 <Class DataInputStream>
dup
aload           7
invokespecial   #110 <Method void DataInputStream(java.io.InputStream)>
astore          8
aload           8
invokevirtual   #114 <Method short DataInputStream.readShort()>
istore          9
iload           9
newarray        int[]
astore          10
iconst_0
istore          11
goto            310
aload           10
iload           11
aload           8
invokevirtual   #118 <Method int DataInputStream.readInt()>
iastore
iinc            11  1
```

Handling Resources

Resources such as images or sound files often claim the largest part of your JAR file. In this section, you'll discover how to tackle resources by including only appropriate resources, decreasing the size of the resources, reducing the number of resources, and removing resources completely.

Using Appropriate Resources

You can reduce the JAR file size by including appropriate resources only. Use the automatic resource assembling capabilities of J2ME Polish for this task.

You can reduce the size of images by using appropriate color palettes. This can also improve the quality of the images on devices that support fewer colors than the original images, because the dithering algorithms behave differently on various devices. You can include different versions of your images for different phones; for example, include high-color images only for devices that support the appropriate color depth. Useful resource folders are *resources/BitsPerColor.12*, *resources/BitsPerColor.16+*, *resources/ScreenSize.128x128*, and *resources/ScreenSize.170+x200+*.

You can also include resources based on several criteria, such as `<fileset dir="resources/sounds" includes="*.mid" if="polish.api.mmapi and polish.sound.midi" />`. Please refer to the "Assembling Resources" section of Chapter 7 for a full discussion of the resource selection with J2ME Polish.

Decreasing the Size of Resources

Resources often contain information that is not needed for playing or displaying them, such as copyright notices or comments.

You can optimize PNG images with the tools Pngcrush (*http://pmt.sourceforge.net/pngcrush*), PNGOUT (*http://advsys.net/ken/utils.htm#pngout*), and PNGGauntlet (*http://numbera.com/software/pnggauntlet.aspx*). These tools remove redundant information and can reduce the image size by several percentage points.

Redundant information can be also found in MIDI files. Some editors allow you to edit the stored headers. Also, some MIDI events, such as the switching of sound banks, are not supported by all J2ME devices, so you can remove those from the files.

Caution Sometimes removing redundant data *increases* the JAR size, because the ZIP algorithm cannot compress the data as efficiently as it could before. Any increase will likely consist of only a couple of bytes, but when you are very close to your target size, you might need to pay attention to this effect.

Reducing the Number of Resources

You can reduce the number of resources by merging them into a single file. This can decrease the size effectively when the resources share common capabilities, for example, when several PNG files use similar color palettes. In such cases, you can create one large image that contains the previous images. Use the `Graphics.setClip()` mechanism to draw the images one by one in your application.

When you store several resources independently into one file, such that the header information is repeated for each resource, you will save some space in your JAR file. The ZIP algorithm can compress headers more efficient when they are repeated in one file, and each file that is stored in the JAR file requires one entry in the contents header of your JAR file; fewer entries result in a smaller file size.

Removing Resources

Sometimes it is feasible to remove some resources completely. You just leave the bare necessities in your JAR file and download the rest when it is needed. An example is to include the resources only for one level of a game, and then download the resources for further levels when the user has finished the first level.

Obfuscating and Packaging Your Application

Last but not least, you can save some space by using obfuscators and specialized packagers.

Obfuscators shrink your classes by renaming them and removing unused code from your application. This is an easy way to save substantially. As an added benefit, your code will be harder to understand for any malicious or curious users interested in decompiling your application. As you learned in the "Obfuscating Applications" section of Chapter 7, you can deploy different obfuscators in J2ME Polish—or even several obfuscators at once. When your budget is tight, go for the free ProGuard obfuscator, but keep in mind that some commercial obfuscators/optimizers can produce even smaller JAR file sizes.

Not all obfuscators can move all classes into the default package. Using the default package brings some additional savings, because the fully qualified class names are stored inside each class. You could just use the default package for all your classes, but this will jeopardize your architecture. J2ME Polish can move all classes of your application into the default package during the preprocessing step. Enable this option by setting the `useDefaultPackage` attribute of the `<obfuscator>` element to `true` in your *build.xml* script. Remember that this approach requires you to use unique class names for all your Java source files.

In the packaging step, all class files and resources are bundled into one JAR file. J2ME Polish uses the default Java ZIP algorithm for packaging the files. Depending on your application and your target devices, you might want to use a different packager. Please refer to the "Packaging Applications" section of Chapter 7 to learn more about your options. Keep in mind that using optimized ZIP-compatible algorithms might result in problems during the installation, so implement this only as a last resort.

Summary

Optimizing your application is the last step for you to create a small, fast, working application. You can optimize for speed, for a reduced memory footprint, and for smaller JAR file sizes. Some optimizations are beneficial for all areas, while others contradict each other. You should consider possible high-level optimizations from the beginning and postpone low-level optimization until the end.

In this book's appendix, you will find details about J2ME Polish and J2ME settings in a condensed format.

PART 4

Appendix

This appendix is a quick reference guide for you to easily find information on settings, attributes, and directives.

Appendix

JAD and Manifest Attributes

MIDP 1.0 Attributes

Table A-1 lists all MIDP 1.0 attributes and shows how to set them using J2ME Polish. When a preprocessing variable with the specified name is defined, it will override the settings made in the <info> section.

Table A-1. *Defining MIDP 1.0 Attributes in J2ME Polish*

Attribute	<info> Attribute	Preprocessing Variable	Description
MicroEdition-Configuration	configuration		The J2ME configuration that is used by the MIDlet, either CLDC-1.0 or CLDC-1.1. You cannot install a CLDC 1.1 application on a CLDC 1.0 device. The configuration is set automatically; use the configuration attribute for overriding this setting.
MicroEdition-Profile	profile		The J2ME profile that is used by the MIDlet, either MIDP 1.0, MIDP 2.0, or MIDP 3.0. You cannot install a MIDP 2.0 application on a MIDP 1.0 device. The profile is set automatically; use the profile attribute for overriding this setting.
MIDlet-<number>			The MIDlet classes in the JAR file, the first of which is defined by the MIDlet-1 attribute. You can set your MIDlet classes with the <midlets> element of the <build> section.

Continued

Table A-1. *Continued*

Attribute	<info> Attribute	Preprocessing Variable	Description
MIDlet-Data-Size	dataSize		The needed space in bytes on the device for additional data. When the available space is not sufficient, the MIDlet will not be installed.
MIDlet-Description	description	${MIDlet-Description}	A description of the MIDlet suite.
MIDlet-Icon	icon	${MIDlet-Icon}	The PNG image used as an icon.
MIDlet-Info-URL	infoUrl	${MIDlet-Info-URL}	A URL that provides additional information about the application.
MIDlet-Jar-Size			The size of the final JAR file size in bytes.
MIDlet-Jar-URL	jarUrl		The URL that provides the JAR file for this JAD file.
MIDlet-Name	name	${MIDlet-Name}	The name of the MIDlet suite.
MIDlet-Vendor	vendorName	${MIDlet-Vendor}	The name of the application vendor.
MIDlet-Version	version	${MIDlet-Version}	The version of the MIDlet suite.

The attributes MIDlet-Jar-Size, MIDlet-<number>, MicroEdition-Profile, and MicroEdition-Configuration are set automatically by J2ME Polish. You can, however, override the configuration and profile settings with the XML attributes configuration and profile of the <info> element. This can be useful when you load classes dynamically for exploiting device-specific functionality in your application.

MIDP 2.0 Attributes

The MIDP 2.0 platform introduces the new attributes listed in Table A-2.

Table A-2. *Defining MIDP 2.0 Attributes in J2ME Polish*

Attribute	<info> Attribute	Preprocessing Variable	Description
MIDlet-Certificate-1-1			The certificate used for calculating the SHA1 hash value.
MIDlet-Delete-Confirm	deleteConfirm	${MIDlet-Delete-Confirm}	A message that alerts the user when the application is removed.

Attribute	<info> Attribute	Preprocessing Variable	Description
`MIDlet-Delete-Notify`	`deleteNotify`	`${MIDlet-Delete-Notify}`	A URL that is called when the application is removed. The user can suppress the calling of this URL.
`MIDlet-Install-Notify`	`installNotify`	`${MIDlet-Install-Notify}`	A URL that is called when the application is installed. The user can suppress the calling of this URL.
`MIDlet-Jar-RSA-SHA1`			The SHA1 hash value of the JAR file.
`MIDlet-Permissions`	`permissions`	`${MIDlet-Permissions}`	The permissions required by the MIDlet for it to work correctly (e.g., `javax.microedition.io.Connector.http`).
`MIDlet-Permissions-Opt`	`optionalPermissions`	`${MIDlet-Permissions-Opt}`	The permissions that are useful for this application to work.

Vendor-Specific Attributes

Some vendors and carriers support additional attributes, as shown in Table A-3. These attributes are created in the same way as user-defined attributes; that is, you need to use the `<attribute>` elements in the `<jad>` element for defining these attributes.

Table A-3. *Vendor- and Carrier-Specific Attributes*

Vendor	Attribute	Description
LG Electronics	`MIDletX-No-Command`	This attribute can deactivate the command bar when it is set to `true`.
LG Electronics	`MIDletX-Big-Icon`	The big (32×32) icon for the application.
LG Electronics	`MIDletX-Medium-Icon`	The medium (18×18) icon for the application.
Motorola	`Background`	MIDlets in which `Background` is `True` (case sensitive) will be able to run in the background as well (e.g., when an incoming call blocks the application).
Motorola	`FlipInsensitive`	When `FlipInsensitive` is `True` (case sensitive), the application continues to run even when the flip is closed. In this case, audio resources are still available to the application.
Motorola	`Mot-Data-Space-Requirement`	The needed size in kilobytes (rounded up) for the application. This attribute is valid for the V60i and V66i devices only.

Continued

Table A-3. *Continued*

Vendor	Attribute	Description
Motorola	`Mot-Data-Space-Requirements`	The needed size in kilobytes (rounded up) for the application on a T720, C370, C450, or C550 device.
Motorola	`Mot-Program-Space-Requirement`	The needed size in kilobytes (rounded up) for the application bundle itself (like the `MIDlet-Jar-Size` attribute). If this is not specified, 16KB is the maximum size of the RMS. This attribute is valid for the V60i and V66i devices only.
Motorola	`Mot-Program-Space-Requirements`	The needed size in kilobytes (rounded up) for the application bundle itself (like the `MIDlet-Jar-Size` attribute) on a T720, C370, C450, or C550 device. If this attribute is not specified, 16KB is the maximum size of the RMS.
Motorola	`MIDlet-Data-Size`	Even though this is not a Motorola-specific property, you should specify `MIDlet-Data-Size` in bytes when your RMS needs more than 16KB.
Nokia, Series 40	`Nokia-MIDlet-Category`	The section on the Series 40 mobile phone into which the application should be installed (e.g., `Game`). This is a JAD-only attribute.
Vodafone	`MIDxlet-API`	The Vodafone API that should be used (e.g., `VSCL-1.0.1` or `VSCL-1.1.0`).
Vodafone	`MIDxlet-Network`	This attribute defines whether network access is needed for this MIDlet. Possible values are `Y` and `N`.
Vodafone	`MIDxlet-Resident`	You can make your application memory resident, so that it runs in the background. It then could act as a screensaver or receive events such as incoming messages. Possible values are `Y` and `N`.
Vodafone	`MIDxlet-Application-Resolution`	The resolution of the application (e.g., *`120-240,130-320`*).

Runtime Properties

You can use runtime properties for determining the capabilities of the device as well as some user preferences during runtime.

System Properties

You can query system properties with the `System.getProperty( String )` method. The device database will also list these properties in future versions. In that case, you can check for specific system properties with the `polish.Property.[property-name]` preprocessing variable (e.g., `//#if polish.Property.microedition.jtwi.version:defined`). You can check many properties with the `SysInfo` MIDlet in *${polish.home}/samples/sysinfo*.

Table A-4 lists common system attributes.

Caution Never assume that a system property is defined—always check whether it is `null`.

Table A-4. *System Properties*

Library	Property	Example Value	Explanation
Location	`microedition.location.version`	`1.0`	Determines whether the Location API (JSR 179) is supported
M3G	`microedition.m3g.version`	`1.0`	The version of the supported Mobile 3D Graphics API (JSR 184)
MIDP	`microedition.configuration`	`CLDC-1.0`	The supported configuration of the device
MIDP	`microedition.encoding`	`ISO8859-1`	The default character encoding of the device
MIDP	`microedition.locale`	`en-UK`	The preferred locale of the user
MIDP	`microedition.platform`	`SonyEricssonK700i/R2A041`	The name and version of the device
MIDP	`microedition.profiles`	`MIDP-1.0 MIDP-2.0`	The supported profile(s) of the device
JTWI	`microedition.jtwi.version`	`1.0`	The version of the supported JTWI version (JSR 185), if supported
MMAPI	`audio.encoding`	`rate=16000&bits=32`	Parameters for recording audio
MMAPI	`microedition.media.version`	`1.1`	The version of the supported Multimedia API, if supported
MMAPI	`supports.mixing`	`true`	Is `true` when the device can play several sounds simultaneously
MMAPI	`supports.audio.capture`	`true`	Is `true` when the device can record audio
MMAPI	`supports.recording`	`false`	Is `true` when the device can record media
MMAPI	`supports.video.capture`	`true`	Is `true` when the device can take pictures or video sequences
MMAPI	`streamable.contents`	`null`	Any formats that can be streamed

Continued

Table A-4. *Continued*

Library	Property	Example Value	Explanation
MMAPI	`video.encodings`	`encoding=JPEG& width=176& height=182`	Parameters for recording video or taking snapshots
MMAPI	`video.snapshot.encoding`	`encoding=JPEG`	Supported image formats for taking snapshots
PDAAPI	`microedition.io.file. FileConnection.version`	`1.0`	The version of the supported FileConnection API (JSR 75)
PDAAPI	`microedition.pim.version`	`1.0`	The version of the supported PIM-API (JSR 75)
Sensor	`microedition.sensor.version`	`1.0`	The version of the Sensor API (JSR 256), if supported
WMAPI	`wireless.messaging.sms.smsc`	`+4912345678`	The number of the used Short Message Service Center (JSR 120)

Bluetooth Properties

Properties of the Bluetooth API (JSR 82), listed in Table A-5, cannot be acquired by calling `System.getProperty()`; they can be acquired only by invoking `LocaleDevice.getProperty()`. Other than that, they behave just like system properties, so you should always check returned values against `null`.

Table A-5. *Bluetooth Properties*

Property	Example Value	Explanation
`bluetooth.api.version`	`1.0`	The version of the Java APIs for Bluetooth wireless technology that is supported
`bluetooth.connected.devices.max`	`1`	The maximum number of connected devices, including parked devices
`bluetooth.connected.inquiry`	`false`	Defines whether an inquiry is allowed while a connection is established
`bluetooth.connected.inquiry.scan`	`false`	Defines whether inquiry scanning is allowed during a connection
`bluetooth.connected.page`	`false`	Defines whether paging is allowed during a connection
`bluetooth.connected.page.scan`	`false`	Defines whether page scanning is allowed during a connection

Property	Example Value	Explanation
bluetooth.l2cap.receiveMTU.max	512	The buffer for receiving MTU in L2CAP
bluetooth.master.switch	false	Defines whether the master/servant roles can be switched during a connection
bluetooth.sd.attr.retrievable.max	1	The maximum number of service attributes to be retrieved per service record
bluetooth.sd.trans.max	1	The maximum number of service attributes to be retrieved per service record

3D Properties

The Mobile 3D Graphics API (JSR 184) defines its own properties (see Table A-6) that cannot be retrieved over the normal `System.getProperty()` mechanism. Instead, a `Hashtable` containing the properties can be retrieved by calling `Graphics3D.getProperties()`. Contrary to other property functions, the stored values are not `Strings`, but `Integers` or `Booleans`.

Table A-6. *3D Properties*

Property	Type	Minimum Value	Explanation
maxLights	Integer	8	The maximum number of concurrent lights.
maxSpriteCropDimension	Integer	256	The maximum size of the actual displayed area of a `Sprite3D`.
maxTextureDimension	Integer	256	The maximum size (width or height) of a `Texture2D`.
maxTransformsPerVertex	Integer	2	The maximum number of transformations for the vertices of a `SkinnedMesh`.
maxViewportDimension	Integer	256	The maximum allowed width and height of the `Graphics3D`'s viewport.
numTextureUnits	Integer	1	The maximum number of textures for an `Appearance`.
supportAntialiasing	Boolean	false	Allows the use of antialiasing to increase the perceived resolution of the screen.
supportDithering	Boolean	false	Allows the use of dithering to increase the perceived color depth of the screen.

Continued

Table A-6. *Continued*

Property	Type	Minimum Value	Explanation
`supportLocalCameraLighting`	`Boolean`	`false`	If local camera lighting is disabled, the direction vector from the camera to the vertex being lit is approximated with `(0 0 -1)`. If local camera lighting is enabled, the direction is computed based on the true camera position.
`supportMipmapping`	`Boolean`	`false`	Defines whether you can filter textures between or within mipmap levels.
`supportPerspectiveCorrection`	`Boolean`	`false`	Allows correction of perspectives in polygons. The lack of perspective correction is especially evident on large, textured polygons; the texture is distorted and seems to "crawl" on the surface as the viewing angle changes.
`supportTrueColor`	`Boolean`	`false`	Allows rendering with an internal color depth higher than what is supported by the device. This is useful in combination with dithering.

Permissions for Signed MIDlets

The MIDP 2.0 standard allows signed MIDlets to request permissions for certain actions during the installation. In that case, the user won't be bothered by screens asking him to permit network connections and so forth whenever the application accesses a security-sensitive resource. You can set permissions with the `permissions` and `optionalPermissions` attributes of the `<info>` section in your *build.xml* script. Table A-7 contains common permissions for a variety of protocols and optional APIs.

Table A-7. *MIDP 2.0 Security Permissions*

Entity	Permission	Explanation
HTTP	`javax.microedition.io.Connector.http`	For establishing HTTP connections
HTTPS	`javax.microedition.io.Connector.https`	For establishing secure HTTP connections
UDP	`javax.microedition.io.Connector.datagram`	For sending UPD datagrams

Entity	Permission	Explanation
UDP	javax.microedition.io.Connector.datagramreceiver	For receiving UPD datagrams
TCP	javax.microedition.io.Connector.socket	For establishing outbound TCP connections
TCP	javax.microedition.io.Connector.serversocket	For accepting inbound TCP connections
SSL	javax.microedition.io.Connector.ssl	For connecting via SSL or TLS
Serial	javax.microedition.io.Connector.comm	For establishing serial connections (e.g., over the infrared port)
Push Registry	javax.microedition.io.PushRegistry	For setting alarms or registering inbound connections
SMS	javax.microedition.io.Connector.sms	For opening a SMS connection in the WM API
SMS	javax.microedition.io.Connector.sms.send	For sending a short message in the WM API
SMS	javax.microedition.io.Connector.sms.receive	For receiving a short message in the WM API
CBS	javax.microedition.io.Connector.cbs	For opening a cell broadcast connection in the WM API
CBS	javax.microedition.io.Connector.cbs.receive	For receiving a cell broadcast in the WM API
MMS	javax.microedition.io.Connector.mms	For opening a MMS connection in the WM API 2.0
MMS	javax.microedition.io.Connector.mms.send	For sending a multimedia message in the WM API 2.0
MMS	javax.microedition.io.Connector.mms.receive	For receiving a multimedia message in the WM API 2.0
Bluetooth	javax.microedition.io.Connector.bluetooth.server	For opening a Bluetooth server connection in the BT API (e.g., Connector.open("btspp://localhost:..."))

Continued

Table A-7. *Continued*

Entity	Permission	Explanation
Bluetooth	`javax.microedition.io.Connector.bluetooth.client`	For opening a client Bluetooth connection in the BT API (e.g., `Connector.open( "btspp://... " )`)
PIM	`javax.microedition.pim.ContactList.read`	For reading a contact list in the PIM API
PIM	`javax.microedition.pim.ContactList.write`	For writing into a contact list in the PIM API
PIM	`javax.microedition.pim.EventList.read`	For reading an event list in the PIM API
PIM	`javax.microedition.pim.EventList.write`	For writing to an event list in the PIM API
PIM	`javax.microedition.pim.ToDoList.read`	For reading a to-do list in the PIM API
PIM	`javax.microedition.pim.ToDoList.write`	For writing into a to-do list in the PIM API
File	`javax.microedition.io.Connector.file.read`	For reading a file in the FileConnection API
File	`javax.microedition.io.Connector.file.write`	For writing a file in the FileConnection API
Location	`javax.microedition.location.Location`	For getting the location in the Location API
Location	`javax.microedition.location.Orientation`	For getting the orientation of the device in the Location API
Location	`javax.microedition.location.ProximityListener`	For adding a proximity listener in the Location API
Location	`javax.microedition.location.LandmarkStore.read`	For reading landmarks in the Location API
Location	`javax.microedition.location.LandmarkStore.write`	For setting landmarks in the Location API
Location	`javax.microedition.location.LandmarkStore.category`	For organizing landmarks in the Location API
Location	`javax.microedition.location.LandmarkStore.management`	For managing landmarks in the Location API

The J2ME Polish Ant Settings

J2ME Polish supports a wide range of elements and attributes that you can use in your *build.xml* scripts.

<info> Section

In the `<info>` section, general information about the project is defined (see Table A-8).

The information given in the `<info>` section defines the JAD and Manifest attributes indirectly. If you need to set attributes that are not supported by the `<info>` section, you can use the `<jad>` element in the `<build>` section.

Table A-8. *Attributes of the <info> Section*

<info> Attribute	Required?	Explanation
`configuration`	No	Normally, J2ME Polish uses the JavaConfiguration capability of the current target device for determining the correct `MicroEdition-Configuration` setting. You can override this by hard-coding the configuration for all target devices. This is useful only in cases when you determine device capabilities during the runtime of the application and want to deliver one application bundle for all target devices.
`copyright`	No	The copyright notice.
`dataSize`	No	The minimum space needed on the device (e.g., `dataSize="120kb"`). The variable `MIDlet-Data-Size` overrides this setting.
`deleteConfirm`	No	The text presented to the user when she tries to delete the application. The variable `MIDlet-Delete-Confirm` overrides this setting; this can be used to localize the application.
`deleteNotify`	No	An HTTP URL that should be called after the application has been deleted from the device. See the explanation of `installNotify`. The variable `MIDlet-Delete-Notify` overrides this setting.
`description`	No	The description of the project. A brief explanation about what this application does should be given here. The variable `MIDlet-Description` overrides the value given here; this can be used to localize the application.
`infoUrl`	No	The URL that contains more information about the application. The variable `MIDlet-Info-URL` overrides this setting; this can be used to localize the application.
`installNotify`	No	An HTTP URL that should be called after the successful installation of the application. This can be useful for tracking how many applications are installed. The user can prevent the install-notify, though. You can use the same variables as for the `jarUrl` attribute. The variable `MIDlet-Install-Notify` overrides this setting.

Continued

Table A-8. *Continued*

<info> Attribute	Required?	Explanation
jarName	Yes	The name of the JAR files that will be created. Apart from the usual J2ME Polish variables, the following variables are especially useful: ${polish.vendor}: The vendor of the device (e.g., Samsung, Motorola, etc.) ${polish.name}: The name of the device ${polish.version}: The version of the project as defined previously ${polish.locale}: The current locale (e.g., en, de_DE, etc.) For example, jarName="Game-${ nospace(polish.vendor)}-${ nospace(polish.name)}-${polish.locale}.jar" translates into *Game-Nokia-6600-en.jar* for an application that has been optimized for the Nokia 6600 and uses the English locale. Use the nospace property function to remove all spaces from the variable values. Define the polish.jarName preprocessing variable for overriding this setting.
jarUrl	No	The URL from which the JAR file can be downloaded. This is either the HTTP address or just the name of the JAR file when it is loaded locally. When no jarUrl is defined, the jarName defined previously is used. Apart from the variables available for the jarName attribute, you can use the name of the JAR file as defined previously: jarUrl="http://www.enough.de/midlets/Game/${polish.vendor}/${polish.name}/${polish.jarName}"
license	Yes	The license under which J2ME Polish is used, either GPL or the commercial license key.
name	Yes	The name of the project. The variable MIDlet-Name overrides this setting. Use this variable to localize the application.
optionalPermissions	No	The permissions that are useful for this application to work. The variable MIDlet-Permissions-Opt overrides this setting.
permissions	No	The permissions needed by this application (e.g., javax.microedition.io.Connector.http). The variable MIDlet-Permissions overrides this setting.
profile	No	Normally, J2ME Polish uses the JavaPlatform capability of the current target device for determining the correct MicroEdition-Profile setting. You can override this by hard-coding the profile for all target devices. This is useful only in cases when you determine device capabilities during the runtime of the application and want to deliver one application bundle for all target devices.
vendorName	Yes	The name of the vendor of this application. The variable MIDlet-Vendor overrides this setting.
version	Yes	The version of the project in the format [major].[minor].[build] (e.g., version="2.1.10"). The variable MIDlet-Version overrides this setting.

Device Requirements Section

The optional `<deviceRequirements>` section is responsible for selecting the devices that are supported by the application. When this section is omitted, the application will be optimized for all known devices (there are more than 300 devices).

Table A-9 presents the attributes and Table A-10 presents the nested elements of the `<deviceRequirements>` section, and Table A-11 presents the attributes of the `<requirement>` elements.

Table A-9. *Attributes of the <deviceRequirements> Section*

<deviceRequirements> Attribute	Required?	Explanation
`if`	No	The name of the Ant property that needs to be `true` or yes to use this `<deviceRequirements>`
`unless`	No	The name of the Ant property that needs to be `false` or no to use this `<deviceRequirements>`

Table A-10. *Nested Elements of the <deviceRequirements> Section*

<deviceRequirements> Element	Required?	Explanation
`<requirement>`	Yes	The requirement that needs to be fulfilled by the device
`<and>`	No	A series of requirements, all of which need to be fulfilled
`<or>`	No	A series of requirements, at least one of which needs to be fulfilled
`<xor>`	No	A series of requirements, one of which needs to be fulfilled
`<not>`	No	A series of requirements, none of which must be fulfilled

Table A-11. *Attributes of <requirement> Element*

<requirement> Attribute	Required?	Explanation
`name`	Yes	The name of the needed capability (e.g. `BitsPerPixel`).
`value`	Yes	The needed value of the capability (e.g., `16+` for a color depth of at least 16 bits per pixel).
`type`	No	The class that controls this requirement. The class must either extend the `de.enough.polish.ant.requirements.Requirement` class, or one of the base types `Size`, `Int`, `String`, `Version`, or `Memory` (e.g., `<requirement name="MaxJarSize" value="100+ kb" type="Memory" />`).

Build Section

With the `<build>` section, the actual build process is controlled. The `<build>` element supports many attributes and nested elements, as shown in Table A-12.

Table A-12. *Attributes of the <build> Section*

<build> Attribute	Required?	Explanation
`apiDir`	No	The folder in which the APIs are stored. It defaults to *${polish.home}/import*.
`apis`	No	The path to the *apis.xml* file. It defaults to *apis.xml* in the project's folder or in *${polish.home}*.
`binaryLibraries` or `binaryLibrary`	No	Either the name of the directory that contains binary-only libraries or the name(s) of the libraries. Several libraries can be separated by colons (`:`) or by semicolons (`;`). When no path is defined, the libraries will be searched within the *import* folder by default. This mechanism can be used only for third-party APIs, which are not available on the phone itself. Device APIs are automatically included, after they have been defined in the *${j2mepolish.home}/apis.xml* file. Alternatively, you can also use the nested `<library>` element, which allows you fine-grained control.
`devices`	No	The path to the *devices.xml* file. It defaults to *devices.xml* in the project's folder or in *${polish.home}*.
`compilerDestDir`	No	Defines where the compiled (and obfuscated) classes should be stored when the compiler mode is activated. The default target directory is *bin/classes*.
`compilerMode`	No	When the compiler mode is activated, J2ME Polish will not package the application and will process only one device. This mode is useful for IDEs that support indirect compilation such as NetBeans. You can select Run in NetBeans, and NetBeans will use J2ME Polish as compiler, package the application, and start the emulator—this saves valuable time during the development phase. You can also use this feature to integrate J2ME Polish with the EclipseME plug-in. In that case, you also need to set the `compilerDestDir` to *preverified* and enable the `compilerModePreverify` option (both attributes are described shortly). Possible values are `true` or `false`. The compiler mode is deactivated (`false`) by default.

<build> Attribute	Required?	Explanation
`compilerModePreverify`	No	Defines whether J2ME Polish should preverify the compiled classes as well. This is needed for using J2ME Polish as a compiler for the EclipseME plug-in. Possible values are `true` or `false`. The preverifying is deactivated (`false`) by default.
`customApis`	No	The path to the *custom-apis.xml* file. It defaults to *custom-apis.xml* in the project's folder or in *${polish.home}*.
`customDevices`	No	The path to the *custom-devices.xml* file. It defaults to *custom-devices.xml* in the project's folder or in *${polish.home}*.
`customGroups`	No	The path to the *custom-groups.xml* file. It defaults to *custom-groups.xml* in the project's folder or in *${polish.home}*.
`customVendors`	No	The path to the *custom-vendors.xml* file. It defaults to *custom-vendors.xml* in the project's folder or in *${polish.home}*.
`destDir`	No	The folder into which the "ready to deploy" application bundles should be stored. It defaults to the *dist* folder.
`encoding`	No	The encoding for the generated JAD and Manifest files. It defaults to `UTF8`.
`full-screen`	No	Defines whether the complete screen should be used for devices that support a full screen mode. Currently these include most MIDP 2.0 devices as well as devices that support the Nokia UI API. Possible values are `no`, `yes`, and `menu`. When the value is `yes`, the complete screen is used but no commands are supported. When the value is `menu`, commands can be used as well. The default setting is `no`. Alternatively, you can define the preprocessing variable `polish.Full-screen`. This allows a fine-grained control, since variables can have conditions.
`groups`	No	The path to the *groups.xml* file. It defaults to *groups.xml* in the project's folder or in *${polish.home}*.

Continued

Table A-12. *Continued*

<build> Attribute	Required?	Explanation
imageLoadStrategy	No	The strategy for loading pictures. Possible values are foreground and background. The foreground strategy loads images directly when they are requested. The background strategy loads the images in a background thread. With the background strategy, the perceived performance of an application can be increased, but not all pictures might be shown right away when the user enters a screen. The definition of the imageLoadStrategy makes sense only when the J2ME Polish GUI is used (usePolishGui="true"). The default strategy is foreground.
javacTarget	No	The target for the Java compiler. By default, the "1.2" target is used, unless a WTK 1.x or Mac OS X is used, in which case the target "1.1" is used. You can also use the nested <compiler> element for further settings.
polishDir	No	The directory containing the sources of J2ME Polish. This is in general used only by developers of the J2ME Polish GUI itself.
replacePropertiesWithoutDirective	No	You can use Ant properties in your source code without using preprocessing when you set replacePropertiesWithoutDirective to true (e.g., String message = "Hello ${polish.Identifier}";).
sourceDir	No	The path to the source directory. The default path is either *source/src*, *source*, or *src*. You can define several paths by separating them with a colon (:) or a semicolon (;): [path1]:[path2]. You can also include source directories based on conditions when the nested <sources> element is used instead.
symbols	No	Project-specific symbols (e.g., showSplash) that you can then check with //#ifdef showSplash in the source code. You can define several symbols by separating them with commas.
usePolishGui	No	Defines whether the J2ME Polish GUI should be used at all. Possible values are true/yes, false/no, and always. When the value is true, the GUI will be used only for devices with the recommended capabilities (e.g., a color depth of at least 8 bits). When the value is always, the GUI will be used for all devices. The default value is true.

<build> Attribute	Required?	Explanation
`vendors`	No	The path to the *vendors.xml* file. It defaults to *vendors.xml* in the project's folder or in *${polish.home}*.
`workDir`	No	The temporary build folder. It defaults to the *build* directory.

Incorporating Different Source Folders: <sources> and <source>

Use the `<sources>` element and its nested `<source>` elements to include different source directories. This can be useful when you include test classes or classes that require specific libraries, as demonstrated in Listing A-1. Table A-13 describes the attributes of the `<sources>` element; Table A-14 describes the attributes of the `<source>` element.

Listing A-1. *Including Source Folder Conditionally*

```
<sources>
   <source dir="source/src" />
   <source dir="source/test" if="test" />
   <source dir="source/bluetooth" if="polish.api.btapi" />
</sources>
```

Table A-13. *Attributes of the <sources> Element*

<sources> Attribute	Required?	Explanation
`if`	No	The Ant property that needs to be `true` for the nested source directories to be used
`unless`	No	The Ant property that needs to be `false` for the nested source directories to be used

Table A-14. *Attributes of the <source> Element*

<source> Attribute	Required?	Explanation
`dir`	Yes	The folder that contains Java source files
`if`	No	The Ant property or the preprocessing term that needs to be `true` for this source directory to be used
`unless`	No	The Ant property or the preprocessing term that needs to be `false` for this source directory to be used

Defining MIDlet Classes: <midlets> and <midlet>

The `<midlet>` element in the `<build>` section defines the actual `MIDlet` class. You can add several `<midlet>` elements or use a `<midlets>` element for grouping the definitions, depending on your preferences. In most cases, you simply need to specify the class:

```
<midlet class="com.apress.example.ExampleMidlet" />
```

Table A-15 lists the attributes of the `<midlet>` element.

Table A-15. *Attributes of the <midlet> Element*

<midlet> Attribute	Required?	Explanation
`class`	Yes	The complete package and class name of the MIDlet.
`name`	No	The name of the MIDlet. The default is the class name without the package. The MIDlet `com.company.SomeMidlet` is named `SomeMidlet`, for example.
`icon`	No	The icon of this MIDlet. When none is defined, the icon defined in the `<info>` section will be used.
`number`	No	The number of this MIDlet. This is interesting only for MIDlet suites that contain several MIDlets.
`if`	No	The Ant property or the preprocessing term that needs to be `true` for this MIDlet to be included.
`unless`	No	The Ant property or the preprocessing term that needs to be `false` for this MIDlet to be included.

Specifying Variables: <variables> and <variable>

Use the optional `<variables>` element to define your own preprocessing variables (see Chapter 8) and to configure J2ME Polish (see Chapters 7, 11, and 12). The `<variables>` element in the `<build>` section contains an arbitrary number of `<variable>` elements, which define the actual variables. You can directly specify variables or load them from files.

Table A-16 lists the attributes of the `<variable>` elements.

Table A-16. *Attributes of <variable> Element*

<variable> Attribute	Required?	Explanation
`name`	Yes, unless `file` is used	The name of the variable.
`value`	Yes, unless `file` is used	The value of the variable.
`file`	No	The file that contains several variable definitions. You can also use J2ME Polish properties in the file name (e.g., `file="config/${ lowercase{ polish.vendor }}.properties"`). This includes variable definitions from *config/nokia.properties* when you're targeting a Nokia device. When you use properties, the file is deemed to be optional, so J2ME Polish will report that it is missing, but it continues the build process nevertheless. In the file, the variable names and values are separated by the equals character (=). Empty lines and lines starting with a hash mark (#) are ignored.

<variable> Attribute	Required?	Explanation
if	No	The Ant property that needs to be true or the preprocessing term that needs to result in true for this variable to be included.
unless	No	The Ant property that needs to be false or the preprocessing term that needs to result in false for this variable to be included.

Controlling the Logging: <debug>

The optional <debug> element in the <build> section controls the inclusion of debugging messages for specific classes or packages when you use the //#debug preprocessing directive. Please refer to Chapter 9 for details.

Table A-17 lists the attributes of the <debug> element.

Table A-17. *Attributes of the <debug> Element*

<debug> Attribute	Required?	Explanation
level	No	The general debug level needed for debug messages. Possible values are debug, info, warn, error, fatal, and a user-defined level. The default level is debug, so all messages will be included.
verbose	No	When the value is true, the time, class name, and line number will be included in each log message. The default is false. When verbose mode is enabled, the preprocessing symbol polish.debugVerbose is defined. In verbose mode, exceptions thrown by J2ME Polish contain useful information. Also, the key handling and animation handling are monitored and error messages are provided.
showLogOnError	No	When the value is true, the log containing all logging messages is shown whenever an exception is logged. The log is shown automatically only when the J2ME Polish GUI is used.
if	No	The name of the Ant property that needs to contain true or yes when this <debug> element should be used. When the <debug> element is activated, the preprocessing symbol polish.debugEnabled is defined.
unless	No	The name of the Ant property that needs to be false or no when this <debug> element should be used.

For finer control over the debugging process, the <debug> element allows the subelement <filter>, which defines the debug level for specific classes or packages. Table A-18 lists the attributes of the <filter> element.

Table A-18. *Attributes of the <filter> Element*

<filter> Attribute	Required?	Explanation
`class`	Yes, unless `package` is used	The fully qualified name of the class.
`level`	Yes	The debugging level for the specified class or for all classes of the specified package. Possible values are `debug`, `info`, `warn`, `error`, `fatal`, and a user-defined level.
`package`	No	The name of the package.

You can also forward messages to log handlers using the nested `<handler>` element, which supports the attributes listed in Table A-19.

Table A-19. *Attributes of the <handler> Element*

<handler> Attribute	Required?	Explanation
`name`	Yes, unless `clientClass` is used	The name of the log handler as registered in *extensions.xml* or *custom-extensions.xml* (e.g., `rms` for storing log entries in the record store)
`clientClass`	No	The name of the class that extends `de.enough.polish.log.LogHandler`

Including Additional Preprocessors: <preprocessor>

You can add your own preprocessors for modifying the source code before it is compiled. Just specify the `<preprocessor>` element in the `<build>` section. You can also invoke specific preprocessors automatically (without the `<preprocessor>` element) by defining the `build.Preprocessor` capability in *${polish.home}/custom-devices.xml*. Please refer to Chapter 13 for more details.

Table A-20 lists the attributes of the `<preprocessor>` element.

Table A-20. *Attributes of the <preprocessor> Element*

<preprocessor> Attribute	Required?	Explanation
`name`	Yes, unless `class` is used	The name of the preprocessor as registered in *custom-extensions.xml*
`class`	No	The fully qualified name of the class that extends `de.enough.polish.preprocess.CustomPreprocessor`
`classPath`	No	The classpath from which the preprocessor can be loaded
`target`	No	Specifies the Ant target that you want to call when you use the `antcall` preprocessor: `<preprocessor name="antcall" target="preprocesstarget" />`

<preprocessor> Attribute	Required?	Explanation
if	No	The Ant property that needs to be true or the preprocessing term that needs to result in true for this preprocessor to be used
unless	No	The Ant property that needs to be false or the preprocessing term that needs to result in false for this preprocessor to be used

As with every extension, you can use nested <parameter> elements to configure the <preprocessor> element: <parameter name="message" value="hello ${polish.Identifier}" />.

Controlling the Compilation: <compiler>

Use the optional <compiler> element in the <build> section to specify any compiler arguments. J2ME Polish normally calls the Java compiler with the appropriate classpath as well as bootclasspath for the current target device. In some cases, you might want to adjust the compiler settings, however, so you can use the nested <compiler> element. Along with all attributes of the standard <javac> task, the <compiler> element also supports the if and unless attributes for selecting to appropriate compiler setting.

Table A-21 lists the available attributes of the <compiler> element.

Table A-21. *Available <compiler> Attributes*

<compiler> Attribute	Required	Explanation
bootclasspath	No	The location of bootstrap class files. J2ME Polish uses either the platform specific library files for the bootclasspath (e.g., *midp1.jar* or *midp2-cldc11.jar*).
bootclasspathref	No	The location of bootstrap class files, given as a reference to a path defined elsewhere.
classpath	No	The classpath to use. J2ME Polish includes all supported libraries of the current target device by default.
classpathref	No	The classpath to use, given as a reference to a path defined elsewhere.
compiler	No	The compiler implementation to use. If this attribute is not set, the value of the build.compiler property, if set, is used. Otherwise, the default compiler for the current VM is used.
debug	No	Indicates whether source should be compiled with debug information. The default is off. If this is set to off, -g:none will be passed on the command line for compilers that support it (for other compilers, no command line argument will be used). If this is set to true, the value of the debuglevel attribute determines the command line argument. J2ME Polish enables debugging only when the <debug> element is active for the current target device.

Continued

Table A-21. *Continued*

<compiler> Attribute	Required	Explanation
debuglevel	No	A keyword list to be appended to the -g command line switch. This will be ignored by all implementations except modern and classic (versions >= 1.2). Legal values are none or a comma-separated list of the following keywords: lines, vars, and source. If debuglevel is not specified, by default nothing will be appended to -g. If debug is not turned on, this attribute will be ignored.
depend	No	Enables dependency tracking for compilers that support this (jikes and classic).
deprecation	No	Indicates whether source should be compiled with deprecation information. The default is off.
destdir	No	The location to store the class files. This defaults to the temporary build directory into which class files are written before they are obfuscated.
encoding	No	The encoding of source files. (Note: gcj doesn't support this option yet.)
excludes	No	A comma- or space-separated list of files (may be specified using wildcard patterns) that must be excluded; no files (except default excludes) are excluded when this attribute is omitted.
excludesfile	No	The name of a file that contains a list of files to exclude (may be specified using wildcard patterns).
executable	No	Complete path to the javac executable to use in case of fork="yes". It defaults to the compiler of the Java version that is currently running Ant. It is ignored if fork="no". Since Ant 1.6, this attribute can also be used to specify the path to the executable when using jikes, jvc, gcj, or sj.
extdirs	No	The location of installed extensions.
failonerror	No	Indicates whether the build will continue even if there are compilation errors. The default is true.
fork	No	Indicates whether to execute javac using the JDK compiler externally. The default is no.
if	No	The Ant property that needs to be true or the preprocessing term that needs to result in true for this compiler setting to be used.
includeAntRuntime	No	Indicates whether to include the Ant runtime libraries in the classpath. The default is false.
includeJavaRuntime	No	Indicates whether to include the default runtime libraries from the executing VM in the classpath. The default is no.
includes	No	A comma- or space-separated list of files (may be specified using wildcard patterns) that must be included. All *.java* files are included when this attribute is omitted.
includesfile	No	The name of a file that contains a list of files to include (may be specified using wildcard patterns).
listfiles	No	Indicates whether the source files to be compiled are listed. The default is no.

<compiler> Attribute	Required	Explanation
memoryInitialSize	No	The initial size of the memory for the underlying VM, if javac is run externally; otherwise, it is ignored. It defaults to the standard VM memory setting (e.g., 83886080, 81920k, or 80m).
memoryMaximumSize	No	The maximum size of the memory for the underlying VM, if javac is run externally; otherwise, it is ignored. It defaults to the standard VM memory setting (e.g., 83886080, 81920k, or 80m).
nowarn	No	Indicates whether the -nowarn switch should be passed to the compiler. The default is off.
optimize	No	Indicates whether source should be compiled with optimization. The default is off.
source	No	The value of the -source command line switch. It will be ignored by all implementations prior to javac 1.4 (or modern when Ant is not running in a 1.3 VM) and jikes. If you use this attribute together with jikes, you must make sure that your version of jikes supports the -source switch. Legal values are 1.3, 1.4, and 1.5; by default, the 1.3 source switch will be used.
sourcepath	No	The sourcepath to use, which defaults to the value of the srcdir attribute. To suppress the sourcepath switch, use sourcepath="".
sourcepathref	No	The sourcepath to use, given as a reference to a path defined elsewhere.
srcdir	No	The location of the Java files. This defaults to the temporary directory to which the preprocessed files are written.
target	No	Generates class files for specific VM version (e.g., 1.1 or 1.2). J2ME Polish uses 1.2 by default when the WTK 2.x is used. The target can also be set with the javacTarget attribute of the <build> element.
tempdir	No	The location where Ant should place temporary files. This is only used if the task is forked and the command line argument's length exceeds 4KB.
unless	No	The Ant property that needs to be false or the preprocessing term that needs to result in false for this compiler setting to be used.
verbose	No	Asks the compiler for verbose output. The default is no.

You can specify additional command line arguments for the compiler with nested <compilerarg> elements. These elements are specified like command line arguments but have an additional attribute that can be used to enable arguments only if a given compiler implementation will be used.

Table A-22 lists the attributes of the <compilerargs> element.

Table A-22. *Attributes of the <compilerargs> Element*

<compilerargs> Attribute	Required	Explanation
`compiler`	No	Only pass the specified argument if the chosen compiler implementation matches the value of this attribute.
`file`	Either `value`, `line`, `file`, or `path`	The name of a file as a single command line argument; will be replaced with the absolute file name of the file.
`line`	Either `value`, `line`, `file`, or `path`	A single command line argument; cannot contain space characters.
`path`	Either `value`, `line`, `file`, or `path`	A string that will be treated as a path-like string as a single command line argument. You can use `;` or `:` to separate path entries.
`value`	Either `value`, `line`, `file`, or `path`	A single command-line argument; can contain space characters.

Processing the Compiled Bytecode: <postcompiler>

After compiling the source code, you can process the bytecode using a postcompiler. An example includes the Floater tool of Enough Software that allows you to use floating-point calculations on CLDC 1.0 devices as well. When you define the `build.Postcompiler` capability in *${polish.home}/custom-devices.xml*, the named postcompiler is invoked automatically for the affected devices. Refer to Chapter 13 for more details about postcompiling.

Table A-23 lists the attributes of the `<postcompiler>` element.

Table A-23. *Attributes of the <postcompiler> Element*

<postcompiler> Attribute	Required?	Explanation
`name`	Yes, unless `class` is used	The name of the postcompiler as registered in *custom-extensions.xml* or the J2ME Polish internal *extensions.xml* file.
`class`	No	The fully qualified name of the class that extends `de.enough.polish.postcompile.PostCompiler`.
`classPath`	No	The classpath from which the postcompiler can be loaded.
`target`	No	Use to specify the Ant target that you want to call when you use the `antcall` postcompiler: `<postcompiler name="antcall" target="postcompiletarget" />`.
`if`	No	The Ant property that needs to be `true` or the preprocessing term that needs to result in `true` for this postcompiler to be used.
`unless`	No	The Ant property that needs to be `false` or the preprocessing term that needs to result in `false` for this postcompiler to be used.

You can use nested `<parameter>` elements for configuring the `<postcompiler>` element: `<parameter name="message" value="hello ${polish.Identifier}" />`.

Shrinking and Obfuscating J2ME Applications: <obfuscator>

Control the shrinking and obfuscation of your applications with the optional `<obfuscator>` element in your `<build>` section. Obfuscation decreases the JAR file size and makes it difficult to reverse-engineer your application. Enable the ProGuard obfuscator with this code snippet:

```
<obfuscator name="ProGuard" useDefaultPackage="true" unless="test" />
```

Table A-24 lists the attributes of the `<obfuscator>` element.

Table A-24. *Attributes of the <obfuscator> Element*

<obfuscator> Attribute	Required	Explanation
`name`	No	The name of the obfuscator that should be used. The default is `ProGuard`; other possible values are `Juicer`, `ProGuard`, `KlassMaster`, `Dasho`, `yGuard`, `RetroGuard`, and `antcall`.
`useDefaultPackage`	No	J2ME Polish can move all classes to the default package for you. This includes the `MIDlet` classes as well and can result in a smaller JAR file size. Please note that you are responsible for preventing class name clashes. You do not need to adjust your `<midlet>` settings; this is done automatically by J2ME Polish. You do need, however, to adjust any `<keep>` settings you have. `useDefaultPackage` defaults to `false`. Use the `classname` property function to adjust the loading of dynamic classes.
`if`	No	The name of the Ant property or the preprocessing term that needs to be `true` if this `<obfuscator>` element should be used.
`unless`	No	The name of the Ant property or the preprocessing term that needs to be `false` if this `<obfuscator>` element should be used.
`class`	No	The class that controls the obfuscator. Each class that extends `de.enough.polish.obfuscate.Obfuscator` can be used.
`classPath`	No	The classpath for this obfuscator. This is useful for integrating a third-party obfuscator, in case you don't want to register it in *${polish.home}/custom-extensions.xml*.
`target`	No	The target in your build.xml file that should be called when you use the `antcall` obfuscator.

You can combine several obfuscators in a project just by defining several `<obfuscator>` elements. Use the nested elements `<keep>` and `<parameter>` to configure the obfuscator.

Excluding Dynamic Classes from Obfuscation: <keep>

Use the nested `<keep>` element to define classes that are loaded dynamically with `Class.forName()`, as demonstrated in Listing A-2. The `<keep>` element supports only the `class` attribute that contains the names of the classes that should be spared from obfuscation. You do not need to add your MIDlet classes, since you have them defined with the <midlet> attributes already.

Listing A-2. *Keeping Dynamic Classes in Your Project*

```
<obfuscator unless="test" enable="true" name="ProGuard" >
   <keep class="com.company.dynamic.SomeDynamicClass" />
   <keep class="com.company.dynamic.AnotherDynamicClass" />
</obfuscator>
```

Configuring an Obfuscator: <parameter>

Use the nested <parameter> element (see Table A-25 for its attributes) to configure any obfuscator, as shown in Listing A-3.

Listing A-3. *Configuring Your Obfuscator*

```
<obfuscator unless="test" enable="true" name="ProGuard" >
   <parameter name="scriptFile" value="../scripts/obfuscate.script" />
</obfuscator>
```

Table A-25. *Attributes of the <parameter> Element*

<parameter> Attribute	Required	Explanation
name	Yes	The name of the parameter
value	Yes	The value of the parameter

Combining Several Obfuscators

Combine several obfuscators by specifying several <obfuscator> elements. When you use <keep> subelements, you need only specify them in one <obfuscator> element.

Specific Obfuscator Settings

ProGuard ProGuard is an excellent obfuscator, shrinker, and optimizer by Eric Lafortune. It is freely available under the GNU General Public License and can be downloaded from *http://proguard.sourceforge.net*. You can use ProGuard by setting the name attribute of the <obfuscator> element to ProGuard.

ProGuard 3.x offers an additional optimization of the bytecode, which is disabled by default. You can enable the optimization by setting the optimize parameter to true, as shown in Listing A-4. This improves the shrinking of the class files a bit.

Listing A-4. *Activating Bytecode Optimizations in ProGuard*

```
<obfuscator name="ProGuard" unless="test" >
   <parameter name="optimize" value="true" />
</obfuscator>
```

A text file that lists all renaming operations is written to *build/[vendor]/[device]/[locale]/obfuscation-map.txt*. This file is useful if you get exceptions in the obfuscated application.

yGuard The yGuard obfuscator by the yWorks GmbH is another interesting obfuscator and code shrinker. J2ME Polish includes the library classes, which are licensed under the GNU Lesser General Public License. The full obfuscator is freely available from *http://www.yworks.de*.

The yGuard obfuscator can be used by setting the `name` attribute of the `<obfuscator>` element to `yGuard`:

```
<obfuscator name="yGuard" unless="test" />
```

RetroGuard RetroGuard is the basis of both yGuard and ProGuard, and was developed by Retrologic Systems/Mark Welsh. It is licensed under the GNU Lesser General Public License and is included in J2ME Polish by default. You can download it from *http://www.retrologic.com*.

You can use RetroGuard just by setting the `name` attribute to `RetroGuard`:

```
<obfuscator name="RetroGuard" unless="test"/>
```

Zelix KlassMaster KlassMaster is a commercial obfuscator available from Zelix Pty Ltd. You can request a free evaluation version at *http://www.zelix.com*.

The KlassMaster integration allows you to specify the following parameters:

- `enableFlowObfuscation`: The flow obfuscation increases not only the security of the application, but the application size as well. It is therefore deactivated by default. Activate it by setting the `enableFlowObfuscation` parameter to `true`.
- `ObfuscateFlowLevel`: You can also set the obfuscation flow level directly (e.g., `none` or `aggressive`). This parameter takes precedence over the `enableFlowObfuscation` parameter.
- `ScriptFile`: You can also set the file containing the full script. In that case, please note that the source JAR file is always *build/source.jar* and the target file is *build/dest.jar*.

Listing A-5 shows a possible invocation of KlassMaster.

Listing A-5. *Using the KlassMaster Obfuscator*

```
<obfuscator unless="test" enable="true" name="KlassMaster" >
   <parameter name="ObfuscateFlowLevel" value="none" />
</obfuscator>
```

DashO Pro DashO Pro is a commercial obfuscator by Preemptive Solutions. You can request a free evaluation version at *http://www.preemptive.com*.

When the DashO Pro obfuscator is used, either the Ant property `dasho.home` or the parameter `DashoHome` needs to be provided. The classpath does not need to be modified.

The DashO Pro obfuscator supports the parameters listed in Table A-26.

Table A-26. *Parameters of the DashO Obfuscator*

Name	Explanation
`ConstantPoolTag`	A tag added to all processed classes. This tag is visible only when a decompiler is used.
`DashoHome`	Needs to point to the installation directory of the DashO Pro obfuscator.
`enableFlowObfuscation`	When the value is `true`, DashO will obfuscate the application flow as well. This is deactivated by default.
`enableOptimization`	When the value is `true`, the bytecode will be optimized by DashO. This feature is activated by default.
`enableRenaming`	When the value is `true`, all possible classes will be renamed. This is activated by default.
`enableStringEncription`	When the value is `true`, `Strings` will be obfuscated by DashO as well. Since this decreases the performance, it is deactivated by default.
`ScriptFile`	The file containing the full script can also be set. In that case, please note that the source JAR file is always *build/source.jar* and the target file is *build/dest.jar*.
`Version`	Needs to correspond to the used version of DashO. The current default version is `3.1`.

A report about the renamed classes as well as methods is written to *build/[vendor]/[device]/[locale]/obfuscation-map.txt*. This file is useful for resolving stack traces in the obfuscated application. Listing A-6 shows you how to use the DashO obfuscator in J2ME Polish.

Listing A-6. *Using the DashO Obfuscator*

```
<obfuscator unless="test" enable="true" name="Dasho" >
   <parameter name="DashoHome" value="/home/user/DashOPro_3.1" />
   <parameter name="Version" value="3.1" />
</obfuscator>
```

Preverifying the Application: <preverifier>

You can use a specific preverifier by defining the `<preverifier>` element in the `<build>` section (see Table A-27 for the `<preverifier>` element's attributes). Alternatively, you can specify the `build.Preverify` capability in *custom-devices.xml*, so that the specified preverifier is used automatically for the affected devices. See Chapter 13 for more details.

Table A-27. *Attributes of the <preverifier> Element*

<preverifier> Attribute	Required?	Explanation
`name`	Yes, unless `class` is used	The name of the preverifier as registered in *custom-extensions.xml* or the J2ME Polish internal *extensions.xml* file. The `none` preverifier skips the complete preverification step.
`class`	No	The fully qualified name of the class that extends `de.enough.polish.preverify.Preverifier`.

<preverifier> Attribute	Required?	Explanation
classPath	No	The classpath from which the preverifier can be loaded.
target	No	Specifies the Ant target that you want to call when you use the antcall preverifier: <preverifier name="antcall" target="preverifytarget" />.
if	No	The Ant property that needs to be true or the preprocessing term that needs to result in true for this preverifier to be used.
unless	No	The Ant property that needs to be false or the preprocessing term that needs to result in false for this preverifier to be used.

Again, you can use nested <parameter> elements for configuring the <preverifier> element: <parameter name="message" value="hello ${polish.Identifier}" />.

Assembling the Resources: <resources>

Use the <resources> element in the <build> section to control the resource assembling as well as the localization of the application, as demonstrated in Listing A-7. Please refer to the "Resource Assembling" section of Chapter 7 for more details.

Table A-28 lists the attributes of the <resources> element.

Listing A-7. *Enabling the Localization and Including Specific Resources*

```
<resources
   dir="resources"
   excludes="*.txt"
>
   <fileset
      dir="resources/multimedia"
      includes="*.mp3"
      if="polish.audio.mp3"
   />
   <fileset
      dir="resources/multimedia"
      includes="*.mid"
      if="polish.audio.midi and not polish.audio.mp3"
   />
   <localization locales="de, en" unless="test" />
   <localization locales="en" if="test" />
</resources>
```

Table A-28. *Attributes of the <resources> Element*

<resources> Attribute	Required	Explanation
`dir`	No	The directory containing all resources. This defaults to the *resources* folder.
`defaultexcludes`	No	Either `yes/true` or `no/false`; defines whether typical files should not be copied in the application JAR bundle during packaging. The files *polish.css* and *Thumbs.db*, any backup files (**.bak* and *~), and the message files used in the localization are excluded by default.
`excludes`	No	Additional files that should not be included in the JAR files can be defined using the `excludes` attribute. Several files need to be separated by commas. Use a star to select several files at once (e.g., `excludes="*.txt, readme*"`).
`locales`	No	The locales that should be supported in a comma-separated list. Alternatively, the nested `<localization>` element can be used. The standard Java locale abbreviations are used (e.g., `de` for German, `en` for English, `fr_CA` for Canadian French, etc.).

Selecting Additional Files: <fileset>

Use the `<fileset>` element to include specific resources. This element behaves like any Ant `<fileset>`, but it offers the additional `if` and `unless` attributes, allowing for fine-grained control.

Table A-29 lists the attributes of the `<fileset>` element.

Table A-29. *Attributes of the <fileset> Element*

<fileset> Attribute	Required	Explanation
`dir`	Yes	The base directory of this file set. This directory needs to exist.
`includes`	Yes	Defines which files should be included (e.g., `includes="*.mid"`).
`if`	No	The Ant property that needs to be `true` or the preprocessing term that needs to result in `true` for this file set to be included.
`unless`	No	The Ant property that needs to be `false` or the preprocessing term that needs to result in `false` for this file set to be included.

Controlling the Localization: <localization>

Control the internationalization of your application with the `<localization>` element. The attributes of this element appear in Table A-30.

Table A-30. *Attributes of the <localization> Element*

<localization> Attribute	Required	Explanation
locales	Yes	The locales that should be supported in a comma-separated list. The standard Java locale abbreviations are used (e.g., de for German, en for English, fr_CA for Canadian French, etc.).
messages	No	The file that contains the translations. This defaults to *messages.txt*.
dynamic	No	Defines whether dynamic translations should be enabled. Dynamic translations can be changed during runtime by calling de.enough.polish.util.Locale.loadTranslations (String url). This requires additional resources and defaults; therefore the default is false.
default	No	The default localization. This makes sense only when dynamic translations are enabled.
if	No	The Ant property that needs to be true or the preprocessing term that needs to result in true for this localization to be used.
unless	No	The Ant property that needs to be false or the preprocessing term that needs to result in false for this localization to be used.

Renaming and Transforming Resources: <copier>

You can rename and transform resources by using the nested <copier> element inside of the <resources> element. The example in Listing A-8 renames files automatically and uses nested <parameter> elements for the configuration. Refer to Chapter 13 for more details about this option. Table A-31 lists the attributes of the <copier> element.

Listing A-8. *Renaming Resources on the Fly*

```
<resources
   dir="resources/default"
   defaultexcludes="yes"
   excludes="*.db"
>
   <copier name="renamer">
      <parameter name="searchPattern" value="\{.*\}" />
      <parameter name="replacement" value="" />
   </copier>
   <localization locales="en" />
</resources>
```

Table A-31. *Attributes of the <copier> Element*

<copier> Attribute	Required?	Explanation
name	Yes, unless class is used	The name of the copier as registered in *custom-extensions.xml* or the J2ME Polish internal *extensions.xml* file.
class	No	The fully qualified name of the class that extends de.enough.polish.resources.ResourceCopier.
classPath	No	The classpath from which the copier can be loaded.
target	No	Specifies the Ant target that you want to call when you use the antcall copier: <copier name="antcall" target="copytarget" />.
if	No	The Ant property that needs to be true or the preprocessing term that needs to result in true for this copier to be used.
unless	No	The Ant property that needs to be false or the preprocessing term that needs to result in false for this copier to be used.

Packaging the Application: <packager>

When your application has been compiled, obfuscated, and preverified, and when all resources have been selected, you are ready to create the JAR package. Usually J2ME Polish uses the default Java ZIP mechanism for doing this, but you can choose different mechanisms with the <packager> element nested inside the <build> section; please refer to the "Packaging" section of Chapter 7 and to Chapter 13 for the details.

Table A-32 lists the attributes of the <packager> element.

Table A-32. *Attributes of the <packager> Element*

<packager> Attribute	Required?	Explanation
name	Yes, unless class or executable is used	The name of the packager as registered in *custom-extensions.xml* or the J2ME Polish internal *extensions.xml* file (e.g., 7zip, kzip or antcall).
executable	No	The external application that should be invoked to create the JAR file (e.g., jar).
arguments	No	The arguments for the packager. Separate arguments with double semicolons (;;). Any Ant properties as well as J2ME Polish variables can be used. Often needed variables are as follows: ${polish.jarPath}: The full path to the JAR file that should be created ${polish.packageDir}: The directory that contains the classes and the resources that should be packaged.
class	No	The fully qualified name of the class that extends de.enough.polish.jar.Packager.

<packager> Attribute	Required?	Explanation
`classPath`	No	The classpath from which the packager can be loaded.
`target`	No	Specifies the Ant target that you want to call when you use the `antcall` packager: `<packager name="antcall" target="jartarget" />`.
`if`	No	The Ant property that needs to be `true` or the preprocessing term that needs to result in `true`, when this packager should be used.
`unless`	No	The Ant property that needs to be `false` or the preprocessing term that needs to result in `false`, when this packager should be used.

You can use nested `<parameter>` elements for configuring the packager. Table A-33 lists the supported parameters of the 7-Zip packager, and Table A-34 lists the possible parameter for the KZIP packager.

Table A-33. *Parameters for Configuring the 7-Zip Packager*

Parameter	Required?	Explanation
`compression`	No	The level of compression, either `maximum`, `normal`, or `none`
`passes`	No	Sets the number of compression runs, a number between `1` and `4`
`fastbytes`	No	Specifies the size of internal compression chunks, a number between `3` and `255`

Table A-34. *Parameter for Configuring the KZIP Packager*

Parameter	Required?	Explanation
`blocksplit`	No	The size of the compressed blocks, a number between `0` and `2048`. Test the values `128`, `256`, `512`, `1024`, and `2048` for best compression.

Specifying and Sorting JAD and Manifest attributes: <jad>, <jadFilter>, and <manifestFilter>

Normal JAD attributes are defined in the `<info>` section, but you can specify additional settings with the `<jad>` element in the `<build>` section. Please refer to the "JAD and Manifest Attributes" section of this appendix for examples of specific attributes and to the "Managing JAD and Manifest Attributes" section of Chapter 7 for more information about handling and sorting such attributes.

Table A-35 lists the attributes of the `<jad>` element.

Table A-35. *Attributes of the <jad> Element*

<jad> Attribute	Required?	Explanation
name	Yes, unless file is used	The name of the attribute (e.g., Nokia-MIDlet-Category).
value	Yes, unless file is used	The value of the attribute.
file	No	The file that contains several attribute definitions. Separate names and values in the file with colons (:). Empty lines and lines starting with a hash mark (#) are ignored. You can also use J2ME Polish variables in the file name (e.g., file="config/${ polish.Vendor } .jad").
target	No	Either jad, manifest, or jad,manifest. A user-defined attribute is added to both, the MANIFEST as well as the JAD, by default. The specification says user-defined attributes should only be added to the JAD file, but there are some devices out there that expect these attributes in the MANIFEST as well.
if	No	The Ant property that needs to be true or the preprocessing term that needs to result in true for this attribute to be included.
unless	No	The Ant property that needs to be false or the preprocessing term that needs to result in false for this attribute to be included.

You can sort JAD attributes by using the nested <jadFilter> element in the <jad> element as demonstrated in Listing A-9. You can use the if and unless attributes for using different filters depending on the current target device.

Listing A-9. *Sorting JAD Attributes with <jadFilter>*

```
<jad>
   <attribute
      name="Nokia-MIDlet-Category"
      value="Game"
      if="polish.group.Series40"
   />
   <jadFilter if="polish.Vendor == Samsung" >
      MIDlet-Name, MIDlet-Version,
      MIDlet-Vendor, MIDlet-Jar-URL, MIDlet-Jar-Size,
      MIDlet-Description?, MIDlet-Icon?, MIDlet-Info-URL?,
      MIDlet-Data-Size?, MIDlet-*, *
   </jadFilter>
</jad>
```

You can also sort Manifest attributes by using a <manifestFilter> in either the <build> section or in the <jad> element. Again, you can use the if and unless attributes to use different filters depending on the current target device. When using a <manifestFilter>, make sure that the Manifest-Version attribute is always included as the first attribute; otherwise, your Manifest won't be valid.

Finishing the Build: <finalizer> and <sign>

After J2ME Polish has created the JAR and the JAD file, it can invoke the optional `<finalizer>` element nested in the `<build>` section. One example of a finalizer is the `jar2cod` finalizer, which automatically converts JAR to COD files for Blackberry devices. You can define the capability `build.Finalizer` to invoke finalizers automatically, without using a specific `<finalizer>` element in your *build.xml* script. Chapter 13 describes further details.

Table A-36 lists the attributes of the `<finalizer>` element.

Table A-36. *Attributes of the <finalizer> Element*

<finalizer> Attribute	Required?	Explanation
`name`	Yes, unless `class` is used	The name of the finalizer as registered in *custom-extensions.xml* or the J2ME Polish internal *extensions.xml* file
`class`	No	The fully qualified name of the class that extends `de.enough.polish.finalize.Finalizer`
`classPath`	No	The classpath from which the finalizer can be loaded
`target`	No	Specifies the Ant target that you want to call when you use the `antcall` finalizer: `<finalizer name="antcall" target="finalizetarget" />`
`if`	No	The Ant property that needs to be `true` or the preprocessing term that needs to result in `true` for this finalizer to be used
`unless`	No	The Ant property that needs to be `false` or the preprocessing term that needs to result in `false` for this finalizer to be used

A specialized finalizer element is `<sign>`, which can also be nested inside of the `<build>` section. Use the `<sign>` element to automate the signing of your MIDP 2.0 applications (see Table A-37 for its attributes). Please see the "Signing Applications" section of Chapter 7 for details.

Table A-37. *Attributes of the <sign> Element*

<sign> Attribute	Required?	Explanation
`key`	Yes	The name of the key that should be used for signing.
`keystore`	Yes	The path to the keystore that contains the signing key.
`password`	Yes	The password for signing. You can use an Ant property like `${pw}` and specify the property on the command line, so that the password is not stored in the *build.xml* file: `ant -Dpw=secret`.
`unless`	No	The Ant property that needs to be `false` or the preprocessing term that needs to result in `false` for the signing to be used.

Emulator Section

The `<emulator>` element is responsible for launching any emulators after your application has been built. Table A-38 lists the attributes of the `<emulator>` element.

Table A-38. *Attributes of the <emulator> Element*

<emulator> Attribute	Required?	Explanation
`wait`	No	Either `yes/true` or `no/false`; defines whether the J2ME Polish task should wait until the emulator is finished. This is needed when any output should be shown on the Ant output; therefore, it defaults to `yes`.
`trace`	No	Defines if any virtual machine activities should be shown on the output. Possible values are `class` for showing the loading of classes, `gc` for garbage collection activities, and `all` for a very extensive output. Several comma-separated values can be provided (e.g., `class,gc`).
`securityDomain`	No	The MIDP 2.0 security domain of the application: either `trusted`, `untrusted`, `minimum`, or `maximum`. In `trusted` and `maximum` mode, all security-sensitive activities are allowed. In `untrusted` mode, the user will be questioned before each security-sensitive activity. In `minimum` mode, no security-sensitive activity will be allowed.
`enableProfiler`	No	Either `yes/true` or `no/false`. When this attribute is activated, the performance will be profiled during the execution of the application. The results will be shown when the emulator itself is closed.
`enableMemoryMonitor`	No	Either `yes/true` or `no/false`. When this attribute is activated, the memory usage of the application will be shown.
`enableNetworkMonitor`	No	Either `yes/true` or `no/false`. When any network activities are done, a monitor will show details of the sent and received data.
`preferences`	No	The file that contains the emulator preferences. When such a file is used, the profiler and monitor settings are ignored. Please consult the WTK documentation for detailed information about the preferences file.
`showDecompiledStackTrace`	No	Either `yes/true` or `no/false`; determines whether a decompiled stack trace should be shown, even when the source code position of an exception could be located.
`if`	No	The Ant property or preprocessing term that needs to be `true` when the `<emulator>` element should be executed.
`unless`	No	The Ant property or preprocessing term that needs to be `false` when the `<emulator>` element should be executed.

You can forward any parameters to the emulator by using nested `<parameter>` elements with name and value attributes (see Table A-39).

Table A-39. *Configuring the Emulator with Nested <parameter> Elements*

<parameter> Attribute	**Required?**	**Explanation**
`name`	Yes	The name of the parameter.
`value`	Yes	The value of the parameter. The value can use any J2ME Polish or user-defined variable. The following variables are especially useful: `${polish.jadName}`: The name of the JAD file `${polish.jadPath}`: The absolute path of the JAD file `${polish.jarName}`: The name of the JAR file `${polish.jarPath}`: The absolute path of the JAR file `${polish.classes.midlet-1}`: The main `MIDlet` class `${polish.classes.midlet-2}`: The second `MIDlet` class, if any `${polish.classes.midlet-n}`: The nth `MIDlet` class, if any When only a command line switch should be defined, just define an empty value (e.g., `<parameter name="-Xsomething" value="" />`).
`if`	No	The Ant property that needs to be `true` or the preprocessing term that needs to result in `true` when this parameter should be used.
`unless`	No	The Ant property that needs to be `false` or the preprocessing term that needs to result in `false` when this parameter should be used.

Standard Preprocessing Variables and Symbols

You can evaluate, compare, and use all values of the J2ME Polish device database (see Chapter 6) in your code by using preprocessing (see Chapter 8). You can also define your project-specific variables and symbols in the *build.xml* script (see Chapter 8). With such variables, you can also configure many aspects of the J2ME Polish GUI (see Chapter 12) as well as the game engine (see Chapter 11).

Device-Specific Symbols

Use preprocessing symbols in the `//#if` preprocessing directives or in the `if` and `unless` attributes of many conditional elements of the `<j2mepolish>` task in your *build.xml* file. Don't forget to check out all available preprocessing symbols of your target device at *http://www.j2mepolish.org/devices-overview.html.* Table A-40 lists the standard preprocessing symbols.

Table A-40. *Standard Device-Specific Preprocessing Symbols*

Symbol	Explanation
`polish.api.[name]`	The target device supports the API `[name]`
`polish.api.3d`	The target device supports the Mobile 3D Graphics API
`polish.api.btapi`	The target device supports the Bluetooth API
`polish.api.mmapi`	The target device supports the Multimedia API
`polish.api.nokia-ui`	The target device supports the Nokia UI API
`polish.api.pdaapi`	The target device supports the PDA API (FileConnection API and PIM API)
`polish.api.wmapi`	The target device supports the Wireless Messaging API
`polish.audio.[name]`	The target device supports the `[name]` audio format
`polish.audio.midi`	The target device supports the Midi audio format
`polish.audio.amr`	The target device supports the AMR audio format
`polish.cldc1.0`	The target device supports the CLDC 1.0 configuration
`polish.cldc1.1`	The target device supports the CLDC 1.1 configuration
`polish.group.[name]`	The target device belongs to the group `[name]`
`polish.group.Series40`	The target device belongs to the Series 40 group
`polish.group.Series60`	The target device belongs to the Series 60 group
`polish.group.Series60E2FP3`	The target device belongs to the Series 60, second edition, feature pack 3 group
`polish.hasCamera`	The target device contains a camera
`polish.hasCommandKeyEvents`	The target device triggers `keyPressed()` events when the user presses a soft key
`polish.hasPointerEvents`	The target device supports a stylus
`polish.image.[name]`	The target device supports the `[name]` image format
`polish.image.jpeg`	The target device supports the JPEG image format
`polish.jtwi`	The target device supports the JTWI specification
`polish.midp1`	The target device supports the MIDP 1.0 profile
`polish.midp2`	The target device supports the MIDP 2.0 profile
`polish.midp3`	The target device supports the MIDP 3.0 profile
`polish.supportSpriteTransformation`	The MIDP 1.0 target device supports sprite transformations in the J2ME Polish game engine
`polish.video.[name]`	The target device supports the `[name]` video format
`polish.video.mp4`	The target device supports the MP4 video format

Device-Specific Variables

Compare the preprocessing variable in the `//#if` preprocessing directives or in the `if` and `unless` attributes of many conditional elements of the `<j2mepolish>` task in your *build.xml* file. You can also include their values in your code with the `//#=` directive. Don't forget to check out all available preprocessing symbols of your target device at *http://www.j2mepolish.org/devices-overview.html.* You can test whether a variable is defined by checking the `[variable-name]:defined` preprocessing symbol. Table A-41 lists the standard preprocessing variables.

Table A-41. *Standard Device-Specific Preprocessing Variables*

Variable	Example Value	Explanation
`polish.BitsPerPixel`	`16`	The number of bits per pixel: `12` are 4,096 colors, `16` are 65K colors, etc.
`polish.CanvasHeight`	`144`	The height of a `Canvas` in pixels.
`polish.CanvasSize`	`176x144`	The size of a `Canvas` in `[width]x[height]`.
`polish.CanvasWidth`	`176`	The width of a `Canvas` in pixels.
`polish.classes.full-screen`	`com.nokia.mid.ui.FullCanvas`	The fully qualified name of the vendor-specific full-screen class.
`polish.Font.large`	`21`	The height of the large font.
`polish.Font.medium`	`16`	The height of the medium font.
`polish.Font.small`	`15`	The height of the small font.
`polish.FullCanvasHeight`	`208`	The height in pixels of a `Canvas` in full-screen mode.
`polish.FullCanvasSize`	`176x208`	The size in `[width]x[height]`of a `Canvas` in full-screen mode.
`polish.FullCanvasWidth`	`176`	The width in pixels of a `Canvas` in full-screen mode.
`polish.HeapSize`	`9MB`	The maximum available heap size; can be `dynamic`. Use the `bytes()` property function to compare this value.
`polish.Identifier`	`Nokia/6630`	The identifier of the target device.
`polish.ImageFormat`	`png, jpeg`	The supported image formats.
`polish.JavaConfiguration`	`CLDC/1.1`	The configuration supported by the target device.
`polish.JavaProtocol`	`udp,socket, server-socket`	The supported protocols for the generic connection framework.
`polish.JavaPackage`	`mmapi,btapi`	Any additionally supported APIs.
`polish.JavaPlatform`	`MIDP/2.0`	The profile supported by the target device.
`polish.Key.ChangeInputModeKey`	`35`	The keycode for the key that changes the input mode in `TextFields`.
`polish.Key.ChangeNumericalAlphaInputModeKey`	`35`	The keycode for the key that switches between the alphabetical and the numerical input. This is only defined when it's different from the `ChangeInputModeKey`.

Continued

Table A-41. *Continued*

Variable	Example Value	Explanation
`polish.Key.ClearKey`	`-8`	The keycode for the clear key.
`polish.Key.LeftSoftKey`	`-6`	The keycode for the left soft key.
`polish.Key.RightSoftKey`	`-7`	The keycode for the right soft key.
`polish.MaxJarSize`	`dynamic`	The maximum allowed size of JAR files. This can be `dynamic`, in which case any size is allowed as long as it fits on the device.
`polish.MaxRecordStoreSize`	`512kb`	The maximum allowed size for record stores.
`polish.Name`	`6630`	The name of the target device.
`polish.OS`	`Symbian OS 8.0`	The name of the used operating system.
`polish.ScreenHeight`	`208`	The height of the screen in pixels.
`polish.ScreenSize`	`176x208`	The size of the screen in `[width]x[height]`.
`polish.ScreenWidth`	`176`	The width of the screen in pixels.
`polish.SoundFormat`	`midi,amr`	The supported audio formats.
`polish.StorageSize`	`10 MB`	The available size for all application.
`polish.Vendor`	`Nokia`	The name of the target device's vendor.
`polish.VideoFormat`	`mp4,3gpp`	The supported video formats.

Configuration Variables

J2ME Polish allows you to tweak the game engine as well as the GUI by defining preprocessing variables in the `<variables>` element or in the *messages.txt* localization files. Table A-42 shows the configuration variables.

Table A-42. *J2ME Polish Configuration Variables*

Variable	Default Value	Explanation
`polish.animationInterval`	`100`	The interval in milliseconds for animating any GUI elements.
`polish.ChoiceGroup.suppressMarkCommands`	`false`	A multiple `List` or `ChoiceGroup` adds the commands "Mark" and "Unmark" by default to the menu. Suppress this by setting the variable to `true`.

Variable	Default Value	Explanation
polish.ChoiceGroup.suppressSelectCommand	false	An implicit or pop-up ChoiceGroup or List usually have a "Select" command that also can be deactivated.
polish.classes.ApplicationInitializer		The class that implements the de.enough.polish.ui.splash.ApplicationInitializer interface. When this variable is set, the interface can be easily removed by the obfuscator, thus saving space.
polish.classes.ImageLoader		Usually J2ME Polish loads all images from the JAR file using the Image.createImage(String url) method. This works fine for most situations, but sometimes images should be retrieved from the RMS or the Internet. In such cases, you can define the polish.classes.ImageLoader variable. The given class (or static field of a class) needs to implement the javax.microedition.lcdui.Image loadImage(String url) throws IOException method, which is responsible for retrieving the image.
polish.command.ok	OK	The label for the OK command that is used when the menu full-screen mode is used.
polish.command.cancel	Cancel	The label for the Cancel command.
polish.command.select	Select	The label for the Select command that is used by an implicit or exclusive List or ChoiceGroup.
polish.command.mark	Mark	The label for the Mark command of a multiple List or ChoiceGroup.
polish.command.unmark	Unmark	The label for the Unmark command item of a multiple List or ChoiceGroup.
polish.command.options	Options	The label for the command that opens the list of available commands.

Continued

Table A-42. *Continued*

Variable	Default Value	Explanation
polish.command.delete	Delete	The label for the Delete command that is used by TextFields.
polish.command.clear	Clear	The label for the Clear command that is used by TextFields.
polish.Container.allowCycling	true	Defines whether the user can cycle to the start of a list when she presses Canvas.DOWN at the very last element.
polish.DateFormat	ymd	The format in which dates should be displayed: any combination of ymd, where y stands for year, m for month, and d for day.
polish.DateFormatSeparator	.	The separator used for dates.
polish.DateFormatEmptyText	YYYY.MM.DD	The text for showing a null date.
polish.Full-screen	false	Selectively activates the full-screen mode. Possible values are true, false, and menu.
polish.GameCanvas.useFull-screen		You can set the full-screen mode of your GameCanvas on MIDP 1.0 devices to either true, false or menu.
polish.jarName		You can define the polish.jarName variable for using a different name for the produced JAR file than defined in the <info> section. This makes sense when a specific target device limits the length of the file name, for example.
polish.MenuBar.useExtendedMenuBar	false	When this variable is set to true, the extended menu bar is activated.
polish.skipArgumentCheck	true	Defines if method arguments should not be checked by the J2ME Polish GUI classes. By default, any incoming values are checked for validity. You can save some cycles by skipping those tests in your final application.

Variable	Default Value	Explanation
polish.ScreenChangeAnimation.backward		The name of the screen change animation that should be shown when the user returns from a screen. This is deemed to be the case when the user triggers a command of the type Command.BACK. Alternatively, you can specify valid Java code, for example to include your own animation: `<variable name="polish.ScreenChangeAnimation.backward" value="new com.apress.ui.MyScreenChangeAnimation" />`.
polish.ScreenChangeAnimation.forward		The name of the screen change animation that should be shown when the user proceeds to a new screen; compare this with backward animation.
polish.TextField.useDirectInput	false	Enables the direct input mode of all TextFields and TextBoxes in your application.
polish.TextField.suppressClearCommand	false	Set this variable to true to disable only the Clear command of TextFields.
polish.TextField.suppressDeleteCommand	false	Set this variable to true to disable only the Clear command of TextFields.
polish.TextField.suppressCommands	false	You can deactivate the Delete as well as the Clear commands by setting this variable to true.
polish.TextField.showInputInfo	true	When this variable is set to false, the indicator of the current input mode is not drawn in direct input mode TextFields
polish.TextField.InputTimeout	1000	The timeout in milliseconds after which a chosen character is inserted into the text automatically.
polish.TextField.charactersKey1	.,!?:/@_-+1	The characters available when the 1 key is pressed.

Continued

Table A-42. *Continued*

Variable	Default Value	Explanation
polish.TextField.charactersKey2	abc2	The characters available when the 2 key is pressed. It might be useful to add locale-specific umlauts here.
polish.TextField.charactersKey3	def3	The characters available when the 3 key is pressed.
polish.TextField.charactersKey3	ghi4	The characters available when the 4 key is pressed.
polish.TextField.charactersKey5	jkl5	The characters available when the 5 key is pressed.
polish.TextField.charactersKey6	mno6	The characters available when the 6 key is pressed.
polish.TextField.charactersKey7	pqrs7	The characters available when the 7 key is pressed.
polish.TextField.charactersKey8	tuv8	The characters available when the 8 key is pressed.
polish.TextField.charactersKey9	wxyz9	The characters available when the 9 key is pressed.
polish.TextField.charactersKey0	" 0"	The characters available when the 0 key is pressed. On Motorola devices, this key is used for switching the input mode.
polish.TextField.charactersKeyStar	.,!?:/@_-+	The characters available when the star key (*) is pressed. On Motorola devices, this key is used for entering spaces.
polish.TextField.charactersKeyPound		The characters available when the # key is pressed. On Sony Ericsson devices, this key is used for entering spaces.
polish.TiledLayer.useBackBuffer	false	Enables the backbuffer optimization for the MIDP 1.0 `TiledLayer` implementation.
polish.TiledLayer.TransparentTileColor	0x000000	Sets the color for transparent tiles when the backbuffer optimization is enabled.
polish.TiledLayer.splitImage	false	Splits the tiled images into single tiles.
polish.TiledLayer.GridType	byte	The primitive used for storing the grid of a `TiledLayer`; can be `byte`, `short`, or `int`.

Variable	Default Value	Explanation
polish.title.input	Input	The title of the native TextBox that is normally used for the actual input of text. This title is used only when the corresponding TextField item has no label. When the TextField has a label, that label is used as a title instead.
polish.usePolishGameApi	false	Forces the usage of the J2ME Polish game engine even for MIDP 2.0-based devices.
polish.usePolishGui	true	Can be used for activating the Polish GUI only for selected devices.
polish.usePolishTitle	false	Uses a "J2ME Polished" title on MIDP 2.0-based devices even when the full-screen mode is not active.

Symbols and Variables for Reading the Settings

You can also evaluate the setup and configuration of J2ME Polish in your source code. This is useful for differentiating between devices for which you don't use the J2ME Polish GUI and vice versa.

Table A-43 lists the preprocessing symbols that are set by J2ME Polish, and Table A-44 lists the variables.

Table A-43. *J2ME Polish Symbols for Reading the Current Setting*

Variable	Explanation
polish.debugEnabled	Is defined when the logging framework is active
polish.debug.debug	Is defined when the debug logging level is active for the current class
polish.debug.error	Is defined when the error logging level is active for the current class
polish.debug.fatal	Is defined when the fatal logging level is active for the current class
polish.debug.info	Is defined when the info logging level is active for the current class
polish.debug.warn	Is defined when the warn logging level is active for the current class
polish.usePolishGui	Is defined when the J2ME Polish GUI is used for the current target device

Table A-44. *J2ME Polish Variables for Reading the Current Setting*

Variable	Example Value	Explanation
`polish.classes.midlet-1`	`com.apress.game.MainMidlet`	For each defined `MIDlet` class, the preprocessing variable `polish.classes.midlet-<number>` is defined.
`polish.sourceDir`	`/home/user/ws/project/src`	Points to the directory that contains the root of the currently processed source code.

Preprocessing Directives

Preprocessing changes the source code before it is compiled. Refer to Chapter 8 for a full discussion. You can also include your own preprocessing directives; please see Chapter 13 for details on this task. Table A-45 lists all available directives,

Table A-45. *Preprocessing Directives*

Directive	Example	Explanation
`#`	`//# return true;`	Hides a statement inside of an `#if` or `#ifdef` block.
`#=`	`//#= int width = ${polish.FullCanvasWidth};`	Includes any Ant properties or preprocessing variables in the following code.
`#abort`	`//#abort Invalid Setup!`	Aborts the complete build process. Use this when you encounter invalid setups.
`#condition`	`//#condition polish.midp2`	Excludes a source file from the compilation when the condition is not fulfilled.
`#debug`	`//#debug error`	Forwards the following `System.out.println()` output to the logging framework.
`#define`	`//#define tmp.MySymbol`	Defines a temporary preprocessing symbol or variable.
`#elif`	`//#elif polish.midp2 && polish.api.3d`	Branches within an `#if` or `#ifdef` directive by checking a preprocessing term.
`#elifdef`	`//#elifdef polish.midp2`	Branches within an `#if` or `#ifdef` directive by checking for a single symbol.
`#elifndef`	`//#elifndef polish.midp2`	Branches within an `#if` or `#ifdef` directive by checking for a single symbol that should not be defined.
`#else`	`//#else`	Branches within an `#if` or `#ifdef` directive.

Directive	Example	Explanation
#endif	//#endif	Closes an #if or #ifdef directive.
#foreach	//#foreach format in polish.SoundFormat	Evaluates several values of one preprocessing variable individually.
#if	//#if polish.midp2 && polish.api.3d	Tests a preprocessing term or a single symbol.
#ifdef	//#ifdef polish.midp2	Checks for a single symbol.
#ifndef	//#ifndef polish.midp2	Checks for a single symbol that should not be defined.
#include	//#include ${polish.source}/code.txt	Includes the defined file. Use the ${polish.sourceDir} property for the root of the source tree.
#message	//#message it's nice!	Prints a message during the build process.
#next	//#next format	Ends a #foreach block.
#style	//#style MainMenu	Applies a CSS style to the following item or screen.
#todo	//#todo implement this case!	Prints a message during the build process that includes the source file and line number.
#undefine	//#undefine tmp.MySymbol	Undefines a temporary preprocessing symbol or variable. This directive is usually not needed since these are undefined automatically when a new source file is processed.

Property Functions

J2ME Polish provides a set of property functions for transforming variable values in preprocessing statements and within any attributes of the <j2mepolish> task. See Chapter 8 for a full discussion of property functions. Table A-46 lists the available property functions.

Table A-46. *Functions for Transforming Variable Values*

Function	Purpose
bytes	Calculates the number of bytes of the given memory value (e.g., 1 kb becomes 1024). The memory value dynamic returns -1.
classname	Retrieves the fully qualified name for the given class. When you activate the useDefaultPackage option of the <obfuscator> element, all source files will be moved into the empty default package. In that case, ${ classname(com.apress.ImageLoader) } returns ImageLoader. When the useDefaultPackage option is not active or the obfuscator is not enabled, the function returns com.apress.ImageLoader.

Continued

Table A-46. *Continued*

Function	Purpose
gigabytes	Calculates the (double) number of gigabytes of the given memory value.
kilobytes	Calculates the (double) number of kilobytes of the given memory value. The value can contain a point and decimal places (e.g., 512 bytes becomes 0.5, 1024 bytes becomes 1, etc.).
lowercase	Translates the given value into lowercase (e.g., AbC becomes abc).
megabytes	Calculates the (double) number of megabytes of the given memory value.
nospace	Replaces any spaces with underscores (e.g., ${ nospace(polish.name) } becomes One_Touch_756 when processing Alcatel's One Touch 756 phone).
number	Retrieves the number of separate values within the variable.
uppercase	Translates the given value into uppercase (e.g., aBc becomes ABC).

The J2ME Polish GUI

You can deploy different background and borders for your Items and Screens by using the background-type and border-type CSS attributes. Depending on the actual type, you can use additional attributes for adjusting the background and border.

Backgrounds

You can place backgrounds for Items as well Screens. The J2ME Polish GUI provides several possible backgrounds, ranging from simple, mono-colored backgrounds to animated, pulsating backgrounds. This section describes each available background in detail.

simple Background

The simple background just fills the background with one color. When no background type is specified, the simple background is used by default, unless the background-image attribute is set. In that case, the image background will be used instead by default. Table A-47 lists the attributes of the simple background, Listing A-10 demonstrates the use of the background, and Figure A-1 displays an example of the background.

Table A-47. *Attributes of the simple Background*

Attribute	Required	Explanation
type	No	The type can be simple
color	Yes	The color of the background; either the name of the color or a direct definition. The simple background supports colors with alpha values as well.

Listing A-10. *Using a Translucent Background for the Currently Focused Item*

```
focused {
   padding: 9;
   font-color: highlightedFontColor;
   background-color: argb( 128, 238, 241, 229 );
   border {
      width: 2;
      color: fontColor;
   }
   layout: expand | center;
}
```

Figure A-1. *Using a translucent simple background for the currently focused item*

round-rect Background

The `round-rect` background paints a rectangular background with round edges. Table A-48 lists the attributes of the `round-rect` background, Listing A-11 demonstrates the use of the background, and Figure A-2 displays an example of the background.

Table A-48. *Attributes of the round-rect Background*

Attribute	Required	Explanation
`type`	Yes	The type has to be `round-rect` or `roundrect`.
`color`	No	The color of the background; either the name of the color or a direct definition. The default color is `white`.
`arc`	No	The diameter of the arc at the four corners. The default is `10` pixels when none is specified.
`arc-width`	No	The horizontal diameter of the arc at the four corners. The default is the `arc` value when none is specified.
`arc-height`	No	The vertical diameter of the arc at the four corners. The default is the `arc` value when none is specified.

Listing A-11. *Using a round-rect Background for the Currently Focused Item*

```
focused {
   padding: 9;
   font-color: highlightedFontColor;
   background {
      type: round-rect;
      color: white;
      arc: 18;
   }
   layout: expand | center;
}
```

Figure A-2. *Using a round-rect background for the currently focused item*

image Background

The `image` background uses an image for painting the background. This background type is used by default when no type is set and the `background-image` attribute is set. Table A-49 lists the attributes of the `image` background, Listing A-12 demonstrates the use of the background, and Figure A-3 displays an example of the background.

Table A-49. *Attributes of the image Background*

Attribute	Required	Explanation
`type`	No	When used, needs to be `image`.
`color`	No	The color of the background; either the name of the color, a direct definition, or `transparent`. The default color is `white`. This color is visible only when the image is not smaller than the actual background.
`image`	Yes	The URL of the image (e.g., `url( background.png )`).

Attribute	Required	Explanation
anchor	No	The anchor of the image. When this is not specified, the image will be centered (horizontal-center | vertical-center). You can use a combination of top, vertical-center (=vcenter), bottom and left, horizontal-center (= hcenter = center), and right: anchor: top | left;.
repeat	No	Either repeat, no-repeat, repeat-x, or repeat-y. This attribute determines whether the background should be repeated, repeated horizontally, or repeated vertically. The default is no-repeat.

Listing A-12. *Using an image Background for the Currently Focused Item*

```
focused {
   padding: 9;
   font-color: highlightedFontColor;
   background {
      image: url( gradient.png );
      color: transparent;
      anchor: top | center;
   }
   layout: expand | center;
}
```

Figure A-3. *Using a gradient image as the background for the currently focused item*

circle Background

The circle background paints a circular or elliptical background. Table A-50 lists the attributes of the circle background, Listing A-13 demonstrates the use of the background, and Figure A-4 displays an example of the background.

Table A-50. *Attributes of the circle Background*

Attribute	Required	Explanation
`type`	No	The type needs to be `circle`.
`color`	No	The color of the background; either the name of the color or a direct definition. The default color is `white`.
`diameter`	No	By using the `diameter` attribute, you can ensure that always a circle and never an ellipse is painted. The diameter then defines the diameter of the circle that is used, regardless of the actual dimensions of the background.

Listing A-13. *Using the circle Background for the Currently Focused Item*

```
focused {
   padding: 9;
   font-color: highlightedFontColor;
   background {
      type: circle;
      diameter: 70;
      color: white;
   }
   layout: expand | center;
}
```

Figure A-4. *Using a circle background for the currently focused item*

pulsating Background

The `pulsating` background animates the color of the background. The color changes from a start color to an end color. Table A-51 lists the attributes of the `pulsating` background, Listing A-14 demonstrates the use of the background, and Figure A-5 displays an example of the background.

Table A-51. *Attributes of the pulsating Background*

Attribute	Required	Explanation
type	No	The type needs to be pulsating.
start-color	Yes	The color of the background at the beginning of the animation sequence.
end-color	Yes	The color of the background at the end of the animation sequence.
steps	Yes	Defines how many color shades between the start color and the end color should be used.
repeat	No	Either yes/true or no/false; determines whether the animation should be repeated. The default is yes.
back-and-forth	No	Either yes/true or no/false; determines whether the animation sequence should be running backward to the start color again, after it reaches the end color. When no is selected, the animation will jump from the end color directly to the start color (when repeat is enabled). The default is yes.

Listing A-14. *Using the pulsating Background for the Currently Focused Item*

```
focused {
   padding: 9;
   font-color: highlightedFontColor;
   background {
      type: pulsating;
      start-color: highlightedBackgroundColor;
      end-color: white;
      back-and-forth: no;
      repeat: no;
   }
   layout: expand | center;
}
```

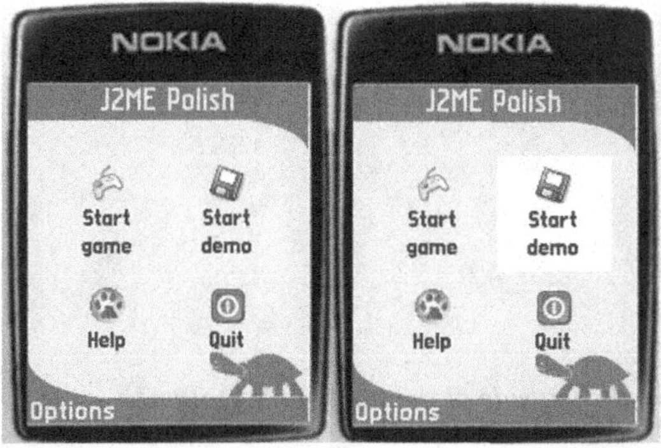

Figure A-5. *The pulsating background in action: on the left side shortly after the start of the sequence and on the right side at the end*

pulsating-circle Background

The `pulsating-circle` background paints a circular background whose size constantly increases and decreases. Table A-52 lists the attributes of the `pulsating-circle` background, Listing A-15 demonstrates the use of the background, and Figure A-6 displays an example of the background.

Table A-52. *Attributes of the pulsating-circle Background*

Attribute	Required	Explanation
`type`	No	The type needs to be `pulsating-circle`.
`color`	No	The color of the background; either the name of the color or a direct definition. The default is `white`.
`min-diameter`	Yes	The minimum diameter of the circle.
`max-diameter`	Yes	The maximum diameter of the circle.

Listing A-15. *Using the pulsating circle Background for the Currently Focused Item*

```
focused {
   padding: 9;
   font-color: highlightedFontColor;
   background {
      type: pulsating-circle;
      color: white;
      min-diameter: 20;
      max-diameter: 75;
   }
   layout: expand | center;
}
```

Figure A-6. *The pulsating-circle background in action: on the left side at the start of the sequence and on the right side at the end*

pulsating-circles Background

The `pulsating-circles` background paints an animated background of ever-growing circles that have different colors. Table A-53 lists the attributes of the `pulsating-circles` background, Listing A-16 demonstrates the use of the background, and Figure A-7 displays an example of the background.

Table A-53. *Attributes of the pulsating-circles Background*

Attribute	Required	Explanation
`type`	No	The type needs to be `pulsating-circles`.
`first-color`	Yes	The first circle color; either the name of the color or a direct definition.
`second-color`	Yes	The second circle color; either the name of the color or a direct definition.
`min-diameter`	Yes	The minimum diameter of the circle.
`max-diameter`	Yes	The maximum diameter of the circle.
`circles-number`	Yes	The number of circles that should be painted.
`step`	No	The number of pixels each circle should grow in each animation phase. Float values like `1.5` are also allowed, even when you target a CLDC 1.0 device. This defaults to `1` pixel.

Listing A-16. *Using the pulsating-circles Background for the Currently Focused Item*

```
focused {
   padding: 9;
   font-color: highlightedFontColor;
   background {
      type: pulsating-circles;
      first-color: white;
      second-color: highlightedBackgroundColor;
      circles-number: 7;
      min-diameter: 10;
      max-diameter: 100;
   }
   layout: expand | center;
}
```

Figure A-7. *The pulsating-circles background in action*

opening Background

The `opening` background paints an animated background that starts at a low height and then increases its height whenever it changes position. Its primary use is for the `focused` style. Table A-54 lists the attributes of the `opening` background, Listing A-17 demonstrates the use of the background, and Figure A-8 displays an example of the background.

Table A-54. *Attributes of the opening Background*

Attribute	Required	Explanation
`type`	No	The type needs to be `opening`.
`color`	Yes	The background color; either the name of the color or a direct definition.
`start-height`	No	The height of the background immediately after it has changed position. This defaults to `1` pixel.
`steps`	No	The number of pixels by which the height should be increased in each animation step. This defaults to `4` pixels. When the height is the same as the normal background, the animation stops.

Listing A-17. *Using the opening Background for the Currently Focused Item*

```
focused {
   padding: 9;
   font-color: highlightedFontColor;
   background {
      type: opening;
      color: white;
      start-height: 6;
      steps: 2;
   }
   layout: expand | center;
}
```

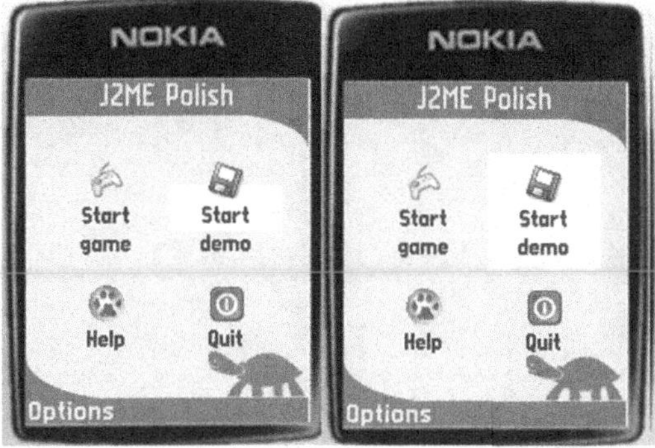

Figure A-8. *The opening background in action: on the left shortly after switching the focused item and on the right side after remaining a while on the focused item*

opening-round-rect Background

The `opening-round-rect` background paints an animated background whose height starts small and then increases whenever it changes position. Its primary use is for the focused-style. Table A-55 lists the attributes of the `opening-round-rect` background, Listing A-18 demonstrates the use of the background, and Figure A-9 displays an example of the background.

Table A-55. *Attributes of the opening-round-rect Background*

Attribute	Required	Explanation
`type`	No	The type needs to be `opening-round-rect`.
`color`	Yes	The background color; either the name of the color or a direct definition.
`start-height`	No	The height of the background immediately after it has changed its position. This defaults to `1` pixel.
`steps`	No	The number of pixels by which the height should be increased in each animation step. This defaults to `4` pixels. When the height is the same as the normal background height, the animation is stopped.
`border-width`	No	The width of the border. The default is `0` (no border).
`border-color`	No	The color of the border. The default is black.
`arc`	No	The diameter of the arc at the four corners. The default is `10` pixels when none is specified.
`arc-width`	No	The horizontal diameter of the arc at the four corners. The default is the `arc` value when none is specified.
`arc-height`	No	The vertical diameter of the arc at the four corners. The default is the `arc` value when none is specified.

Listing A-18. *Using the opening-round-rect Background for the Currently Focused Item*

```
focused {
   padding: 9;
   font-color: highlightedFontColor;
   background {
      type: opening-round-rect;
      color: white;
      start-height: 0;
      steps: 2;
      border-width: 2;
      border-color: fontColor;
      arc: 18;
   }
   layout: expand | center;
}
```

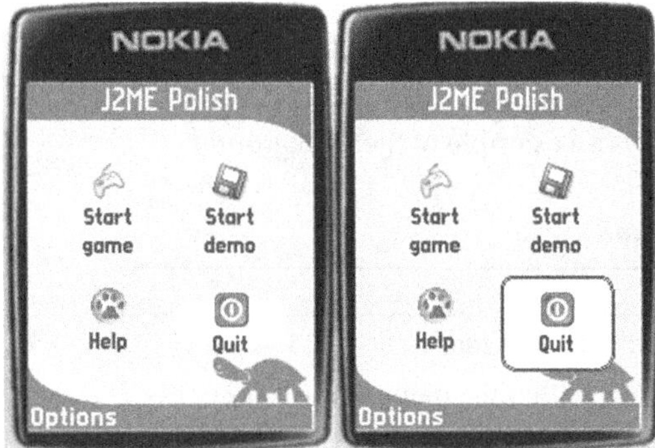

Figure A-9. *The opening-round-rect background in action: on the left shortly after switching the focused item, and on the right side after remaining a while on the focused item*

round-tab Background

The round-tab background paints a rectangular background where the top edges are rounded. Its main use is for `TabbedForms` (compare Chapter 12). Table A-56 lists the attributes of the `round-tab` background, Listing A-19 demonstrates the use of the background, and Figure A-10 displays an example of the background.

Table A-56. *Attributes of the round-tab Background*

Attribute	Required	Explanation
`type`	Yes	The type needs to be `round-tab`.
`color`	No	The color of the background; either the name of the color or a direct definition. The default color is `white`.
`arc`	No	The diameter of the arc at the four corners. The default is `10` pixels when none is specified.

Attribute	Required	Explanation
arc-width	No	The horizontal diameter of the arc at the four corners. The default is the arc value when none is specified.
arc-height	No	The vertical diameter of the arc at the four corners. The default is the arc value when none is specified.

Listing A-19. *Using the round-tab Background in a TabbedForm*

```
tabbar {
   background-color: white;
   layout: expand;
   padding-bottom: 0;
   tabbar-scrolling-indicator-color: black;
}

activetab {
   background-type: round-tab;
   background-color: silver;
   background-arc: 8;
   font-color: white;
   padding-left: 10;
   padding-right: 8;
}

inactivetab {
   padding-left: 6;
   padding-right: 4;
   margin-left: 2;
   margin-right: 2;
   background-type: round-tab;
   background-color: gray;
   background-arc: 8;
   font-color: silver;
}
```

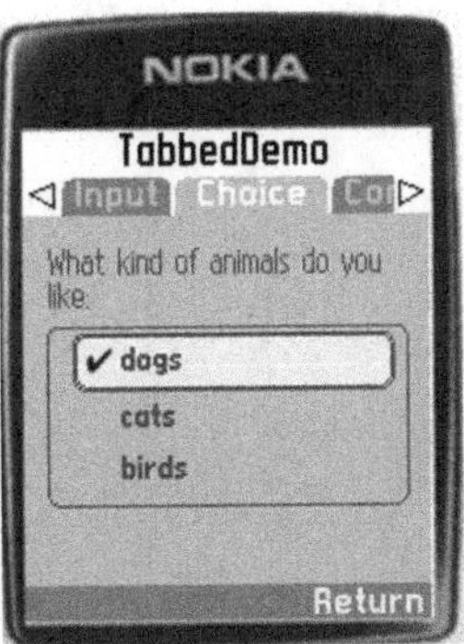

Figure A-10. *The round-tab background in a TabbedForm*

Borders

You can set borders for any `Items`. The J2ME Polish GUI provides several possible borders, which are described in this section.

simple Border

The `simple` border paints a rectangle border in one color. The type attribute does not need to be set for the `simple` border, since this is the default border. Table A-57 lists the attributes of the `simple` border, Listing A-20 demonstrates the use of the border, and Figure A-11 displays an example of the border.

Table A-57. *Attributes of the simple Border*

Attribute	Required	Explanation
`color`	Yes	The color of the border; either the name of the color or a direct definition.
`width`	No	The width of the border in pixels. The default is `1`.

Listing A-20. *Using a simple Border for the Currently Focused Item*

```
focused {
   font-color: highlightedFontColor;
   background: none;
   border-width: 2;
   border-color: black;
   layout: expand | center;
}
```

Figure A-11. *Using a simple border for the currently focused item*

round-rect Border

The round-rect border paints a rectangular border with round edges. Table A-58 lists the attributes of the round-rect border, Listing A-21 demonstrates the use of the border, and Figure A-12 displays an example of the border.

Table A-58. *Attributes of the round-rect Border*

Attribute	Required	Explanation
type	Yes	The type needs to be round-rect or roundrect.
color	Yes	The color of the border; either the name of the color or a direct definition.
width	No	The width of the border in pixels. The default is 1.
arc	No	The diameter of the arc at the four corners. The default is 10 pixels when none is specified.
arc-width	No	The horizontal diameter of the arc at the four corners. The default is the arc value when none is specified.
arc-height	No	The vertical diameter of the arc at the four corners. The default is the arc value when none is specified.

Listing A-21. *Using a round-rect Border for the Currently Focused Item*

```
focused {
   font-color: highlightedFontColor;
   background: none;
   border {
      type: round-rect;
      width: 2;
      color: black;
      arc: 18;
   }
   layout: expand | center;
}
```

Figure A-12. *Using a round-rect border for the currently focused item*

shadow Border

The shadow border paints a shadowy border. Table A-59 lists the attributes of the shadow border, Listing A-22 demonstrates the use of the border, and Figure A-13 displays an example of the border.

Table A-59. *Attributes of the shadow Border*

Attribute	Required	Explanation
type	Yes	The type needs to be shadow, bottom-right-shadow, or right-bottom-shadow.
color	Yes	The color of the border, either the name of the color or a direct definition.
width	No	The width of the border in pixels. The default is 1.
offset	No	The offset between the corner and the start of the shadow. The default is 1 pixel.

Listing A-22. *Using a shadow Border for the Currently Focused Item*

```
focused {
   font-color: highlightedFontColor;
   background-color: highlightedBackgroundColor;
   border {
      type: shadow;
      width: 2;
      color: black;
      offset: 5;
   }
   layout: expand | center;
}
```

Figure A-13. *Using a shadow border and a simple background for the currently focused item*

top, bottom, left, and right Borders

These borders paint a simple border on one side of the corresponding item. Table A-60 lists the attributes of the borders, Listing A-23 demonstrates the use of the `bottom` border, and Figure A-14 displays an example of the `bottom` border.

Table A-60. *Attributes of the top, bottom, left, and right Borders*

Attribute	Required	Explanation
`type`	Yes	The type needs to be `top`, `bottom`, `left`, or `right`
`color`	Yes	The color of the border; either the name of the color or a direct definition
`width`	No	The width of the border in pixels. The default is `1`.

Listing A-23. *Using a bottom Border for the Currently Focused Item*

```
focused {
   font-color: highlightedFontColor;
   background-color: highlightedBackgroundColor;
   border {
      type: bottom;
      width: 2;
      color: black;
   }
   layout: expand | center;
}
```

Figure A-14. *Using a bottom border for the currently focused item*

circle Border

The `circle` border paints a round or elliptical border. Table A-61 lists the attributes of the `circle` border, Listing A-24 demonstrates the use of the border, and Figure A-15 displays an example of the border.

Table A-61. *Attributes of the circle Border*

Attribute	Required	Explanation
`type`	Yes	The type needs to be `circle`.
`color`	Yes	The color of the border, either the name of the color or a direct definition.
`width`	No	The width of the border in pixels. The default is `1`.
`stroke-style`	No	Either `solid` or `dotted`. It defines the painting style of the border and the default is `solid`.

Listing A-24. *Using a circle Border for the Currently Focused Item*

```
focused {
   font-color: highlightedFontColor;
   background-color: highlightedBackgroundColor;
   border {
      type: circle;
      width: 2;
      color: black;
      stroke-style: dotted;
   }
   layout: expand | center;
}
```

Figure A-15. *Using a dotted circle border for the currently focused item*

J2ME Polish License

J2ME Polish is licensed under the open source GNU General Public License (GPL, *http://www.gnu.org/licenses/gpl.html*) as well as a proprietary license (*http://www.j2mepolish.org/licenses.html*). You can use the complete build features along with the device database in your commercial, closed-source application, without any restrictions, for free. If you want to use parts of J2ME Polish that are linked with your application, such as the utility classes, the GUI, or the game engine, you need to either publish your application under the GPL or obtain a commercial license. For details and pricing, please refer to *http://www.j2mepolish.org/licenses.html*.

Abbreviations Glossary

In the wireless Java world you will encounter many acronyms; some of these are listed in Table A-62.

Table A-62. *Abbreviations and Acronyms in the Wireless Java World*

Abbreviation	Explanation
3G	Third Generation. A term describing UMTS and similar advanced network technologies.
3GPP	Third Generation Partnership Project. A worldwide collaboration project established in 1998 to create and standardize advanced network technologies (*http://www.3gpp.org*).
AMS	Application Management Software. Software responsible for installing and running the application and for forwarding events to the application.
CBS	Cell Broadcast Service. A GSM service for sending messages to all devices reachable from a certain cell or a group of cells.
CDC	Connected Device Configuration. A configuration that provides an environment similar J2SE.
CLDC	Connected Limited Device Configuration. The common J2ME configuration defining the minimal requirements for a J2ME device. The CLDC 1.1 release introduced floating-point calculations and weak references to the J2ME world.
CSS	Cascading Style Sheets. The standard to design websites and now also J2ME applications.
GCF	Generic Connection Framework. A framework that provides an abstract system for establishing I/O connections to arbitrary data streams.
GUI	Graphical user interface. The application components visible to the user.
IMEI	International Mobile Equipment Identity. A globally unique identification number of the mobile device.
IMP	Information Module Profile. A profile for embedded devices. Basically, it's MIDP without the user interface.
IMSI	International Mobile Subscriber Identity. The identification number of the subscriber to a carrier network. The IMSI is stored on the SIM card.
J2EE	Java 2 Enterprise Edition. A runtime environment for server applications (*http://java.sun.com/j2ee*).

Continued

Table A-62. *Continued*

Abbreviation	Explanation
J2ME	Java 2 Micro Edition. A runtime environment for restricted devices (*http://java.sun.com/j2me*).
J2SE	Java 2 Standard Edition. A runtime environment for desktop applications (*http://java.sun.com/j2se*).
JAD	Java Application Descriptor. A text file containing information about the application that itself is in the JAR file. The JAD file can allows the device to check the requirements listed in the JAD before the (much bigger) JAR file is downloaded.
JAM	Java Application Manager. Another name for the AMS.
JAR	Java ARchive. A ZIP file that includes Java classes, resources, and a Manifest.
JCP	Java Community Process. Responsible for creating Java-based standards (*http://www.jcp.org*)
JSR	Java Specification Process. A standardization request within the JCP.
JTWI	Java Technology for the Wireless Industry. A standard that tries to limit device fragmentation by setting minimum requirements for J2ME devices (JSR 185).
JVM	Java Virtual Machine. A standardized machine usually realized in software.
KVM	Kilobyte Virtual Machine. The name of the JVM for the Connected Limited Device Configuration. Originally *K* stands for Kuaui, but now it stands for kilo, as in kilobyte, to emphasize its small size.
MIDlet	An application written for the MIDP profile.
MIDP	Mobile Information Device Profile. A profile that adds basic networking, user interface, and persistence functionality to the CLDC.
MMS	Multimedia Message Service. A GSM service for sending enhanced text messages that can contain multimedia elements such a photos or sounds. Some devices accept Java applications to be deployed via MMS.
OTA	Over The Air (Provisioning). A specification for downloading and installing J2ME application over a wireless network.
PIM	Personal Information Manager. Software for managing personal information such as address books, calendars, to-do lists, and so on.
PNG	Portable Network Graphics. The default, patent-free format for images on J2ME devices.
RMS	Record Management System. A persistence mechanism offered by the MIDP and IMP profiles.
SIM	Subscriber Identity Module. The SIM card is used to identify the mobile phone owner to the network. The SIM card contains the IMSI.
SMS	Short Message Service. A GSM service for sending short text or binary messages to devices.
UMTS	Universal Mobile Telephone System. One of the Third Generation (3G) mobile systems.
WAP	Wireless Application Protocol. A network agnostic protocol for wireless connections. Is often used to download J2ME applications and forms the basis for sending MMS messages.
WML	Wireless Markup Language. An XML-based markup language for structuring content for WAP browsers.

Index

Symbols

! operator
    see not (!) operator
#*xyz* preprocessing directives
    see preprocessing directives
&& operator
    see and (&&) operator
= directive
    see equals (#=) directive
^ (xor) operator, 107
|| (or) operator, 107

Numbers

3D Graphics API, 359–360
3GPP (Third Generation Partnership Project), 417
3gpp group
    assembling resources, 71
55/65/75 groups
    Siemens devices, 289
7-Zip packager, 15, 79
    parameters, 385
    using, 79

A

a selector, StringItem, 186
abbreviations glossary, 417
abort directive, 398
abstract classes
    design phase, 31
abstraction
    high-level performance tuning, 330
access modifiers
    low-level performance tuning, 338
acronyms glossary, 417
activetab style
    designing TabbedForms, 213
    predefined styles, 184
address book
    managing contacts in, 134
after attribute
    common design attributes, CSS, 197–198
    structure of style definition, 189
AHNAPI (Ad Hoc Networking API)
    optional packages for MIDP devices, 278
algorithms
    high-level performance tuning, 334
allowCycling variable, Container, 394
alpha blending
    colors, 195
amr group
    assembling resources, 71
AMR's Jazelle
    MIDP platforms, 293
AMS (Application Management Software), 417
    detecting interruptions, 320
anchor attribute
    image background, 403
and (&&) operator, 73, 107
and nested element
    deviceRequirements element, 365
animate method
    Border class using, 269
    creating client-side Background class, 265
animationInterval variable, 164, 392
    SpriteItem constructor arguments, 179
animations
    designing Tickers, 227–228
    programming SpriteItem, 178
    repeat-animation attribute, 208, 209
    screen-change-animation attribute, 229
    using, 228–229
Ant, 9, 55–58
    build.xml elements, 363–389
        build section, 366–369
        compiler element, 373–375
        compilerargs element, 375, 376
        copier element, 383–384
        debug element, 371–372
        deviceRequirements section, 365
        emulator element, 388
        fileset element, 382
        filter element, 371–372
        finalizer element, 387
        handler element, 372
        info section, 363–364
        jad element, 385–386
        jadFilter element, 386
        keep element, 377–378
        localization element, 382–383
        manifestFilter element, 386
        midlet element, 369–370
        midlets element, 369–370
        obfuscator element, 377
        packager element, 384–385
        parameter element, emulator, 389
        parameter element, obfuscator, 378
        postcompiler element, 376–377
        preprocessor element, 372–373
        preverifier element, 380–381
        resources element, 381–382
        sign element, 387
        source element, 369
        sources element, 369
        variable element, 370–371
        variables element, 370–371

build.xml file, 55
properties, 56
creating "Hello World" application, 58–64
determining name of properties file, 57
integrating Eclipse IDE with, 20–21
J2ME Polish Ant settings, 363–389
online documentation for, 56
online list of external tasks, 56
properties, 56
activating/deactivating logging framework, 127
loading, 57
setting Ant properties, 238
write-once capability, 57
target dependencies, 58
targets, 55
copying resources, 246
extending build phases, 237
using custom packagers, 246
tasks, 55
antcall
additional Ant properties for obfuscator, 245
implementing custom preverifier, 245
integrating finalizers, 247
integrating unsupported obfuscators, 96
postcompiler, 244
using custom preprocessor, 243
anti-aliasing
using for bitmap font, 142
Apache Ant
see Ant
api element, apis.xml, 45
apiDir attribute, build element, 366
APIs
controlling vibration and display light, 156
design phase, 31
device control, 156
device-specific preprocessing symbols, 390
integrating binary third-party APIs, 93
integrating device APIs, 94
integrating source code third-party APIs, 92
integrating third-party APIs, 92–94
optional packages for MIDP devices, 276–278
porting low-level graphics operations, 152
porting sound playback, 155
Series 80 Nokia devices, 287
apis attribute, build element, 366
apis element, apis.xml, 45
apis.xml, 45–47
device database file, 39
specifying libraries in, 46
Aplix's JBlend JVM
MIDP platforms, 293
append method, Form class
additional FramedForm methods, 177
additional TabbedForm methods, 174
designing ChoiceGroups, 216
integrating CSS into custom items, 256
application bundle
specifying files not to include in, 70
application life cycle, 30
build phase, 31–32, 64–68
deployment phase, 31, 33
design phase, 30–31
implementation phase, 30, 32
optimization phase, 31, 33
testing phase, 31–32
updating application, 36
ApplicationInitializer variable, 393
applications
building localized applications, 84
configuring application, 74
debugging applications, 96–99
obfuscating applications, 94–96
optimizing applications
see optimizing applications
untrusted applications, 77
appliesTo attribute
registering custom CSS attributes, 260
arc attribute
opening-round-rect background, 409
round-rect background, 401
round-rect border, 413
round-tab background, 410
arc-height attribute
opening-round-rect background, 409
round-rect background, 401
round-rect border, 413
round-tab background, 411
arc-width attribute
opening-round-rect background, 409
round-rect background, 401
round-rect border, 413
round-tab background, 411
architecture
design phase, 31
high-level performance tuning, 330–331
optimization phase, 33
area element, bugs.xml, 47
arguments
skipArgumentCheck symbol, 164
arguments attribute, packager element, 384
using third-party packagers, 78
arithmetic operations
low-level performance tuning, 336
array data
bytecode instruction storing integer array, 346
loading array data from resource file, 348
storing array data in strings, 347
storing to improve class model, 345–348
arrayCopy method, System class
low-level performance tuning, 335
ArrayList class, 134–135
low-level performance tuning, 335
synchronization, 134
arrays
splitting text into String array, 135
ASCII-String data type
Binary Editor, 141

aspect-oriented programming
J2ME apps. on multiple devices, 102
preprocessing, 300
asterisk
attribute name ending with, 76
AT&T Wireless
carrier modifications, 292
attribute-value pairs
CSS declaration, 187
attributes
design attributes, 189–199
grouping, CSS, 187
name ending with asterisk, 76
name ending with question mark, 76
optional attributes, 76
overriding attribute values, 74
registering custom CSS attributes, 259
selecting all remaining, 76
selecting several, 76
specifying, 74
audio
device-specific preprocessing symbols, 390
audio.*xyz* properties
system properties, 357
authentication
high-level performance tuning, 332
HTTP networking, 312
automatic resource assembling
device database, 49
available method, InputStream
defensive programming, 304

B

back buffer optimization
optimizing game engine, 148–149
back-and-forth attribute
pulsating background, 405
background attribute
structure of style definition, 189
Background class
client-side, 265–267
server-side, 267–268
background-color attribute
pop-up ChoiceGroups, 221
background-type attribute, 199
backgrounds
background converter, 267
circle background, 403–404
creating Background class
client-side, 265–267
server-side, 267–268
creating custom, 265–269
custom background, 268–269
designing screen background, 199
designing, CSS, 199
image background, 402–403
moving background, 265
using in polish.css file, 268
not required, 198
opening background, 408–409
opening-round-rect background, 409–410
pulsating background, 404–405
pulsating-circle background, 406
pulsating-circles background, 407–408
round-rect background, 401–402
round-tab background, 410–411
simple background, 400–401
translucent backgrounds
currently focused item, 401
porting low-level graphics, 153
backgrounds section, polish.css file, 189
Backlight functionality
device control, 156
backward variable, ScreenChangeAnimation, 395
before attribute, 189, 197–198
behavior, configuring GUI, 164–167
benchmarking tests, 328, 329
bin folder, 15
Mac OS X system, 139
binary data files
creating/manipulating, 138
managing level files, 139
Binary Editor, 139–141
editing data with, 140
predefined types of, 141
binaryLibrary attribute, build element, 366
bitmap attribute, 196
bitmap fonts, 142
common design attributes, CSS, 197
BitMapFont class, 136–138
customizing fonts, 133
BitMapFontViewer class
displaying messages, 136
layout method, 137
paint method, 137
BitsPerColor groups
assembling resources, 71
BitsPerPixel 391
device database, 42
preprocessing symbols and variables, 115
selecting target devices to build for, 82
BlackBerry
see RIM BlackBerry
blocksplit parameter
KZIP packager, 80, 385
Bluetooth API
deployment phase, 33
device identification, 319
networking problems, 310
permissions for signed MIDlets, 361
properties, 358–359
Series 40/60 Nokia devices, 286
boolean data type
Binary Editor, 141
boolean operators
evaluating terms, 107
bootclasspath attribute
compiler element, 373
bootclasspathref attribute
compiler element, 373
border attribute, 189
Border class, 269

border-color attribute, 409
border-type attribute, 199
border-width attribute, 409
borders
  adding custom borders, 269
  circle border, 416
  designing, CSS, 199
  not required, 198
  round-rect border, 413
  shadow border, 414
  simple border, 412
  top, bottom, left, and right borders, 415
borders section, polish.css file, 189
bottom animation, 229
bottom border, 415
bottom layout, 193
bottomframe style, 185
box model
  CSS box model, 191–192
branching code
  if directive, 105
BREW (Binary Runtime Environment for Wireless), 293
bug element, bugs.xml, 47
bugs
  optimization phase, 33
  preprocessing symbols and variables, 115
Bugs capability
  device database, 43
bugs element, bugs.xml, 47
bugs.xml, 47–48
  clarifying device bugs in, 47
  device database file, 39
build element, build.xml
  attributes, table of, 366, 368
  building a MIDlet with J2ME Polish, 61
build extensions, 231–248
  accepting parameters in, 233
  Ant targets, invoking, 237–238
  build phases summarized, 231–232
  compiler, changing/configuring, 243–244
  configuring, 233–235
  configuring extension with conditional parameters, 234
  creating custom preprocessor, 239–243
  emulators, integrating, 247–248
  extension mechanism, 231–238
  Extension superclass, 232
  finalizers, integrating, 247
  obfuscator, integrating custom/third-party, 244–245
  packagers, using custom, 246
  parameter elements, 233
  postcompiler, using, 244
  Preprocessor class, implementing, 239–243
  preverifier, integrating, 245
  property functions, creating, 248
  registering extensions, 235, 236
  resources, copying and transforming, 245–246
  using extensions, 237
  using extensions conditionally, 236
  using in build.xml file, 235–236
build framework, 30
build phase, 64–68
  application life cycle, 31–32
  building for multiple devices, 80–84
  building localized applications, 84–91
  compilation phase, 66–67
  extending
    see build extensions
  extension points of, 232
  invoking emulators, 68
  minimizing number of target devices, 83–84
  obfuscation phase, 67
  packaging phase, 68–80
    managing JAD and Manifest attributes, 74–77
    resource assembling, 68–73
    signing MIDlets, 77–78
    using third-party packagers, 78–80
  preprocessing phase, 66
  preverification phase, 68
  selecting devices to build for, 80–83
  selecting target devices, 65–66
  summarized, 231–232
build section, build.xml, 366–369
build tools
  Ant, 55–58
  extending build phases
    see build extensions
  Make, 55
build.xml file, 16
  activating specific log levels, 124
  activating the GUI, 161–162
  activating/deactivating logging framework, 128
  Ant, 55
  Ant properties, 56
  building a MIDlet, 60
  configuring build extensions, 233–235
  configuring GUI, 162–170
  controlling logging framework, 125
  controlling GUI, 161–170
  creating a "polished" application, 161
  debugging applications, 96
  defining symbols and variables, 116
  device-specific preprocessing symbols, 389–390
  device-specific preprocessing variables, 390–392
  deviceRequirements element, 50
  elements and attributes, 363–389
  full-screen mode, using GUI in, 163–164
  integrating J2ME Polish into IDEs, 19
  optimizing game engine, 146
  project tag, 56
  setting symbols and variables, 115
  testing sample applications, 16
  using extensions in, 235–236
  using registered extension in, 236
button appearance mode, 186
button selector, StringItem, 186

byte data type
  Binary Editor, 141
bytecode modification, 244
  avoiding known issues, 307–308
  storing integer array, 346
bytes property function, 118, 399

C

caching
  high-level performance tuning, 331
calculations
  low-level performance tuning, 336
Cancel command variable, 166
  label for Cancel command, 393
  localizing J2ME Polish GUI, 90
cancel-image attribute, menubar, 204
CanvasHeight variable, 391
CanvasSize, 391
  device database, 43
  preprocessing symbols and variables, 115
  selecting target devices to build for, 82
CanvasWidth variable, 391
capabilities, 41
  cumulative effect, 48
  defining supported libraries, 45
  determining canvas height with, 52
  device database, 42
  if directive, 51
  inheritance, 49
  precedence between xml files, 48
  preprocessing, 51–52
  selecting target devices to build for, 82
capabilities.xml
  device database file, 39
  implicit groups, 42
capability element
  devices.xml, 41
  groups.xml, 44
  vendors.xml, 44
capture property, MMAPI, 357
caret-char attribute, TextFields, 225
caret-color attribute, TextFields, 225
carrier modifications
  differences between devices, 279
carriers
  carrier specific attributes, 355
CBS (Cell Broadcast Service), 417
  permissions for signed MIDlets, 361
CDC (Connected Device Configuration), 417
  J2ME configurations, 275
center layout
  aligning items with layout attribute, 193
certificates
  root certificates, 318
  signing MIDlets, 77
  vendor certificates, 318
ChangeInputModeKey variable, 391
ChangeNumericalAlphaInputModeKey variable, 391
CHAPI (Content Handler API)
  optional packages for MIDP devices, 277
characters supported
  JTWI specification, 278
charactersKey variables, TextField, 165–166, 395–396
  configuring the TextField, 168
charactersKeyPound variable, 166, 396
charactersKeyStar variable, 166, 396
check box-selected attribute, ChoiceGroups, 220
checkbox
  available dynamic styles, 186
  ChoiceGroups, 219
checkbox-plain attribute, ChoiceGroups, 220
choice-color attribute, ChoiceGroups, 217, 220
ChoiceGroups
  attributes for, 216
  available dynamic styles, 186
  designing, 215–222
  designing exclusive, 216–219
  designing multiple, 219–221
  designing pop-up, 221–222
  insertion points for style directives, 172
  preprocessing variables, 165
  types of, 215
ChoiceItem class, 186
chunk-width attribute, Gauge class, 223
circle background, 403–404
circle border, 416
circles-number attribute
  pulsating-circles background, 407
class attribute
  copier element, 384
  filter element, 127, 372
  finalizer element, 387
  keep element, 378
  midlet element, 370
  obfuscator element, 377
  packager element, 384
  postcompiler element, 376
  preprocessor element, 372
  preverifier element, 380
  using extensions in build.xml file, 235
class model, improving
  grouping functionalities, 344–345
  minimizing size of JAR files, 344–348
  removing classes and methods, 345
  storing array data, 345–348
classes
  changing class inheritance, 51, 119
  design phase, 31
  directive including/excluding, 109
  ImageLoader preprocessing variable, 164
  obfuscator removing unused classes, 133
  removing to improve class model, 345
  working on multiple devices, 101
classname property function, 399
  transforming variables with, 118
  using/avoiding interfaces, 331
classPath attribute
  compiler element, 373
  copier element, 384
  finalizer element, 387

integrating custom background, 268
obfuscator element, 377
packager element, 385
postcompiler element, 376
preprocessor element, 372
preverifier element, 381
using extensions in build.xml file, 235
classpath element
registering project extensions, 236
classpathref attribute
compiler element, 373
CLDC (Connected Limited Device Configuration), 274, 417
device-specific preprocessing symbols, 390
J2ME configurations, 275
CLDC 1.0 profile
writing portable code, 295
cldc groups
assembling resources, 70
clean build
building a MIDlet, 61
Clear command variable, 166
label for Clear command, 394
localizing J2ME Polish GUI, 91
suppressClearCommand variable, 165, 168
ClearKey variable, 392
client framework, 30
clientClass attribute
handler element, 372
clock resolution
JTWI specification, 278
code
adjustments, avoiding known issues, 305–308
manipulating bytecode, 307–308
using preprocessing, 305–307
writing portable code, 294–303
using different source files, 300–303
using dynamic code, 295–298
using lowest common denominator, 295
using preprocessing, 298–300
color attribute
available font attributes, 196
circle background, 404
circle border, 416
Gauge items, 223
image background, 402
opening background, 408
opening-round-rect background, 409
pop-up ChoiceGroups, 221
pulsating-circle background, 406
round-rect background, 401
round-rect border, 413
round-tab background, 410
shadow border, 414
simple background, 400
simple border, 412
top, bottom, left, and right borders, 415
colors
alpha blending, 195
building a MIDlet, 63
caret-color attribute, TextFields, 225
defining, 194
defining colors, CSS, 193–195
designing normal menu bar, 202
naming conventions, 194
predefined colors, 193
Series 40 Nokia devices, 284
Series 60 Nokia devices, 286
colors section, polish.css file, 189, 194
columns attribute
arranging items on screen, 206
ChoiceGroups, 216
using with view types, 207
columns-width attribute
arranging items on screen, 206
ChoiceGroups, 216
"Command not found"
sample application error messages, 17
commandAction method
MIDlet showing a menu, 59
CommandListener interface
minimizing classes in JAR files, 344
commands
Cancel command variable, 166
Clear command variable, 166
command preprocessing variables, 166
configuring TextField commands, 168
configuring, J2ME Polish GUI, 164–167
Delete command variable, 166
hasCommandKeyEvents, 163, 390
keytool command, 77
leftcommand style, 204
Mark command variable, 166
OK command variable, 166
Options command variable, 166
rightcommand style, 204
Select command variable, 166
suppressClearCommand variable, 165
suppressCommands variable, 165, 168
suppressDeleteCommand variable, 165
suppressMarkCommands variable, 165
suppressSelectCommands variable, 165
Unmark command variable, 166
comment characters
preprocessing directives, 104–105
comments
Cascading Style Sheets, 188
Commercial/None-GPL license, 12
comparison operators, 108
compilation
see build phase
compilation phase, 66–67
build phase extensions, 232
using J2ME Polish as compiler, 67
compiler attribute
compiler element, 373
compilerargs element, 376
compiler element, 373–375
attributes, table of, 373–374
debugging applications, 99
extending build phases, 243

compilerargs element, 375, 376
compilerDestDir attribute
  build element, 366
compilerMode attribute
  build element, 366
compilerModePreverify attribute
  build element, 367
components
  build framework, 30
  client framework, 30
  IDE plug-ins, 30
  installing, 13
  layers of components, 29
  stand-alone tools, 30
compression parameter
  7-Zip packager, 79, 385
condition directive, 398
  description, 105
  implementing StringListItem class, 255
  include/exclude classes/interfaces, 109
conditional parameters
  configuring an extension with, 234
  using extensions conditionally, 236
conditions
  debugging applications using, 96–98
configuration attribute, info section, 363
configuration property, MIDP, 357
configuration variables, 392–397
configurations
  Connected Device Configuration, 274
  Connected Limited Device Configuration, 274
  differences between devices, 274–275
  J2ME configurations, 275
  Nokia devices, 285
  Siemens devices, 289
  Sony Ericsson devices, 291
configurations.xml, 39
configure method, 234
Connected Device Configuration
  see CDC
Connected Limited Device Configuration
  see CLDC
connections
  see also networking
  telecom market, 280
ConstantPoolTag parameter
  DashO Pro obfuscator, 380
constructors
  integrating CSS into custom items, 256
  setting style, 257
containers
  low-level performance tuning, 335
contents property, MMAPI, 357
cookies
  HTTP networking, 312
  tracking number of times installed, 34
copier element, resources, 383–384
  attributes, table of, 384
  extending build phases, 245
copyright attribute, info section, 363
Count definition, 140
countries
  ISO country code, 89
  localized country name, 89
createNewStatement method
  background converter, 268
CSS (Cascading Style Sheets)
  see also polish.css file
  aligning items with layout attribute, 192–193
  backgrounds and borders, 198–199
  before and after attributes, 197–198
  bitmap fonts, 197
  brief description, 417
  comments, 188
  common design attributes, 189–199
  creating server-side Background class, 267
  CSS box model, 191–192
  CSS declaration, 187
  CSS syntax, 187–188
  defining colors, 193–195
  designing the GUI, 181–229
  designing with font attributes, 196
  effect of different polish.css files, 169
  grouping attributes, 187
  labels, 197
  naming conventions, 187
  registering custom CSS attributes, 259
  structure of polish.css file, 189
  structure of style definition, 189–191
CSS styles
  see also styles
  applying in MIDlet constructor, 63
  applying to a form, 171
  components of, 182
  defining in resources/polish.css file, 172
  handling custom items, 256
  integrating into custom items, 256
  referring to other styles, 188
  setting, 113
currencies
  code for used currency, 89
  localization, 88
  symbol of translation's currency, 89
current setting
  symbols for reading current setting, 397
currently focused item
  using bottom border for, 415
  using circle background for, 404
  using circle border for, 416
  using image background for, 403
  using opening background for, 408
  using opening-round-rect background for, 410
  using pulsating background for, 405
  using pulsating-circle background for, 406
  using pulsating-circles background for, 407
  using round-rect background for, 402
  using round-rect border for, 413
  using shadow border for, 414
  using simple border for, 412
  using text of list item as title, 211–212
  using translucent background for, 401

currentTimeMilis method, System class, 328
custom items
  see customizations
custom log levels, 127
custom-css-attributes.xml file, 259
custom-extensions.xml file, 270
customApis attribute, build element, 367
customDevices attribute, build element, 367
customGroups attribute, build element, 367
CustomItem class
  writing custom items, 248
CustomItems
  troubleshooting Sony Ericsson devices, 291
customizations
  backgrounds, 265
  borders, 269
  custom items, designing, 256, 261
  custom items, handling, 255–261
  custom items, writing, 248–261
  extending build tools
    see build extensions
  finalizer, integrating, 247
  logging framework, extending, 269–270
  obfuscator, integrating, 244
  packagers, using custom, 246
  preprocessor, 239–243
  preverifier, integrating, 245
  problems implementing low-level GUI, 309
  property function, 248
  registering custom CSS attributes, 259
  scrollable list item, 248
customVendors attribute, build element, 367

D

damping attribute, dropping view, 208
DashO Pro obfuscator, 379
  combining several obfuscators, 95
  parameters, 380
DashoHome parameter, 380
data
  editing data with Binary Editor, 140
data files
  creating/manipulating binary data files, 138
data protocols
  HTTP networking, 311
data types
  Binary Editor, 141
dataSize attribute, info section, 363
DateField class
  available dynamic styles, 186
DateFields
  additional attributes for, 226
  designing DateFields, 226–227
DateFormat variable, 394
DateFormatEmptyText variable, 394
DateFormatSeparator variable, 394
dates
  date formatting, 138
  formatDate function, 88
  localization, 88
debug attribute, compiler element, 373
Debug class, 138
debug directive, 398
  description, 105
  logging framework, 113
  logging messages, 123
  priority level of messages, 124
debug element, build.xml, 371–372
  attributes, 127, 371
  controlling logging framework, 125–126
  debugging applications, 96
  debugging applications using conditions, 98
  enabling benchmark log level, 329
debugEnabled preprocessing symbol
  detecting if logging framework active, 129
debugging, 96–99
  adding debug code for log levels, 125
  compilation phase, 67
  controlling logging framework, 125
  symbols for reading current setting, 397
  tracking bugs on real devices, 127
  using conditions, 96–98
  using J2ME Polish as compiler, 98–99
debuglevel attribute, compiler element, 374
default attribute
  localization element, 383
  project element, 56
  registering custom CSS attributes, 260
default package
  obfuscating applications, 95
default style, 184
defaultexcludes attribute, resources element, 382
defaultFrameIndex
  arguments of SpriteItem constructor, 179
defensive programming, 304–305
define directive, 105, 398
  defining/removing symbols/variables, 109
definition files, 139
  Count definition, 140
  saving definition files, 141
Delete command variable, 166
  label for Delete command, 394
  localizing J2ME Polish GUI, 90
  suppressDeleteCommand variable, 165, 168
delete method
  additional TabbedForm methods, 174
deleteConfirm attribute, info section, 363
deleteNotify attribute, info section, 363
depend attribute, compiler element, 374
dependencies
  Ant targets, 58
deployment phase
  application life cycle, 31, 33
deprecation attribute, compiler element, 374
description attribute, info section, 363
  registering custom CSS attributes, 260
description element
  apis.xml, 45
  bugs.xml, 47
design phase
  application life cycle, 30–31

designs
applying desired design styles, 171
design definitions, 181
sample application in dark design, 170
sample application in default design, 169
sample application in pop design, 169
storing design settings and files, 181
using different designs for application, 168
destDir attribute
build element, 367
compiler element, 374
Development Platform 2.0
Series 40 Nokia devices, 284
device database, 39–53
automatic resource assembling, 49
avoiding problems, 121
changing and extending, 52
common capabilities, 42
defining capabilities and features, 48–49
defining devices, 40–43
defining groups, 44–45
defining issues, 47–48
defining libraries, 45–47
defining vendors, 44
determining canvas height with device capabilities, 52
optimizing target devices, 51
preprocessing, 51
resource assembling, 50
selecting devices to build for, 82
selecting resources for target devices, 50
selecting target devices, 49–50
using, 49–52
using several variable values individually, 111
XML files described, 39
XML format, 39–49
device element, devices.xml, 40
supportsPolishGui attribute, 42
device groups
defining in groups.xml, 45
designing the GUI for, 182–183
device identification
accessing native functionality, 320
MSISDN, 319
retrieving Globally Unique ID, 319
solving common problems, 318
device libraries
Nokia devices, 285
optional packages for MIDP devices, 276–278
porting low-level graphics operations, 152
Siemens devices, 289
Sony Ericsson devices, 291
specifying default path of, 46
specifying file names of, 46
specifying supported libraries, 45
specifying libraries in apis.xml, 45–46
specifying name, 45
supported library not defined in apis.xml, 45
using floating-point emulation libraries, 315
using optional/device-specific libraries, 118
DeviceControl class, 138
allowing for device vibration, 156
deviceRequirements element, build.xml, 50, 365
attributes, table of, 365
building a MIDlet with J2ME Polish, 61
debugging applications using conditions, 98
nested elements, table of, 365
selecting devices to build for, 80–83
selecting target devices for build phase, 65
devices
see also target devices
activating GUI for, 161
applying filter for specific, 76
building for multiple, 80–84
carrier modifications, 292
controlling GUI, 161
controlling vibration and display light, 156
designing GUI for, 182–183
differences between devices, 273–280
carrier modifications, 279
configurations, 274–275
emulators, 280
firmware versions, 279
formats, 279
hardware, 273–274
profiles, 275–276
directories for specific, 70
distinguishing between, 66
integrating device APIs, 94
JAR size variation, 273
JTWI specification, 278–279
manufacturers of, 281
MIDP device packages, 276–278
Mobile Service Architecture, 278–279
preprocessing symbols and variables, 114
device-specific symbols, 389–390
device-specific variables, 390–392
real devices, 127–130
selecting devices to build for, 80–83
setting variables for, 117
testing capabilities of, 143
using hard-coded values, 120
using optional/device-specific libraries, 118
vendor characteristics, 283–292
LG Electronics, 290
Motorola, 287–288
Nokia, 283–287
RIM BlackBerry, 291
Samsung, 288–289
Siemens, 289–290
Sony Ericsson, 290–291
working on multiple, 101
devices attribute, build element, 366
devices element, devices.xml, 40
devices.xml, 40–43
defining capabilities and features, 48
defining emulator arguments in, 247
defining generic phone in, 40
defining Nokia 6600 phone in, 40
defining supported libraries, 45
device database file, 39

diameter attribute
  circle background, 404
dir attribute
  fileset element, 382
  resources element, 69, 382
  source element, 369
direct input attribute, TextFields, 224
direct input mode, 168
direct-input CSS attribute, 168
directives
  see preprocessing directives
display area, 133
dist directory
  building a MIDlet, 61
distribution
  see also vendors
  minimizing target devices, 83
doc folder, 15
DoJa platforms, 294
  vendor forums, 322
downloads
  Ant, 9
  Eclipse IDE, 8
  J2ME Polish installer, 11
  J2SE, 7
  JBuilder, 8
  NetBeans, 8
  vendor-specific emulators, 10
  Wireless Toolkit, 8
drawRGB method, Graphics class
  avoiding known issues using preprocessing, 306–307
drawRgbOrigin bug
  porting low-level graphics operations, 153
dropping view, 208
DSAPI (Data Sync API)
  optional packages for MIDP devices, 277
dynamic attribute, localization element, 383
dynamic classes
  excluding from obfuscation, 377
  keeping in project, 378
dynamic coding
  writing portable code, 295–298
dynamic image loading, 261–265
dynamic styles
  available dynamic styles, 186
  designing GUI, 183, 185–186
  integrating CSS into custom items, 258
  naming conventions, 185
  programming GUI, 173
  static styles compared, 64

E

Eclipse IDE, 8
  implementation phase, 32
  installing J2ME Polish plug-ins, 22
  integrating J2ME Polish into, 20–22
  integrating with Ant, 20–21
  naming conventions, 21
  using different source files, 302–303
  writing portable code using preprocessing, 299
elif directive, 105, 398
  see also if directive
  checking for multiple preprocessing symbols, 107
elifdef/elifndef directives, 104, 398
  see also if directive
  checking for single preprocessing symbols, 106
else directive, 104, 398
  see also if directive
  checking for multiple preprocessing symbols, 107
  checking for single preprocessing symbols, 106
emulation phase
  build phase extensions, 232
emulator element, build.xml, 388
  attributes, table of, 388
  building a MIDlet with J2ME Polish, 61
  debugging applications using conditions, 98
emulators
  defining emulator arguments in devices.xml, 247
  differences between devices, 280
  downloading, 10
  extending build phases, 247
  floating-point emulation libraries, 315
  invoking, 68
  measuring performance on target devices, 328
  Siemens devices, 289
  testing phase, 32
  WTK emulator, 326
enableFlowObfuscation parameter
  DashO Pro obfuscator, 380
  KlassMaster obfuscator, 379
enableMemoryMonitor attribute
  emulator element, 388
enableNetworkMonitor attribute
  emulator element, 388
enableOptimization parameter
  DashO Pro obfuscator, 380
enableProfiler attribute, emulator element, 388
  measuring performance in WTK emulator, 326
enableRenaming parameter
  DashO Pro obfuscator, 380
enableStringEncription parameter
  DashO Pro obfuscator, 380
encoding attribute
  build element, 367
  compiler element, 374
encoding property, MIDP, 357
encoding property, MMAPI, 357–358
end-color attribute
  pulsating background, 405
endif directive, 104, 399
  see also if directive
  checking for multiple preprocessing symbols, 107
  checking for single preprocessing symbols, 106
environment variables
  setting, 9
equals (#=) directive, 105, 398
  including values of variables in code, 110

equals (==) comparison operator, 108
error messages
  logging framework, 113
  sample applications, 17
errors
  tracking errors, 123
escaping
  escaping special characters in translations, 89
Evaluation license, 12
event handling
  design phase, 31
  DoJa platforms, 294
  minimizing number of classes in JAR files, 345
  problems implementing user interface, 308
exceptions
  logging an exception, 129
  logging framework, 124
  passing errors to logging framework, 127
  stack traces of exceptions, 124
  verbose debugging mode, 124
excludes attribute
  compiler element, 374
  resources element, 382
    files not to include in application bundle, 70
    saving definition files, 141
excludesfile attribute, compiler element, 374
exclusive ChoiceGroups
  additional attributes for items in, 217
  designing, 216–219
  radio boxes and, 216
  with standard selection marker, 218
exclusive lists, 211
exclusive view type
  designing exclusive ChoiceGroups, 217, 219
executable attribute
  compiler element, 374
  packager element, 384
    using third-party packagers, 78
expand layout
  aligning items with layout attribute, 193
explicit groups, 51, 72
  groups.xml, 44
extdirs attribute, compiler element, 374
extending build phases
  see build extensions
extending J2ME Polish, 248–269
  extending logging framework, 269–270
extends keyword
  extending styles, 182
Extension class
  extending build phases, 232
external tools
  installing, 15

F

face attribute
  available font attributes, 196
failonerror attribute, compiler element, 374
fastbytes parameter
  7-Zip packager, 79, 385
FC (File Connection) API
  optional packages for MIDP devices, 277
Feature Packs 1, 2, and 3
  Series 60 Nokia devices, 286
Feature requirement
  selecting target devices to build for, 83
features element
  devices.xml, 41
  groups.xml, 44
  vendors.xml, 44
feedback to users
  improving perceived performance, 339–340
file attribute
  compilerargs element, 376
  jad element, 386
  parameter elements, 233
  variable element, 370
file XML attribute, 75
FileConnection API
  permissions for signed MIDlets, 362
files
  creating/manipulating binary data files, 138
  definition files, 139
  managing level files, 139
files element, apis.xml, 46
fileset element, resources, 382
  attributes, table of, 382
  resource assembling, 72, 73
filter element, debug, 127, 371–372
  attributes, table of, 372
  log levels for classes/packages, 125
final modifier
  using access modifiers, 338
finalize phase
  build phase extensions, 232
finalizer element, build.xml, 387
  attributes, table of, 387
  extending build phases, 247
firmware versions
  differences between devices, 279
first-color attribute
  pulsating-circles background, 407
Flash for mobile devices
  J2ME competitors, 282
flexible folders
  solving common problems, 303
Floater tool, 316
floating-point calculations
  bytecode modification, 244
  floating-point calculation, 314
  floating-point emulation libraries, 315
  Series 60 Nokia devices, 286
  solving common problems, 314
  using integer instead of, 314
  using only integers, 315
flushGraphics method
  running game in full-screen mode, 148
Focused item
  designing, 228

focused style/focused-style attribute
designing ChoiceGroups, 216
designing menus, 200
predefined styles, 184
structure of style definition, 189
folders
flexible folders, 303
font attributes
designing with, CSS, 196
structure of style definition, 189
Font Editor, 142–143
converting True Type into bitmap, 142
creating bitmap font with, 142
Font variables, 391
font-bitmap attribute, 197
fonts
bitmap fonts, 197
BitMapFont class, 136
converting True Type into bitmap, 136, 142
custom fonts displaying messages, 133
customizing, 133
font attributes, 196
font faces, 136
font sizes, 136
font styles, 136
J2ME font support, 136
Motorola devices, 287
specifying font settings, 196
fonts section, polish.css file, 189
foreach directive, 105, 399
finishing #foreach block, 111
using variable values individually, 111
foreground image, 210, 211
fork attribute, compiler element, 374
Form class
append method, 256
available dynamic styles, 186
Form elements
insertion points for style directives, 172
formatDate function, 88
formats
differences between devices, 279
forms
applying CSS Style to, 171
designing, 213
designing FramedForms, 214
designing TabbedForms, 213
programming FramedForm, 176
programming SpriteItem, 178
programming TabbedForm, 174
using dynamic styles, 173
forums, 321, 322
forward variable, ScreenChangeAnimation, 395
FP (Foundation Profile) devices
J2ME profiles, 276
FPLib library, 315
frame style, 185
FramedForm class
additional methods, 177
available dynamic styles, 186
designing lower frame, 214
programming, 176–178
using, 177, 215
FramedForms
designing, 214
full-screen attribute, build element, 367
full-screen mode
activating, 394
enabling, 163
events for soft keys, 164
optimizing game engine, 147–148
troubleshooting Sony Ericsson devices, 291
avoiding known issues using preprocessing, 305
using different source files, 301
using dynamic coding, 296
using GUI in, 163–164
using preprocessing, 298
full-screen variable, 391
FullCanvas class
needsNokiaUiForSystemAlerts bug, 305–306
FullCanvasHeight variable, 391
FullCanvasSize, 391
device database, 43
preprocessing symbols and variables, 115
selecting target devices to build for, 82
FullCanvasWidth variable, 391
fullscreen attribute, build element
running game in full-screen mode, 147
using GUI in full-screen mode, 163
FullScreen variable, 166
using GUI in full-screen mode, 163
FullScreenPreprocessor extension
registering extensions, 236
using in build.xml file, 235
functionalities, grouping
improving class model, 344–345

G

game engine
defining Grid Type of TiledLayer, 149
how not to use, 146
optimizing, 146–150
porting MIDP 2.0 game to MIDP 1.0 device, 152–157
controlling vibration and display light, 156–157
porting low-level graphics operations, 152–155
porting sound playback, 155–156
running game in full-screen mode, 147–148
splitting image into single tiles, 149
using, 145–146
using back buffer in TiledLayer, 148–149
using for MIDP 2.0 devices, 150
working around limitations of, 150–151
game programming, 145–157
measuring performance of typical game loop, 328
GameCanvas
running game in full-screen mode, 147–148

gap-color attribute, Gauge class, 223
gap-width attribute, Gauge class, 223
Gauge class/items
  additional attributes for, 223
  available dynamic styles, 186
  designing Gauge items, 222–224
  improving perceived performance, 340
GCF (Generic Connection Framework), 417
General Public License
  see GPL
getBooleanProperty method, 259
getColor method, 255
getFont method, 255
getHeight method, 297, 299
getIntProperty method, 259
getKeyStates method, 150
getObjectProperty method, 259
getPrefContentHeight method, 251, 255
getPrefContentWidth method, 251, 255
getProperty method, 259
getSelectedTab method, 174
gigabytes property function, 400
  transforming variables with, 118
glossary
  abbreviations/acronyms glossary, 417
GPL (General Public License), 12, 417
graphics
  low-level performance tuning, 335
  porting low-level graphics, 152
Graphics class
  porting low-level graphics, 152
greater than (>) comparison operator, 108
GridType variable, TiledLayer, 396
  defining Grid Type of TiledLayer, 149
group element, groups.xml, 44
grouping functionalities
  improving class model, 344–345
groups
  device-specific preprocessing symbols, 390
  explicit groups, 51, 72
  groups for assembling resources, 70
  hierarchical ordering of, 72
  implicit groups, 41, 51, 72
groups attribute, build element, 367
groups element
  devices.xml, 41
  groups.xml, 44
groups.xml, 44–45
  defining capabilities and features, 48
  defining device groups in, 45
  defining supported libraries, 45
  device database file, 39
  explicit groups, 44
GUI (Graphical user interface), 417
  see also J2ME Polish GUI
GUI items
  see items

H

h.263 group
  assembling resources, 71
handler element, debug, 372
  activating log handlers, 130
  attributes, table of, 372
hard-coded values, 120
hardware
  differences between devices, 273–274
hasCommandKeyEvents feature
  device-specific preprocessing symbols, 390
  MIDP 2.0 devices supporting menu mode, 163
heap size
  Motorola devices, 287
  optimizing applications, 325
  Series 40 Nokia devices, 284
heaps
  JTWI specification, 278
HeapSize, 391
  device database, 43
  preprocessing symbols and variables, 115
  selecting target devices to build for, 83
height attribute
  DateFields, 226
  Gauge items, 223
  TextFields, 224
help
  getting help, 321
helper classes
  minimizing classes in JAR files, 345
hex value
  defining colors, 195
hideNotify method, Canvas
  detecting interruptions, 320
  pauseApp method, 321
  Series 40 Nokia devices, 284
hiding statements, 112
high-level GUI
  problems implementing, 308
high-level performance tuning, 329–334
  algorithms, 334
  architecture, 330–331
  networking, 332
  protocols, 331–332
  record stores, 332–334
  reducing abstraction, 330
  reusing and caching objects, 331
  threading, 331
HTTP networking
  networking problems, 311
    authentication, 312
    cookies, 312
    data protocols, 311
    sessions, 312
  permissions for signed MIDlets, 360
hyperlinks appearance mode, 186

I

iAppli platforms, 294
IBM's WEME virtual machine, 293
icon attribute, midlet element, 370
icon-image attribute
  exclusive ChoiceGroups, 217
  list items, 213
  multiple ChoiceGroups, 219
icon-image-align attribute
  exclusive ChoiceGroups, 217
  list items, 211, 213
  multiple ChoiceGroups, 219
IconItem class
  available dynamic styles, 186
icons
  Motorola devices, 287
  Samsung devices, 288
IDE plug-ins, 30
identifier element, devices.xml, 41
Identifier requirement
  target devices to build for, 83
Identifier variable, 391
IDEs, 8
  Eclipse, 20–22
  integrating J2ME Polish into, 19–26
  IntelliJ, 24–25
  JBuilder, 24
  NetBeans, 23–24
if attribute
  adding attribute for current target devices, 75
  applying filter for specific devices, 76
  compiler element, 374
  copier element, resources, 384
  debug element, 127–128, 371
  deviceRequirements element, 365
  emulator element, 388
  fileset element, resources, 382
  finalizer element, 387
  jad element, 386
  localization element, resources, 383
  midlet element, 370
  obfuscator element, 377
  packager element, 385
  parameter elements, 233
  parameter element, emulator, 389
  postcompiler element, 376
  preprocessor element, 373
  preverifier element, 381
  selecting devices to build for, 81
  source element, sources, 369
  sources element, 369
  variable element, 371
if directive, 105, 399
  branching code, 105
  capabilities, 51
  checking for multiple preprocessing symbols, 107
  checking for multiple symbols, 106
  checking for single preprocessing symbols, 105
  commenting out statement in if block, 105
  comparing variables, 106
  comparing variables and constants, 107
  nesting directives, 114
ifdef directive, 104, 399
  checking for single preprocessing symbols, 106
  commenting out statement in ifdef block, 105
ifndef directive, 104, 399
  checking for single preprocessing symbols, 106
image attribute
  foreground image, 210
  Gauge items, 223
  image background, 402
  pop-up ChoiceGroups, 221
image background, 402–403
Image class, 152
ImageFormat variable, 391
ImageItem class, 186
ImageItems
  designing, 215
ImageLoader class
  getting images from web server, 262
  integrating custom, 264
  loading images dynamically, 262
ImageLoader preprocessing variable, 164, 393
imageLoadStrategy attribute, build element, 368
images
  available dynamic styles, 186
  device-specific preprocessing symbols, 390
  JTWI specification, 278
  loading images dynamically, 261–265
  minimizing size using appropriate resources, 349
  setting a foreground image, 210
  solving common problems, 303
IMAPI (Instant Messages API)
  optional packages for MIDP devices, 277
IMEI (International Mobile Equipment Identity), 417
  device identification, 318
IMP (Information Module Profile), 275, 417
  J2ME profiles, 276
implementation phase, 30, 32
implicit groups, 41, 51, 72
import folder, 15
import statements
  fully qualified class names, using instead of, 95
  using correct, 170–171
  using game engine, 146
IMSI (International Mobile Subscriber Identity), 417
  device identification, 318
inactivetab style
  designing TabbedForms, 213
  predefined styles, 185
include directive, 105, 399
  including external code, 112
includeAntRuntime attribute, compiler element, 374
includeJavaRuntime attribute, compiler element, 374

includes attribute
  compiler element, 374
  fileset element, resources, 382
includesfile attribute, compiler element, 374
info element, build.xml, 363–364
  attributes, table of, 363–364
  building a MIDlet, 61
  specifying attributes, 74
info style, 184
infoUrl attribute, info section, 363
inheritance
  capabilities, 49
  changing class inheritance, 51, 119
  devices, 48
  parent libraries, 46
init target, 126
initialization
  handling custom items, 255
input
  direct input attribute, TextFields, 224
  InputTimeout variable, 165
  showInputInfo variable, 165
  useDirectInput symbol, 165
input modes
  configuring the TextField, 167
input title variable, 166
  localizing J2ME Polish GUI, 91
  title of TextBox, 397
InputStreams, Bluetooth
  Series 60 Nokia devices, 286
InputTimeout variable, TextField, 165, 395
insertion points
  style directives, 172
installation directory folders, 15
installations
  J2ME Polish, 4, 11–15
  J2SE, 7
  status codes, 35
  third-party tools, 15
  tracking number of times installed, 34
  Wireless Toolkit, 8
installNotify attribute, info section, 363
instance variables
  low-level performance tuning, 337
  this keyword, 21
int data type, Binary Editor, 141
integration
  integrating J2ME Polish into IDEs, 19
IntelliJ
  integrating J2ME Polish into, 24–25
interaction modes
  handling custom items, 255
interfaces
  design phase, 31
  designing user interfaces, 160
  directive including/excluding, 109
  GUI
    see J2ME Polish GUI
  interface concepts, 160
  reducing abstraction, 330
interruptions
  detecting, 320
intervals
  animationInterval symbol, 164
issues
  see troubleshooting
Item constructors
  insertion points for style directives, 172
items
  arranging items on screen, 206
  custom items, handling, 255–261
  designing, 215–228
  designing ChoiceGroups, 215–222
  designing DateFields, 226–227
  designing Focused item, 228
  designing Gauge items, 222–224
  designing ImageItems, 215
  designing StringItems, 215
  designing TextFields, 224–226
  designing Tickers, 227–228
  static styles, 184

J

J2EE (Java 2 Enterprise Edition), 7, 417
J2ME (Java 2 Micro Edition), 7, 418
  competitors, 282
J2ME applications
  build framework for, 30
J2ME market, 282
J2ME Polish
  application life cycle, 30
  downloading, 4
  forums, 321, 322
  installation directory folders, 15
  installing, 4, 11–15
  installing components, 13
  licensing, 11, 417
  running, 4
  sample applications, 15–17
    error messages, 17
    testing, 16
J2ME Polish GUI
  activating, 161–162
  backgrounds, 400–411
    circle background, 403–404
    image background, 402–403
    opening background, 408–409
    opening-round-rect background, 409–410
    pulsating background, 404–405
    pulsating-circle background, 406
    pulsating-circles background, 407–408
    round-rect background, 401–402
    round-tab background, 410–411
    simple background, 400–401
  backgrounds, creating custom, 265–269
    client-side Background class, 265–267
    integrating, 268–269
    server-side Background class, 267–268
  borders, 412–416
    circle border, 416
    creating custom, 269

round-rect border, 413
shadow border, 414
simple border, 412
top, bottom, left, and right borders, 415
changing appearance/logic of, 164
configuring, 162–170
commands, labels, and behavior, 164–167
different designs for application, 168–170
full-screen mode, 163–164
TextField, 167–168
with preprocessing variables and symbols, 167
controlling, 161–170
creating professional GUIs, 159
custom items, 248–261
applying a style, 256
designing, 256–261
designing custom item, 261
initialization, 255
interaction modes, 255
registering custom CSS attributes, 259
designing, 181–229
common design attributes, 189–199
extending styles, 187
for devices and device groups, 182–183
items, 215–228
reviewing CSS syntax, 187–188
screens, 199–215
using animations, 228–229
using dynamic, static, and predefined styles, 183–186
drawback, 160
extending, 248–269
images, loading dynamically, 261–265
introduction and warning, 159
problems implementing, 308
using high-level GUI, 308
using low-level GUI, 309
programming, 170–181
FramedForm, 176–178
porting MIDP 2.0 applications to MIDP 1.0 platforms, 173
setting styles, 171–173
SpriteItem, 178–181
TabbedForm, 174–176
using correct import statements, 170–171
using dynamic styles, 173
using predefined styles, 173
Scrollable List item, creating, 248–255
usePolishGui preprocessing variable, 166
J2ME Polish installer, 11
J2SE (Java 2 Standard Edition), 7, 418
installing, 7
JAD (Java Application Descriptor)
glossary of abbreviations, 418
JAD and Manifest attributes, 353–356
defining in messages.txt file, 88
device identification, 319
managing, packaging phase, 74–77
MIDP 1.0 attributes, 353–354
MIDP 2.0 attributes, 354–355
sorting and filtering attributes, 75–77
sorting with jadFilter element, 386
target XML attribute specifying, 75
troubleshooting Samsung devices, 288
vendor and carrier specific attributes, 355–356
Jad decompiler, 15
stack traces in emulators, 124
jad element, build section, 385–386
attributes, table of, 386
specifying attributes, 74
JAD files
configuring applications, 119
JTWI specification, 278
web servers configuring, 34
jadFilter element, 386
sorting and filtering JAD attributes, 75–76
default JAD filter, 77
JAM (Java Application Manager), 418
JAR (Java ARchive) files, 418
JTWI specification, 278
minimizing size of, 78, 344–350
handling resources, 349–350
improving class model, 344–348
minimizing number of classes, 344
obfuscating and packaging application, 350
using appropriate resources, 349
web servers configuring, 34
JAR packager, 78
JAR size
DoJa platforms, 294
Motorola devices, 287
variation between devices, 273
jarName attribute, info section, 364
adjusting JAR name, 89
localizations, 85
jarName variable, 394
jarUrl attribute, info section, 364
Java 2 SDK (Software Development Kit)
editions of, 7
"Java Compiler cannot be found"
sample application error messages, 17
Java line comment characters, 104
Java platforms
Sony Ericsson devices, 290
Java Verified initiative, 318
carrier modifications, 292
minimizing target devices, 84
permissions, 77
javac-target
compilation phase, 66
JavaConfiguration, 391
standard preprocessing symbols and variables, 115
device database, 43
selecting target devices to build for, 82
javacTarget attribute, build element, 368
compilation phase, 67
JavaPackage, 391
device database, 43
preprocessing symbols and variables, 115
selecting target devices to build for, 82

JavaPlatform, 391
  device database, 43
  preprocessing symbols and variables, 115
  selecting target devices to build for, 82
JavaProtocol, 391
  device database, 43
  preprocessing symbols and variables, 115
  selecting target devices to build for, 82
JavaRanch forum, 322
javax.microedition.lcdui package, 159
  configuring the TextField, 167
JAVA_HOME variable, 9
Jazelle, 293
Jbed platform, Esmertec's, 293
JBlend JVM, 293
  accessing native functionality, 320
JBuilder IDE
  download for, 8
  integrating J2ME Polish into, 24
JCP (Java Community Process), 418
JMFP library, 315
JNI (Java Native Interface)
  accessing native functionality, 320
JSR (Java Specification Process), 418
JTWI (Java Technology for the Wireless Industry), 418
  device-specific preprocessing symbols, 390
  differences between devices, 278–279
Juicer optimizer, 331
JVM (Java Virtual Machine), 418

K

keep element, obfuscator, 377–378
KEITAI-L mailing list, 322
key attribute, sign element, 387
keys
  charactersKey variables, 165–166
  charactersKeyPound variable, 166
  charactersKeyStar variable, 166
  generating a temporary key, 77
  invalid Locale calls, 89
  soft keys, 164
keystore attribute, sign element, 387
keytool command
  generating a temporary key, 77
kilobytes property function, 400
  transforming variables with, 118
KlassMaster obfuscator, 379
known issues
  see troubleshooting
KVM (Kilobyte Virtual Machine), 418
KVM-INTEREST mailing list, 322
KZIP packager, 15, 79–80
  parameters, 385

L

label style, 184
label-style attribute, 197
labels
  arguments of SpriteItem constructor, 179
  common design attributes, CSS, 197
  configuring, J2ME Polish GUI, 164–167
language
  ISO language code, 88
  localized language name, 89
LAPI (Location API)
  optional packages for MIDP devices, 277
layout attribute
  aligning items with, 192–193
  available layout values, 193
  structure of style definition, 189
layout method
  BitMapFontViewer class, 137
lcdui classes
  using correct import statements, 171
left animation
  screen change animations, 229
left border, 415
left layout
  aligning items with layout attribute, 193
leftcommand style, 204
leftframe style, 185
LeftSoftKey, 163, 392
length
  show-length attribute, TextFields, 225
less than (<) comparison operator, 108
level attribute
  debug element, 127, 371
  filter element, debug, 372
level files
  managing level files, 139
LG Electronics
  vendor characteristics, 290
  vendor-specific attributes, 355
libraries
  see device libraries
libraries element, build section
  integrating binary third-party APIs, 93
license attribute, info section, 364
licensing
  J2ME Polish, 11, 417
line attribute, compilerargs element, 376
List class
  available dynamic styles, 186
list elements
  insertion points for style directives, 172
list items
  creating scrollable list item, 248
List screen
  designing screen background, 200
listfiles attribute, compiler element, 374
lists
  additional attributes for list items, 213
  designing, 211
  exclusive lists, 211
  multiple lists, 211
  using text of currently focused list item as title, 211–212
local variables
  low-level performance tuning, 338
Locale class, 138
locale property, MIDP, 357

locales
  defining locales, 85
  invalid Locale calls, 89
  locale specific methods, 138
  localizing applications, 86
  resources folder, 85
  supporting several locales, 84
locales attribute
  localization element, resources, 383
  resources element, 382
localization
  adjusting JAR name, 89
  avoiding common mistakes, 89–90
  building localized applications, 84
    using locale for, 86
  currencies, 88
  dates, 88
  escaping special characters in translations, 89
  invalid Locale calls, 89
  localizing J2ME Polish GUI, 90–91
  managing translations, 85–88
  resources element controlling, 381
  setting localized variables, 88
  using locale specific resources, 72
  using localized attributes, 88
localization element, resources, 382–383
  attributes, table of, 383
  building localized applications, 84–85
  debugging applications using conditions, 98
  supporting several locales, 84
Location API
  permissions for signed MIDlets, 362
log handlers
  activating, 130
  creating, 131
  extending logging framework, 269–270
  RMS log handler, 130
log levels
  adding debug code for, 125
  custom log levels, 127
  enabling benchmark log level, 329
  enabling different, for classes/packages, 125, 127
  predefined levels, 127
  testing for specific log level, 125
  which levels apply when level set, 125
log viewer
  building and installing, 130
  filtering messages, 131
  finding shared record store, 130
logging
  exceptions, 129
  showing log automatically, 128
  showing log automatically on error, 127
  showing log manually, 129
  symbols for reading current setting, 397
  testing phase, 32
logging framework, 113, 123–131
  activating, 126–128
  adding debug code for log levels, 125
  adding exceptions, 124
  advantage of, 131
  controlling, 125–128
  deactivating, 125–128
  detecting if active, 129
  extending, 269–270
  forwarding log messages, 130
  logging messages, 123–124
  measuring performance on target devices, 328
  printing stack trace, 124
  stack traces of exceptions, 124
  viewing log on real devices, 128–130
logging messages, 123–124
  debug preprocessing directive, 123
  disadvantages, 123
  viewing logged messages, 123
LogHandler class
  creating log handlers, 131
LogViewerMidlet
  viewing log entries, 130
long data type
  Binary Editor, 141
loops
  low-level performance tuning, 337
  performance of game loop, 328
  unrolling, 337
low-level GUI
  problems implementing, 309
low-level optimizations, 325
low-level performance tuning, 335–338
  accelerating loops, 337
  access modifiers, 338
  containers, 335
  graphics, 335
  instance fields, 337
  loops, 337
  optimized arithmetic operations, 336
  precalculating data, 336
  switch statement, 336–337
lowercase property function, 400
  transforming variables with, 118

M

M3GAPI (Mobile 3D Graphics API)
  optional packages for MIDP devices, 277
Mac OS X
  bin folder, 139
  Wireless Toolkit for, 8
mailing lists, 322
Make
  build tools, 55
Manifest attributes
  see JAD and Manifest attributes
manifestFilter element, 386
  default Manifest filter, 77
  Manifest-Version as first element, 76
  sorting and filtering Manifest attributes, 75–76
manufacturers
  see vendors

margin attribute
  CSS box model, 192
  defining simple margins, 192
  structure of style definition, 189
Mark command variable, 166
  label for Mark command, 393
  localizing J2ME Polish GUI, 90
market
  J2ME market, 282
  telecom market, 280–281
MathFP library, 315–316
max-diameter attribute
  pulsating-circle background, 406
  pulsating-circles background, 407
max-width attribute
  achieving a tabular arrangement with, 207
  max-width CSS attribute, 197
  structure of style definition, 189
maximum attribute, dropping view, 208
MaxJarSize, 392
  device database, 43
  preprocessing symbols and variables, 115
maxLights property
  Mobile 3D Graphics API, 359
maxperiode attribute, dropping view, 208
MaxRecordStoreSize variable, 392
maxSpriteCropDimension property
  Mobile 3D Graphics API, 359
maxTextureDimension property
  Mobile 3D Graphics API, 359
maxTransformsPerVertex property
  Mobile 3D Graphics API, 359
maxViewportDimension property
  Mobile 3D Graphics API, 359
MBSAPI (Mobile Broadcast Service API)
  optional packages for MIDP devices, 278
megabytes property function, 400
  transforming variables with, 118
memory consumption
  measuring, 341–342
  reducing, 341–344
  reducing number of objects, 342
  using recursion, 343
memory leaks, 343
memoryInitialSize attribute, compiler element, 375
memoryMaximumSize attribute, compiler element, 375
menu bars
  designing, 202
  extended menu bars
    activating, 203
    designing, 202, 204
    predefined styles for, 204
  menubar style, 204
menu mode
  MIDP 2.0 devices supporting, 163
  running game in full-screen mode, 147–148
  using GUI in full-screen mode, 163
menu style
  designing menus, 200
  predefined styles, 184
menubar style, 204
  additional attributes of, 204
menubar-color
  designing menu bar, 202
menuItem style
  designing menus, 200
  predefined styles, 184
menus
  designing, 200
message directive, 105, 399
  analyzing preprocessing phase, 112
messages
  defining translations in resources/messages.txt, 86
  displaying, 136
  forwarding log messages, 130–131
  logging, 138
  retrieving localized, 138
  specifying priority level of, 124
  using custom fonts for displaying, 133
  viewing logged, 123
messages attribute, localization element, 383
messages.txt file
  defining default translations, 87
  defining JAD and Manifest attributes in, 88
  defining translations in, 86
  defining variables in, 117
  localizing J2ME Polish GUI, 91
  setting localized variables, 88
methods
  removing to improve class model, 345
MIAPI (Mobile Internationalization API)
  optional packages for MIDP devices, 277
MicroEdition-*Xyz* attributes
  MIDP 1.0 platforms, 353
microedition.*xyz* properties
  system properties, 357–358
MicroFloat library, 315–316
midi group
  assembling resources, 71
midlet element, build.xml, 369–370
  attributes, table of, 370
midlet-*n* variable, classes, 398
MIDlet-*Xyz* attributes
  MIDP 1.0 platforms, 353
  MIDP 2.0 platforms, 354
  vendor-specific attributes, 356
MIDlet.getAppProperty
  configuring applications, 119
MIDlets, 418
  applying CSS styles in MIDlet constructor, 63
  building with J2ME Polish, 60
  certificates, 77
  creating "Hello World" application, 58–64
  detecting interruptions, 320
  execution of, 279

JTWI specification, 278
LogViewerMidlet, 130
MIDP 1.0 attributes, 353
MIDP 2.0 attributes, 354
permissions for signed MIDlets, 360–362
showing a menu, 58
signing MIDlets, 77–78, 317
SysInfo MIDlet, 143
trusted MIDlets, 317
midlets element, build.xml, 369–370
MIDletX-*Xyz* attributes
vendor-specific attributes, 355
MIDP (Mobile Information Device Profile), 275, 418
device-specific preprocessing symbols, 390
J2ME profiles, 276
optional packages for, 276–278
MIDP 1.0 devices
porting a MIDP 2.0 game to, 152–157
using game engine for, 145
MIDP 1.0 platforms
attributes, 353–354
MIDP platforms, 293
porting MIDP 2.0 applications to, 173
updating application, 36
writing portable code, 295
MIDP 2.0 devices
porting game to MIDP 1.0 device, 152–157
using game engine for, 150
MIDP 2.0 platforms
attributes, 354–355
MIDP platforms, 293
porting to MIDP 1.0 platforms, 173
security permissions, 360, 362
updating application, 36
writing portable code, 295
midp groups
assembling resources, 70
midp2 view
arranging items on screen, 209
MIDPSysInfo MIDlet, 143
MIDxlet-*Xyz* attributes
vendor-specific attributes, 356
min-diameter attribute
pulsating-circle background, 406
pulsating-circles background, 407
min-width attribute
achieving a tabular arrangement with, 207
structure of style definition, 189
mixing property, MMAPI, 357
MMAPI (Mobile Media API)
optional packages for MIDP devices, 276–277
playing background music with, 313
mmapi group
assembling resources, 71
MMAPI support
JTWI specification, 279
MMS (Multimedia Message Service), 418
permissions for signed MIDlets, 361
Mobile 3D Graphics API
properties, 359–360
Mobile Game Developer forum, 322
mode attribute, Gauge class, 223
modifiers
low-level performance tuning, 338
modules
design phase, 31
Modulo operations
optimizing applications, 325
Mot-*Xyz* attributes
vendor-specific attributes, 355
Motorola
device identification, 318
known device issues
available method, InputStream, 304
vendor characteristics, 287–288
vendor-specific attributes, 355
vendor-specific emulators, 10
mp3 group
assembling resources, 71
mpeg-4 group
assembling resources, 71
MSA (Mobile Service Architecture)
differences between devices, 278–279
MSAPI (Mobile Sensor API)
optional packages for MIDP devices, 278
MSISDN (Mobile Subscriber ISDN Number)
device identification, 319
MTA (Mobile Telephony API)
optional packages for MIDP devices, 278
MUICAPI (Mobile User Interface Customization API)
optional packages for MIDP devices, 278
multimedia
JTWI specification, 278–279
Multimedia Messaging Service (MMS)
deployment phase, 34
multiple ChoiceGroups
additional attributes for items in, 219–220
checkboxes and, 219
designing, 219–221
multiple devices
building for, 80–84
multiple lists, 211

N

name attribute
copier element, resources, 384
finalizer element, 387
handler element, debug, 372
info section, 364
jad element, 386
midlet element, 370
obfuscator element, 377
packager element, 384
parameter element, emulator, 389
parameter element, obfuscator, 378
parameter element, preprocessor, 233
postcompiler element, 376
preprocessor element, 372
preverifier element, 380
registering custom CSS attributes, 260

requirement element, 365
using registered extension in, 236
variable element, 370
name element
apis.xml, 45
bugs.xml, 47
groups.xml, 44
registering extensions for several projects, 236
vendors.xml, 44
Name variable, 392
naming conventions
Cascading Style Sheets, 187
colors, 194
directories for specific devices, 70
dynamic styles, 185
Eclipse IDE, 21
predefined styles, 184
referring to J2ME Polish properties, 238
native functions
accessing native functionality, 320
needsNokiaUiForSystemAlerts bug, 306
nesting preprocessing directives, 114
NetBeans IDE
download for, 8
implementation phase, 32
integrating J2ME Polish into, 23–24
netiquette, 321
networking
high-level performance tuning, 332
networking problems, 310
Bluetooth, 310
HTTP networking, 311
short message service (SMS), 310
newline-after layout
aligning with layout attribute, 193
newline-before layout
aligning with layout attribute, 193
next directive, 105, 399
Nextel
carrier modifications, 292
Nokia
device identification, 319
main features of Nokia devices, 285
Series 40 devices, 284
Series 60 devices, 286
Series 80 devices, 287
Series 90 devices, 287
vendor characteristics, 283–287
vendor forums, 322
vendor-specific attributes, 356
vendor-specific emulators, 10
nokia-ui group
assembling resources, 71
nospace property function, 400
not (!) operator
boolean operators for evaluating terms, 107
XML encoding, 73
not equal to (!=) comparison operator, 108
not nested element
deviceRequirements element, 365
nowarn attribute, compiler element, 375
number attribute, midlet element, 370
number property function, 400
transforming variables with, 118
numTextureUnits property
Mobile 3D Graphics API, 359

O

O2
carrier modifications, 292
ObfuscateFlowLevel parameter
KlassMaster obfuscator, 379
obfuscation, 94–96
additional Ant properties for antcall obfuscator, 245
combining several obfuscators, 95, 378
configuring an obfuscator, 378
excluding dynamic classes from, 377
extending build phases, 244
integrating unsupported obfuscators, 96
minimizing size of JAR files, 350
obfuscators, 378–379
specific obfuscator settings, 378–380
useDefaultPackage option, 95
using default package, 95
yguard Ant task, 237
obfuscation phase, 67
build phase extensions, 232
obfuscator element, build.xml, 377
antcall obfuscator, 244
attributes, table of, 377
debugging applications using conditions, 98
obfuscators
DashO Pro obfuscator, 379
KlassMaster obfuscator, 379
ProGuard obfuscator, 378
RetroGuard obfuscator, 379
yGuard obfuscator, 379
object-oriented approach
design phase, 31
offset attribute
shadow border, 414
OK command variable, 166
label for OK command, 393
localizing J2ME Polish GUI, 90
opening background, 408–409
opening-round-rect background, 409–410
operating systems
Motorola devices, 287
Nokia devices, 285
Siemens devices, 289
Sony Ericsson devices, 290
optimization phase, 31, 33
optimize attribute, compiler element, 375
optimizing applications, 325–350
game engine, 146
heap size, 325
JAR file size, 344–350
low-level optimizations, 325
memory consumption, 341–344
overview, 325–326

performance improvements, 326–341
measuring performance, 326–329
perceived performance, 338–341
performance tuning, 329–338
target device constraints, 325
optionalPermissions attribute, info section, 364
options command variable, 166
label for Options command, 393
localizing J2ME Polish GUI, 90
options-image attribute, menubar, 204
or (||) operator
boolean operators for evaluating terms, 107
or nested element
deviceRequirements element, 365
OS (operating system)
preprocessing symbols and variables, 115
OS variable, 392
OTA (Over The Air) provisioning, 418
OTA download, deployment phase, 33

P

p selector
dynamic form p style, 186
StringItem class, 186
package attribute
filter element, debug, 127, 372
packager element, 384–385
attributes, table of, 384
extending build phases, 246
using third-party packagers, 78
packagers
7-Zip packager, 79
custom packagers, 246
KZIP packager, 79
third-party packagers, 78
packages
optional for MIDP devices, 276–278
packaging phase, 68–80
build phase extensions, 232
managing JAD and Manifest attributes, 74–77
sorting and filtering attributes, 75–77
minimizing size of JAR files, 350
resource assembling, 68–73
fine tuning, 72–73
including group specific resources, 70–71
selecting and loading resources, 72
using locale specific resources, 72
using vendor/device specific resources, 70
signing MIDlets, 77–78
third-party packagers, 78–80
padding attribute
CSS box model, 192
defining percentage padding, 192
structure of style definition, 189
paint method
BitMapFontViewer class, 137
StringListItem class, 255
paintScreen method
game in full-screen mode, 148
PAPI (Payment API)
optional packages for MIDP devices, 277
parameter element
emulator, 389
obfuscator, 378
packager, 385
preprocessor, 233
preverifier, 381
parameters
invalid Locale calls, 90
parent element
apis.xml, 46
devices.xml, 42
groups.xml, 44
passes parameter, 7-Zip packager, 79, 385
password attribute, sign element, 387
path attribute, compilerargs element, 376
path element, apis.xml, 46
PATH variable, setting, 9
pauseApp method
detecting interruptions, 320
hideNotify method supported, 321
Series 40 Nokia devices, 284
PBP (Personal Basis Profile) devices
J2ME profiles, 276
PDAPI
optional packages for MIDP devices, 277
performance
improving, 326–341
measuring performance, 326–329
on target devices, 327–329
typical game loop, 328
WTK emulator, 326–327
optimization phase, 33
perceived performance, improving, 338–341
ensuring responsiveness, 340
feedback to users, 339–340
splash screen, 339
performance tuning, 329–338
high-level, 329–334
low-level, 335–338
permissions
Java Verified initiative, 77
MIDP 2.0 security, 360, 362
signed MIDlets, 360–362
trusted MIDlets, 317
permissions attribute, info section, 364
Personal Java profile
accessing native functionality, 320
PIM (Personal Information Management) API, 418
optional packages for MIDP devices, 277
permissions for signed MIDlets, 362
pixel-level collision detection
working around limitations of game engine, 150
plain appearance mode, 186
plain layout
aligning items with layout attribute, 193
platform property, MIDP, 357
platforms
DoJa platform, 294
MIDP platform, 293
mobile Java platform, 292–294
WIPI, 294

platforms.xml
device database file, 39
plug-ins
Eclipse plug-ins, 22
plus sign
selecting target devices to build for, 82
PNG (Portable Network Graphics), 418
PNG-Image data type
Binary Editor, 141
Pngcrush, 15, 349
PNGGauntlet, 15, 349
PNGOUT, 15, 349
pointer events
checking for, 51
pointerPressed method
StringListItem class, 255
polish.css file
see also CSS (Cascading Style Sheets)
backgrounds section, 189
using moving background, 268
borders section, 189
building a MIDlet, 62
cascading character of, 183
colors section, 189, 194
comments, 188
complete polish.css file, 189
custom item, designing, 261
defining CSS style in resources/polish.css file, 172
design definitions, 181
devices and device groups, designing for, 183
dynamic styles, 185
fonts section, 189
structure of, 189
style definition, structure of, 189, 191
basic style definition in resources, 183
polish.*xyz* configuration variables, 392–397
polish.*xyz* preprocessing symbols, 390
polish.*xyz* preprocessing variables, 391–392
polish.*xyz* symbols for reading current setting, 397
polishDir attribute, build element, 368
popup
available dynamic styles, 186
pop-up ChoiceGroups
additional attributes for items in, 221
designing, 221–222
porting
DoJa platforms, 294
interface concepts, 160
MIDP 2.0 to MIDP 1.0, 152–157, 173
using high-level GUI, 308
writing portable code, 294–303
postcompilation phase
build phase extensions, 232, 244
postcompiler element, build.xml, 376–377
attributes, table of, 376
PP (Personal Profile) devices
J2ME profiles, 276
predefined colors, 193
transparent, 194
predefined styles
designing GUI, 183, 184–185
naming conventions, 184
programming GUI, 173
supported predefined styles, 184
preferences attribute, emulator element, 388
preprocessing, 101–121
adding debug code for log levels, 125
avoiding problems, 121, 305–307
capabilities, 51–52
changing class inheritance, 119
configuring applications, 74, 119
configuring preprocessor extension, 233
using custom preprocessor, 243
custom preprocessor, creating, 239–243
defining symbols and variables, 114
embedded translations after, 87
hard-coded values, using, 120
J2ME apps. on multiple devices, 102
libraries
using optional/device-specific, 118
parent libraries, 46
reasons for, 101–104
reducing abstraction, 330
target devices, optimizing, 51
transforming variables with property functions, 117
using and avoiding interfaces with, 330
writing portable code, 298–300
preprocessing directives, 104–114, 398–399
boolean operators for evaluating terms, 107
hiding statements, 112
include/exclude classes/interfaces, 109
including external code, 112
Java line comment characters, 104
logging framework, 113
nesting directives, 114
setting CSS styles, 113
preprocessing phase, 66
analyzing preprocessing phase, 112
build phase extensions, 232
preprocessing symbols
checking for multiple, 106
checking for single, 105
configuring GUI, 164
defining/removing, 109
symbol element, apis.xml, 45
table listing, 389–390
using, 114
preprocessing variables
comparing variables, 106, 108
comparing variables and constants, 107
configuration variables, 392–397
configuring GUI, 164, 166
controlling GUI, 161
defining/removing, 109
device-specific, 390–392
including variable values in code, 110
optimizing game engine, 146
overriding attribute values, 74, 353

setting variables for devices, 117
specifying attributes, 74
using, 114
using several variable values individually, 111
Preprocessor class
implementing, 239–243
preprocessor element, build.xml, 372–373
attributes, table of, 372
preverification phase, 68
build phase extensions, 232, 245
implementing custom preverifier, 245
skipping the obfuscation step, 245
WIPI platforms, 294
preverifier element, build.xml, 380–381
attributes, table of, 380
println statement
viewing logged messages, 123
priority level, messages, 124
problems
see troubleshooting
profile attribute, info section, 364
profilers
enabling WTK profiler, 326
profiles
differences between devices, 275–276
differentiating between, 276
J2ME profiles, 276
Nokia devices, 285
Siemens devices, 289
Sony Ericsson devices, 291
profiles property, MIDP, 357
programming
game programming, 145–157
progress indicators
see Gauge class/items
ProGuard obfuscator, 15, 378
combining several obfuscators, 95
obfuscating applications, 94
project tag, build.xml, 56
projects
registering extensions for several projects, 236
properties
Bluetooth API properties, 358–359
Mobile 3D Graphics API, 359–360
naming conventions, 238
retrieving from a style, 259
runtime properties, 356–360
system properties, 356–358
property functions
build phase extensions, 232
creating custom, 118, 248
extending build phases, 248
table listing, 399–400
transforming variables with, 117
protocols
high-level performance tuning, 331–332
public access modifier
low-level performance tuning, 338
pulsating background, 404–405
pulsating-circle background, 406
pulsating-circles background, 407–408
PushRegistry
permissions for signed MIDlets, 361
troubleshooting Siemens devices, 290

Q

question mark
attribute name ending with, 76
quotation marks
escaping special characters in translations, 89

R

radio boxes
exclusive ChoiceGroups, 216
radiobox
available dynamic styles, 186
radiobox-plain attribute, ChoiceGroups, 217
radiobox-selected attribute, ChoiceGroups, 217
real devices
tracking bugs on, 127
tracking errors on, 128
viewing log on real devices, 128–130
Record Management System
see RMS
record stores
filtering and sorting, 332–333
creating temporary objects by, 332
high-level performance tuning, 332–334
recording property, MMAPI, 357
recursion
memory consumption, 343
reflection
dynamic coding, 295
repeat attribute
image background, 403
pulsating background, 405
repeat-animation attribute
dropping view, 208
shuffle view, 209
repeatAnimation
SpriteItem constructor, 179
replacePropertiesWithoutDirective attribute
build element, 368
requirement element, deviceRequirements, 365
requirement elements
checking capabilities, 83
selecting devices to build for, 81
selecting target devices to build for, 82
resource assembling, packaging phase, 68–73
automatic, 303
device database, 50
distinguishing between formats, 72–73
fine tuning, 72–73
fileset element, 73
including group specific resources, 70–71
resources element controlling, 381
screen sizes, 274
selecting and loading resources, 72
solving common problems, 303
using locale specific resources, 72
using vendor/device specific resources, 70

resourcecopier element
  build phase extensions, 232
resources
  decreasing size of, 349
  loading array data from resource file, 348
  minimizing size of JAR files, 349–350
  reading incorrectly, 304
  reading, using defensive techniques, 305
  reducing, 349–350
  removing, 350
  removing redundant information, 349
  renaming, 383
  Series 40 Nokia devices, 284
  solving common problems, 303
  using appropriate resources, 349
resources directory
  directories for specific devices, 70
  group specific resources, 70
  groups for assembling resources, 70
  hierarchical ordering of resources, 72
  selecting resources for target devices, 50
resources element
  copying and transforming resources, 245
  renaming resources, 246
resources element, build.xml, 381–382
  attributes, table of, 382
resources folder, 16
  loading images dynamically, 261
  locales, 85
  managing data files in, 69
  resource assembling, 68
  saving definition files, 141
  specify which folder is used as, 69
  subdirectories, 72
  switching used resources, 168
resources.txt file
  defining variables in, 117
resources2 folder, 16
responsiveness
  improving perceived performance, 340
RetroGuard obfuscator, 379
return statements
  hiding statements, preprocessing, 112
reusing objects
  high-level performance tuning, 331
reverse engineering
  obfuscation, 67, 94
RGB data
  porting low-level graphics operations, 152, 153
  troubleshooting Sony Ericsson devices, 291
RGB value
  defining colors, 195
right animation
  screen change animations, 229
right border, 415
right layout
  aligning items with layout attribute, 193
rightcommand style, 204
rightframe style, 185
RightSoftKey variable, 163, 392
RIM BlackBerry
  device identification, 319
  vendor characteristics, 291
  vendor forums, 322
RMS (Record Management System), 418
RMS log handler, 130
RMS log viewer
  filtering messages, 131
root certificates, 318
root directory, 15
rotation and reflection functionality
  porting low-level graphics operations, 153
round-rect background, 401–402
round-rect border, 413
round-tab background, 410–411
runtime properties, 356–360
  Bluetooth API properties, 358–359
  Mobile 3D Graphics API, 359–360
  system properties, 356–358

S

sample applications, 15
  error messages, 17
  testing, 16
samples directory, 15
Samsung
  vendor characteristics, 288–289
  vendor forums, 322
  vendor-specific emulators, 10
scale-factor attribute, list items, 213
scale-steps attribute, list items, 213
scaling functionality
  porting low-level graphics, 153
Screen constructors
  style directive insertion points, 173
screen size
  Nokia devices, 285
    Series 40, 284
    Series 60, 286
    Series 80, 287
    Series 90, 287
  Siemens devices, 289
  solving common problems, 303
  Sony Ericsson devices, 290
screen-change-animation attribute, 229
  Series 90 Nokia devices, 287
ScreenChangeAnimation, 395
ScreenHeight, 392
  selecting target devices to build for, 82
screens
  arranging items on, 206
    dropping view, 208
    midp2 view, 209–210
    shuffle view, 209
    using tables, 206–207
  designing, 199–215
    Focused item, 228
    forms, 213
    FramedForms, 214
    lists, 211
    menus, 200

menu bars, 200, 202
screen background, 199
scroll indicator, 210
TabbedForms, 213
TextBoxes, 215
titles, 200
foreground image, setting, 210
FullScreen preprocessing variable, 166
JTWI specification, 278
programming FramedForm, 176
resource assembling, 274
screens used, 281
setScreenStateListener method
FramedForm, 177
TabbedForm, 174
static styles, 184
using GUI in full-screen mode, 163–164
ScreenSize, 392
device database, 42
groups for assembling resources, 71
preprocessing symbols and variables, 115
selecting target devices to build for, 82
ScreenWidth, 392
selecting target devices to build for, 82
ScriptFile parameter
DashO Pro obfuscator, 380
KlassMaster obfuscator, 379
scroll indicator, 210
setting color of scrolling indicator, 213
scrollable list item, 248
second-color attribute
pulsating-circles background, 407
security
see permissions
securityDomain attribute, emulator element, 388
Select command variable, 166
label for Select command, 393
localizing J2ME Polish GUI, 90
select-image attribute, menubar, 204
SelectionListenerImplementation
using and avoiding interfaces with preprocessing, 331
selectors
CSS declaration, 187
serial connections
permissions for signed MIDlets, 361
Series 40 Nokia devices, 284, 285
Development Platform 2.0, 284
Series 60 Nokia devices, 285, 286
activating the GUI, 162
Feature Packs 1, 2, and 3, 286
Series 80 Nokia devices, 285, 287
Series 90 Nokia devices, 285, 287
sessions
HTTP networking, 312
set method
accepting parameters in build extensions, 233
additional TabbedForm methods, 174
setFrameSequence method
SpriteItem, 178
setFullScreenMode method, Canvas class
avoiding known issues using preprocessing, 305–306
setParameters method
accepting parameters in build extensions, 233
configuring extension with conditional parameters, 234
setScreenStateListener method
additional FramedForm methods, 177
additional TabbedForm methods, 174
setStyle method
integrating CSS into custom items, 259
shadow border, 414
shared record store
log viewer finding, 130
short data type
Binary Editor, 141
short message service (SMS)
networking problems, 310
show-image-and-text attribute, menubar, 204
show-length attribute, TextFields, 225
show-value attribute, Gauge class, 223
showDecompiledStackTrace attribute
emulator element, 388
showInputInfo variable, 165, 395
showLog method, 129
showLogOnError attribute, debug element, 127, 371
showing log automatically, 128
shrink layout
aligning items with layout attribute, 193
shuffle view, 209
Siemens
55/65/75 groups, 289
device identification, 318
SX1, 289
vendor characteristics, 289–290
vendor forums, 322
vendor-specific emulators, 10
sign element, build.xml, 387
attributes, table of, 387
signing MIDlets, 77
signed MIDlets
permissions for, 360–362
signing
minimizing number of target devices, 84, 318
signing MIDlets, 317
SIM (Subscriber Identity Module), 418
SIM card, device identification, 318
simple background, 400–401
simple border, 412
SIMPLEAPI
optional packages for MIDP devices, 277
SIPAPI (Session Initiation API)
optional packages for MIDP devices, 277
size attribute
available font attributes, 196
skipArgumentCheck variable, 164, 394
SMS (Short Message Service), 418
permissions for signed MIDlets, 361
smsc property, WMAPI, 358

SOAP
    networking issues, 311
soft keys, 164
    dynamic coding, 297
    implementing low-level GUI, 309
    using correct keycodes for, 309
solution element, bugs.xml, 47
Sony Ericsson
    avoiding known issues using preprocessing, 305
    device identification, 318
    vendor characteristics, 290–291
    vendor forums, 322
    vendor-specific emulators, 10
SoundFormat, 392
    device database, 43
    preprocessing symbols and variables, 115
    selecting target devices to build for, 83
sounds
    playing background music with MMAPI, 313
    solving common problems, 313
source attribute, compiler element, 375
source code
    implementing Preprocessor class, 241–243
    translating into binary bytecode, 66
source files
    writing portable code, 300–303
source element, sources, 369
    attributes, table of, 369
    using different source files, 300
sourceDir attribute, build element, 368
    integrating source code third-party APIs, 92
sourceDir variable, 398
sourcepath attribute, compiler element, 375
sourcepathref attribute, compiler element, 375
sources element, build.xml, 369
    attributes, table of, 369
Spacer class
    available dynamic styles, 186
spaces
    available dynamic styles, 186
speed attribute
    dropping view, 208
    shuffle view, 209
splash screen
    improving perceived performance, 339
splitImage variable, TiledLayer, 396
Sprint
    carrier modifications, 292
Sprite transformations
    working around limitations of game engine, 151
SpriteItem class
    arguments of SpriteItem constructor, 179
    available dynamic styles, 186
    programming SpriteItem, 178–181
    setFrameSequence method, 178
sprites
    arguments of SpriteItem constructor, 179
    device-specific preprocessing symbols, 390
    troubleshooting Sony Ericsson devices, 291
src folder, 16
srcdir attribute
    compiler element, 375
    build element, 268
SSL connections
    permissions for signed MIDlets, 361
stack trace
    logging framework printing, 123–124
stack traces
    in emulators, 124
    of exceptions, 124
start-color attribute
    pulsating background, 405
start-height attribute
    opening background, 408
    opening-round-rect background, 409
state
    determining internal application state, 123
statements
    hiding, 112
static final variables
    J2ME apps. on multiple devices, 102
static modifier
    using access modifiers, 338
static styles
    designing GUI, 183–184
    dynamic styles compared, 64
    integrating CSS into custom items, 256
status codes
    installations, 35
step attribute
    pulsating-circles background, 407
    Tickers, 227
steps attribute
    opening background, 408
    opening-round-rect background, 409
    pulsating background, 405
StorageSize, 392
    device database, 43
    preprocessing symbols and variables, 115
streamable.*xyz* properties
    system properties, 357
String entries field
    implementing StringListItem class, 255
StringBuffers
    memory consumption, 344
StringItem class
    available dynamic styles, 186
StringItems
    designing StringItems, 215
StringListItem class
    creating scrollable list item, 248
    designing custom item, 261
strings
    creating unnecessary, 343
    StringBuffer reducing temporary objects, 343
    storing array data in, 347
stroke-style attribute
    circle border, 416
style attribute
    available font attributes, 196

style definition
  designing exclusive ChoiceGroups, 217
  structure of, 189–191
style directive, 105, 399
  applying desired design styles, 171
  designing ChoiceGroups, 216
  dynamic styles, 185
  insertion points for, 172
  setting CSS styles, 113
  specifying styles directly for GUI items, 182
  static styles, 184
  using dynamic styles, 173
styles
  see also CSS styles
  applying desired design styles, 171
  basic style definition in resources/polish.css, 183
  design definitions, 181
  designing GUI
    dynamic, static, and predefined styles, 183–186
    extending styles, 182, 187
  handling custom items, 256
  predefined styles, 184
  programming GUI
    setting styles, 171–173
    dynamic, and predefined styles, 173
  retrieving a property from a style, 259
  simple style definition, 182
  specifying styles directly for GUI items, 182
  static styles, 184
supportAntialiasing property, M3GAPI, 359
supportDithering property, M3GAPI, 359
supportLocalCameraLighting property, M3GAPI, 360
supportMipmapping property, M3GAPI, 360
supportPerspectiveCorrection property, M3GAPI, 360
supports.*xyz* properties
  system properties, 357
supportsPolishGui attribute
  device element, 42
supportTrueColor property, M3GAPI, 360
suppressClearCommand variable, 165, 395
suppressCommands variable, 165, 395
suppressDeleteCommand variable, 165, 395
suppressMarkCommands variable, 165, 392
suppressSelectCommands variable, 165, 393
SVGAPI (Scalable 2D Vector Graphics API)
  optional packages for MIDP devices, 277
switch statement
  low-level performance tuning, 336–337
SX1
  Siemens devices, 289
Symbian
  vendor-specific emulators, 10
  known device issues
    available method, InputStream, 304
Symbian operating system
  MIDP platforms, 293
symbol element, apis.xml, 45
symbols
  defining, 114
  preprocessing symbols
    checking for multiple, 106
    checking for single, 105
    device-specific, 389–390
    using standard, 114
  setting, 115
  symbols for reading current setting, 397
symbols attribute, build element, 368
  defining symbols, 115
synchronization
  ArrayList class, 134
  using access modifiers, 338
SysInfo MIDlet, 143
  testing capabilities of devices, 143
system properties, 356–358
  assuming defined, 357
System.out stream
  viewing logged messages, 123

T

T-Mobile
  carrier modifications, 292
tabbar style
  designing TabbedForms, 213
  predefined styles, 184
TabbedForm class
  additional methods, 174
  available dynamic styles, 186
  illustrated, 176
  programming TabbedForm, 174–176
  using, 174, 214
TabbedForms
  designing, 213
tables
  arranging items on screen, 206–207
  attributes for table arrangements, 206
target attribute
  compiler element, 375
  copier element, resources, 384
  finalizer element, 387
  jad element, 386
  packager element, 385
  postcompiler element, 376
  preprocessor element, 372
  preverifier element, 381
target dependencies, Ant, 58
target devices
  see also devices
  adding attribute for current, 75
  adjusting J2ME apps. to work on multiple, 101
  checking capabilities of, 103
  device-specific preprocessing symbols, 390
  information about specific devices, 49
  measuring performance on, 327–329
  minimizing number of, 83–84
  minimizing size of JAR files, 344–350
  optimizing, 51
  optimizing applications, 325

- selecting, 49–50
- selecting devices to build for, 80–83
- selecting for build phase, 65–66
- selecting resources for, 50
- targetable devices, 66
- with integrated camera, 273

target XML attribute
- specifying attributes, 75

targets
- Ant, 55
- build.xml file, 56
  - invoking, 57

taskdef element, build.xml
- building a MIDlet, 61
- integrating custom background, 268

tasks
- Ant, 55
- build.xml file, 56

TCP connections
- permissions for signed MIDlets, 361

telecom market, 280–281
- mobile sales European and worldwide, 281

tempdir attribute, compiler element, 375

temporary objects
- creating by filtering/sorting record store, 332
- reducing number of objects, 342–343

Term requirement
- selecting target devices to build for, 83

test target
- activating/deactivating logging framework, 126

testing
- testing capabilities of devices, 143

testing phase
- application life cycle, 31–32

text
- fitting text within display area, 133
- painting text, 137
- splitting text into String array, 135
- wrapping text to fit display area, 133

TextBox class
- available dynamic styles, 186

TextBoxes
- designing, 215
- using correct import statements, 171

TextField class
- available dynamic styles, 186
- configuring, 167–168
- configuring TextField commands, 168
- configuring GUI, 167–168
- preprocessing variables, 165–166

TextFields
- additional attributes for, 224
- designing, 224–226

texts
- dynamic form p style, 186

TextUtil class, 135–136
- fitting text within display area, 133
- wrapping text to fit display area, 133

third-party APIs, 92–94

third-party packagers, 78–80

this keyword
- naming conventions, 21

threads
- DoJa platforms, 294
- high-level performance tuning, 331
- JTWI specification, 278
- synchronizing ArrayList class, 134

Tickers
- additional attribute for, 227
- designing Tickers, 227–228

TiledLayer
- back buffer optimization, 148–149
- defining Grid Type of a TiledLayer, 149
- splitting image into single tiles, 149

time zones
- JTWI specification, 278

timeouts
- InputTimeout preprocessing symbol, 165

TinyLine
- integrating binary third-party APIs, 93

title style, 184

titles
- designing titles, 200
- input preprocessing variable, 166
- using text of currently focused list item as, 211–212

TLS connections
- permissions for signed MIDlets, 361

todo directive, 105, 399
- analyzing preprocessing phase, 112

tools
- installing, 15
- stand-alone tools, 30

top animation
- screen change animations, 229

top border, 415

top layout
- aligning items with layout attribute, 193

topframe style, 185

trace attribute, emulator element, 388

translations
- defining translations, 87–88
  - in resources/messages.txt, 86
- embedded after preprocessing, 87
- escaping special characters in, 89
- inserting in application, 86–87
- localizing J2ME Polish GUI, 91
- managing, 85–88
- setting localized variables, 88
- using localized attributes, 88

translucent backgrounds
- porting low-level graphics operations, 153
- using for currently focused item, 401

transparent color
- alpha blending, 195
- designing normal menu bar, 202
- predefined colors, 194

TransparentTileColor variable, 396
- activating back buffer optimization, 149

traverse method
 handling custom items, 256
 implementing StringListItem class, 255
troubleshooting
 avoiding known issues, 304–308
 avoiding problems, 121
 common problems, 303–321
 defensive programming, 304–305
 device identification, 318–321
 floating-point calculations, 314–317
 getting help, 321–322
 LG Electronics devices, 290
 Motorola devices, 287
 networking, 310–312
 Nokia devices, 284, 286
 Samsung devices, 288
 Siemens devices, 290
 Sony Ericsson devices, 291
 sounds, 313–314
 trusted MIDlets, 317–318
 user interface, 308–310
 using appropriate resources, 303
True Type font
 converting into bitmap font, 142
TrueTones sound
 porting sound playback, 155
trusted applications, 77
trusted MIDlets
 permissions, 317
 signing MIDlets, 317
 solving common problems, 317
type attribute
 circle background, 404
 circle border, 416
 image background, 402
 opening background, 408
 opening-round-rect background, 409
 pulsating-circle background, 406
 pulsating-circles background, 407
 registering custom CSS attributes, 260
 round-rect background, 401
 round-rect border, 413
 round-tab background, 410
 shadow border, 414
 simple background, 400
 top, bottom, left, and right borders, 415
type attribute, requirement element, 365
 checking capabilities, 83
 pulsating background, 405
type element
 registering extensions for several projects, 236

U

UMBAAPI (Unified Message Box Access API)
 optional packages for MIDP devices, 278
UMTS (Universal Mobile Telephone System), 418
undefine directive, 105, 399
 defining/removing symbols/variables, 109
unless attribute
 adding attribute for current target devices, 75
 applying filter for specific devices, 76
 compiler element, 375
 copier element, resources, 384
 debug element, 127–128, 371
 deviceRequirements element, 365
 emulator element, 388
 fileset element, resources, 382
 finalizer element, 387
 jad element, 386
 localization element, resources, 383
 midlet element, 370
 obfuscator element, 377
 packager element, 385
 parameter element, 233
 parameter element, emulator, 389
 postcompiler element, 376
 preprocessor element, 373
 preverifier element, 381
 selecting devices to build for, 81
 sign element, 387
 source element, sources, 369
 sources element, 369
 variable element, 371
Unmark command variable, 166
 label for unmark command, 393
 localizing J2ME Polish GUI, 90
unsigned byte data type
 Binary Editor, 141
unsigned short data type
 Binary Editor, 141
untrusted applications, 77
UPD datagrams
 permissions for signed MIDlets, 360
updating application, 36
uppercase property function, 400
 transforming variables with, 118
useBackBuffer variable, 396
useDefaultPackage attribute
 obfuscating applications, 95, 377
useDirectInput variable, 165, 395
 configuring the TextField, 168
useExtendedMenuBar variable, 394
 designing extended menu bar, 203
useFull-screen variable, GameCanvas, 394
usePolishGameApi variable, 397
 using game engine for MIDP 2.0 devices, 150
usePolishGui attribute, build element, 42, 368
 activating the GUI, 161–162
usePolishGui variable, 166, 397
usePolishTitle variable, 397
user input, evaluation of
 limitations of game engine, 150
user interfaces
 see also interfaces; J2ME Polish GUI
 problems implementing user interface, 308
user-defined attributes
 configuring application, 74

user-defined log levels, 127
UTF-String data type
  Binary Editor, 141
utilities, 138–143
  Binary Editor, 139–141
  Font Editor, 142–143
  SysInfo MIDlet, 143
utility classes, 133–138
  ArrayList class, 134–135
  BitMapFont class, 136–138
  BitMapFontViewer class, 136
  Debug class, 138
  DeviceControl class, 138
  Locale class, 138
  obfuscator removing unused classes, 133
  TextUtil class, 135–136

V

value attribute
  compilerargs element, 376
  jad element, 386
  parameter elements, 233
  parameter element, emulator, 389
  parameter element, obfuscator, 378
  requirement element, 365
  variable element, 370
value-align attribute, Gauge class, 223
values
  using hard-coded values, 120
values attribute
  registering custom CSS attributes, 260
variable element, build.xml, 370–371
  attributes, table of, 370
  defining symbols and variables, 116
variables
  comparing, 108
  configuration variables, 392–397
  defining, 114
  device-specific preprocessing variables, 390–392
  functions transforming variable values, 399–400
  including values of preprocessing variables in code, 110
  retrieving number of separate values within, 111
  setting, 115
  transforming with property functions, 117
  using several variable values individually, 111
  using standard preprocessing variables, 114
  variables for reading current setting, 398
variables element, build.xml, 370–371
  defining variables, 115
  localizing J2ME Polish GUI, 91
vcenter layout
  aligning items with layout attribute, 193
Vector class, 133
vendor certificates, 318
vendor element, vendors.xml, 44
Vendor requirement
  selecting target devices to build for, 83
vendor-specific emulators, 9
Vendor variable, 392
vendorName attribute, info section, 364
vendors
  directories for specific vendors, 70
  mobile device manufacturers, 281
  vendor-specific attributes, 355
vendors attribute, build element, 369
vendors element, vendors.xml, 44
vendors.xml, 44
  defining capabilities and features, 48
  defining Nokia and Siemens in, 44
  defining supported libraries, 45
  device database file, 39
verbose attribute
  compiler element, 375
  debug element, 127, 371
verbose debugging mode
  exceptions, 124
verification
  Java Verified initiative, 318
version attribute, info section, 364
version control systems
  integrating J2ME Polish into IDEs, 19
Version parameter
  DashO Pro obfuscator, 380
version property
  JTWI, 357
  Location API, 357
  M3G, 357
  MMAPI, 357
  PDAAPI, 358
  Sensor API, 358
vexpand layout
  aligning items with layout attribute, 193
Vibrate functionality
  device control, 156
video
  device-specific preprocessing symbols, 390
video.*xyz* properties, 358
VideoFormat, 392
  device database, 43
  preprocessing symbols and variables, 115
  selecting target devices to build for, 83
view types
  arranging items on screen, 206
  using with columns attribute, 207
view window
  Siemens devices, 290
view-type attribute, ChoiceGroups, 216, 217
  arranging items on screen, 206
viewer class
  BitMapFontViewer class, 136
Vodafone
  carrier modifications, 292
  vendor-specific attributes, 356
vshrink layout
  aligning items with layout attribute, 193

W

WAAPI (Web Services API)
  optional packages for MIDP devices, 277
wait attribute, emulator element, 388
WAP (Wireless Application Protocol), 418
WAP gateway
  networking problems, 311
wav group
  assembling resources, 71
web server
  ImageLoader getting images from, 262
WEME (WebSphere Everyplace Micro Environment) virtual machine, 293
width attribute
  circle border, 416
  DateFields, 226
  Gauge items, 223
  round-rect border, 413
  shadow border, 414
  simple border, 412
  TextFields, 224
  top, bottom, left, and right borders, 415
WIPI (Wireless Internet Platform for Interoperability), 294
wireless gaming market, 282
Wireless Markup Language (WML)
  deployment phase, 33
Wireless Toolkit
  see WTK
wireless.*xyz* properties, 358
WMAPI (Wireless Messaging API)
  optional packages for MIDP devices, 276–277
WML (Wireless Markup Language), 418
workDir attribute, build element, 369
  setting, 128
wrapper classes
  using game engine, 146
wrapping text
  splitting text into String array, 135
  TextUtil class, 133
write-once capability
  Ant properties, 57
WTK (Wireless Toolkit)
  for Mac OS X, 8
  installing, 8
  selecting installation directory, 12
  versions, 8
WTK emulator
  measuring memory consumption, 341
  measuring performance, 326–327
  running J2ME Polish, 4

X

x attribute, foreground image, 210
XML format
  build.xml file, 58
  device database, 39–49
    changing and extending, 52
XML protocol
  networking issues, 311
xor (^) operator
  boolean operators for evaluating terms, 107
xor nested element
  deviceRequirements element, 365

Y

y attribute, foreground image, 210
yguard Ant task
  obfuscating application, 237
yGuard obfuscator, 379

Z

zoomInAndHide/zoomOut animations
  screen change animations, 229